Genocide in the Age of the Nation-State

Volume I
The Meaning of Genocide

Genocide in the Age of the Nation-State

Volume I:
The Meaning of Genocide

Mark Levene

I.B. TAURIS
LONDON · NEW YORK

Published in 2005 by I.B. Tauris & Co. Ltd
6 Salem Road, London W2 4BU
175 Fifth Avenue, New York NY 10010
www.ibtauris.com

In the United States of America and Canada
distributed by Palgrave Macmillan a division of St Martin's Press
175 Fifth Avenue, New York NY 10010

ISBN 1 85043 752 1
EAN 978 1 85043 752 9

A full CIP record for this book is available from the British Library
A full CIP record is available from the Library of Congress

Library of Congress Catalog Card Number: available

Typeset in Garamond by JCS Publishing Services
Printed and bound in Great Britain by
TJ International Ltd, Padstow, Cornwall

Contents

For Alejandro Chueca
a true friend and fighter for a better world

Flectere si nequeo superos, Acheronta movebo
If I can't move the gods, I'll stir up hell

Acknowledgements

This work has been a long time in the making. It owes, at the outset, a great debt of gratitude to Ronnie Landau and Iradj Bagherzade, who were fundamental to its pursuit. And so, too, over now more than a dozen years, to various bodies who wittingly, or unwittingly, gave their support and assistance. I would like to thank the university libraries of Warwick, Southampton and Oxford, most particularly in the form of the Bodleian, plus the British Library, for being there. I am also grateful to Warwick University, alongside the Nuffield Foundation, for useful research grants, to the Herbert and Valmae Freilich Foundation for enabling participation in an important 'genocide' colloquium in Australia, and to the British Academy, for making possible attendance at the biennial conference of the International Assocation of Genocide Scholars.

It has often been through the Association that I have been able to keep abreast of burgeoning developments in this peculiar field of study. Indeed, in critical respects, this work rests heavily upon and and would not have been possible without the groundwork and, indeed, often ground-breaking studies of Helen Fein, Roger W. Smith, Jack Nusan Porter, Israel Charny, Robert Melson, Frank Chalk, Kurt Jonassohn, Rabbi Steve Jacobs, Colin Tatz and Henry Huttenbach, all of whom were so important to the Association's foundation. I would like to thank all of them for their generosity of spirit and, in similar vein, acknowledge Eric Markusen, Ben Kiernan, Jacques Kornberg, Jacques Sémelin, Al Alvarez, Alex Hinton, David Wilkins, Herb Hirsch and David Kopf who have made these and other conferences on 'genocide' something other than simply morose and depressing events.

Turning this into a roll-call could end up becoming rather tedious for all concerned, yet the more this author ponders on it, the more he would like to acknowledge those who helped stimulate this work or kept it on track towards its ponderous completion. Two names, for instance, which come instantly to mind, on the former score, are Gil Eliot and Norman Cohn, the first for an entirely mould-breaking work on the sheer scale of exterminatory violence in our contemporary age, the latter for daring, as an historian, to engage with its psycho-social underpinnings. I read their respective works when I was rather young and at a time when I could not conceivably guess that I would one day myself be similarly engaged. I have had the pleasure of meeting Gil, though not Professor Cohn. Both have been important influences on this work.

Many other people have given a great deal of time, effort and enthusiastic support for this project. Thanks on this score are especially due to Ruth Parr and Anne Gelling at OUP, both Lester Crook and the wonderful Kate Sherratt at I.B. Tauris, Steven Howe, Eric Weitz and two further unknown readers for their kind as well as purposefully critical commentary. Donald Bloxham, Dirk Moses and Dan Stone have not only ploughed through unwieldy chunks of manuscript but have been really good friends and constructive critics. Their encouragement, plus their own work, has been immeasurably important to my own writing and thinking process.

Many, many other colleagues, scholars and friends have given of their time and help. In no particular priority, or hierarchical order (!) I would like to acknowledge the help of Mark Mazower, Alexander Prusin, Steven Jensen, Michael Freeman, Ara Sarafian, Barbara Rosenbaum, Rouben Adalian, Vahakn Dadrian, Hans-Lukas Kieser, Heather Goodall, Robert Cribb, Colin Richmond, Sean Bourke, Simon Norfolk, Anne Mackintosh, Robin Okey, Chris Read, Penny Roberts, Alan James, Colin Jones, Henry Cohn, Chris Clark, Anne Gerritsen, David Hardiman, Steve Hindle, Peter Marshall, Hussein Mohamed, Cheryl Burgess, Sarah Pearce, Trish Skinner, David Cesarani, Kendrick Oliver, Nils Roemer, Neil Gregor, Alistair Duke, Elisa Miles, Tony Kushner, Julie Gammon, Peter Gray, Brian Golding, George Bernard, John Oldfield, Waltraud Ernst, Adrian Smith, Mishtooni Bose, David Glover, Nadia Valman, Clive Gamble, Yannis Hamilakis, John Schofield, Roger Winterbottom, Louise Revell, Liz Dore, Tony Campbell, and my late, dear friend, and much lamented colleague, Callum MacDonald. Plus all the many students, at Warwick and Southampton universities, who have not flinched from engagement with both me and this unremittingly awful subject.

That said, sometimes it requires native common sense to cut to the chase. So, thanks to Andy Daly for proving that lay people often have a much more intuitive grasp of the heart of the matter than a host of academics. And also to somebody else with native grit and intuition, not to say extraordinarily steadfast patience; namely Jenny Ivory, who has not only been behind and party to this project since day one but, most recently, has provided the sort of help with the bibliography and index without which I would have despaired. Jessica Cuthbert-Smith, too, who has been the very model of a sharp-eyed, sensitive and creative copy-editor with whom it has been a pleasure and joy to work.

Finally, a heartfelt thank you to those who have survived this project while helping to maintain a sense of proportion for its author. Somewhere in the process of writing, I became seriously ill. The mainstream medical profession could not provide answers. Two fine acupuncturists were rather critical in restoring good order. That said, there is no substitute in the health and happiness stakes for family and close friends. So thanks to all those in recent years, Karen, Jeannie, Helen S., family Doniach-Durant, Pauline and Saul, parents Helen and Alf, and siblings Betty and Simon, who have been steadfast, loyal, kind and true.

ML
Kineton, Warwickshire,
Summer 2004

Preface

Writing about genocide is not like writing about other matters, even historical ones where the subject so often bespeaks human horror and misery. Genocide is not simply a sustained version of this. It is not even simply about mass murder. At its most elemental level, it is about all the processes by which some human beings are both willed and empowered to deprive and deny other human beings, both individually and as part of broader familial and communal groupings, of their basic human dignity. Grand agendas for societal betterment and progress have a terrible danger of losing sight of what that can mean for peoples' lives. Equally disturbing, however, might be the idea that somebody can set him or herself up – in this case the former – as an authority on the subject and breezily write about the deaths of millions, before sitting down in an armchair, in his well-appointed home, for morning tea. And, all the time, not once considering that somebody out there, God forbid, might stop his monthly pay-cheque, let alone knock down the door of his well-appointed home and forcibly march him out of it forever.

This opening statement, for all its clumsy artlessness, has to be made if only to highlight the reasons for this act of writing, and the problems which immediately arise from it. Most people to whom one talks about genocide, whoever they are, usually agree that this is a very important subject with implications for all of us, and, therefore, that it *ought* to be written about. Yet why write *another* when, in the last decade, enough tomes on one particular genocide, the Holocaust, have been published to fill a large removal van? Part of the answer might be to question why this one genocide has received so much attention while other cases have received so little. Representations of the Holocaust as not simply the 'genocide of genocides' but as even the defining event of the twentieth century have, in recent years, become sufficiently pervasive in Western consciousness and culture that one sometimes wonders at what point discussion about the possibilities of a broader landscape of genocide is going to surface properly. Even closely related Second World War killings, such as that which befell Europe's Roma (gypsies), with losses arguably proportionate – in terms of population numbers – to that of the Jews, are rarely treated as little more than a footnote to the fundamental story. Try and find a book on what happened to a range of other ethnic groups under the Nazis, or, for that matter, the Soviet regime, and one would have to start searching in specialist libraries and area studies periodicals for the information.

It is not, then, that books on other genocides, some of which are accessible to a broad educated public, do not exist. Nevertheless, there is a relative paucity compared with what has been written in recent times on the specifically Nazi destruction of the Jews, while many fewer consider the linkages between this and other possible genocides. A dominating tendency within Holocaust scholarship, insisting on the absolute incomparability and uniqueness of this particular genocide, would certainly appear to be one obstacle to progress on the latter score, though, arguably, this is an obstacle as much for the way its strictures have influenced, instructed and informed Western opinion formers and policy makers, as for its impact on strictly academic circles. Thus, while, on the one hand, the Holocaust has come to be commonly treated as the yardstick for all that might be described as 'evil' in our world, on the other, it is – despite the obvious contradiction involved – a subject notably cordoned off and policed against those who might seek to make connections.

Academic attempts to change these ground rules have not always been helpful, or even motivated by discernibly honourable intentions. In the early 1980s, for instance, one notably tortuous if not perplexing effort was by the otherwise distinguished German historian, Professor Ernst Nolte. He sought to argue that the Nazi extermination of the Jews, through gas chambers, was a reactive response to the threat of a 'Bolshevik-Asiatic' Gulag being carried out against the Germans, implying, thereby, not only that the Nazi accusation of Jewish responsibility for Soviet bolshevism had some substance but that the Jews were also in some way responsible for their own Holocaust fate. Divorced from any empirical evidence to back up his claim, Nolte's effort was to turn the ensuing German historians' debate: the *Historikerstreit* – an occasion for what might have been a very important reappraisal of the place of the Holocaust in an *age* of genocide – into something akin to an albatross. Indeed, instead of further explorations of the historical relationships between genocides – including those committed by both Soviets and Nazis – becoming the order of the day, it was rather the opposing Holocaust-centric tendency which now forcefully came to the fore, charging that the historians' debate, *tout ensemble*, was an attempt to relativise, trivialise and even decriminalise a human catastrophe in an entirely extraordinary and singular class of its own.[1]

Paradoxically, though equally problematically, it is this very continuing cultural hegemony of Holocaust *as* genocide, and the resistance to contenders which this often engenders, which repeatedly acts as a magnet to advocates of other human catastrophes, clamouring to make the point that the 'g-word' applies to theirs, too. Demonstrate that what happened to 'your' group was comparable to what happened to the Jews under the Nazis, or that its perpetrators were similarly impelled by a racist worldview, and you have made the case. All the more so if there are powerful governments (sometimes aided and abetted by academics and opinion formers) intent on denying, refuting or rubbishing the very validation you most fervently seek. A growing bibliography on the destruction of the Armenians in 1915–16 suggests something of this tendency.[2] Not that there are not now some first-rate books on the subject, but it often appears as if so much energy has to be expended on proving that what happened to the Armenians *was* genocide (it was – enough said) and the Holocaust so very often used as the legitimising reference point, that consideration of the former's own 'unique' historical background, not to say the significance of that history in a broader context, has been repeatedly either overlooked, or overwhelmed.

Supposing, however, that there had been no Holocaust? The very statement has the potential to be seriously misunderstood, where it is not treated as a malicious sacrilege pure and simple. But just supposing, for one moment, that this was the case. Would our global, historical canvas still not be littered with the murdered corpses of the Armenians and Assyrians of eastern Anatolia, the Tutsi of Rwanda, Hutu in Burundi, Kurds in northern Iraq, Chams in Cambodia, Herero in Namibia, Yuki of California, Pequots of New England, the Brautauolong of south-east Australia, the peoples collectively known as jumma in Eastern Bangladesh, East Timorese, Tibetans, Chechens, Circassians and many, many scores, possibly hundreds more, including all those people labelled as a communal entity, even where they subscribed to no such group identity? Would we still not need a common word we could use to refer to what had happened to all of them? Or some way of understanding not simply what were the specifics of their individual destructions but a framework in which it might all make some sense?

This is hardly, then, a proposition for omission of the Holocaust from the proper study of modern genocide, nor for avoiding issues of comparability with it, when so many are manifest. That this particular genocide looms grotesquely large in the overall picture there is no doubt. And the consequent scholarship which its study has engendered equally offers multitudinous methods and insights into how we might consider and evaluate other genocides. To this scholarship this author, amongst others, is greatly in debt, not least in the development of this particular study. But the result should not be that all the highways and byways relating to the phenomenon must lead inexorably forwards or backwards toward this single event. We can, and certainly will, find in these pages many grounds for comparison between Armenia and the Holocaust, or between it and Rwanda. In fact, we might venture further, that there are historical patterns and processes which particularly connect all three. But by the same token there are connecting threads between Rwanda and events in 1972 Burundi, just as more distantly there are between Rwanda and 1965 Indonesia, or, for that matter, between this latter genocide and the beginnings of another wave, ten years later, both in Cambodia and East Timor. Interrogate the data more widely still and we would find more localised examples of genocide, or at least its potentiality, across much of south-east Asia in this period, not least against the region's hill peoples. This might, in turn, open up the question of why it is, throughout much of the history of the last few hundred years, that it has been relatively small groups of indigenous peoples, across the globe, who have been most exposed and vulnerable to genocide. The highways can lead us to lost or forgotten byways, and, through the very process, towards a recognition that what we imagined were only byways are actually critical indicators of the phenomenon writ large.

This projected four-volume study thus seeks, as its justification, a better understanding not simply of acts of systematic, exterminatory violence – which, sometimes, quite consciously as a function of Western political and cultural priorities, more often out of sheer ethnocentrism, have been mislaid or marginalised – but, equally importantly, of the way individual genocides, instead of being treated in worthy isolation (or not at all), need to be seen as part of a whole. One might prosaically call it joining up the dots, or, as Dirk Moses has more provocatively and persuasively put it, trying to imagine the subject as 'part of a single process rather than merely in comparative (and competitive) terms'.[3] The case, to date, has not been properly demonstrated. This is an attempt to do so.

As such, our study seeks to understand the processes and patterns that link genocides from the early modern centuries to the present day. Embraced in this reckoning are waves of colonial exterminations, particularly from the sixteenth to nineteenth centuries, alongside other great twentieth-century genocidal eruptions more firmly fixed in our our contemporary consciousness. Some of these latter incidents have emanated from the very centre of European power. Yet, whether it is metropolitan events, or those taking place on distant colonial, post-colonial, or neo-colonial peripheries, there is an underlying assumption here that these can only be understood within a single frame of reference, the beginnings of which are rooted in the development of Western, initially European power bases, and the extrusion of that power into the wider world.

If this, then, is a controversial – as well as ambitious – thesis, there will be other grounds, too, on which it is likely to be contested. Within the discipline of history, stepping outside an area or period speciality to make comparisons or generalised assertions, especially when operating at second hand, or without the full linguistic equipment for the task, is often treated as risky, even where it is not roundly condemned as a cardinal sin. This enterprise, by seeking to draw together elements from across a very wide historical and geographical range certainly runs risks, and it will be for fellow historians to judge the results. It is ironic, however, that this is a subject crying out for a thorough historical interpretation, albeit with broad brushstrokes on a large canvas, supported by a good dose of cross-disciplinary awareness and assistance. While historians dominate the specific field of Holocaust studies, it is noteworthy that practically the entire groundwork involved in charting the broader parameters of genocide has been achieved to date by sociologists, political scientists and psychologists, even while many of these have continued to lament the lack of interest in the phenomenon from the vast majority of their own disciplinary colleagues. Nevertheless, unencumbered by the self-denying ordinances of historians, it is these frontrunners who have built upon Raphael Lemkin's original 1940s definition and explanation of genocide,[4] and to whom this author is again indebted for the results. That said, even in these quarters, not all scholars will find welcome the proposition that there is an overarching analytical framework, transcending political and cultural, as well as more obvious spatial and temporal boundaries within which the phenomenon needs to be understood.

Equally problematic will be this study's reception amongst not only the defenders of Holocaust singularity but all those who would start from a premise of the specialness of their group's victim status. Necessarily, *Genocide in the Age of the Nation-State* deals with groups who have become victims of mass murder. But while this statement implicitly carries with it an interest in, not to say enthusiasm for the cultural, linguistic and ethnographic diversity of humankind, this does not translate into advocacy, or, for that matter, emotional investment on behalf of any such particular group. In this sense, the writer Ian Buruma's view that: 'There are no dangerous peoples; there are only dangerous situations, which are the result, not of laws of nature, or history, or of national character, but of political arrangements',[5] is very much one with which this author concurs. Not only, as will be argued, are the very terms 'perpetrators' and 'victims' inadequate in explaining the state–group interactions which lead to genocide, they also give an entirely false impression that there are essentially only two immutable types of human being in the world; one which is wrongdoing, the other which is perpetually on its receiving end.

Unfortunately, it is exactly such notions which can legitimise and, thus, per-petuate cycles of violence, including genocide. It is a paradox that genocidal perpetrators always claim that it is actually *they* who are the victims. But if, by the same token, the group which has genuinely suffered has its victimhood validated by the 'international community', it may equally use this status to either justify or absolve itself of its own malodorous actions, even several gen-erations down the line. One important aspect in the very failure to break free from this dangerous transmission belt is the way our contemporary Western culture appears to privilege 'victimhood' with a celebrity cachet or kudos. It follows that the now common tendency to valorise, or even sacralise, the memory of one's *own* catastrophe, as genocide, is a logical next step.[6] By either emulating the singularity of the Holocaust, or alternatively denigrating it in favour of one's own distinct suffering, candidates can participate in a competi-tion where the rules of the game are that you prove that your 'genocide' was worse than your neighbour's, and in return receive undoubted cultural recog-nition, possibly economic compensation, and, quite probably, political unction in the form of support for your current post-genocide agendas, and from states which, henceforth, would not dream of challenging your credentials.

Fortunately, there *are* countervailing tendencies. Paradoxically again, the way an increasingly multicultural Western society has, in the last decade, taken on board the full magnitude of the Holocaust – at least in so far as what happened to European Jewry is concerned – has opened up possibilities for an increasing receptivity and openness to the wider vistas of genocide, though not least, alas, by dint of the fact that genocides keep on happening. Entitlement to a hearing should not have to be dependent on an unseemly jockeying for position on the hierarchy of suffering. Especially, one might add, now that a new body of scholarship is emerging which refuses to take as its starting point the 'my genocide better (worse) than yours' game of assertion and counter-assertion which has characterised 'the polemical turn' in Holocaust and geno-cide studies in recent years.[7] It is time, instead, says Moses, 'for historians in the field to play by other rules, namely, those of the community of scholars, dedicated to presenting evidence directed to the world at large, rather than primarily to an ethnic or political group'.[8] If there has remained, at the back of my mind, an uncertainty as to whether the current political and cultural cli-mate is quite ready for a work of this nature, it is at least with some renewed realisation that I am not entirely alone.

That said, and for all the contentiousness involved in critically charting and analysing the course of modern genocide, at all, there does remain an urgent and overriding rationale for this effort. Genocide is not ultimately containable within geographical, political and cultural boundaries, any more than it is essentially about bad, mad or sad societies 'out there' in godforsaken countries which have nothing to do with 'ourselves' in the West. On the contrary, the world we now live in is one that has been radically reshaped and transformed by the dominant political and economic forces emanating out of the West in the last few hundred years, and genocide is one authentic by-product of that process. Thus, this study is intended to provide some small insight not only into the nature of the beast itself but, equally importantly, into the nature of an historical development which spawned it and where that same historical development might be taking us. In getting to grips with genocide, the aim is certainly not to pardon but to understand better. But over and beyond that, the real challenge is how understanding might provide us with the tools to turn the tables on what, at the beginnings of the twenty-first century, are regularly regurgitated as the inevitable directions for human progress – themselves encompassed within increasingly hegemonic wisdoms – in order, instead, to create genuinely just, sustainable and gentle conditions within which we can fulfil the potential we *all* have for the good. This author is a convinced non-Marxist. But the words of the prophet still have a very contemporary resonance: '… the philosophers have only interpreted the world in various ways; the point however is to change it'.[9]

An Introduction to *Genocide in the Age of the Nation-State*

Rationale

The late Leo Kuper, widely revered as the doyen of genocide studies, doubted the feasibility of developing 'a general theory of genocide', on grounds of 'the great variety of historical and social contexts' in which genocides occur.[1] To attempt to contain any of these catastrophes in preordained boundaries would be not simply to denude each of its unique qualities but to create 'a single general process' where none otherwise exists.[2] Citing the Holocaust and Gulag Archipelago as commonly misappropriated models, Helen Fein has warned equally that 'comparisons based on ... a single archetype which assume there is one mechanically recurring script are bound to be misleading'.[3]

Historians would readily agree with most if not all of these prescripts, practically by second nature. Historical process is not only moulded by specific political and economic conditions which will differ markedly from region to region, country to country, and continent to continent but by strata upon strata of cultural and social distinctiveness developed over time and space. Add that critical human ingredient, contingency, and it is no wonder that the Holocaust and Rwanda, for instance, will *seem* not simply several thousand miles, and fifty years but more like planets apart. Even so, we do not have to conclude from this that they have nothing in common. To compare two events, argues Charles Maier, 'does not entail claiming that one caused the other. Comparison is dual process that scrutinizes two or more systems to learn what elements they have in common, and what elements distinguish them. It does not assert identity; it does not deny unique components'.[4]

If finding similarities between cases of genocide is not primarily what this work is about – even in some instances where these may be quite striking – nor, actually, however, is it driven by the search for comparison, as Maier describes. Certainly, genocide studies has become strongly associated, in recent years, with a comparativist approach and accompanying methods. Fein's warning about the phenomenon having no recurring script, thus, has not precluded her own vanguard search for features, elements or ingredients which separate cases have in common, nor, through this method, to the many attempts, mostly by sociologists and political scientists, to conceive what genocide *is*. The outcome has been various, if often quite conflicting attempts at definition but, also alongside this, efforts at categorisation of types of genocide, as if, having built up a general picture of the phenomenon, it then has to be broken down into the quite distinct pathways by which it occurs. If this would be simply to repeat Kuper's initial warning that genocide cannot be treated as a whole, nevertheless, it does amount to a basic theory of genocide.

Genocide, thus, is taken to be a both radically criminal and aberrant act, outside of, and distinct from, the dominant and accepted norms of liberal state and society. Such theorisation assumes some particular causative agent, such as racism or totalitarianism, which is responsible for this aberration, though equally indicative of this approach is an emphasis on the intentionality – described by Moses as the radical voluntarism[5] – of the prime organising actors to accomplish the act. Necessarily, therefore, the wilful wickedness of those who engage in genocide contrasts not simply with the detached (if compassionate) observation of the genocide researcher but the latter's implicit intention, through discovering the grounds for causation, to help such damaged societies towards paths of restoration. As Frank Chalk and Kurt Jonassohn have succinctly put it, 'the major reason for doing comparative research on genocides is the hope of preventing them in the future'.[6]

This proposition is entirely worthy and honourable. Nor, in itself, does it preclude, as Chalk and Jonassohn have themselves apprised, a recognition that it 'must be based on an understanding of the social situations and the social structures and the processes that are likely to lead to genocides'.[7] But what if the underlying theoretical premise is itself at fault? That is, that it is not so much the particularly aberrant and hence isolated social structures and situations which are at the root of the persistence and prevalence of the phenomenon but, rather, the very process of historical development out of which our entire, global, political-economic system has emerged. Put differently, the primary distinction, thus, between this work and leading wisdoms in the field might be expressed as follows: the dominant scholarship operates on the notion that genocide is an essentially extraneous, ill-fitting nugget in a broader rock-face which can be prised out from it through careful manipulation. Our proposition argues that it is the nature of the rock-face, or rather the process by which a recent vein became deeply embedded into its strata, which is the essential problem. Hence, attempting to bash away at the discernible nuggets is likely to expose the instability of the entire cliff. Indeed, until we have more fully understood how the strata were laid in the first place, offering any suggestions on how to proceed further might be decidedly premature.

The analogy may be a poor one, though at least it might suggest that the distinction between myself and the mainstream is not an insuperable one. We are, after all, in essential agreement that we are looking at the same rock-face, as we are also in agreement that there is something wrong with it. The difference, thus, is primarily one of degree and hence what can be done about it. Chalk and Jonassohn, like others, aspire to prevention. The position here is not entirely one of a contrasting counsel of despair. It is simply one which proposes that the problem of genocide is much deeper, and more intractable, than we might imagine. Indeed, the issue goes to the heart of the evolution and crystallisation of the modern world as we know it and, not least, the current international system of nation-states which emanated from it. Genocide, in short, is not properly amenable to cure until we come to terms with and seek to do something about that system's actually very dysfunctional nature.

Insisting, however, that the problem of genocide lies in the very nature of modernity – of which more below – is not, in itself, novel. The most prescient and perspicacious of Central European Marxist thinkers, especially those like Max Horkheimer and Theodor Adorno, associated with the Frankfurt School, were wrestling with aspects of the relationship during the Second World War.[8] The issue, too, has been repeatedly invoked in more recent studies. Richard L. Rubenstein, for instance, believes that genocide is an expression of 'some, though obviously not all, of the dominant trends in contemporary civilisation'.[9] More pointedly, and indeed, in some respects, taking up the cue where the Frankfurt polymaths left off, Zygmunt Bauman has specifically described the Holocaust as 'a rare, yet significant and reliable test of the hidden possibilities of modern society'.[10] Much of these discourses are richly philosophical and theoretical. This much more limited work remains essentially grounded in historical empiricism.

That said, a full-blown history of genocide cannot proceed without a degree of theoretically inclined conceptualisation which is the primary focus of this first volume. This also carries with it an implication that we might need to consider not so much the specific conditions pertinent to each genocide but rather the broader preconditions out of which genocide has arisen in the modern world. Even before we begin on this difficult task, however, we need to delineate those essential constituent elements which, we argue, are responsible for the instability of our rock-face in the first place.

What is immediately odd is that it is these very same interlinked elements which, far from being interrogated as responsible for an intrinsic dysfunctionality, are usually treated as the normative, if not positively benign underpinnings of 'international society'. Indeed, to state that these elements are the 'rise of the West', 'modernity', 'the nation-state' is simply to regurgitate what most history students would take as a given: that together they represent, on the one hand, the most profound shift in human development since the Iron Age and, on the other, key fundaments upon which contemporary (or at least Western) society's peace, security and well-being have become largely assured.

Let us, therefore, consider their relevance to *Genocide in the Age of the Nation-State.*

The Rise of the West

A recent historical study states the matter succinctly: 'Massive expansion of European interference with non-European societies and the forging of wholly new forms of dependency worldwide'.[11] The rapid outgrowth and outreach of increasingly mercantilist and, later, overtly capitalist economies from a Western European core into the far corners of the globe, from the late fifteenth century onwards, were either accompanied, where they were not directly accomplished, by military coercion and conquest. The process can be traced back earlier still, in terms of the frontier expansion of this core region's own hinterlands. The result, even where direct destruction or supplanting of indigenous polities and societies through European colonisation and settlement did not take place, was the serious if not total disruption, destabilisation or displacement of existing patterns of social and economic relationship, as these were forcibly reorientated towards the hegemonic interests of the new 'core' metropolitan centres. Former world empires found themselves subservient to an emerging world economy.[12] Human communities operating on the basis of time-honoured, reciprocal obligations, or customary usages which ensured their conditions for survival according to their own localised 'habitus', now found themselves, instead, either forced to participate according to (in the worst cases through slavery), or alternatively marginalised by, economies of profit, in turn founded on reified concepts of property.[13] Nowhere was entirely untouched by these trajectories in what also had every appearance of, and indeed was broadcast by its creators as, 'a unilinear historical process'.[14]

Moreover, what was of undoubted advantage to the dominant elites and, eventually, the masses of the core metropolitan societies through the near-monopolisation of a global market and resource base, became not only a recipe for implicit structural violence for the vast 'peripheralised,' or 'semi-peripheralised' regions on the receiving end. It also galvanised those societies – whether nominally independent of the West, or, at a later stage, released from direct imperial bondage – to react, rethink and reformulate themselves, in order to compete with, or somehow circumvent the dominant dispensation. While the rise of the West was accompanied by no overarching political agenda for the annihilation of foreign peoples, it did create a broader cultural discourse in which such annihilation was considered perfectly conceivable;[15] in which exactly such annihilations sometimes took place, not to mention further multitudinous interactions, tensions and fractures between, and within, extra-Western polities and societies which, in the long run, also carried an almost incalculable potential for extreme, exterminatory violence.

The obvious and necessary follow-on question: how did this all arise? fortunately, is not one which has to be directly addressed in a work which is about a by-product of this development, not its cause. Nevertheless, the rise of West, clearly, is closely intermeshed with emerging Western thought systems and epistemologies, or, more prosaically put, ways of seeing, understanding and explaining the world. It is this which is primarily meant here by modernity, the second element in our dangerous rock-face.

Modernity

Again, use of this term should not be construed as meaning the same thing as modernisation, which, while integral to our overall thesis, is primarily understood here as referring to processes and outcomes of state efforts to engineer programmes of economic, political and social change. In this sense, however, modernisation can be seen as one outcome of modernity, given the latter's essential Enlightenment foundations as an organising principle for a scientifically informed and rational awareness of the world. The immediate Enlightenment result was 'a veritable obsession to categorise and classify'.[16] Indeed, according to Edward Said, in order to respond and above all regulate the planet in the most efficacious and utilitarian manner, modernity became a quest to 'divide, deploy, schematise, tabulate, index and record everything in sight (and out of sight) and ... make out of every observable detail a generalisation and out of every generalisation an immutable law'.[17] In this way, modernity has posited, and continues to posit, not only that all things are knowable but that all things are possible.[18]

Moreover, what can be applied to things, can and must also be applied to people. Thus, just like other living species, human beings too can be 'apprehended, classified and theorised'.[19] The magistrate, working in the backwater village in nineteenth-century British colonial Bengal, who ventures upon the fingerprint as the perfect identifying mark of individual difference,[20] is, in this way, working from essentially the same utilitarian premise as the Nazi institute researchers categorising and hierarchising whole groups of Eastern European peoples, on the basis of their 'biosocial attributes'.[21] The anthropologist of genocide, Alexander Hinton, has variously described these tendencies as the reifying, essentialising, biologising and manufacturing of difference.[22] But while there is now a general recognition that these tendencies, in so far as Nazism is concerned, throw light on the dark side of modernity, part of the paradox Hinton is further driving at is that these are equally founded on those basic self-referential Enlightenment wisdoms by which the world at large is supposed to be made a better, healthier, more productive and, one might crucially add, more efficient place. Modernity's positivist meta-narrative of progress, thereby, logically links back to the economic requirements of a Western world order. But it also carries with it implicit assumptions about those allegedly problematic human individuals or groups, who fail to fit, or are insufficient to the demands of, or, indeed, are surplus to the requirements of that ordering.

Even before one reaches this point, however, modernity's very method of aggregating human beings within single, fixed, unchanging and irreducibly essentialised categories should be warning sign enough. That we normatively name people as members of given tribes, nations, races, religions, or whatever, is thus testament, on the one hand, to modernity's facility for reducing and simplifying complex phenomena – humans included – 'into a more manageable and schematised form',[23] and, on the other, to its intrinsic failure (or, alternatively, obdurate refusal) to imagine human beings as potentially possessing multi-layered identities and loyalties. Clinical, 'scientific', and hence impersonal in its approach, the end result can be, as Gerard Libaridian has noted of some of the historiography of the Armenian genocide, a situation where:

> analysis revolving around conflicts over irreducible categories such as race and religion turn history into a field where, instead of human beings interacting, abstract concepts do battle. It is as if hordes of individuals think and act as prescribed by ideologies of nationalism, religion, or race. Terminology then comes to reconfirm the view imposed by the genocide that, ultimately, one need not account for real Armenians leading real lives whose disappearance from their homes and from history must be accounted for; one is comforted by the thought that Armenians can be reduced to a corollary of a concept.[24]

Libaridian's charge of human abstractisation, however, is hardly peculiar to extreme events such as genocide. Race, in the nineteenth century, became a 'master concept' for the very reason that it offered a scientific way – backed by a then new battery of technological paraphernalia – for ostensibly measuring and, hence, administratively managing groups of people, independent of their 'personal idiosyncracies'.[25] Just as James Scott has recently pointed to the way one tangible outcome of the modernity project, cadastral surveys of land, have tended to overlook or consciously ignore aspects of fields or forests which either are not regular or do not enhance their commercial value, the dominance of race in biology, and ethnos in anthropology, have served well for so long for essentially the same epistemological reason; they bring into 'sharp focus certain limited aspects of a far more complex and unwieldy reality'.[26] This, however, still leaves open the question of the spatial arena – the nation-state in which, as Scott argues, these selective reality/'tunnel vision' tendencies[27] manifest themselves.

The Nation-State

Our third element, thus, relates to the normative framework of political organisation within the modern world. But, yet again, to cite this element as part of the structural instability out of which genocide is derived goes against the essential grain of a positive and comforting narrative most of us have imbibed, as well as generating some seriously critical thinking on the subject. Thus, the idea of the nation both tells us who we are, while conjoined to the state, and it provides us with the promise, if not absolute guarantee, that our daily lives will be lived free from the threat of serious violence against our persons. Indeed, according to Norbert Elias, a major twentieth-century figure in the study of social transformations from the pre-modern to the modern world, the emergence of the modern state provided for a two-fold linked benefit on this very score. On the one hand, it reined in human propensities towards aggression, demanding of the individual a greater degree of self-control and ensuring, in turn, that everyday social encounters were less likely to be marred by violent confrontation. On the other hand, it gave monopolistic powers to universally recognised and legitimised authorities – most notably the police and the judiciary – to help confirm and ensure that social peace while at the same time punishing those who continued to transgress against it. The consequent retreat of daily intrusions against our safety, thought Elias, powerfully enhanced the potential for a civilising process.[28] True, other historical sociologists have pointed out that significant break-points in the transition, at least in the specific modernising trajectories of particular states, have led to moments of extreme violence.[29] Yet, until relatively recently, few have questioned whether, once achieved, the monopolisation of violence – which was such a central outcome of the nation-state forming process – was in itself problematic, except in those most obvious cases where recognisably anti-democratic and overtly violent groups seized the apparatus.

This, however, is grossly to ignore, or avoid, both the general characteristics of what it is to be a modern – or more specifically nation-state, and/or its broader implications. The modern state, after all, presupposes an unmediated and absolutely uniform authority for its military and policing, as well as its legal, fiscal and administrative functions throughout the fixed, precisely bounded and (internationally) recognised territory which is its sovereign domain. This entails that all the land, natural and material resources, movable and immovable property, are exactly, as appropriate, surveyed, mapped, weighed up, collated and assessed as statistical unitary values equally and without reservation or exception. It is this which Scott has described as the modern state's aspiration to make a 'society legible' in order to control and manipulate it in the state's interests.[30] Logically, thus, what would apply to cadastral surveys would also apply to human resources, most obviously through simple administrative procedures such as registration of births, marriages and deaths, as well as regular censuses. However, while some of these procedures clearly preceded the advent of modernity in some traditional state systems, the tendency not only to ascribe to each registered individual human being an equal statistical number for the cross-referencing purposes of the administrative, fiscal and military apparatus but also to ascribe uniform rights and responsibilities – at least on paper – to go with it, was both quite novel and fundamentally revolutionary. The concept of individual citizenship emanating most obviously out of the specific 'moment' of the French Revolution and, with it, of an equality before the law – with, arguably, as a logical extension of that, the notion of universal suffrage – thus is generally hailed as a fundamental benefit for the human condition, as latterly inscribed in the 1948 United Nations Declaration of Human Rights.[31]

If, then, these are allegedly liberating features associated with this new political formulation of state – and man's place within it – wherein does the inherent danger lie? Firstly, by defining each human being as an individual citizen, the state effectively subordinates all previous, traditional, and often multi-layered loyalties – whether to extended family, clan, tribe, community, sect, estate, or whatever – to itself, repudiating in the process the authority of these bodies to act as meaningful mediators or negotiators vis-à-vis the state, on behalf of those who otherwise might have understood themselves as component elements of exactly such social organisms. This might not be to render such bodies redundant in cultural, economic or social terms, but it would be to do so politically, given that only the atomised citizen, henceforth, would be recognised as a valid member of the body-politic. An exception, of course, might be made where either the state itself, or other states, in international compact, intervened specifically to allow such bodies 'group rights'. However, the very notion that such 'group', or alternatively, 'minority' rights might exist, would represent not simply a dispensation but a significant departure from what otherwise would be considered normative.[32] Equally importantly, while modern nation-state primacy would automatically override religious authority in any competing temporal jurisdiction – even where religion had been fundamental to the previous, traditional organisation of that polity – the nation-state's very affinity to modernity's (albeit terrestrially bound) principle of omniscience and omnicompetence would mean that any challenge to the state's political authority, coming from a spiritual source, would be technically as inadmissible as that coming from any other dissenting social, ethnic, or other voice. While, thus, there is no intrinsic reason why the nation-state has to be a secular one, the general point holds: the modern state's primacy is absolute, regardless of religious authority or sanction, and hence to challenge it, whatever the manner or source of that opposition, is potentially to expose oneself to its monopoly of violence in whatever form the state might choose to respond.

Secondly, moreover, the dangers inherent in this situation are bound, and, indeed, amplified, by the modern state's ineluctable drive to development. How else can we envisage the modern state except through its ongoing project to bring about a better, more productive, more healthy society? That the modern state is based on the assumption of an ever upward trajectory – that it is 'going somewhere' – confirms its basic debt to modernity. Yet if this is its very *raison d'être,* it also carries with it both an implicit, if not explicit, mandate to organise its fiscal, human, technological and extractive resources in the pursuit of these firmly terrestrial goals. A radically laissez-faire state, such as today's United States, might protest that it is exempt from this agenda. Yet laissez-faire is simply a route for contracting out these powers to private companies. It does not detract from a basic modern state interest – whether organised around the liberal free market or a closely planned command economy – to mobilise its resources, including human resources, in order to compete within an increasingly universal frame of equally modernising nation-states. If people find their complete participation most keenly required under emergency conditions, such as war, the general rule prevails; it is the modern state which determines need and, hence, the right to socially engineer its way towards that achievement. In short, the modern polity provides itself with a totalising capacity largely undreamt of in the pre-modern world, the resulting options available to its subjects being of a zero-sum nature. As a group, or an individual, one can either be enthusiastic, obeisant or acquiescent in response to the state's mobilising demands, or, if one dissents or demurs, one ultimately, again, has to reckon with its monopoly of violence.

Thirdly, and finally, there is the danger inherent in the modern polity in its dominant mode: not so much the nation-state *per se* but certainly the homogeneous state-society. Not all modern states have automatically insisted on a legitimisation of their existence around the idea of the nation. Nor even, when this has been the case, need we assume a grounding based on an ethnic monoculture. Avant-garde nation-states, such as Britain and the United States, have been notably hybrid in their national attributes. Others, such as a diversely ethnic Brazil, are almost entirely colour-blind. If in many (though certainly not all) cases of actual genocide the issue, thus, would seem to turn on conflicts of ethnicity or race, the underlying issue here is rather the modern state's premium on social coherence. We have already hinted that this requirement relates critically to a broader problem of how modern polities can operate and sustain themselves effectively within a fiercely competitive international system of other such nation-states. In other words, external pressures, as much as internal ones, act as the primary driving force towards concepts of unity and uniformity. The outcome, however, is unequivocal; polities intent on long-term sustainability in the modern, international political economy are those which, as a matter of necessity, demand that their citizens, or subjects, accommodate and/or assimilate themselves to a set of social, cultural, economic and often linguistic norms, as determined by the state. This usually means, in short, recognising oneself as a member of the national – or some other state-defined notion of collective and unified – community.

As a result, living on its geographical, or even emotional margins no longer remains acceptable as a means of avoiding compliance. Indeed, these avoidance tactics become increasingly implausible as the state's modernising economic imperatives kick into play. Those who will not voluntarily assimilate are in these circumstances likely to be forcibly encapsulated, not least through the inculcation of 'national' values in universal programmes of state schooling – another fundamentally critical indicator of the arrival of the modern nation-state. Others, who might claim exemption on grounds of, for instance, religious nonconformism, are also likely to find their room for manoeuvre keenly circumscribed. Again, the recourse to minority group status, possibly via negotiation with the authorities, might represent one possible bolt-hole, though one that would simply confirm a fixed, subordinate and subservient status vis-à-vis the state. Any group which thus holds out against these norms is likely to find itself branded as pariahs, outsiders, troublemakers, or where simply individuals are concerned, as insane.[33] Even where states are very obviously multi-ethnic in character and the state elite's behaviour entirely manipulative in order to ensure the ethnic dominance of its own group over one or more others, the rhetoric of the unified nation provides the most obvious tool with which to do down or marginalise its competitors.[34]

All this said, nowhere in this litany have we considered more obviously genocidal possibilities: where, for instance, the state-national community sets out to extrude a group on account of its alleged irreconcilable 'otherness' or where a group itself, unable to embrace the arrangements of its existence as set down by the nation-state, actively seeks secession from it.[35] Rather, danger from the nation-state's monopoly of violence is implicit in *all* its fundamental arrangements.

None of this, however, is to suggest that any one thing must *inevitably* lead to genocide, any more than it is a proposition that all modern states are identical. As our later discussion will develop, genocide can only occur as a result of the coming together of a matrix of usually quite specific ingredients under contingent, nearly always crisis conditions. Equally, however, we should be wary of imagining that some states, because of their allegedly more benign development, are automatically exempt from this potentiality. Argues Carole Nagengast:

> Few states especially liberal democracies, typically or openly exercise their power over their constituency through unmediated violence, though it is always held in reserve. Rather they try to ensure conformity to a set of images that create the illusion of unity, the illusion of consensus about what is and what is not legitimate, what should and should not be suppressed.[36]

Nagengast goes on to emphasise her point by enlisting the verdict of the influential social anthropologist, Pierre Clastres: 'The refusal of multiplicity, the dread of difference ... is the very essence of the state.'[37] Even if one were not to subscribe absolutely to this final statement, our sketch review of the emerging nation-state, alongside the rise of the West, and that of modernity, has attempted to demonstrate that the fundamental reconfiguration of human society which these developments inaugurated was the harbinger of *universal* conditions in which genocide, as we understand it, became possible.

Again, this is certainly not to imply an inbuilt teleology. Or that the synchronisation of our three key constituent elements in the making of our contemporary world landscape provides us with an 'ur' genocide. It may be tantalising, of course, to ask such questions. If, for instance, we were to take the Holocaust as our yardstick for all genocides, or alternatively, as a culmination of tendencies in this direction, it might be logical to work backwards to some event, or series of events, which we could then take as its precursors. In this way, we might alight, as many scholars do, on the attempted annihilation of the Herero people of South-West Africa, an event conveniently situated at the very outset of a recognisably genocidal twentieth century and an event, moreover, which, because it was committed by Germans, would seem to provide us, at first sight, with grounds for assuming a particularly Teutonic state propensity, or disorder. The problem is that what the Germans were doing in Africa (not just South-West Africa, in fact) has close parallels with British actions in the same regional context a few years earlier, American ones almost simultaneously in the Philippines, or, for that matter, Dutch ones in a far-flung corner of their East Indies colonies, at that precise moment. These other exterminatory assaults may be at the margins of genocide scholarship but they are more immediately and obviously relatable to the fate of the Herero than anything to do with the Holocaust. Our thesis may readily accept that what took place in its fullest, most decipherable form in the twentieth century was either lacking, or protean, in earlier centuries but what is more problematic is to deduce from this that all roads must in some unilinear way lead towards a single cataclysmic event, or, that again, 'obscure' genocides committed on the frontiers of colonial empires are only of relevance as signposts to the really fundamental and 'total' ones (sic.) perpetrated in contemporary European, or near-European heartlands.

So, *Genocide in the Age of the Nation-State* is not able to propound a chronological sequence which neatly begins with A and ends with Z. For instance, we may find what happened in the Vendée, in year 2 (1793–4) of the Jacobin supremacy in revolutionary France, to be a significant, even prototypical version of genocides more regularly associated with the nation-state more than a century later. But the very fact that there is such a *longue durée* between this event and its would-be, latter-day competitors must in itself give us pause, just as by the same token, from the vantage point of 1794, the Vendée might equally be taken as a summation of a particular set of dangerous tendencies associated with the gestation and formation of early modern Europe, even when here, arguably, this might take us back yet another six or seven hundred years.[38] Add to all this the small matter of political geography – the Vendée was clearly a domestic event within the confines of the nation-state, those committed by both Europeans and non-Europeans on distant frontiers were most often a statement about their strengths and weaknesses as empires – and it should be fairly obvious that the only way we can make sense of the phenomenon in its entirety is by applying a much larger historical framework of analysis.

But then again, all that this may ultimately tell us is that the study of history has its own inherent limitations. It cannot predict, only offer explanations from hindsight. Nor is its ability to penetrate into the minds of humankind, and its multitudinous societies, comprehensive by any means. As for the intentions and behaviour of men and women themselves, the very way these so often get turned, through the vagaries of contingent events, into entirely unintended or unexpected courses of action, further conspires to make history a very imprecise explanatory system.

Organisation of Work

For all these shortcomings, however, the purpose of *Genocide in the Age of the Nation-State* is to consider our phenomenon, at least in its modern and contemporary manifestations, from a world historical standpoint; that is, in the broadest conceptual as well as chronological terms. This assumes a treatment over several volumes. This first more theoretically inclined volume, *The Meaning of Genocide* will be succeeded by a second, *The Rise of the West*, much of the pre-1914 colonial as well as European terrain of which is rarely considered in mainstream studies of genocide. Indeed, a basic aim of the overall project is to introduce non-specialist readers to broad patterns, processes and interconnections between what may often be quite unfamiliar instances of genocide. At first sight, this lack of general familiarity may appear less the case with a third volume which will treat the years 1914–45, encapsulated in critical part by the two great global, yet still significantly European-centred, wars. The Holocaust, hence, will be a dominant aspect of this volume. Even so, this will not be to exclusion of a much wider picture of exterminatory violence. If this implicitly returns to our original preface remarks about what is, and what is not, part of our general Western cognitive map when it is comes to this subject, a fourth post-1945 volume will up the ante further by arguing for an even more persistent and universal landscape of genocide emanating from repeatedly labyrinthine conflicts associated with post-colonialism, the Cold War, its demise, and yet a further lurch into a new era of global uncertainties.

Indeed, at this point, the very turbulence of the contemporary era, not least in the breakdown and, or collapse of nation-states in specific regions of the second and third worlds, even while the international political economy becomes more tightly organised around a single hegemonic master, may merit a further, final but shorter sequel. All four volumes, up to this point, will feed into a generalising thesis as to genocide's close affinity to, and linkage with, the evolution and ultimate crystallisation of an international system of nation-states. However, the possible end of the nation-state trajectory, and the potential disintegration of its universal applicability, may lead, in this additional volume, to an assessment of how genocide is either metamorphosing into, or literally being replaced by, a new framework of exterminatory violence, while still acting as a critical by-product of a partially post-nation-state world.

However, in returning to the organisation of this opening volume, we will not be able to pursue any of this broad survey until we have confronted and attempted to overcome one fundamental conceptual problem: what is genocide? To state that the phenomenon has a certain elusive quality, that despite a United Nations Convention which purports to define it there is precious little consensus among scholars or researchers in support, is actually to put the matter mildly. Ward Churchill, himself a notably controversial scholar of the subject, poses the problem acerbically: 'At the most fundamental level ... we presently lack even a coherent and viable description of the processes and circumstances implied by the term genocide.'[39] With this in view, *The Meaning of Genocide* attempts to pin down the broad conceptual nature, dynamics and historical framework of our phenomenon.

This is developed through three linked chapters. The first charts the origins of the term and the way it has come to be used. By two specific routes, one considering genocide as a form of warfare, the other as an 'ideal type' it seeks to determine for the entire work our own understanding of the phenomenon. There is an awareness in this process that the most familiar examples of genocide can provide a heuristic way of explaining the shape, form and contours of our subject. Concentration on the Holocaust, Armenia and Rwanda, thus is not because these examples have to be accepted as archetypal but more because they are generally understood in this way. However, given that this author does not accept that concepts of race or ethnicity, of themselves, can be a basis for a proper definition of the target group in this particular form of communal mass murder, the heuristic exercise is developed through additional use of two other examples, the Soviet attack on the 'kulaks', and the Khmer Rouge assault on the people of its 'Eastern Zone'. These are consciously intended to problematise traditional methods of approaching the phenomenon while, at the same time, *not* abandoning the essential *genos* element – that is the biological connectedness of those targeted and murdered – in genocide.

Having established how we should approach the subject, our second chapter is primarily concerned with understanding what we mean by perpetrators and victims, even though these terms may ultimately be inadequate to describe the nature of the real or perceived state versus communal interactions at play. In particular, it argues that utilitarian, or instrumental explanations for the state's drive towards the systematic extermination of a communal 'aggregate' lack conviction on their own, requiring a further psycho-social dimension encompassing regime leadership, plus often significant sections of the dominant society, to translate the genocidal potential into its actualisation.

The third, and final chapter of this conceptual presentation, however, demands that all this needs to be placed within a firm historical context and that, while other closely related forms of mass murder are deeply embedded in history, there is good reason to argue that the specific explosion of genocide onto the world stage is closely associated with the coming – and crisis – of the modern age. Much of this presentation is developed discursively indeed as it will be throughout all four volumes, with an emphasis less on detailing an exact chronological plot and more with developing a thematic approach to the history of modern genocide.

Methodological Problems and Related Issues

This, then, is a macro-study of genocide which effectively starts from the premise that causation is to be found in grand Great Power geo-strategic calculations, as much as in the political thinking, cultural mores, or economic environment of particular societies. But, as stated right at the outset of this project, this carries with it an almost imponderable moral dilemma. It is human beings who suffer (as well as commit) genocide. Surely to treat them as abstractised items in some grand narrative is to be as guilty of the same clinical mindset with which we have already been at pains to charge a complicit modernity.

On one level, there is simply no adequate answer to this dilemma. All one can do, perhaps, is spell out what this work cannot do. It cannot offer solace. It cannot bring people back. Nor can it in any sense offer genuine insight into what it feels like to suffer humiliation and personal loss, let alone brutality and violent death. Neither, actually, can it directly answer the two most often repeated questions asked by my students: 'how is it that people can do these sort of things?' and, as its corollary, 'how can other people stand by and let it happen?' The nearest this work can come to responding, on the former score, is to propose that the question needs replacing by the somewhat different and certainly more detached question: 'why is it that people, in certain circumstances, do such things?' To this the answer might then be: read on. That said, anyone who is seeking, in these pages, a tranche of moral judgements is likely to be disappointed. Genocide is an authentic by-product of the dominant political and economic forces which – whether we like it nor not – determine and shape our lives. It is not the exclusive prerogative of evil men, however often in this work we will have to confront the clearly pathological in the human condition.

As for the latter question about bystanders, this is something with which this work chooses not to engage directly. This is not because it is an irrelevant question. Indeed, it touches upon arguably the fundamental *practical* issue associated with this work: how can ordinary people genuinely take control of their social and economic environments and, in such affirmative and life-sus- taining ways, that they can, in so doing, neutralise the conditions out of which genocide might arise, *before* it arises? This clearly places this author amongst those who see any future hope for mankind in actions and transformations shaped and determined from the grass-roots rather than, for instance, in reac- tive recourse to international juridical formulae. That said, genuine genocide prevention has to be grounded in a proper understanding of how we got here in the first place. It is not, then, that the heroism, the nobility or indeed the basic humanity of the rescuer – as of the resister – does not matter to this author, simply that it has to be secondary in a work whose immediate and pri- mary focus is on the etiology and transmission (hence, epidemiology) of the disease.

That still, however, does not adequately answer the problem of how one actually writes a history of genocide when the subject matter is so clearly obscene.[40] Or how one can represent the dehumanisation, degradation and extreme violence which is at its core without engaging inadvertently, or other- wise, in a form of sensationalist, even pornographic voyeurism.[41] Alternatively, is not the effect of writing of millions of disparate personal, familial and com- munal tragedies, as if they were part of a seamless whole, to turn each and every one of them into the undifferentiated mass of the perpetrator's wish- fulfilment?[42] Under these circumstances, questions of a balanced account, or elegant style, might be fairly preceded by the more acerbic question: why is one contemplating this exercise at all? The only justification that can be offered in response is that, until we more fully and effectively understand the root mechanisms of this all too prevalent and persistent phenomenon, silence on the matter may be equally unsatisfactory. This does not mean that the moral questions go away, simply that more immediate, methodological ones have to interpose.

Let us then consider the most intractable of these. Everybody in the West, of school age or beyond, has – however hazy – some idea of what happened to European Jewry in the Holocaust. And consequently every one is likely to be aware, once they have given the issue a modicum of thought, of the impact of that event upon the individual psyches and collective consciousness of Jewish survivors and their descendants. But this itself assumes some very basic knowledge of the event, knowledge which in turn presupposes not usually direct access to archival material but repeated communication of that material via bona fide historical accounts, supported by a much broader willingness, from the popular media, to engage with and promote information about the Holocaust, through television, cinema, internet, radio, in newspaper items and magazine stories; and all on a regular basis. Bit by bit, this process has become self-reinforcing, the subject not only having become integral to our Western consciousness and even sense of identity[43] but tangibly developed through university degrees and modules in the humanities and social sciences, as well as through integration into the national curricula of many countries, including Britain. Holocaust memorials, museums, days of commemoration are, thus, testament to the way an essentially private, interiorised part of Jewish collective mourning has been transformed into a very public, yet normative part of our general culture.

It is not our interest here to consider the exact process by which this has happened, nor to enter into the controversy associated with, for instance, Norman Finkelstein's charge that a 'Holocaust Industry' exists primarily to serve a Zionist agenda.[44] It is well known that, for more than a decade after the destruction of European Jewry, public silence on the subject dominated and even Raul Hilberg, latterly recognised as producing the magisterial and still paradigmatic study of the bureaucratic mechanisms driving the 'Final Solution', had difficulty finding a publisher for it.[45] This rather confirms that being Jewish, in itself, has hardly provided an automatic basis for Holocaust dissemination. However, the fact that, in recent decades, the Jewish demographic profile worldwide has come to correlate more closely with the relatively open, pluralist societies of the affluent West – especially in North America, where increasing Jewish economic success has generally combined with social acceptability and educational mobility[46] – has clearly played a seminal role in the manner in which this particular genocide has gradually seeped into broader popular consciousness. Jews are amply represented in Western universities and research institutes, where writing books and learned articles is a *sine qua non*. Beyond the ivory towers, publishing and media opportunities abound. The preconditions for a perfectly understandable Jewish predisposition to study and understand their own seminal catastrophe being translated into something more universally accessible are, in these conditions, neither mystery nor conspiracy. And this, regardless, of the undoubted political influence and power which some Jews, individually, and as part of collective lobby groups possess, particularly in the contemporary USA, in ways which would have been unimaginable fifty years ago.

The point which is being laboured here with regard to methodological approach is a simple one. Any attempt to assess the history of genocide in the broader sense, or to treat examples of the phenomenon as if they were equally relevant figures, as might be viewed on a level playing field, are massively handicapped at the outset by the fact that so much of the field has already been staked out by the custodians of one or more genocides who may, actually, additionally claim that the entire field legitimately belongs to them.[47] Nor, indeed, are such assertions, or assertiveness, dependent on access to the corridors of power *alone*. For instance, a parallel case to the Jewish one is that of the Armenians who, for nefarious political reasons, have been repeatedly disallowed official Western recognition of the *Aghet* – *their* genocide. This might be argued to represent a muzzle on Armenian progress, compared to which Holocaust custodians remain unencumbered. Arguably, however, the opposite is true. The very refusal to accept the truth of the matter, compared with the institutionalisation of the Holocaust, in the form of the US Holocaust Memorial Museum, in Washington DC –at the heart of the public life and space of the most powerful country in the world – actually provides the most potent goad for Armenian institutes and educational foundations to intensify their efforts to detail to the world the full horror of the 1915–16 events. The point though, is that while this clearly has the effect of turning genocide recognition into a competition, the Armenians are able to be serious and successful competitors in it, by dint of a social, educational and occupational diaspora profile highly resembling the Jewish one.[48]

Thus, such contemporary communal strengths, allied to favourable geographical and social opportunities, paradoxically confer a notable advantage to particular narratives of genocide, while also having the obverse effect of blanking out other less accessible ones. Alexander Solzhenitsyn, in *The Gulag Archipelago*, claims that we remember the Soviet mass killings of 1937–8 as if they were 'a whole Volga of the people's grief' yet forget 15 million peasants in 'a good river Ob' of destruction in 1929–30, let alone a Yenisei of the 1944 to 1946 wave, in which whole *nations* were dumped 'down the sewer pipes not to mention millions and millions of others'.[49] Why? asks Solzhenitsyn. Because it was intellectuals, educated people, party people, the sort who suffered in 1937, who could write, speak, give literary voice to their plaint. Simple people, in the other cataclysms, remained silent: they did not write memoirs.

But if Solzhenitsyn's point is valid – and it surely is – how much more is this so for fated peoples around the globe who do not have even a Solzhenitsyn to speak for them? At the chalk-face, in a British university, one is repeatedly reminded that Kurds, East Timorese, Chechens, Rwandans or even, for that matter, Armenians, offer no resonances whatsoever for the vast majority of the decent but largely white, middle-class young adults who are one's primary constituency. Imagine their consideration of the native inhabitants of the remote jungles of Amazonia, or the desert regions of sub-Saharan Africa, and the discrepancy becomes all the more gaping. In the late 1960s and early 1970s, the Aché people of Paraguay suffered a man-created catastrophe of such proportions that only a small proportion of them survived. We must surely assume that the searing impact of this disaster upon the individual psyches and collective consciousness of the survivors and their dwindling descendants was no less profound than the effect of the *Aghet*, or the Holocaust, had been on theirs. But then the Aché could hardly compete in the sort of numbers nightmare conjured up by Solzhenitsyn. Fatalities, all told, were certainly less than 1,000.[50] Does that mean, therefore, that we should only accord the Aché, or other small bands of wiped out 'native' peoples, passing consideration, our rule of prioritisation operating according to strictly quantitative criteria? Or is this again to skew the picture fatally by an implicit ethnocentric bias. Mark Mazower has perceptively voiced the anxiety thus:

> I think there may also have been a widely-held assumption that the mass killing of African or American peoples was distant and in some sense an 'inevitable' part of progress while what was genuinely shocking was the attempt to exterminate an entire people in Europe. The assumption may rest upon an implicit racism, or simply upon a failure of historical imagination; it leads, in either case, to the view that it was specifically with the Holocaust that European civilisation – the values of the Enlightenment, a confidence in progress and modernisation – finally betrayed itself.[51]

Mazower's comment is not intended to dispute, or in any sense downplay, the Holocaust – or, for that matter, the *Aghet* – any more than it conceals a covert effort to succour the ravings of denialists, on either score. The same is completely true of this work. Not only is denialism entirely reprehensible and nasty, but in the face of the overwhelming documentary, forensic, film, photographic, archaeological and architectural evidence, plus the plenitude of cross-referential eyewitness and survivor testimony detailing the Jewish and Armenian genocides, utterly ludicrous. But there's the rub. We have a corpus of facts around these events. They have been carefully, indeed meticulously, researched and validated. And their purveyors, primarily, if not exclusively, Jewish and Armenian scholars, are from communities which, while in the not so distant past, were reviled or ignored, have attained a status in the contemporary West where their professional elites are, for the most part, not only heard but listened to with respect.

The problem in writing a comprehensive history of modern genocide, thus is not a straightforward issue of creating some balance between the big 'metropolitan' genocides against supposedly smaller ones, on some geographical periphery. It is rather how we surmount this mindset, as predicated by Mazower, in the first place.[52] But even with the best will in the world such a drive to a fuller, more holistic, perspective has to acknowledge some critical problems en route.

The case of the Aché is an interesting, if ugly, illustration in point. That we know something of their fate actually says more about the fact that a handful of Western anthropologists happened to be there to witness and report on it than it does about the atrocity itself. Some of the anthropologists, plus the London-based NGO, Survival International, claimed that manhunts carried out by incoming settlers and military against the tribe amounted to a policy of organised and systematic genocide, a charge which actually was contested not only by the Paraguayan authorities but also by other anthropologists and advocacy groups. While, thus, nobody on the scene denied that Aché numbers were being fast decimated to the point where extinction seemed probable, a controversy nevertheless ensued over whether genocide was an appropriate description of what was happening.[53] Moreover, in no sense were the Aché themselves protagonists in this argument. In so far as they had had an opportunity to convey their story in their own words at all, it was at second hand, through the assistance of Western, educated professionals. Paradoxically, however, the nature of this transmission, inadvertently or otherwise, served to highlight the Aché as a special case, even though scores of other tribes were suffering then, as now, a remarkably similar process of degradation and destruction all across what remains of Amazonia.[54]

To propose that a production of history of this kind is thus dependent on certain unspoken yet intrinsic assumptions about the nature of power is perhaps to state the obvious. Except that it would seem to apply to a predicament – namely that of victimhood – where we might expect the mobilisation of such power to be divorced from the equation. In practice, however, what the Amazonian experience might instead highlight is that there could be many cases of unreported genocide – or at least cases to which the term genocide might apply, if we had the opportunity to give them the benefit of the doubt – not so much because they disappeared down some convenient memory hole but rather because that memory could not be manufactured into 'history' in the first place, the most important and credible reporters of the events being *entirely* disinherited and, hence, powerless.[55] True, an alternative reading might argue that most such modern genocides are ultimately recoverable for posterity but at the price of being reported either by the perpetrators, or, as we have already suggested, at second, or third hand. Even in the latter case, however, while the ensuing narrative might not be intent on fragmenting or distorting the whole truth of the story, as it would in the former, it would more than likely be predicated on a worldview at considerable odds with that of the actual victims.

Such considerations are extraordinarily perplexing for a work of this nature which, because of the very scope of its undertaking, is dependent on the writings of others. Equally problematic, however, might be cases where a group has suffered genocide – or alleges to have done so – but then has survived, regrouped, re-empowered itself, and then sought memorialisation of the event but closely aligned with more contemporary political agendas. This could be true of parts of the Jewish and Armenian communities, both of which today have both 'minority' diasporic as well as state dimensions.

Let us take another example, a case of contested genocide within the boundaries of what became the post-1945 federal communist state of Yugoslavia, which has since fragmented into other smaller nation-states, two of which, Serbia and Croatia, fought a vicious sequence of wars with each other in the early 1990s. Both in the immediate decade before, and during these events, scholars as well as politicians from either side of the divide invested a great deal of energy to offer markedly different versions of what had happened in the Nazi-sponsored Croatian *ustashi* state, during the Second World War, and, more particularly, in its major concentration camp, at Jasenovac. For former Yugoslav historians and then, more specifically, Serbian commentators, a figure of some six or seven hundred thousand mostly Serb, as well as Jewish and Roma fatalities was repeatedly cited, and endorsed in state literature, as its consequence.[56] Other, most particularly Croat writers, however, repeatedly downgraded these figures, often by a factor of more than ten but also by inferring that a significant proportion of those killed in the camp, or elsewhere, were Croat.[57] For a writer such as this one, operating at second hand, which version then does he accept: the one which proposes the larger fatality figure, because it sounds grander and more serious, or the one which offers a smaller number, because it appears more careful and cautious? Alternatively, does he decide both figures are suspicious and that the only thing is do a cross-check, requiring in turn his considerable investment in learning Serbo-Croat for the purpose? Or does he give up entirely, convinced that each of these narratives is only really indicative of its propagandist or polemical value?

There may be no simple and straightforward answer to such conundrums, though, as a matter of fact, the Jasenovac example potentially points us in directions out of the dark tunnel of political agendas. Two rigorous and meticulously prepared quantitative studies, in the 1980s, one by a Croat, Vladimir

Žerjavic, the other by a Bosnian Serb, Boguljub Kočović, came to remarkably similar conclusions about the demographic losses suffered by a range of ethnic groups in wartime Yugoslavia. The fact that they found that these were not nearly as high as were broadcast in nationalist or state versions in no sense detracted from the extent of the disaster wrought on all affected communities, while equally demonstrating that mature, honest and entirely independent researchers were quite capable of rising above ethnic backgrounds and were not impelled in their assessments by some unrelenting axe to grind.[58]

There is, of course, a dreadful irony in this story, in that, by the late 1980s, nobody much in Yugoslavia was listening to these calm but compassionate voices. If people want to believe something is true, even when the evidence points in very different directions, there is usually very little those with authentic information can do about it. Indeed, it is exactly such obdurate refusal to recognise a usually complex reality, especially when it is about people, or peoples about whom one has already made up one's mind, which is such a powerful ingredient in the continuing transmission belt of genocide. For a book such as this, however, it is exactly the purveyors of complex truths who provide it with its lifeline. Writing history, at the best of times, involves a form of adjudication. One considers, evaluates and weighs up the evidence and attempts to come to some conclusion about its significance within a broader context, usually by selecting from the available material that which one considers most salient or pertinent. Doing this at second hand, on the basis of other people's work, is hardly a recipe for perfection. One is, thus, doubly reliant on specific studies of genocide, or, for that matter, non-genocide, which one assumes to be sound and, hence, dictated by research itself founded on honesty and integrity. Unfortunately, this does not necessarily reduce the problems of adjudication. What may have been a wisdom twenty or thirty years ago, may have changed in the light of new information, as well as changing perspectives on the specific subject matter.

New information, of course, may be an unadulterated bonus. When, in March 1991, in the immediate aftermath of the first Gulf War against Ba'athist Iraq, Kurdish *peshmerga* in the north of the country were briefly able to take over offices and buildings formerly controlled by the Mukhabarat, the feared secret police, they uncovered vast archives in which the regime's 'astonishing penchant for documentation of its own terror' was revealed.[59] Without all the hundreds of thousands of reports and video recordings adumbrating the surveillance, rape and torture of their victims, not to say a more specific corpus of military communications and tape recordings, the 1993 Middle East Watch report, extensively charting and analysing Saddam Hussein's 'Anfal' campaigns for the annihilation of the Kurds five years earlier, would have had to have been developed primarily on the basis of guesswork.[60] One may, in the same vein, hope that the opening of, for instance, Chinese, Indonesian or Turkish archives may, one day in the future, reveal a great deal more for the historian of genocide.

That said, this does not always resolve the issue of how one positions oneself between strikingly different approaches to particular cases of genocide, or alleged genocide, whether based on fresh documentary evidence or not. It is easy enough to repudiate the charge made by historian and Nazi apologist, David Irving, that because no written Führer order to command the initiation of the 'Final Solution' has ever been found, it therefore follows that Hitler either did not know of, or by extension never intended to exterminate European Jewry.[61] So much other documentary evidence is available which throws light on the connection, so minutely analysed by scores of authoritative experts, that we hardly need detain ourselves with regard to a commentator so obviously motivated by plain malice.[62] This does not mean, of course, that no questions on this score remain. The lack, disappearance, or wilful destruction of key pieces of decodable evidence may determine, for instance, that conclusive proof as to an exact moment for the launching of the 'Final Solution' may never be recoverable and, hence, will continue to remain open to intelligent, interpretative speculation. The organisers of genocide are usually very careful to keep their annihilatory orders secret and encoded. In the Nazi case, indeed, this was compounded by a conscious and systematic effort on the part of the perpetrators to erase much of the material evidence of what they had done.[63] Yet, in spite of this, we have considerable (indeed vast) documentary evidence on the Holocaust and a vast body of scholars willing to invest time and energy in its scrutiny.

What is arguably much more difficult to evaluate are cases where the opening up of archives has given rise to quite new revisionist approaches, often radically at odds with wisdoms provided by an earlier generation of – by now – very renowned scholars. For instance, the absolute totalitarianism of the Stalinist regime, and the many millions of Soviet deaths which were allegedly testimony to it, were adumbrated not only in *The Gulag Archipelago* but in Robert Conquest's ground-breaking studies, originally in the 1960s and 1970s.[64] Twenty years later, a new generation of Western scholars, with an access to the Soviet archives not available to Conquest, arrived on the scene and proceeded, amongst other things, to downgrade the casualty figures drastically.[65] At stake here, however, was not just a numbers dispute, the like of which we have already encountered in the Jasenovac case. Interrogating Conquest's – or for that matter Solzhenitsyn's – figures could, in these twilight years of Soviet communism, also be interpreted as somehow condoning or even giving succour to what to the revisionists were now claiming was an actually rather shambolic regime, when the conventional scholarly wisdom all the way through the long and lethal years of the Cold War had been characterising it as the very epitome of evil. Should this influence a synoptic study of this nature in favour of one interpretation or the other? By the same token, looking back at an earlier moment in history, if we were to accept that what happened in the Vendée is deserving of the appellation 'genocide', might this not appear to align us with often very ultra-conservative French groupings whose very advocacy of its commemoration seems to be, at least in part, guided by an outrage at the central place of the Holocaust in contemporary culture and, obversely, by an attempt to overturn that implicit hierarchy in favour of a quite different set of closed, exclusive and ethnocentric values?[66]

If this author thus, on the one hand chooses to listen seriously to what the revisionist scholars of the USSR have been saying alongside that of more traditional sources and, on the other, to accept that the Vendée *is* a case of genocide, it is simply because he has attempted to assess the evidence as cogently as possible, and come to some sort of conclusions on that basis. Seeking the truth, in all its forms, however discomfiting those truths are, may be a somewhat old-fashioned pursuit. In cases where the charge is genocide, it is certainly to acknowledge that one may run into all manner of disputes and controversies in the process. This is not to assume, however, that one can set oneself up as some sort of arbiter, not least when what is being articulated is not rocket science but history, that is – amongst other things – the study of human folly, foible and capriciousness. Nor does this specific study make any claims towards some detached, disinterested neutrality, as if this is what the historian's highest virtue can be. Too much is actually at stake here: those parts of the record which have been repeatedly but erroneously denied, or relegated to a footnote, possibly because little information on them exists, or more damningly, perhaps, because they do not neatly fit onto a Western cognitive map.[67] Or equally, there are those parts of the record which are consciously airbrushed out, because they are about a particular type of victim, whose mass deaths cannot be blamed on an official enemy but may be the fault of our 'own' side.

Desiring to piece together this massive jigsaw in the face of perpetrator cover-up, subterfuge and blatant disinformation, whoever that perpetrator may be, can hardly be accomplished by an insouciant disinterest. Whether it can be accomplished by a transparent honesty is another matter. But there is no doubt that such honesty has to be a *sine qua non* for this study. Because one might agree that numbers may be open to interpretation, or, indeed, posit that numbers games in themselves may not be what the study of genocide ought most fundamentally be about, is not to repudiate that *many* genocides, for instance, took place in a Soviet context. Similarly, to confirm the Vendée as a genocide is not, thereby, to diminish the Holocaust. Nor, as it happens, is it to demand that these, or any other examples, have to be considered in some sort of uneasy counterpoint with one another. On one level, all genocides need to be treated with regard (and respect) to their particular dynamic, their peculiar, necessarily individual and unrepeatable features.

The challenge, implicit in this study, however, is the degree to which we can successfully stand back from the fray in order to see the wood for the trees. Our premise remains that genocide is not so much a series of isolated, aberrant and essentially unconnected events but is at the very heart of modern historical development. Paradoxically, this is why, while maintaining a rigorous definition of genocide, we have so much subject matter with which to engage. Doubly paradoxically, part of our intrinsic challenge will also be to delineate – as far as is possible – the degree to which we are dealing with an identifiably discrete phenomenon within a much broader and, indeed, unremittingly scarred landscape of mass exterminatory violence, a consideration which, instead of extracting it into an entirely separate category of its own, might demand some additional effort in framing its specific morphology, as well as in locating its more particular psycho-social and political, etiology. That said, the appearance of fuller data may, in time, change the specific contours of this investigation, just as rigorous counter-analysis may challenge or undermine its basic conception. It should go without saying that responsibility for any failings rests entirely at this author's door.

The Meaning
of Genocide

1. Definitional Conundrums

Opening Shots

> Genocide occurs when a state, perceiving the integrity of its agenda to be threatened by an aggregate population – defined by the state as an organic collectivity, or series of collectivities – seeks to remedy the situation by the systematic, *en masse* physical elimination of that aggregate, *in toto*, or until it is no longer perceived to represent a threat.[1]

How should we understand the term genocide? The above formulation is not a definition as such. It is an attempt – consistent with the historical grounding of this account – to provide both a conceptual and contextual frame of reference for a phenomenon which has *repeatedly* taken place in the modern world. Why not then begin with the official version, the 1948 United Nations Convention on the Prevention and Punishment of Genocide (hereafter UNC)? The Convention's key article – Article II – does clearly define genocide: as 'acts committed with intent to destroy in whole or in part, a national, ethnical, racial or religious group.'[2] Many scholars in the field have found this definition flawed and unsatisfactory while others have deferred to it simply because in international law it *is* canonical.[3] This author also disputes the value of the UNC as a tool for understanding the nature of genocide. Whether it has any value as a means for either preventing or punishing human rights violations is for others to decide.[4]

However, my interest here in offering an alternative formulation is primarily to do with historical process. The UNC would appear to define genocide as something which has a pre-existing teleology, almost to the point where the actors responsible for genocide were governed by a fixed and given blueprint of what they were going to do. It may be in many, if not the majority of such cases, that there exists – at least in the actors' heads, if not on paper – a pre-script of this sort. But translating it into action is contingent on events, very often events which, far from being expected or foretold, actually, literally, came out of the blue. This is not to deny, then, that intention may not be a key factor in the act; it is simply to propose that the actuality of genocide, in practice, like all human-made catastrophes, is dependent on a form of collision between the avowed interests and intentions of the actors and the very complex, not to say capricious nature of contingency.

Does this mean, then, that genocide is just a convenient term for entirely 'disparate phenomena' which just happen to have 'superficial characteristics in common'?[5] My answer to this proposition, however, would be a very definite no. It is worth studying the many instances of genocide, as a totality, for the very reason that they do have a not only remarkably common but also consistent set of causative ingredients. This does not mean that the study of genocide can be an exact science reducible to a mathematical equation. But it is, nevertheless, chartable as a phenomenon (albeit one that also repeatedly merges into others along a continuum of extreme violence) and, in so doing, links similar cases across time and space into a sinuous yet discernible pattern.

Proper sense cannot be made of this pattern, however, without foregrounding the very actor – the modern state – notable by its remarkable absence in the UNC, even though again, as we will see, what exactly constitutes a state in cases of genocide might itself be open to further scrutiny. By the same token, while agreeing that the *genos* in genocide, as a term for representing the biological connectedness of those killed, is the most appropriate term available with regard to the phenomenon, our formulation would dispute that using a series of fixed labels – ethnical, racial or whatever – tells us very much about what turns state actors genocidal or who it is that is the object of their wrath. That said, our formulation is of a particular type of mass murder: one which is directed against 'some', not 'any', and involves direct physical killing of the targeted population. It also infers, though perhaps less explicitly spells out, that genocide has spatial and temporal characteristics that cannot be simply equated to a single episode of mass murder but, rather, point to a definite sequence of killing taking place in different, if usually geographically linked locations, though also at some juncture coming to a definite end. Above all, it is a formulation which seeks implicitly to suggest that this is a particular type of experience which has emerged out of a broader process of historical development and which has shaped not only how we understand ourselves as social organisms but also our place in the world.

What follows are a series of discussions around which this formulation has emerged. In part, what is being signposted here are lines of thinking which have been weighed up and then either eliminated or discarded as insufficient for the task in hand. In more major part, however, two distinct routes are more fully developed. The first follows and expands upon Raphael Lemkin's interest in the relationship between genocide and war. The second is an attempt via five key examples of genocide – three generally accepted, two more bitterly contested – to determine what genocide is, as if it were 'an ideal type'. These routes effectively provide the ground rules by which the subject of genocide will be pursued in subsequent chapters and volumes.

The Problem of Genocide

Let us begin with a paradox. Genocide is neither an obscure nor remote term for the majority of people in the Western world. It may have been invented only in the 1940s but it has rapidly – particularly in recent years – become part of our normal linguistic currency and, indeed, an important facet of our sense of the world and what happens in it. That that should be so, on one level, ought to be treated very positively, as it would appear to show a general awareness of the acute malfunction of not just particular societies but of our global community writ large. Yet the fact is that the term now is so broadly used and abused that it has become much less a tool for understanding and much more a millstone around our necks.

This is not a study of the way genocide has become part of our cultural baggage. Nevertheless, it is well for a moment to consider the ubiquity of its usage. Death on the roads, abortion, AIDS, man's inhumanity to animals, as well as the dangers of nuclear warfare, are all regularly claimed by different interest groups to be forms of genocide.[6] The phenomenon, as a result, says David Moshman, has become 'the ultimate human rights catastrophe and thus the measure of all such catastrophes.'[7] Using the term, in other words, effectively is to make an accusation against whatever it is that one thinks is the very worst thing imaginable. The accusation is not only levelled at present crimes and evils. The Atlantic slave trade is often charged as a genocide.[8] This author recalls being harangued at a workshop for not calling apartheid a genocide.[9] By refusing to do so my own political and social credentials were put on the line. Of course, what is, and is not, to be classed in this way, may depend heavily on the company one keeps. For some, particularly many Jewish people, to suggest that any event, or item, is a genocide, other than the Holocaust, would be equally wrongheaded, not to say sacrilegious.[10] To steer a course between these two extremes, the one, where everything bad is genocide and the other, where everything bad is encapsulated in one terrible series of events, is akin to being caught between Scylla and Charybdis. Whatever position one takes, the result will be an offence to somebody. One can only conclude that 'genocide' has become, on the one hand, so ubiquitous a term, yet on the other, so unmalleable to interrogation, that is has completely lost any descriptive value.

Significantly, however, the problem is not just a layman's one. Much scholarly entrenchment reflects how perilously one might have to risk a trip across 'no man's land' in order to recover the term for fresh analysis. The barrage en route is most likely to come from two entirely polarised but fixed positions. The first is from the inclusivist camp: one that treats genocide as a very broad phenomenon, effectively embracing it thereby as the measure of all human rights catastrophes. The exclusivity camp, by contrast, would restrict usage of the term to a very small, if not sole example of the phenomenon which is also tightly ringfenced from any inference of comparability with further possible examples.

The former position is most obviously exemplified in the work of Israel W. Charny. Charny has been among the first and most vociferous exponents of comparative genocide studies. He also has consistently argued from the moral high ground and considers it both humanistic and commonsensical to aver 'that, unless clear-cut self-defence can be reasonably proven, whenever a large number of people are put to death by other people, it constitutes genocide.'[11] This 'self-evident truth', as Charny puts it, would certainly receive the plaudits of all those who would not exclude anything from the genocide list. But leaving aside the tricky problem that all genocide perpetrators would argue that their actions are motivated by clear-cut self-defence, the efficacy of Charny's explication would have to lead to writs being served against the world's major multi-national corporations on the grounds of their responsibility for the annual death of millions in the third world as a result of the structural inequalities they cause.[12] Perhaps, inadvertently, Charny has a point. The problem here, however, is straightforward: why should one substitute the term 'mass murder' with 'genocide' when the former is not only perfectly adequate but actually much less open to interpretation? Indeed, one might charge that the amplification of this introduced term when we already have massacre, civil war, coup, revolution, man-made famine, total war and nuclear obliteration as guides to the politically-inspired violent deaths of possibly 187 million people this last century,[13] can only serve to muddy the water.

What then of the alternative approach: to try and define genocide in such a way that it can only refer to a very limited number of case histories? A starting point here might be the leading Holocaust scholar, Yehuda Bauer. Surprisingly, however, despite his many – and often quite diverse – pronouncements on the subject, Bauer has never offered a particularly categorical formulation suggesting how the anatomy, etiology or morphology of genocide is markedly distinct from other exterminatory *modus operandi*. His 1984 statement, for instance, that genocide is 'the planned destruction, since the mid-nineteenth century, of a racial, national or ethnic group',[14] while mirroring the UNC emphasis on intent against specific groups, provides more questions than answers. The chronological watershed inferring that genocide only began to take place after c. 1850 might be a valuable signpost if it could be shown that this was the case, alongside whatever new criteria made this so. This volume will certainly support the contention that there are mid-nineteenth-century genocides – in Central Asia, the Americas and the antipodes – the one and major proviso being that it will also argue that there were many other genocides, some in quite different locations, considerably earlier. The key problem with Bauer, however, is that while he is prepared to countenance that a limited number of groups, notably the Ottoman Armenians, suffered from what he calls this 'loosely termed "genocide"',[15] he is very grudging to place these examples in the same category as the Holocaust, which he considers an altogether more thoroughgoing and ideologically motivated affair. Bauer's position, in short, is that while genocide exists as an isolated phenomenon specific to the mass killing of particular and identifiable groups, the only one really compelling example is actually so extraordinary that similarities between it and other examples are entirely outweighed by the differences.[16]

The problem is that if the Holocaust is utterly singular, not to say 'unique', it actually has the effect of subverting any attempt to define a more general category of genocide. Bauer, however, is not a lone voice. Saul Friedlander, another major Holocaust historian, for instance, repudiates the very notion that the Holocaust can be placed 'within the framework of explanatory categories of a generalising kind':

> The absolute character of the anti-Jewish drive of the Nazis makes it impossible to integrate the extermination of the Jews, not only within the general framework of Nazi persecutions, but even within the wider aspects of contemporary ideologico-political behaviour such as fascism, totalitarianism, economic exploitation and so on.[17]

Interestingly, Friedlander is not refuting – as some do – that historical factors and trends caused the Holocaust. But his singularity argument, not unlike that of Bauer's, either leaves us in the rather bizarre predicament where genocide exists minus the Holocaust or, alternatively, has to be squarely confronted as the *only* example of the phenomenon.

This is the more recent thesis of Steven T. Katz who, to date, has completed only the first massive volume in a projected multi-volume work which ranges exhaustively across ancient, medieval and modern history to prove the point. Katz offers a more thoroughgoing definition of genocide than does Bauer, yet also one which appears superficially to mirror the conventional UNC wisdom. Genocide should be employed, Katz proposes, with regard to the intent to murder 'any national, ethnic, racial, religious, political, social, gender or economic group, as these groups are defined by the perpetrator, by whatever means'.[18] Actually, this rubric, considered more closely, would appear to be not only more expansive but also more rigorous than that of the UNC, providing for inclusion of groups which do not appear in it, as well as utilising an important aspect of other scholars' insights on the nature of perpetrator projection.[19] So far so good. Where Katz shifts into an entirely different gear is in his assertion that the notion of genocide should only be applied to 'the *actualisation* of the intent, however successfully carried out, to murder in its totality' (my emphasis).[20] In other words, Katz not only makes intentionality absolutely fundamental to his defintion but also in effect demands that any advocate for the inclusion of a prospective case in his genocide 'list' would need to demonstrate that the perpetrators had moved beyond design to attempt the entire physical extermination of the targeted group.

Katz's restrictive definitional parameters, of course, have a quite explicit purpose; namely, to prove that what he calls the 'phenomenological incommensurability'[21] of the Nazi drive against the Jews was the only event of its kind in history. Ironically, even by his own frame of reference, this may be seriously flawed, given the not wholly consistent thrust towards the 'Final Solution'. Obversely, if one were to put aside the entire historical record up to 1994[22] – the date of publication of his first volume – Katz would be hard pressed to demonstrate that, again, even by his own criteria, the events in Rwanda of that year were *not* a genocide.[23]

It is the recent confrontation of a Western public with events in Rwanda and Bosnia, however, which makes the ongoing efficacy of the 'Holocaust equals genocide' camp that much more difficult to sustain. Whether expressed as the 'prototypical' genocide to which others, if they are to be considered as genocides have to conform,[24] or, alternatively, as an event so extraordinary that its definitional relationship to other mass murders becomes practically insurmountable, neither of these paradigms would seem particularly adequate in the face of the mounting empirical evidence that specific group-exterminations have been running at a post-1945 average of around one a year.[25]

This does not necessarily mean that scholars with this more contemporary historical focus have the answer to the fundamental problem of conceptualisation. Indeed, Barbara Harff and Ted Gurr, who have, in particular, charted cases of state violence against subject populations in a contemporary timeframe, have, if anything, signalled the insufficiency of the term genocide by proposing that 'communal characteristics i.e. ethnicity, religion or nationality', cannot meet the growing corpus of cases in which 'the victim groups are defined primarily in terms of their hierarchical position or political opposition to the regime and dominant groups'.[26]

Whatever one may think about their proposal for filling this gap with a new term 'politicide' – to sit alongside that of genocide – what is clearly devastating about the Harff and Gurr studies is the globally endemic, not to say recidivist, quality and quantity of organised exterminatory assaults by states on elements of their *own* populations since the Second World War. With fatalities running into many millions, arguably in excess of those from international and civil wars in this same period, these sort of studies do seem to raise (in contradistinction to Friedlander's Holocaust-centric rebuttal) the possibility that genocide is actually a symptom of particular types of social, economic or political environment. However, while the Harff–Gurr studies alongside those of Helen Fein,[27] show that the majority of cases have been associated with totalitarian, authoritarian or ethnically dominant regimes, we would be going down a cul-de-sac if we were to infer from this that genocide *itself* is a system. Putting aside the appropriateness of terms such as 'totalitarian' to describe, for instance, a wide range of Soviet bloc regimes, even acceptance of the criteria would not explain why it is that many, possibly the majority of such regimes have *not* committed genocide in the last fifty years. By the same token, extending the time-frame back over the last hundred, or two hundred years could equally be challenging if we were then to discover that the list of perpetrator states included those we might otherwise label as liberal-democratic (and this leaving aside the more recent complicity of such states in genocides committed elsewhere). In short, being able to identify a state regime as a particular political type, does not *of its own* advance description, conceptualisation or explanation of our phenomenon. Genocide is not something fixed in the make-up of regimes. It is, however, something which *different* types of regimes *do*.

Nevertheless, if, as is being inferred, the phenomenon of genocide, both before and after the Holocaust divide, is actually a relatively common – as opposed to entirely exceptional – feature of the modern world, a formulation which leaves the potential for the act entirely in the realm of chance, would seem equally unsatisfactory. Claiming, as the UNC does, its intention to outlaw this 'odious scourge' it is particularly fascinating then how scrupulously its definition avoids the one most tangible element in the perpetration of genocide, not to say the one that so utterly grounds it in the modern world – the sovereign state. Need we remind ourselves that the UNC was created by the *United Nations* on the very cusp of the creation of a globalised, contiguously interlocking system of such *nation*-states and on the principle, however spurious in practice, that each and every one of them, whether Burkina-Faso, or the United States of America, was an equally independent, internationally recognised sovereign entity? Indeed, the drafters of the UNC were operating in the immediate wake of the ratification of the United Nations Charter, a supposed recipe for peace, global governance and international cooperation which was first and foremost a compact neither between individual human beings nor communal groups but again, this very self-same club of actual or (in light of the post-colonial record) would-be sovereign states.[28] The reason, thus, that the UNC defintion omits any reference to its constituent members is not only because this would bring the club itself into public disrepute but because it would effectively deny to each and every one of its number 'as an integral part of its sovereignty the right to commit genocide, or engage in genocidal massacres against peoples under its rule'.[29]

Leo Kuper's shocking insight should explain why any rigorous conceptual treatment of genocide based on the UNC is impossible. Indeed, if the avowed antidote to the reality of genocide is actually framed in such a way that it leaves the actual or potential perpetrator out of the equation, is it any wonder that 'the UN definition of genocide is responsible for much of the confusion that plagues scholarly work in the field'?[30] If we are to make further progress it is perhaps time to retrace our steps from where we have come; that is back to the moment in time when the term 'genocide' was invented.

The Lemkin Thesis

Genocide's first public appearance can be attributed to a book, published in 1944, under the auspices of the Washington-based Carnegie Endowment for International Peace, and entitled *Axis Rule in Occupied Europe*. Its author was a Polish-Jewish jurist and expert in international law, Raphael Lemkin, who had fled war-torn Europe in 1941 by an extraordinarily difficult and circuitous route and who, hardly surprisingly, spent the rest of the war wracked with anxiety and guilt about the fate of the family he had left behind.[31] However, neither Lemkin's book nor his new term – from the Greek *genos* meaning 'race' or 'tribe' and the Latin, *cide* indicating killing – was, as is often commonly assumed, exclusively about the Nazi extermination of the Jews. To a certain degree this was a straightforward matter of information, or rather its lack. Lemkin knew that European Jewry was suffering a 'process of liquidation' and that this involved starvation methods, deportations and ghetto massacres.[32] However, like the vast majority of even well-informed people in the United

States and Britain, he did not realise the full import of the 'Final Solution' perpetrated through *Einsatzgruppen* operations and the death camps.

Even had that been the case it is doubtful from what we know of Lemkin that he would have restricted his study accordingly. For more than a decade prior to *Axis Rule* and entirely on his own account, Lemkin had been charting and attempting to analyse both contemporary examples of ethnic group destruction, such as the Armenians, as well as ostensibly similar but more ancient historical case-studies; a project which had he lived longer would certainly have led to the first comparative history of genocide.[33] Yet Lemkin's scholarship was hardly of an ivory tower nature. It was entirely geared towards the prevention of such onslaughts in the future, an agenda that, given the jurist's professional expertise and liberal universalist optimism, led to a literally one-man obsession to have the League of Nations and, latterly, the United Nations take up the issue. His first lobbying efforts, presented to the 1933 League International Conference in Madrid, for the Unification of Criminal Law, proposed that an international treaty oulaw attacks on national, religious and ethnic groups as 'a crime of barbarity'.[34] Despite the recent assault by the newly sovereign Iraqi state on its Assyrian (Nestorian) community, Lemkin's proposal went entirely unheeded. *Axis Rule* represented a redoubling of the effort. With a European landscape in which the Nazi 'destruction of *peoples*'[35] provided all the chapter and verse Lemkin would ever need for his argument, he proceeded in the crucial chapter 9 of his book to restate his case, but this time forearmed with a new concept.

Genocide, said Lemkin, is 'a coordinated plan of different actions aiming at the destruction of the essential foundations of the life of national groups, with the aim of annihilating the groups themselves'. This, he continued, did not necessarily have to entail '*immediate destruction*' but was part of an overall plan to cause '*the disintegration of the political and social institutions of the group*', including the 'destruction of the personal security, liberty, health, dignity, and *even the lives of the individuals* belonging to such groups' (my emphases).[36] Lemkin's argument, therefore, is two-fold. The perpetrator's ultimate aim is 'the destruction of the *biological* structure' of such national groups, Lemkin making it clear that in the context of Nazi-occupied Europe this signified their supplanting by the German 'nation'. However, Lemkin also infers here that the routes by which this goal would be reached might be manifold and varied.[37] For instance, Lemkin perceived a number of synchronous Nazi strategies at work: direct mass murder of whole populations, especially of Russians, Poles and Jews, certainly, but also the softening up of these populations and others by the extermination or deportation of their intelligentsia. A conscious strategy of starvation was another possibility, particularly if it could be engineered to lowering the survival capacity of children.[38] If this might not entail immediate destruction, a further linked but more medium-term strategy could involve arresting the reproductive capacities of a group. Lemkin, at this point, quoted Hitler's own recorded 'table-talk' thoughts on this score:

> ... by remove I don't necessarily mean destroy: I shall simply take systematic measures to dam their great natural fertility. For example, I shall keep their men and women separated for years. Do you remember the falling birthrate of the [first] world war? Why should we not do quite consciously and through a number of years what was at the time merely the inevitable consequence of the long war? There are many ways systematical and comparatively painless or at any rate bloodless, of causing undesirable races to die out.[39]

German 'techniques', to this end, argued Lemkin, included not only the deportation of fit men for forced and life-threatening labour but also, in areas such as Alsace-Lorraine and Luxembourg, earmarked for 'Germanisation', the abolition of local law courts, the removal of traditional street signs and the banning in schools of French or Letzeburgesch. Even encouraging excessive alcohol consumption and the substitution of 'vocational education for education in the liberal arts' could be part of this genocidal package.[40] Lemkin was not being trite. Indeed, he was being entirely consistent with his 1933 proposals where the crime of 'barbarity'; namely, direct physical destruction of population groups, had its counterpoint in the crime of 'vandalism', where the groups found themselves emasculated through the stifling of their culture, language, national feelings, religion and economic existence.

Very specific acts of destruction could, arguably, act as a bridge between the two forms. Lemkin specifically cited the burning of the great Talmudic library, in Lublin in March 1941 as indication of an intent to obliterate, in this case, Jewish people's culture through the destruction of their most precious communal artefacts and collective written memory.[41] This same line of reasoning prevailed in the brief but significant period after *Axis Rule* in which Lemkin found himself being listened to in the highest corridors of power.[42] Charged with responsibility by the recently formed UN Secretariat for drafting an instrument for the prevention and punishment of the crime of genocide – recognised by that name in a UN General Assembly Resolution in December 1946 – Lemkin confirmed its different but interrelated physical, biological and cultural components. Direct physical annihilation – one might say the fast-speed approach – had its corollary in measures aimed at reducing the biological base of a population, while the will of the group to live as a group could ultimately be sapped and finally extirpated by a battery of coercive measures aimed at making that impossible. Ultimately, argued Lemkin this 'composite of different acts of persecution or destruction' could all constitute genocide.[43]

Lemkin's logic remains in attenuated form in the version of the UNC finally agreed and unanimously adopted by its General Assembly in December 1948. Attenuated for the simple reason that Lemkin had been pushed out of the last stages of drafting by big and small state players who wanted nothing in the text which would have the UNC rebounding against them.[44] The degree to which the red pen was applied, however, is rather noteworthy. Practically the whole cultural element of Lemkin's package, including 'prohibition of the use of the national language, destruction of books, documents, monuments, and objects of historical, artistic or religious value'[45] was deleted or withdrawn. This was not only the work of major players such as the United States and France. Delegates on the so-called *ad hoc* drafting committee, including members from South Africa, Sweden, New Zealand and Brazil, also played their part, the Brazilian, for instance, warning that cultural protection in the Convention would have some minorities using it 'as an excuse for opposing perfectly normal assimilation'.[46] State sensitivities when it came to immigrants, indigenous peoples, or those simply deemed outside the national community also ensured that measures against both forced exile and population mass displacement – or in today's parlance, ethnic cleansing – were energetically resisted by the majority of states, which is hardly surprising considering that a significant number were, at this very juncture either in the throes of, had just completed, or were heavily complicit in major programmes of this nature.[47] Most significantly of all, perhaps, 'political groups' which Lemkin had included in his original rubric of potential victims, as part of his Secretariat draft submission,[48] were also cut, though not solely at the behest of the USSR, as is normally assumed, but with the support of a wide range of delegates, including that, ultimately, of the United States.[49]

This left Article II referring to acts of genocide against national, ethnic, racial or religious groups by:

a) Killing member of the group;
b) Causing serious bodily or mental harm to members of the group;
c) Deliberately inflicting on the group conditions of life calculated to bring about its physical destruction in whole or in part;
d) Imposing measures intended to prevent births within the group;
e) Forcibly transferring children of the group to another group.[50]

Clearly a cursory view of this list suggests the degree to which it had been eviscerated. That said, enough survives as a legacy to Lemkin's original formulation of genocide as a series of interlinked components. In short, if the UNC itself is deeply flawed, Lemkin's groundwork is less easily dismissible. Its most compelling feature is the identification of named annihilatory policies perpetrated against specific groups. Equally persuasive is the way Lemkin demonstrates that annihilation as such can never be viewed in isolation but has a developmental, cumulative trajectory in which a variety of coercive strategies might be applied to the targeted group by way of 'preparatory' measures. A key element of Lemkin's secretariat draft, for instance, before its removal by the hatchet men, refers to 'all forms of propaganda tending by their systematic and hateful character to provoke genocide, or tending to make it appear as a necessary, legitimate or excusable act'.[51] How can one conceive of the Nazi 'Final Solution' against Jews and Roma except against a backdrop of government-fostered as well as societally embedded hate? Or of all the other preparatory measures against these targeted groups: removing their citizenship rights, shutting off their ability to make a living, expropriating their property, isolating them from the rest of the population, terrorising their persons, incarcerating them in prisons, ghettos and camps, and so on. Similarly, how could one consider events in Kosovo, in the late spring and early summer of 1999, with all their ingredients for a *potential* mass onslaught on the ethnic Albanian population, except by reference to 'arguably the worst human rights abuses in the whole of Europe'?[52]

Yet if that is the case, where exactly do we locate the onset of these actual or potential genocides? In the Kosovo case is it in 1989, with the repudiation of its autonomy within the Yugoslav federation and the imposition of draconian and martial rule by the Milosevic regime in Belgrade? Surely this would meet one of Lemkin's many elucidations of genocide as a 'synchronised attack on different aspects of the life of captive peoples'.[53] Or is it even earlier, in 1912, for instance, when Serbia achieved firm control of the province and attempted – largely unsuccessfully – to ethnically cleanse it of Albanians by massacre and forced deportation? By the same token, we may have no difficulty in discerning an accumulating array of anti-Jewish and anti-Roma laws and practices from the commencement of Nazi rule in Germany in 1933 (and indeed in the Roma case long before then) which, while they do necessarily connote the aim to bring about the 'destruction of the biological structure'[54] of these groups, were manifestly motivated by a desire *to get rid of them*. Are we to assume, therefore, that Nazi genocide begins in 1933 as opposed to a generally accepted date of sometime during the course of 1941? If this is so, should we be thinking of a genocide not so much as a spasm or sequence in which group extermination is massively unleashed but rather as an ongoing process, in which the peaks of mass violence should be understood as only the most overt of the instruments calculated to bring about the group's physical destruction?

This author would argue that, while Lemkin is providing a very sound basis here for understanding a genocidal process which may – *under certain circum-*

stances – lead to genocide *per se*, the ultimate result of his conception is a somewhat misconceived conflation of the two. This does not mean that Lemkin's interpretation is not vitally important for the study of genocide. On the contrary, many elements and components to genocidal process that he describes and develops in *Axis Rule* are hardly peculiar to Nazism but represent a major, one might even propose a regular, or 'normative' facet of modern political behaviour. This is particularly the case with regard to the cultural degradation and emasculation that he describes. Whether Lemkin intended that this form of 'denationalisation' *of its own* – that is in the absence of biological and physical destruction – should be taken to constitute genocide is open to question.[55] Yet, what surely matters here is the distinction between a process which is actually all too common and a consequence which, *while all too frequent*, is much less so. It is also the distinction which puts the 1999 events in Kosovo on one side of a divide and the Holocaust on the other; not because genocidal mechanisms were not at work in both cases or that those in Kosovo could not have led to genocide. But the point is they did not. The component elements that Lemkin describes as 'genocide' may have all been there – the coordinated and synchronised plan of different actions aiming at the destruction of the essential foundations of the life of the ethnic Albanian community – but these, whether through luck, design, deflection, avoidance, abortion of plan, or a contingent mixture of these and other factors, ultimately did not end up producing a systematic programme of attempted extermination of people. The challenge thus before us – unless we want to return to the looser and arguably less rigorous usage of the term as presented in Lemkin – is not to deny that genocides come out of genocidal processes but rather to understand how, in particular conditions, the ingredients in the latter are translated into the specificity of the former.

Let us return for an instance to one example Lemkin cites, to try and unravel this conundrum of connection but distinction. One group that the Nazis attempted to denationalise, after the invasion and occupation of northwest Europe, in 1940, were the Letzeburgesch, the inhabitants of a previously independent Luxembourg. The German method was one of forced assimilation. Political, linguistic and cultural autonomy were denied, the expectation being that the Luxembourgers would simply acquiesce in the death of their separate identity and henceforth *become* Germans. This was clearly an attack not only on their individual but their national group rights. But one might also argue that it was one which was closely comparable with the main long-term thrust of English/British 'nation building' with regard to its 'Celtic fringe' and, certainly, post-revolutionary French policy towards the state's Bretons, Basques or, for that matter, southern Occitans.[56] These examples, the

Letzeburgesch included, carry with them the assumption on the part of those who were dominant in these respective states that the subordinate populations in question, by dint of their specific cultural or social distinctiveness, represented an impediment or even danger to these states' political and societal well-being. The assimilationary premise, however, also assumes that the perceived impediment can be resolved, in principle, without recourse to annihilation but rather through people-incorporation or, to use another term, 'encapsulation'[57] into the majority population. This starting point, of course, is at marked variance from the Nazi mindset with regard to Jews where the initial premise was to overturn and do away with a century-old state policy of assimilation, a policy which, with regard to the Roma, had never been seriously entertained at all.

Thus, this might suggest that a necessary critical element for a trajectory from embryonic persecution to annihilatory culmination pre-existed in the Jewish and Roma cases in a way which was ruled out in the Letzeburgesch one. This might also suggest that forced assimilation and true genocide, though they might arise from a single *Weltanschauung* – the Nazi racial ideology of this particular case – are in practice distinct, non-transferable, categories. The Letzeburgesch might have been denied a separate existence but at least they were not mass murdered. Jews and Roma were. But is it all so cut and dried? Is Nazi racial ideology on its own sufficient to act as the driving force from the genocidal A to the Z of the 'Final Solution'? Is there, indeed, a teleological logic which demands 'cumulative radicalisation' towards inevitable annihilation in these two cases but not in the third? Under what circumstances – if any – might genocide be called off or reversed? Or deflected onto a different less violent path? Or even toned down a gear, for instance, by replacing mass murder with forcible deportation or exclusion? This would hardly be anything other than another aspect of 'genocidal process', but it might also suggest that more than one variable might be required to launch that process into direct, full-blown physical annihilation. Many German historians speak of a 'twisted road to Auschwitz',[58] thereby questioning the assumption of predetermined inevitability. By the same token, is it not conceivable that, with a slightly different set of variables, the forced assimilation of the Letzeburgesch could have been ratcheted up to become genocide?

Suppose, for instance, that the Letzeburgesch had attempted to resist assimilation. A common assumption is that a targeted group facing acute discrimination and persecution is not only passive but has no bearing on how the perpetrator acts towards them. At the critical point of genocidal delivery, of course, this is true because the group has become completely powerless. This should not assume, however, that there is never any victim–perpetrator dynamic in the longer prequel to this moment, even, where paradoxically, as with the Nazis vis-à-vis the Jews, it is played out almost entirely in the perpetrators' heads. If the reactive behaviour of the victim group may thus intensify already latent feelings of contempt or hatred felt by the perpetrator towards them, we might expect not a lessening so much as an exacerbation of the genocidal processes already in train. Enforced harmonisation presupposes that the perpetrator considers that there is nothing worth maintaining in the social or cultural arrangements of the targeted group. They, in turn, or at least some elements within them, are likely to resist the process tenaciously. All the more so, as they come to recognise that what is on offer in the new imposed situation, far from creating benefits or opportunities for them, is only likely to lead beyond political disempowerment to economic subservience and social marginalisation. As stated earlier, these tendencies are not so much uncommon in the contemporary world as the developmental *norm* and, though they may frequently lead to ethnic conflict, they mostly do not lead to genocide.

However, consider the most acute and toxic of these tendencies as they apply to today's most genocidally vulnerable peoples. Systematic expropriation if not actual physical destruction of the territorial space of 'fourth world' groups, whether the space in question is the Amazonian rainforests, or the near-deserts of central Sudan, denies to such groups both an independent economic sustenance and that all-important sense of continuity which gives cultural-symbolic meaning to their existence. The use of the term ethnocide, which UNESCO currently employs to denote the denial of an ethnic group's right to 'enjoy, develop and transmit its own culture and language',[59] would seem insufficient to describe these cases when the consequences go beyond dispossession to material and psychological deprivation, destitution and massive demographic collapse. Moreover, such onslaughts are often accompanied by a basic ambiguity on the part of the perpetrator about the means by which the extinction of the group is to be brought about. Forced assimilation often blurs in such instances into much more direct and obviously eliminationist strategies aimed at what Helen Fein speaks of as the 'interdiction of the biological and social reproduction of group members'.[60] This is the same as Lemkin's biological genocide. For Fein, too, this *is* genocide. But direct *physical* annihilation – the mass killing of fourth-world groups – most often occurs in quite specific circumstances, most particularly in response to the one thing one might expect peoples to do in such intolerable conditions: *fight back.*

If, applied to our subject at large, this suggests that a perpetrator–victim dynamic may indeed be one important factor in understanding how a genocidal process culminates in a specific moment of systematically organised and *extended* mass killing, it must also raise the possibility that such a result is not necessarily preordained but will come out of a concatenation or matrix of ingredients and contingencies, almost as, using a physics analogy, the critical mass needed to explode an atomic bomb is dependent on a particular chain reaction. A critical mass with regard to the Letzebergesch was never very likely given, not only the Nazi perception of them as potentially like 'us', but their own essential passivity in the face of Germanisation. Yet had it been otherwise, in the specific circumstances of unrestrained war, when the Nazis were increasingly responding to national resistance – particularly in eastern Europe and the Balkans – by repeated massacre, the possibility that this broader killing momentum might have provided the impetus for the Luxembourgers also being *sucked in* is not entirely implausible. The point, however, is not about this example *per se*, given that it is something of a red herring, but rather about the nature of genocide at large. In Lemkin's framework, genocide cannot be isolated or pinned down to a specific sequence of mass killing. In Harff and Gurr's view it is exactly this: an 'episode' of sustained and coherent group destruction perpetrated by a state regime.[61]

While it seems to this author that this is the only way genocide can be distinguished as *sui generis,* the fact that genocide usually arises out of an extremely long and laboured gestation and, indeed, is itself only at the extreme end of a continuum of repressive state strategies including marginalisation, forced assimilation, deportation and even massacre – all of which might share the latent if not explicit aim of 'getting rid' of the perceived 'problem' population – confirms that the problem of giving clear definition to its beginning, middle and end – in other words its exact shape – remains a stark one. One might also add, just to complicate the picture, that one genocide discussed at length in the next volume – that against the people of the Vendée – evinces a gestation period so short as to put in question the absolute necessity for the actual event to *always* be preceded by a prolonged genocidal process. By the same token, longer-term trajectories which seem to lead inexorably towards this apparent final destination are often aborted or, possibly, succeeded by a return to other carrot-and-stick strategies of forcible integration or exclusion, even in some instances running in parallel to, if never quite in tandem with genocide itself. In recent history, one can think of some extraordinary examples of this kind of trajectory. For instance, after the first major effort of the Iraqi Ba'athist regime in 1974 to extirpate the support population of the Kurdish *peshmerga,* some of the Kurdish groupings sat down to attempt to negotiate a settlement with the Ba'ath, though in this case only for the latter to resume a more lethal agenda culminating in a thoroughgoing genocide a decade later.[62] Alternatively, the Turkish war *à outrance* versus the newly created state of Armenia in 1919–20, just three years after an attempted Turkish mass extermination of the Armenian people, represents a state commitment to pursue genocide but, in changed circumstances, by a somewhat different route.[63]

If this shifting ground thus makes for a certain unsatisfactory, even contradictory, messiness to the exact parameters of our subject, perhaps we would do well to remember that it is, after all, an outcome of highly fluid situations created by human beings acting in the real world – and so not required purposefully to fit theoretical models supplied by politicial scientists or the strictures of jurisprudence textbooks. Nevertheless, the fact that everything described so far points to the phenomenon *only* crystallising in specific and usually quite extraordinary circumstances of acute state and societal crisis is surely noteworthy. Indeed, it would suggest that the specificity of genocide emanates not simply from a marked escalation in the conflictual relationship between polity and communal adversary (whether caused by one or both parties) but requires some sudden, exceptional energy spasm or release to finally precipitate its protagonists literally – and irrevocably – over the edge.[64] As the film-maker Claude Lanzmann, pondering on the launching of the 'Final Solution', has remarked: 'Between the conditions that allowed the extermination and the extermination itself – the *fact* of extermination – there is a discontinuity, a gap, a leap, an abyss.'[65] The implication – and insight – is not just of rupture but of the necessity of a trigger. Find the trigger and maybe one can unravel the whole plot. Is, then, that trigger war?

War and Genocide

The whole thrust of Lemkin's conceptualisation of genocide in *Axis Rule* suggests a phenomenon which does not simply take place within a war context but is itself a form of warfare. For Lemkin, the primary distinction lay in *who* the war was being waged against. While 'normal' understanding of war – at least in the traditional international legal canon – assumes conflict between states, Lemkin argued that this did not allow for the sort of onslaught being perpetrated by the Nazis, i.e. a state waging war against – and with the purpose of destroying – *nations*. In this sense what Lemkin was attempting to do was to extend the international legal framework, with reference 'to the underlying moral principles of just-war theory',[66] to cover a whole category of *war crimes* which up to that point had been excluded because they fell outside prevailing principles associated with sovereignty.[67] That he succeeded in this immediate aim is most obviously adduced by the terms of the agreement arrived at by the victorious Allied powers in August 1945, to set up a juridical instrument, the International Military Tribunal (IMT), to try Nazi – and later Japanese – war crimes. In subsequently bringing the Nazi leadership to account at Nuremberg on the grounds of conspiracy to commit war, crimes against peace (the waging of war), and crimes associated with the treatment of POWs, the legal drafters of the IMT were working within already well-recognised and accepted juridical parameters. In adding a fourth plank to the prosecution case, namely crimes against humanity, defined under Article 6 of the IMT statute as that which included: 'assassination, extermination, enslavement, deportation and all other inhuman acts committed against civilian populations before or during the course of war as well as involving persecution on political, religious or racial grounds'[68] they were, however, breaking new ground, and in effect paving the way – though the term itself would only be retrospectively used with regard to the 1946 Nuremberg final judgement – for the recognition of genocide as a further war crime treatable under international law.[69] Ironically, the formulation of the 1948 UNC contains no specific reference to war, which commentators, such as William Schabas, have lauded as a major juridical advance for the very reason of its application to non-military situations.[70] If, however, we were to take Lemkin's original *Axis Rule* description of genocide as an aspect, albeit a clearly delineated and particularly criminal aspect, of more general war, the Nuremberg conceptualisation does little or nothing to demonstrate the link between the two. That genocide is *usually* associated with war is evident from its post-1945 incidence.[71] But does this therefore mean that the two are so inextricably intertwined that any attempt to unravel their causal relationship becomes a lost cause?

There is a corpus of scholarly writing which does come close to adopting a formula of genocide equals modern war and vice versa. The works of Robert Lifton and Eric Markusen and also Markusen with David Kopf,[72] in particular, see so many parallels in the motivation, rationalisation and practice of strategic bombing in both the Second World War and beyond compared with the conveyor-belt annihilations of the Holocaust that they conclude that such similarities can hardly be purely coincidental but are the result of a common specifically modernist mindset. They label this 'the genocidal mentality', believing that it can be equally applied to Nazi doctors conducting medical experiments in the death camps or US technocrats planning for nuclear conflagration. Their argument is predicated on the notion that in addition to key instruments of modernity – science, technology, rational calculus and bureaucratic organisation – supplying contemporary man with the wherewithal to mass murder on a mega-scale quite unimaginable in pre-modern times, the psychological repositioning which goes with this enables such mass killing to be conducted in a fashion entirely devoid of restraint or remorse. With the targeted victims a series of dehumanised statistics and the actual killing often technically 'distanced' from the perpetrators by deliveries which omit the necessity to personally engage in murder, or even see the results, the whole process becomes impersonal and even sanitised. Also, the very bureaucratised and segmented nature of killing orders, down complex chains of command, further cocoons individual participants from either responsibility for the killing decision or the dilemmas which might go with it. On the contrary, through what Lifton has called 'the killing–healing paradox', mass murder is actually justified. Bureaucratic, jargonised and entirely euphemistic language, for instance, deeming the obliteration of inhabited areas in aerial bombing campaigns as 'collateral damage', provides for added psychological displacement. The ultimate result is what one might call the 'banality of evil' syndrome, the term Hannah Arendt applied to the 1961 Jerusalem trial of Adolf Eichmann for his role as chief bureaucratic organiser of the 'Final Solution'.[73]

While thus Lifton, Markusen and Kopf stop short of suggesting that the aerial obliteration of Dresden, Hamburg, Tokyo or Nagasaki is essentially the same thing as the killing processes of the Holocaust, they do not stop far short. If the deliberate massacre of unarmed, innocent, defenceless Jewish and Roma women and children is genocide, the deliberate massacre of 'unarmed', 'innocent', 'defenceless' Japanese or German women and children, for Markusen and Kopf, is 'genocide in the course of war'.[74] The inference is clear: what is different about these killings is less important than what they share. And what that is is 'the willingness of national governments to plan, prepare for and carry out the extermination of masses of innocent people'.[75] Genocide, in other words, is a single facet of a more general exterminatory thrust of late-modern man en route to nuclear nemesis.

There is surely much to be said for subsuming genocide within this larger framework. The statistics of modern mass murder are largely self-evident. Not only are civilians much more likely to be killed than combatants in modern conflicts but the trajectory is unmistakably upwards. During the Korean War of 1950–3, the ratio of combatant to civilian deaths was 1:5. A decade later in Vietnam it was 1:13. Unicef data from 1989 suggested that 90 per cent of all war victims since the Second World War had been women and children.[76] That the culprit for all this 'lethal violence' is primarily and overwhelmingly the modern state has also been conclusively demonstrated. Back in 1972, an independent writer, Gil Eliot, particularly acknowledged by Markusen as a pathfinder in the field, surveyed twentieth-century political conflict and cautiously estimated a resulting 110 million deaths.[77] For Eliot, the totalisation of war, for which only states had the full technological, military and administrative systems with which to undertake it purposefully, was a key driving force. But in considering, for instance, China and Russia, his survey of 'macro-violence' also encompassed circumstances which were not strictly of a war type but in which, nevertheless, whole populations succumbed to privation, attrition and ultimate liquidation. Thus, Eliot's thesis was about something other than *simply* war. R. J. Rummel, a scholar with a similar penchant for statistics, somewhat later shifted the ground even further from the specific war focus by proposing that the vast majority of twentieth-century 'mega-deaths' should be laid at the door of 'totalitarian' regimes, by which he particularly meant Soviet and Chinese polities, in addition to the Nazis. Interestingly, and perhaps quite significantly, Rummel abjured the use of the word 'genocide' as his theoretical tool for this task, pointing out that it alone could hardly cover the whole range of mass deaths which these regimes 'habitually and systematically' perpetrated.[78] In its place Rummel proffered the term 'democide', by which he meant *any* government action which through its 'intentionality' led to the death of people.

Rummel's emphasis on the concept of 'totalitarian' regimes – especially when contrasted with what seems an almost wilful myopia about mass murders committed directly or indirectly by liberal democratic regimes – lays him open to serious challenge from this author, amongst other students of genocide. Nevertheless, his very questioning of the term is bold and salutary on at least one important score. Recognising that the range of mass violence he was describing included murder through hyper-exploitation and starvation either *in situ* or through deportation to faraway slave camps, not to say against victims who could not always be bracketed within an identifiable ethnic or social group, Rummel chose neither to be wedded to the term 'genocide' for its own sake or to bend its meaning to serve his own agenda. Instead, by offering a different term for his analysis of all forms of government killing (albeit with its limited 'totalitarian' focus), he deftly avoided conflating war and genocide while implicitly offering to those jurists seeking to nail all state perpetrators, a restatement by a different route of the IMT's catch-all Crimes against Humanity statute.[79] By contrast, Lifton, Markusen and Kopf's insistence on the 'genocidal' nature of *both* genocide and modern war would seem to veer, inadvertently or otherwise, too obviously in the direction of a Charny-style inclusivism and thereby to that broader, contemporary Western cultural disposition to embrace all manner of criminal acts under the umbrella of genocide.

One might wish to counter in response: why should mass killings of any nature be any the less deplorable or criminal for *not* being genocide? Cannot *different types of mass killing* be equally criminal? Yet the persistence of 'genocide' as the ultimate yardstick of depravity has also led to particular cases of modern warfare being more closely interrogated for their genocidal content. Take as one example the US bombing of Indochina, in the 1960s and early 1970s. Here the asymmetry of the struggle between the United States and its Vietcong and other opponents – with murderous and devastating consequences for the population of the region as a whole – is blatantly self-evident. In addition to a ground war of counter-insurgency and 'free-fire' zones, 14 million tons of bombs were dropped on the region in this period, some seven times the tonnage deployed by the Allies in the whole of the Second World War. The bombing campaign culminated in 1972, when much of eastern Cambodia and Laos, along with Hanoi and Haiphong, suffered a bomb tonnage equivalent to that used in the atom bomb attacks on Hiroshima and Nagasaki.[80] Already, in 1968, Jean-Paul Sartre, as president of the Russell War Crimes Tribunal was adducing that 'genocidal intent is implicit in the facts' but adding 'It is not necessarily premeditated.'[81] Similarly, in an evaluation by Hugo Adam Bedau in 1974 for a non-governmental international war crimes tribunal which had accused the US of committing genocide in Vietnam through indiscriminate bombing of civilians, Bedau considered that 'the gap between the results of the present discussion and a verdict of genocide is not very wide.'[82] That said, however, Bedau concluded that, though the indiscriminate killing of Vietnamese civilians was common, the charge of genocide could not ultimately be sustained, at least not under the terms of the UNC, as there was no evidence that the US *had intended* to destroy the Vietnamese in whole or in part. A further study by Ron Aronson, another activist critic of US policy as well as genocide scholar, thought the US bombing campaign a 'variant of genocide', yet one which was 'disguised by the fact that its purpose was neither oppression nor extermination as such, but *winning the war*'.[83]

This Indochina example illustrates a quite common route by which the war–genocide connection is developed, only then to be partially retracted through one or more riders. Clearly, each of the commentators here are convinced (in line with writers like Markusen or for that matter Lemkin himself) that there is a close connectedness, though quite where it begins and ends ultimately would seem to be elusive. Yet if this really is the case; if there is no way of isolating what is specifically genocide in war, out of it, or beyond it, we might as well admit that the distinction cannot be properly made and so use the terms interchangeably. Have we, thus, once more hit the definitional doldrums? Or is Lemkin again at hand to come to our rescue? Let us not forget that Lemkin's formulation of genocide is as *a type* of state-organised modern warfare in which the perpetrating party is the state itself and the victim target a national, ethnic or some comparable population. This might suggest that rather than focusing on the end results of both genocide and warfare in which indiscriminate, mass non-combatant death is the critical similarity the emphasis should rather be on creating a typology of state warfare, attempting to compare what Lemkin's genocidal type either does or does not share with the others. The further questions that then might logically arise are *causal* questions: why do states go to war with these different types of 'enemies' in the first place and in what circumstances?

Starting then from Lemkin's premise that genocide is a *type* of warfare but one which would appear to involve the (unlawful) actions of a sovereign state waging war against a non-sovereign national or other group, the obvious contrast would be with sovereign states who go to war with other sovereign states, this type of conflict being considered 'normative' and acceptable, at least in a Clausewitzian sense.[84] Certainly, this would be to leave to one side a great many other types of warfare, including communal conflicts in which states may not be primary actors, or in which the question of who represents the state is the actual disputed point of conflict. These may also be relevant to our discussion. However, in keeping with Lemkin's basic parameters, let us concentrate on the issue of state-organised warfare while proposing that actually what we are dealing with here are not two types but actually three, albeit with the additional type – not least because of its very fluidity – providing an important bridge between the other two.

Thus the three relevant types would be:

1 Type One: State war against other sovereign states.
2 Type Two: State war against other sovereign states or nations who are perceived to be 'illegitimate'.
3 Type Three: State war *within* the boundaries, or other territories, controlled by the sovereign state, against national or other groups who are perceived to be illegitimate.[85]

Before saying something on each of these, a further few words on their common denominator, i.e. war conducted by the state. Though not all warfare has emanated from this source, throughout history the ability of a state to wage war has been both a prime indicator of its status vis-à-vis other states and of its power structure with regard to its domestic populace. Additionally, a recourse to war tells us much about the self-perception of a state leadership and of its willingness – ideologically motivated or otherwise – to pursue what it considers to be the state's interests or agendas by these means. Yet, by definition, war is also a high-risk strategy, which, even where carefully prepared, can be comprehensively demolished by contingent events. It also requires prodigious inputs of manpower, resources and capital. If the war fails these may be lost in part or entirety to the great if not fatal detriment of the state. Alternatively, successful war may result in great material and psychological benefits. This may be true for Type Three warfare as much as for Types One and Two. Indeed, especially in contemporary history, Type Three warfare has been on many occasions conducted simultaneously, or, in parallel, with the other types. In other words, despite the diversity of the perceived state enemies, this might suggest common causal roots.

*

In modern times, Type One warfare is waged between sovereign states, recognised as such within an international system of nation-states. There may be major disparities in such conflicts given that one militarily powerful state may be ranged against a group of others, or, for geographical or technical reasons, may not be able to inflict the same degree of damage on its adversaries as they can inflict on it. One thinks of the asymmetry of the Allied campaign against Iraq in the Gulf War of 1990, where Iraq attacked targets in 'neutral' Israel in lieu of being able to bombard the United States (the asymmetry was even more transparent in the 2003 Allied invasion), or, for that matter, those aspects of the Pacific theatre in the final stages of the Second World War, where Japanese cities were obliterated by US conventional or nuclear bombing, while urban populations in America slept peacefully at night. Nevertheless, a prime hallmark of these inter-state twentieth-century conflicts has been both the intent and, perhaps more importantly, the increasing technological ability of participants, not only to annihilate whole enemy armies in the field, or even devastate regions in which those armies were operating, but to strike at the enemy or enemies' very heartlands with weapons of sophisticated but mass destruction.

Back in 1921, in the ebb of the first global war of that century where the potential for such no-holds-barred logic was already becoming apparent, the Italian airpower theorist, Guilio Douhet, in his influential study, *Command of the Air*, noted: 'Today it is not armies but whole nations which make war; and all the citizens are belligerents and all are exposed to the hazards of war.'[86] In stating the issue thus, Douhet was signalling the obsolescence of codes of military conduct, either traditionally grounded in 'just war' theory or more recently formulated by international agreements, which were supposed not only to act as brakes on unlimited warfare but also to protect non-combatants.[87] In effect, Douhet was saying that the distinction between combatant and civilian was – in his words – 'outmoded' or, to put it more harshly, extinct. This is, of course, very pertinent for the Markusen–Kopf line of argument –

despite their insistence on the existence of a category of innocent non-combatants – in that it supports their contention that modern military planners no longer feel required to make such a distinction. In a century where the leading world states mobilised their adult populations to supply and equip armies around the clock and from year to year in two totalised global wars and in the knowledge that that these had to be fought for the highest, life or death, stakes, the ground was indeed being logically set for the ultimate type of inter-state warfare: superpower nuclear missile exchange – with the possibility of global population wipe-out.

Having offered this utterly bleak picture, two caveats are in order, one of which distinguishes Type One war from Type Two, and both of which distinguish Type One from Type Three. In Type Three warfare the disparity between the state's military capacity to kill the targeted population and the latter's ability to resist is usually so marked that the state's killing operatives can undertake their task not only for the most part with a high degree of impunity but often with no serious threat to their physical existence whatsoever. The warfare, in other words, is highly unequal to the point where it is arguable that it is warfare at all in the normal sense of the term. This is not usually the case in War Type One, at least not until one side has gained a major and decisive military advantage over the other, at which point the war may, anyway, actually cease. Thus, for instance, considering the strategic bombing campaigns of the Second World War, both the British and Germans attempted to bomb each other's cities with devastating effect, both sides also lost thousands of their air crews in the process – at various points putting in doubt their ability to continue these campaigns – while both sides also attempted to transcend the limitations implicit in these military failings by developing new nuclear or missile technologies which they were, at least in principle, prepared to use against each other right up to the bitter end.[88]

Having said that, however, there is no evidence that the German state set out to exterminate the majority British population, or vice versa, as *their war aim* but only to defeat the other in order to confirm their respective positions of power within the post-war world order. Thus, even where, in this particular case, one side was demanding the other's unconditional surrender, there remained – however residually – the Clausewitzian notion that the struggle was between 'legitimate' state adversaries and that at the end of the day negotiation rather than extermination would determine the ongoing relationship between victor and vanquished. The assumptions implicit in this are a) the role of state enemy is an ephemeral one for the duration of the war *only*; and b) once the war is over there is no basic impediment preventing former adversaries from co-existing peacefully and without malice or danger to one another.

Paradoxically, even in the most extreme case of the potentiality of Type One warfare this century, namely the Cuba Missile Crisis of 1962, while on the one hand both the USA and USSR prepared for mutual annihilation, there is nothing in the behaviour of either leadership to suggest that they desired the elimination of the other's population or – had nuclear warfare resulted – would have pursued it (however blackly absurd this may seem) for anything other than statist, classically limited and 'realist' Clausewitzian ends.[89]

What, of course, spoils the straightforwardness of this argument is the assumption that Type One conflicts are somehow ideologically neutral, i.e. that states who enter into warfare are engaging in conflict with adversaries whom they believe to be essentially like themselves or, at least, are assumed to be fighting according to a mutually agreed set of rules. This might have been the case between Germany and Britain at the outset of war in 1914, but by its end, after four years of mutual attempts at attrition through starvation and aerial bombardment, not to mention the use of poison gas against each other's combatants, the assumption was in tatters. A global war later, certainly from the period of the Blitz in late 1940, there could similarly be no question of Britain living alongside a defeated *Nazi* state, the proclaimed aim being rather to remove the regime, which meant in effect subjugating Germany and *its people*. If this immediately suggests that ideological colouring might be an important factor potentially exacerbating tendencies towards unrestrained, exterminatory warfare, the specifically British–German conflict still falls dramatically short of others from both world wars where the aim was the Carthaginian-style liquidation of adversary states. The Western Allies, after all, after the defeat of the Nazis, still assumed the existence of *a* Germany and its people. When the Nazis attacked Poland in 1939, or even more overtly Soviet Russia in 1941, the aim was to do away with these polities forever. Both states were perceived by the Nazis to be illegitimate, in other words, to have no right to exist. As for their populations, in so far as they were to be allowed their lives at all – which, given the racial underpinning of Nazism, was itself debatable – their purpose would be only to serve German interests. Similar assumptions were held by the Japanese when, in 1937, they began their main onslaught on China. The fact that at least two of these allegedly 'illegitimate' states were relatively powerful ones within the international system proved no barrier to their adversaries' liquidatory programmes. However, the refusal of either China or Russia to simply disintegrate under the impact of the respective Japanese and German onslaughts on them and indeed to take the war to the enemy by partisan action behind their lines, provided classic conditions for the development of Type Two warfare.

The main characteristics of this warfare type are the dispensing entirely of Geneva Convention-informed restraints by the supposedly 'legitimate' side, on the grounds that the armed opposition that they are dealing with are no more than 'terrorists', 'saboteurs' or 'bandits' who are incapable of fighting conventional 'civilised' war and worse, are succoured by a native population whose cultural and social level is beneath contempt. Racism invariably confirms this judgemental verdict. In the circumstances, all 'necessary' measures for the liquidation of resistance are allowable; mass aerial bombardment, scorched earth, counter-insurgency, mass deportation, environmental devastation as well as repeated retributive or disciplinary massacre – often without regard to the age or gender of victims. Indeed, *worst* cases of this type of warfare may well take on *'genocidal'* characteristics in the systematic persistence with which the allegedly 'illegitimate' state's population is attacked and destroyed. Common 'legitimate state' rationalisations for these attacks: blaming the 'enemy' for their obdurate unwillingness to submit – itself often taken as evidence of the latter's propensities to both inflict and suffer extreme pain and violence – and thereby impeding against reason or logic the just cause or even integrity of the 'legitimate' state, also bear close resemblances or actually dovetail with perpetrator rationalisations in more recognised cases of genocide.

Yet if powerful states, such as Russia and China, have been on the receiving end of Type Two warfare in recent times, what is equally noteworthy is how most often it has been powerful states (Russia and China included) who have opted for its practice against relatively much weaker ones. The British struggle against the Boer states at the opening of the twentieth century is a case of Warfare Type Two, even though, as we will see in Volume II, on a continuum of violence it was arguably not as severe as, for instance, that meted out by Austria against the Serbian nation from August 1914 onwards. Further down the 'power' spectrum, one might argue that the Nigerians vis-à-vis a briefly secessionist Biafra from 1967 to 1970, Pakistan versus Bangladesh in 1971, or most recently still post-1991 Yugoslavia pitted against an independent Bosnia, also arguably fall within this category. Each raises questions about the point at which War Type Two merges into a War Type Three, not least given that Biafra was largely unrecognised as a sovereign state, Bangladesh had mostly to wait for this status until after the war, and Bosnia's war had strongly internecine elements. By the same token, America's war in Vietnam in the 1960s and early 1970s was only partially a War Type Two against the sovereign North when so many of its 'Vietcong' adversaries were citizens of a supposedly allied South Vietnam. The discrepancy is even more stark in the 1980s Soviet struggle with the Afghani *mujahideen,* all of whom were 'rebels' against the indubitably pro-Soviet state of Afghanistan.

The diversity of the above examples may also warn us that too much can be made of their common features. Some of these wars were certainly more vicious – more *genocidal* – than others. As a general rule, however, what they have in common is a dynamic in which perpetrator-state violence leads to tenacious *people* resistance, provoking in turn a ratcheting up of the perpetrator's response, usually accompanied by self-justificationary apologia that it is the behaviour of the victims that compelled it – the 'legitimate' state – to fight the war *à outrance* and without mercy. Indeed, when this point is reached, Helen Fein's proposition that what distinguishes the victims of genocide from those in war is a case not of 'where they are but who they are'[90] rather loses its edge. By the same token, however, so too does the Markusen–Lifton model of war-genocide as so technically advanced that the perpetrators are largely distanced from the mass murders they are committing. While, certainly, sophisticated weaponry, as in Vietnam or Afghanistan, may be integral to most Type Two wars, such instruments are nearly always supplemented by thoroughly hands-on and 'dirty' warfare on the ground conducted with an intimacy, crude technology and barbarism recognisable in any historical period.

This is, of course, very much in tune with Lemkin's *Axis Rule* – informed understanding of genocide as a return to some earlier historical phase of wars of people-extermination, against the grain of what he believed to be the civilising, genocide-free thrust of modern international society. There is, certainly, an irony here as this study will repeatedly examine cases where the military legitimisation for exterminatory assault was founded on the firm conviction that the adversary society-state was the savage or barbarian antithesis of the civilised or civilising state. But this can only tend to reinforce the similarity of ingredients and outcomes between Type Two wars and Lemkin's version of genocide. Where there is arguably a critical distinction is in Lemkin's elucidation of genocide as *a policy* of conscious, systematic and outright elimination, compared with most Type Two wars which usually entail a *strategy* of defeating the 'illegitimate' enemy. There is nothing, of course, to prevent what begins as a strategy shifting through the war's escalation to an indiscriminate killing *policy*. Few Type Two wars, however, cross this Rubicon, a reality underscored in the case of the Biafran war, for instance, where, after a ghastly conclusion brought about by the systematic effort by the Nigerian army to starve the breakaway state into submission, its people were fully and comprehensively readmitted into the federal west African polity. If genocide had been the Nigerian policy it would have been implemented at this critical moment when the Biafrans had surrendered and, thus, were in no position to resist further.[91] Even in much less palatable scenarios where the defeat of the 'illegitimate' state leads to its complete dismantling and subjugation of its people, rarely is this a prelude to systematic and synchronised onslaught of the sort that Lemkin describes.

Nevertheless, the fact that it can occur, especially in a case like that of Poland after 1939, when its population found itself no longer classed as members of an illegitimate state but more as an illegitimate, stateless community, poses the question more starkly still whether War Type Three is *ipso facto* genocide. Given that, on one crucial level, what is at stake here is what Vahakn Dadrian has called the issue of 'preponderant access to overall resources of power',[92] one might be inclined to answer in the affirmative. By definition, an 'illegitimate' national community within state boundaries or imperial territory is likely to be weaker in politico-military terms than its opponent and, thus, will make itself highly vulnerable if it, or elements of it, should attempt armed conflict against that state. However, must this lead inexorably towards genocide?

Take a classic example suggesting an alternative trajectory. The Irish national liberation struggle against British control culminated in an authentic War Type Three, in the period 1919 to 1921. Many of the necessary ingredients which we would associate with genocide were undoubtedly here: a several hundred years long bitter legacy of religiously informed, massacre-punctuated conflict which included late-sixteenth- and seventeenth-century English state efforts to ethnically cleanse parts of the island of their indigenous population in favour of Anglo-Scottish settlers; significant structural discrimination; a state contempt for the Irish Catholic peasant masses, often verging on racism; a previously aborted path to local autonomy (Home Rule); and, finally, an escalating, increasingly vicious armed struggle – during, and more particularly in the wake of the First World War – in which possibilities of compromise had been jettisoned, and inflamed passions against a series of British atrocities had mobilised a significant proportion of the Irish national community as participants in the struggle. The nature and scale of this challenge, moreover, put the integrity of the British state as it was understood by its dominant elites in acute jeopardy. In such conditions of crisis, something had to give: an almost textbook narrative on the preconditions for genocide. However, this scenario did not materialise. Certainly, had it so decided, Whitehall could have found additional resources and manpower reserves with which to pursue the military struggle, and ultimately, if it had so sought, could have imposed its monopoly of violence by quashing the insurrection. But this could only have been achieved in the circumstances of 1919, or 1920, by fighting an all-out war against the Irish *qua* Irish. Such a war could well have been, indeed probably would have been genocidal. Whether Lloyd George's government ever seriously contemplated such a possibility we do not know.[93] It is surely significant that they probably did not, and when faced with the actual reality of the situation in which they had to recognise that they could not win by conventional military means, they opted in the summer of 1921 to find another diplomatic strategy involving a high degree of compromise, the result of which radically altered the entire political map, not just of Ireland but of Britain.[94]

That genocide could have emanated from this War Type Three but, in practice, did not, would suggest that the two are not automatically identical or congruent. Inherent institutional – including fiscal – restraints, humanitarian sensibilities, a parliamentary democratic system acting as an inertial force handicapping – though not necessarily ultimately preventing – the government from acting with impunity, a civil society including a strong free press in which human rights interests were often vocally articulated, anxiety about international, particularly American outrage at the conduct of the war, all, in this instance, impeded the momentum towards genocidal inevitability. That said, it is perhaps significant that the one region of Ireland where its potential came closest to realisation was in the north, in Ulster, where Lloyd George's acceptance of a mini-Protestant and Unionist state in opposition to the majority, effectively independent Catholic one in the south, led to an assault on its Catholic enclaves by Ulster's official and semi-official forces, including paramilitary, in the early months of 1922, hardly held in check by the London government.[95] The episode again shows the degree to which settler-loyalist defence and defiance of a metropolitan agenda represents a critical variable in some Type Three wars. Certainly, the much more violent and savage French struggle against the Algerian independence movement in the 1950s and early 1960s had its strongest potential for lurching over the precipice in the form of the actions of settler *pieds noirs*, a possibility which, paradoxically, had to be ultimately stymied by what amounted to a Gaullist, right-wing coup in the French capital geared towards negotiating peace with the Algerian revolutionary leadership.[96]

In other instances the brakes on genocide may be more prosaic, for instance, where the state's ability to deliver genocide is not limited so much by lack of will but because its military or resource capacity to do so is insufficient, often in the face of a relatively strong communal insurgency. Post-colonial struggles in southern and western Sudan, Iraqi Kurdistan, the Karen and other hill-tribe regions of Burma, or the northern Tamil part of Sri Lanka, all have displayed these inertial tendencies while in no way negating their high and in some cases continuing potential for genocide.[97] Indeed, the frustration associated with state failure to reassert its authority in the regions controlled by the insurgents – and with it a state monopoly of violence – may be itself a significant, if not the ultimate goad driving such regimes towards genocidal denouement.

What these War Type Two and War Type Three examples confirm, therefore, is that total wars in which the perpetrator is the state and victim population a national or some other communal group (whether an autonomous political community or not) have characteristics close to those of genocide. Indeed, genocide not only is a form of total warfare in the same way as these are[98] but would appear to emanate in many cases out of these very same 'total war' scenarios. In this and succeeding volumes repeated reference to War Types Two and Three will be a reminder of these interconnections and relationships.

However, there still remains a somewhat problematic lacuna here. Genocide, argues Fein, involves a perpetrator's purposeful action to destroy physically a collectivity, and action 'sustained regardless of the surrender or lack of threat offered by the victim',[99] while Chalk and Jonassohn up the ante in their definition by arguing that genocide is 'a form of one-sided mass killing'.[100] The best-known examples of twentieth-century genocide would certainly appear to confirm some or all of this verdict. The only Jews *qua* Jews who participated in armed resistance, let alone insurrection, in Nazi-dominated Europe were reacting against a genocide already well in train. Whether or not one agrees with or disputes that there was an armed dynamic between Armenians and Turks in 1915, the vast majority of the Armenians exterminated in the Ottoman assault of that year were genuinely defenceless, unarmed, not to say entirely *innocent* men, women and children. The same is true of Rwanda of 1994. There was a violent, armed dynamic between a Tutsi-dominated invasion force and the Hutu-dominated government, but the victims of the genocide were almost exclusively non-participants in this armed struggle. Where there were native Tutsi attempts to defend themselves against the Hutu Power regime they were isolated, belated and desperately last-ditch efforts in the face of overwhelming force. Just as with Armenians and Jews, so here too, these efforts made little or no difference to the outcome. Indeed, for the most part, Armenians, Jews and Rwandan Tutsi offered no physical resistance in the face of genocide.

This may be to assume that these specific cases have features which are not repeatable elsewhere. Alternatively, it may suggest that there is something about genocides more generally which is peculiar in the history of warfare. It is not that they are *not* conducted as military operations – they most certainly are. But if a state nevertheless proceeds in this way against a communal group whose observable threat to its integrity or agenda would appear to be either negligible or non-existent, there must be something about the nature of the state–community dynamic that cannot be purely or wholly assessed in straightforward political or military terms. An all-important psycho-social ingredient will be central to the discussion of the next chapter. However, in terms of formulating what genocide is, or is not, giving it an equivalence to Type Two or Type Three warfare – when it has already been demonstrated that many such examples do not result in genocide – can clearly only take us so far. Our argument, paradoxically, would seem to be confirming that genocide does represent these types of warfare in their most extreme manifestation, while at the same time having rather discrete qualities that ultimately also make it definable as something different again. But in that case, perhaps, what we need to do is to develop a somewhat differently organised if complementary approach; one which considers afresh the component elements of our phenomenon and how it is that, configured into a fissile matrix, we end up with something we can squarely recognise as genocide.

Genocide as an Ideal Type

When Roger Griffin attempted to provide a definition of fascism, a notably intractable concept for which there remains no scholarly consensus, he turned for assistance to the notion of the 'ideal type' propounded by the great German sociologist, Max Weber. As nobody could agree on what it was they were describing – rather like genocide – Griffin considered that the only way one could put a handle on what it really meant, was not by ploughing through all the often conflicting, multitudinous information which existed on the subject, but rather by using this Weberian tool to construct a conceptual model based on its common properties and shared patterns. This 'ideal type' is, in Weber's own words, 'an internally consistent thought picture' whose 'conceptual purity cannot be found empirically anywhere in reality, it is a utopia'.[101] Thus, as Griffin adds, given that 'it does not exist empirically but only at the level of abstraction in an intellectual world stripped of the heterogeneity ... and "messiness" of real phenomena' its purpose is not to offer *definitive* taxomonic categories, but only to provide a useful, heuristic framework 'in which significant patterns of fact can be identified, causal relationships investigated and phenomena classified'.[102] A guide, if one prefers, to help spot and classify examples of the phenomenon, rather than claiming it to be the phenomenon itself.

Genocide, as we have seen, is difficult to pin down, not only because it comes out of a genocidal process which is *not* in itself genocide but also because the various ingredients in that process are entirely dependent on necessarily fluid and contingent circumstances enabling it to either crystallise into our discrete phenomenon or, alternatively, to be stymied or even transformed into something akin but nevertheless distinct. Even then, few scholars agree on where and when this crystallisation has occurred, in practice resulting in only a limited number of examples of mass murder where there is *general agreement* that the term 'genocide' should apply. However, by focusing on these few examples and selecting their most salient features and common ingredients, we might be able to build up that elusive Weberian-style 'idealisation' as it may exist in our heads. The value of this exercise is that with this in hand we might then be able to apply this conceptualisation as a tool for the study of genocide in history.

As for the examples which, by general consensus, are referred to as genocide, the Holocaust, specifically meaning the attempted extermination of European Jewry between 1941 and 1945, whether this is accepted as the example *par excellence* or not – bearing in mind some recent quite legitimate caveats which doubt its prototypicality[103] – is almost universally accepted as *a* genocide. The only dissenters from this viewpoint are those who wilfully ignore or deny the empirical facts, usually for very specific political motives. There are more dissenters of this ilk with regard to the attempted extermination of Ottoman Armenians between 1915 and late 1916, as there are those who make a point of ringfencing the Holocaust as the only genocide. Our sole concern here, however, is not current vested interests but only the phenomenon itself, the vast majority of scholars of the subject confirming that what happened to the Armenians in this specific period constitutes genocide. Again, only those with current political agendas would deny the 1994 extermination of Tutsi in Rwanda as anything other than a case of genocide. These three examples, indeed, are sometimes referred to as 'total' genocides, i.e. acts which assume not simply a conscious attempt on the part of the perpetrators to mass murder these targeted groups as groups but, so far as it was possible to do so, to the point of their complete annihilation.[104]

It also should not escape our notice at this point that these three generally agreed cases are in historical terms ultra-modern, all indeed, despite their wide geographical diversity, events of the twentieth century. None of this is to repudiate earlier genocides, for instance in the Americas and antipodes, as the basis for an idealised formulation and – other than the lack of scholarly consensus in their favour – there is no good reason why some of these could not provide a legitimate starting point.[105] That said, unless it can be shown that it is our historical memory which is at fault (an issue which will be debated further in Chapter 3), a case will be made for why it is in the most recent strata of modern-cum-contemporary history that our phenomenon *has taken on its sharpest crystallisation*. With this proposition in view, this author would add to the Holocaust, Armenia and Rwanda two other specific twentieth-century cases to assist us in creating our ideal type: case 4, the Soviet state assault against the *so-called* 'kulaks', between 1929 and 1933, and case 5, Khmer Rouge killings in 1978 Cambodia, specifically against their 'Eastern Zone' population. These examples are certainly far from consensually accepted cases of genocide. Certainly, they would fall outside the parameters of the UNC and hence from most genocide scholarship which follows its guidelines. However, our decision to include them should not be taken as indicative of a desire to find a more all-encompassing formula for mass murder, following, for instance, Rummel's democide criteria. Nor is it to specifically nail the role of communist regimes in the perpetration of genocide. On the contrary, our aim is entirely heuristic; namely to identify characteristics evident in these cases, alongside those of the other three, which can help to sharpen more clearly our conceptually idealised model.

To develop this proposition our aim here is not to offer potted histories, not least given that all these cases will be studied in depth in future volumes. What follows is a consciously outline, sparsely footnoted schema with a view to identifying in each instance salient features and critical components. We begin with the three generally agreed cases.

The Holocaust (Shoah): The Nazi extermination of European Jewry

Timespan: 1941–5: Continuous throughout.

Geographical range: Entire European continent in territories directly or indirectly under Nazi control, with epicentre of killing operations in Poland/western USSR – i.e. areas of largest Jewish concentration.

Organiser of genocide: Nazi German leadership headed by Adolf Hitler. More specifically regime's security organisation (SS) with connivance and involvement of wider German state apparatus and that of satellite and puppet states.

Perpetrators: Spearheaded by specially designated units of SS assisted by German military, para-military, technical and administrative staff drawn from all levels of German society. Support operatives also recruited from subject populations, especially but not exclusively from the ex-Soviet Russian borderlands.

Targeted population status as defined by genocide organisers: *All* Jews by race, encompassing immediate offspring of mixed marriages between Jews and Gentiles (*Mischlinge*), Jews who were Christian converts and religiously non-practising Jews. Racial difference of Jewish group visible, according to genocide organisers, in terms of physiognomy, anatomy, mental traits etc.

Targeted population status as self-defined: No agreed self-definition, Jewish diasporic group loyalties existing on basis of diverse formulations of religion, ethnicity, nationality and race, in large part dependent on cultural and geographical location and/or social status of individual Jews. In western and central Europe, including Germany, through to the advent and beyond of Nazi rule, Jewish primary identification was often with the countries of their birth with marked tendencies towards acculturation and exogamy. Cultural and linguistic separateness remained most visible and marked within the more traditional of the demographically significant Jewish centres in eastern Europe.

Targeted population status as defined in law: In Germany, before 1933, Jews were citizens. With the Nazi Reich Citizenship (Nuremberg) Law of 1935, Jews and half-Jews were disqualified from citizenship on the basis of genealogy and with reference to Jewish *religious* communal records. Individuals including converts, who did not consider themselves 'full' Jews had to prove their exemption credentials by these criteria but there was no Nazi attempt to provide an alternative racial methodology, in spite of the regime's insistence that Jews and 'Aryans' were racially distinct. Jewish juridical separateness throughout Nazi-controlled Europe was restated in November 1939 with the public requirement that Jews wore a yellow star.

Warning signs (genocidal process): The openly anti-Semitic Nazi regime, from its 1933 elevation to power in Germany, geared itself towards the civil disenfranchisement, economic immiseration and social segregation of the less than 1 per cent of its population that was Jewish. Police and party persecution plus physical assault were common but dramatically escalated from the period of near-war crises involving the annexation of Austria and dismemberment of Czechoslovakia to culminate in the country-wide Kristallnacht pogroms of November 1938. Compulsory expropriations of German-Jewish properties and businesses, mass internments in concentration camps and a state policy now officially geared towards deportation ensued. With the advent of general European war and the German invasion and liquidation of Poland in September 1939, anti-Jewish policy was ratcheted up with diverse programmes for the mass removal of all Jews from Nazi-occupied territories. Forced ghettoisation, sporadic massacres, executions and the beginnings of significant attrition of the Jewish population through conscious starvation and hyper-exploitation became commonplace. However, these symptoms of a now emerging regime-plan for a general or 'Final Solution of the Jewish Question' do not conclusively provide evidence for a systematic programme of extermination before sometime in 1941.

Trigger/immediate catalyst: Not agreed by scholars. Approximate consensus that the trigger was either build-up to, or initiation and initial success of Operation Barbarossa, the Nazi invasion of the USSR, beginning on 22 June 1941, or its military failure in the high summer/early autumn.[106] Throughout this period, the assault on Soviet Jews engulfed by Nazi invasion radically escalated into systematic extermination. A decision for a continent-wide 'Final Solution', meaning systematic and total extermination of all European Jews may have been catalysed by the German declaration of war on the USA, in December 1941 or earlier.[107]

Wider context: Escalation and radicalisation of War Type One with Western powers (1939) into life and death War Type Two struggle with USSR (summer 1941) and further war with USA later that year. Allies henceforth jointly committed to the unconditional surrender and liquidation of Nazi Germany.

Nature of genocide: Repeated military-style massacres of entire Jewish communities in the Russian borderlands, as of summer/autumn 1941, partially superceded by a deportation programme of all Jews under direct or indirect Nazi jurisdiction to specially created killing plants – incorporating gas chambers for the killing itself – on former Polish territory, from late 1941/early 1942 onwards. Mass murder through starvation, hyper-exploitation in labour camps, plus ongoing massacres, remained major adjuncts to the core exterminatory programme.

Organiser-perpetrator defence/rationalisation: The 'Final Solution' aimed to eliminate the international Jewish conspiracy (sic.): the primary but all-pervasive threat to the German national community, the resurgence of that community on the global stage and its defence of Western civilisation. The conspiracy operating through manifold, multi-layered forces of subversion and pollution, including Bolshevism, capitalism, cultural modernism, sexual contamination, racial emasculation and disease had already been responsible for Germany's defeat and humiliation in 1918. In the context of apocalyptic, global war the destruction of those who were attempting to destroy Germany demanded nothing less than their complete biological extirpation.

Actual target population danger to state: Only in the realms of imagination. Jews as a ubiquitous, stateless, dispersed population posed no collective threat to Germany. An attempt by 'worldwide' Jewish communities to boycott Germany, in 1933, in response to Nazi anti-Semitism had been an unmitigated failure. In the context of world war, Jews – *qua* Jews – were not part of any geo-strategic or geo-economic equation. Jews in Nazi-occupied Europe were entirely defenceless, powerless and dependent on outside forces to deliver them from extermination.

Exemptions: Bar occasional bureaucratic anomalies and specific 'liberations' of German *Mischlinge* on special orders from Hitler,[108] there were no exemptions.

Other related killings: The death camp exterminations were partly prefigured in the so-called T-4 operations, from September 1939, aimed at the 'mercy killing' (sic.) of German and Polish mental institution and sanatoria inmates. Widespread massacres, deportations and labour camp hyper-exploitation decimated vast swathes of Polish, Ukrainian and other particularly Slavic populations. Roma (gypsies) suffered more specific death camp exterminations, often alongside or in close parallel to the Jewish genocide.

Termination of genocide: Nazi regime's absolute defeat and extirpation by the combined military power of the USSR and the Western Allies, in May 1945. Jewish extermination pursued to the bitter end by the Nazis.

Estimated deaths: Between 5 and 6 million, an estimated 72 per cent of the Jewish population of the countries under Nazi hegemony.[109]

The Armenian genocide (the *Aghet*): Attempted extermination of the Ottoman Armenians

Timespan: 1915–16, eighteen near-continuous months of killing.

Geographical range: Primarily in main Armenian population concentrations in eastern Anatolia and southwards into Syrian desert both along and at termini of mass deportation routes.

Organiser of genocide: Inner committee of the Committee of Union and Progress (CUP) governing regime with connivance of limited number of other key military and political figures in the Ottoman state apparatus.

Perpetrators: Military and para-military forces of state including specially but covertly organised forces for this purpose. Additionally, armed auxiliaries drawn from wider spectrum of diverse Ottoman populations, notably from many Kurdish tribes.

Targeted population status as defined by genocide organisers: Armenian religious and political collectivity, separate from rest of population by dint of economic practice and political mindset.

Targeted population status as self-defined: A native, linguistically distinct population in an ethnically mixed region, with historical sense of cohesion particularly founded on fourth-century Armenian Church. Growing tendencies towards a sense of modern cultural and political nationhood linked many Ottoman Armenians to other Armenians across Russian border and in broader diaspora. However, in actuality a socially, occupationally and culturally diverse population with different religious as well as political alignments, including, for many, allegiance to the Ottoman state.

Targeted population status as defined in law: Belonging to one of two historically 'tolerated' – but inferior – Christian self-governing millets within the Ottoman-Muslim empire[110] with Catholic and Protestant Armenians also more recently allowed their own separate millets. Paradoxically, at the time of the genocide Armenians were also entitled to citizenship alongside other national groups within a multi-national Ottoman empire, given the CUP commitment, in principle, to full equality before the law.

Warning signs (genocidal process): Worsening Armenian situation since at least 1870s – some four decades prior to CUP seizure of power in 1908 – running in close parallel to ongoing crisis of Ottoman state. Communal depredations, in eastern region, at hands of Kurdish tribes, went unpunished while Ottoman imperial authorities also increasingly responded to Armenian revolutionary groups with persecution and escalating violence against whole Armenian communities. These culminated in extensive state-sponsored massacres in 1894–6. In the wake of the CUP coup the situation was expected to improve but actually led to further massacres, in Cilicia in 1909, and a deterioration in government–community relations during the years of Ottoman territorial haemorrhage before the First World War. As the CUP regime became more stridently nationalistic in a Turkish sense and looked to develop this agenda by entering the First World War on the side of Germany and the Central Powers, in late 1914, the Armenians became the butt of their antipathies. By early 1915, with eastern Anatolia transformed into a largely lawless war zone, the Armenian position was becoming extremely perilous in the face of repeated assassinations and local massacres.

Trigger/immediate catalyst: Matrix of events centring around period 20–5 April 1915, with expected, imminent Anglo-French landings on the Gallipoli coast, close to the Ottoman capital at Constantinople, coinciding with an apparent insurrection mounted by the Armenian population of Van, close to the eastern Ottoman front with the Russians. The CUP response was to arrest, deport (and later kill) hundreds of leading Armenians in Constantinople. This was succeeded by a series of general orders issued by the interior minister, Talaat Pasha in the following months, authorising the mass deportation of Armenians from eastern and central Anatolia into the Syrian desert.

Wider context: Life and death struggle of residual Ottoman empire for survival against Entente powers; CUP leadership both attempting to transform the country under these total war conditions into a modern 'national' state and at the same time break out from its perceived geo-strategic straitjacket, via military campaigns into (Turkic) Central Asia, with eastern Anatolia as the projected bridgehead.

Nature of genocide: Liquidation of whole communities *in situ*, in designated districts of eastern region, including mass burnings and drownings in the summer of 1915, in parallel to, or succeeded by a much wider process of extermination through repeated massacre and atrocity of communities on forced marches to the desert. With most able-bodied male Armenians dispatched simultaneously in their Ottoman army units, it was the old, the young and most particularly women who were the primary victims of the death marches. Tens of thousands of survivors were subsequently liquidated by mass burning and asphyxiation at desert camps, and other killing sites throughout late 1915 and 1916. Tens of thousands more died through starvation and disease, or through hyper-exploitation working in slave gangs on military roads, or on a section of the Berlin–Baghdad railway.

Organiser-perpetrator defence/rationalisation: Legitimate defence by sovereign state – at the moment of its greatest danger – against an actual or projected general Armenian uprising in favour of Russia and Western Allied invasion of Ottoman heartlands. Treasonable nature of Armenians already proven by decades of their revolutionary party activities against the state and – notwithstanding the 1908 change of regime – the continued willingness of Armenians to act as fifth column agents of malevolent foreign powers. The CUP argued, however, that the deportation orders were not an intent to exterminate but to remove specific Armenian communities from eastern theatre of operations where they posed a danger. The Armenian 'uprising' at Van, in the second half of April 1915, was regularly cited by the regime at the time, as evidence of Armenian malice and sabotage of the war effort.

Actual target population danger to state: Debatable. Armenian revolutionary groups *had* perpetrated terror acts during the previous Hamidian regime. Their continuing activity posed some potential threat, especially in eastern Anatolia in the context of war. Equally, there were some Armenian Ottoman volunteers serving in the Russian army in the Caucasus. However, the degree to which the specifically Van uprising was premeditated or rather reactive in the face of already perpetrated atrocities against Armenians is a subject of some scholarly dispute.[111] Overall, there is little evidence of a general Armenian threat in the eastern region, at least compared with the behaviour of some overtly insurrectionary Kurdish tribes. Armenian religious and political leaders in 1914–15 were actually preaching loyalty and passivity as well as encouraging young men to fulfil their Ottoman army obligations. Moreover, the vast majority of Armenians remained unpoliticised. What Armenian resistance there was appears to have been localised, desperate and *reactive* in the face of liquidation.

Exemptions: Many young women and children survived the deportations through forcible Islamicisation at the hands of their captors, or purchasers, requiring them as brides or other useful chattel. The genocide mostly did not extend – bar leading elite figures – to major Armenian metropolitan communities in Constantinople and Smyrna.

Other related killings: Smaller schismatic Christian communities in eastern Anatolia caught up in assault. Hakkari Nestorians (Assyrians) also a specific target.

Termination of genocide: From late 1916, as destruction of Armenian society and culture in eastern Anatolia was completed.

Estimated deaths: Out of a pre-war Ottoman Armenian population of not more than 2 million, between 800,000 and 1 million were directly or indirectly killed.[112] These figures exclude deaths from subsequent post-war Turkish campaigns against them and/or the putative independent Armenian state on the former Russian side of the border.

Rwandan Genocide: Extermination of Rwandan Tutsi

Timespan: April–early July 1994 (c. 100 days).

Geographical range: All areas of central and southern Rwanda under control of Hutu Power governing regime.

Organiser of genocide: Newly installed Hutu Power regime involving elements of previous National Republican Movement for Development (MRND) government, other party leaders, senior military chiefs plus palace clique centring around wife of former President Habyarimana.

Perpetrators: The Presidential Guard, Rwandan army and police, specially organised militias acting as strike-force, elements from all sections of dominant (Hutu) population including peasantry, the latter often acting on the directives of the local prefects and administrators.

Targeted population status as defined by genocide organiser: Anybody who was classified by their identity papers as a Tutsi or looked like a Tutsi or was believed to oppose the killings of Tutsi. Tutsi themselves characterised as a racially alien population from a different part of Africa who, in recent historic times, had invaded and usurped the political and economic rights of of the authentic, indigenous majority.

Targeted population status as self-defined: Far from clear, not least due to fact that Tutsi shared the same culture, customs and language of those Rwandans (Banyarwanda) defined as Hutu with whom they lived and worked. Historic pre-colonial cleavages associated with caste, lineage, wealth and power were reformulated towards the end of Belgian colonial rule and through later politicisation to give rise to a specific sense of Tutsi identity as separate, even arguably superior to the Hutu. None of this proved a blanket impediment to intermarriage, which was common.

Targeted population status as defined in domestic law: While minority Tutsi were full Rwandan citizens alongside Hutu majority, their ethnic distinctiveness was inscribed in the universal identity card system which the Belgians had introduced in 1933–4, and which was maintained by the post-colonial Hutu-dominated governments.

Warning signs (genocidal process): Arguably, seriously unravelling at the end of Belgian colonial rule in the late 1950s, when the traditionally Belgian-supported Tutsi dominance in Rwanda was overthrown, along with the king, by a popular, grass-roots Hutu revolution (1959–62). The failure to create a common Rwandan identity subsuming both groups stems from this period as well as a legacy of anti-Tutsi violence. Tutsi efforts to hold on to or reclaim land and power were bloodily resisted. Many fled, particularly to neighbouring Uganda and Tutsi-controlled Burundi. Those who remained – generally accepted as some 15 to 20 per cent of the population[113] – were removed from political and administrative office and suffered sporadic bouts of grass-roots, or more commonly, government-orchestrated ethnic violence, often in direct response to Tutsi anti-Hutu violence in Burundi. However, inter-communal relations only deteriorated massively in 1990, when the Tutsi-dominated Rwandese Patriotic Front (RPF) invaded Rwanda from Uganda, at a juncture when the country was already reeling from economic crisis and pressures from international lenders (on whom the regime was wholly dependent) to democratise. Further, the international community leant on the government to negotiate an arrangement with the RPF, who were already in control of much of the north of the country, and had displaced as many as 1 million of its inhabitants in the process.[114] Against this background of massive dislocation and uncertainty as to the country's future, political positions polarised and the indigenous Tutsi became scapegoats in a flurry of covertly state-organised massacres between 1991 and 1993.

Trigger/immediate catalyst: The downing of the presidential plane by a missile on 6 April 1994, as President Habyarimana returned with his Burundian opposite number to the Rwandan capital, Kigali, after the signing of the Arusha accords. The agreement was intended to provide for MRND power-sharing with the RPF, supervised by the UN. Whoever was responsible for the assassinations – which remains an open question – the occasion provided the moment for the anti-Arusha – Hutu Power – elements in the regime and in opposition parties to seize power, repudiate the accords and initiate a preplanned programme for the elimination of all internal opposition. The early massacre of twelve Belgian peacekeepers also helped ensure the rapid removal of most UN forces from the scene.

Wider context: The events of early April 1994 represented the greatest crisis of Rwandan state and society since its post-colonial inception. With the RPF cancelling its ceasefire and resuming its advance on Kigali, the goals of the 1959 revolution appeared to be on the verge of being undone. This combined with radical Hutu fears that Rwanda was about to go the same way as Burundi, whose brief honeymoon with democracy had been smashed the previous year with the military assassination of its first Hutu president, and a repeat of major anti-Hutu massacres. The UN made no serious attempt to halt what followed.

Nature of genocide: Initial elimination of opponents of Hutu Power in Kigali rapidly became a country-wide hunting down of all Tutsi, leading to executions at roadblocks, often using machetes and other blunt instruments, and to huge massacres where the targeted people had taken sanctuary, particularly in churches. The grass-roots nature of the killing stands out, with participants often violating, disembowelling and murdering neighbours, friends and fellow church-goers.

Organiser-perpetrator defence/rationalisation: The Rwandan Tutsi could not be trusted. They had attempted an 'invasion' from Burundi in the early 1960s, while the willingness of the Tutsi in that country to indiscriminately massacre Hutu who resisted their minority hold on power was further evidence of what was in store if the RFP took over in Rwanda. In short, the Tutsi were foreigners who had no just claim to Rwandan Hutu home and hearth but who would certainly seize them and massacre their owners, unless the Hutu got in their retaliation first.

Actual target population danger to state: The RPF undoubtedly *were* a threat to the Hutu-dominated state. But this was primarily an exile organisation with little or no connection to Tutsi living within Rwanda. The latter's insurrectionary potential was negligible to the point of non-existence. The degree to which these Rwandan Tutsi identified with and supported the RPF is also open to question.

Other related killings: Hutu who were opposed to Hutu Power or willing to protect Tutsi; also members of the smaller minority Twa group.

Exemptions: There were a few prominent genocide organisers and perpetrators who were Tutsi by birth. Some Hutu husbands protected their Tutsi wives.

Termination of genocide: The genocide stopped in the south of the country, on the arrival of French troops, in June. A final end came when the RPF won their complete military victory, their Hutu Power adversaries plus some 2 million of their Hutu support population fleeing, as refugees, into neighbouring Zaire.

Estimated deaths: Between half a million and 800,000 primarily Tutsi (but also Hutu and Twa) out of a total Rwandese population of some 8 million.[115]

*

On the basis of these three most generally acknowledged genocides a preliminary statement as to their common attributes might run as follows:

1 A government, or regime in control of a state, committed to the extrusion of a communal group or groups for political purposes and with the logistical and resource capacity to undertake this by means of direct physical extermination.
2 An occasion in which this is possible with minimum hindrance or outside interference.
3 A heightened sense of crisis when this occurs, the government believing that there is extreme danger to itself and the state.
4 A prolonged but continuous sequence of killing over time and space, with the enactment of genocide not reducible to a single act of mass murder.
5 Killing pursued regardless of age or gender distinctions.

6 The employment of state-organised, usually professional military and para-military personnel to spearhead the killing and other elements of the dominant population to participate in it.

7 An inability on the part of targeted group or groups to defend themselves or strike back in such a way as to noticeably halt or impede the killing.

8 A sense on the part of the government that the communal group is a genuine and serious threat to the well-being of the state and/or dominant society then, now and in the future, regardless of the coherence or cohesive unity of the group as a group.

Now, one might wish to note at this point that the centrality of the state in this set of attributes cuts across both its complete (and conscious) absence in the UNC text and a recent, important definitional examination of genocide in which its author, Scott Straus, has argued that there is no *prima facie* case why the genocidal agent *has to be* a state. That said, Straus also notes that it would be 'hard to imagine a modern annihilation campaign without state involvement'.[116] This statement, in itself, would seem to raise further legitimate questions about the relationship between genocide's primary organisers and those secondary agencies of state who might be its implementers. Or then again, occasions when this transmission belt is not so abundantly clear. Indeed, one might wish to go on from there to question what it is that we understand by the term 'state'. Is it a fixed entity? Does it have a beginning and end? Can one imagine genocides at either of such moments of formation or implosion? Does authorisation for genocide have to come from the very centre of power or could it come, for instance, from a colonial governor? These are relevant questions to which we need to return. Nevertheless our idealisation, so far, would seem to point to a fundamental 'state' role in the conception, organisation and execution of our phenomenon.

However, our attributes would hardly seem to endorse genocide as an internally consistent aspect of state behaviour. Points 2 and 3, for instance, clearly pull in quite contradictory directions, as do points 7 and 8. If each is true, and so, in relation to the other, paradoxical, the best we can do, at least at this moment, is to accept the paradox. Nor should we be sidetracked by each and every detail of our three genocides, most of which are specific to their particular case and, thus, not transferable across to the 'ideal' type. Clearly, sequences of killing which range from four full years, to two years, to a hundred days are different. The fact that in the last the rate of killing far exceeded anything in the previous two also says something quite extraordinary about Rwanda, though it also perhaps rather significantly suggests that relatively sophisticated apparatus for killing large numbers of people is *not* a necessary requirement for modern genocide. Patrick Brogan, referring to the events of 1915 might assert that 'though countless Armenians were massacred by Turkish troops … Turkey's object was its own security, not genocide. There were no gas chambers',[117] thereby misleads on two counts. Low-level weaponry may have been the norm in the Turkish and, even more notably, in the Rwandan case, but proved quite adequate to the genocidal actions of each. Similarly, any notion that where these actions involve the perceived self-defence of state interests the term genocide should not be applicable is negated by each of our cases. Even the Holocaust was built on a premise of self-defence – albeit of the most preposterous kind. Nevertheless, that this premise is an absolutely critical ingredient of our phenomenon is confirmed by Helen Fein's own first and highly influential reading of the 'unifying necessary conditions underlying all types of genocide':

> Genocide is the calculated murder of of a segment or all of a group defined outside the universe of the perpetrator, by a government, elite, staff or crowd representing the perpetrator in response to a crisis or opportunity *perceived to be caused by or impeded by the victim* [my emphasis]. Crises and opportunities may be a result of war, challenges to the structure of domination, the threat of internal breakdown or social revolution and economic development … Motives may be ideological, economic and/or political … Genocides, as are other murders, may be premeditated or an ad hoc response to a problem or opportunity.[118]

What Fein would appear to be propounding here is that genocide is the outcome of a specific relationship between perpetrator and targeted group – however much that might be based on an entirely false, imaginary or confabulated reading of that relationship on the part of the perpetrator. Moreover, Fein confirms that the phenomenon crystallises only in particular, not to say extraordinary circumstances. Indeed, her implicit tension between crisis and opportunity is even more apt if one were to understand 'crisis' as the Chinese read it on the basis of two characters, one meaning 'danger' the second 'opportunity'. Indeed, Fein's would be as good a working formulation as any, were it not for two lacunae. One is her uncertainty about the primacy of the state, even though in this formulation she gets within a hair's breadth of accepting it. The second relates to a certain unwillingness to develop what is meant by a (victim) group in the context of her own implicit insight that what matters is the perpetrator's perception of it.

The problem, far from peculiar to Fein, has actually dogged many scholars since Lemkin attempted to denote the socio-biological connectedess of a group through use of the term *genos*. Or, as aptly put by Straus, its 'biological immutability, hereditary qualities … and … possibility of reproduction'.[119] But restricting a definition as does the UNC, to 'stable, permanent groups whose membership is determined by birth'[120] – as if groups *really* are fixed in this way – flies so obviously in the face of evidence to the contrary, that the recent International Criminal Tribunal on Rwanda found itself having to tweak the original UNC interpretation in order that the exterminated Tutsi could be meaningfully encompassed within its definition.[121]

As proposed by Pieter Drost, the Dutch legal expert and early authority on the UNC, as well as its critic, there is a neat and elastic way around the problem. Drost argued that the 'group' was an entirely self-defining one composed of any body of individuals who saw themselves as part of a collectivity.[122] The notion is undoubtedly highly inclusive and would allow not only for political groups – a particular Drost cavil – to be incorporated in the 'victim' rubric but indeed any group from antique stamp collectors to Esperanto speakers (who might also be Jewish-born Christian converts). Yet under what circumstances such a body of individuals becomes a socially identifiable, let alone biologically reproducing, group is less clear. Unfortunately, however, Drost's efforts are entirely academic as this is a case of viewing the genocide phenomenon through the wrong end of telescope. Our three case studies confirm that *it is the perpetrator, not the victim (or bystander) who defines the group*.

It may also be, of course, that the targeted group is perfectly capable of its own self-definition; though this would immediately confront us in the Jewish case, if not the others, with some serious internal disagreement on the matter. Alternatively, we might seek professional adjudication, social anthropologists surely being able to offer some guidelines to suggest how Jews, Tutsi and Armenians, even under changing modern circumstances of greater integration with, and acculturation to other human populations, have retained at least a modicum of ethnic distinctiveness. They would surely point to occupational, social, religious, culinary and linguistic traits, patterns of domicile, not to mention those of marriage and child-rearing to underscore these distinctions. They would even more forcefully note traditions of social group cohesion based on prejudices against outsiders, penalties against boundary crossing, and, most strictly enforced of all, endogamy, whose transgression would most critically sap the biological intactness of the group. Yet no sooner had they done this than they would start throwing in all sorts of caveats, noting how Jewish–Gentile intermarriage in pre-1933 Germany, for instance, was already well on its way to dissolving Jewish identity in the broader mass,[123] how some Ottoman Armenians in remote areas had, through Islamicisation, become practically indistinguishable from neighbouring Kurds,[124] how the Tutsi–Hutu cleavage was never obviously amenable to a general set of lineal rules.[125] In short, the expert advice would be that an ethnic group is *never* a fixed entity. It changes over time and place.[126]

That changes of this sort have become more marked in contemporary history, that traditional boundaries between groups have consequently blurred or even disintegrated, and that these changes have been noted by people who would become both perpetrators and victims in genocide is undoubtedly all very relevant to our broader study. But it does not determine the issue here at hand. In 1915, Armenians who were Catholics and Protestants were at a critical point – and even though thousands had already been killed – exempted from the general deportation, on order of the Interior Ministry.[127] By contrast, half-Jewish central Europeans who thought themselves safe from Nazi extermination on account of their diluted *Mischling* status found themselves, towards the end of the war, being herded onto transports to Theresienstadt and beyond as the 'Final Solution' began to be applied to them, too.[128] As for Rwanda, though identity cards which 'bore the precious inscription Hutu (or Twa)' were meant to distinguish them from Tutsi singled out for death, at militia- or army-guarded roadblocks what the cards said proved no protection for Hutu or Twa 'whose skin was a bit too light, who were a bit too tall or whose necks were a bit too long'.[129] In other words, if they looked like Tutsi, they might as well be Tutsi. Ultimately, no social or any other science can determine how perpetrators define a group, whether this has some relationship to social reality, or is entirely something which has developed in their own heads.

But does this effectively mean that the notion of *genos* has no actual salience to the phenomenon Lemkin was trying to describe? Our two further cases are certainly not examples where the targeted groups could be obviously identified as distinctly national, ethnical, racial or religious. Indeed, in terms of the broader histories of genocide under Stalinist and Khmer Rouge regimes, they are not the most clear-cut examples that come to mind. They do, however, amply illustrate something of how a perpetrator can conceive a group as an organic collectivity *in spite of itself.* Again, the aim here is to offer only outline schema in so far as it develops our conceptual effort.

Soviet State Against the 'Kulaks'

Timespan: 1929–33.

Geographical range: Throughout USSR.

Organiser of genocide: Communist Politburo as dominated by Party Secretary Stalin.

Perpetrators: Secret police (OGPU), army, ordinary police militias, specially enrolled Communist party cadres including Komsomol (youth movement) usually assisted by local party activists, including poor peasants.

Targeted population status as defined by perpetrator: No clear definitional boundaries as 'kulak' was a highly elastic, constantly shifting category. In pre-Soviet times the literal ascription kulak – i.e. 'tight-fisted' – had come to denote independent peasant proprietors. This was the focus of post-1917 Communist Party distaste and antipathy. However, with social distinctions on the land dramatically levelled in the wake of the revolution, attempts to delineate a specific kulak 'class', as separate from the rest of the majority peasant population, were constantly being 'redefined by statisticians to suit the political circumstances, or redefined by politicians who ordered the statisticians to produce appropriate figures to prove their point'.[130] A 1927 commission of investigation found that some 3.9 per cent of peasant households were kulaks representing some 4.9 million people.[131] Later on, as the 'dekulakisation' campaign in the countryside got under way, kulak could mean just about anybody – peasant or otherwise – who was opposed to collectivisation, or was considered suspect either by the regime, or by local denunciation.

Targeted population status as self-defined: No such self-definition. Those who were so defined, however, would normally have been part of interrelated peasant households and broader communities.

Targeted population status as defined in law: Technically, citizens of USSR until such time as labelled as 'kulaks', in which case liable to disenfranchisement and punishment.

Warning signs (genocidal process): Repudiation of previous state-party policy (New Economic Policy: NEP) encouraging essentially free peasants to sell their grain on the open market in favour of direct and violent forced seizure of grain (Stalin's 'Urals–Siberian method'), during 1928 and 1929. The resulting collapse of NEP, along with internal party opposition, provided the opportunity for the initiation of the crash-course Five Year Plan to create a total command economy in which a collectivised countryside would be harnessed to the needs of a forced-pace programme of industrialisation. A special Politburo commission rapidly put together recommendations both for the forcible collectivisation of peasant communes and dekulakisation.

Trigger/immediate catalyst: 27 December 1929, Stalin announcement in party paper, *Pravda*, of the regime's intent to liquidate the kulaks as a class in the USSR.

Wider context: Backdrop of violent rupture with past tsarist regime, in 1917, and of an ongoing crisis situation in which replacement, strictly doctrinaire Marxist–Leninist regime, having failed to catalyse world revolution, saw itself both in a state of siege from, and in ideological and physical competition with, the advanced capitalist world. Ability to survive in this hostile environment perceived by Stalin and other party leaders as requiring an accelerated programme of social and economic change – the projected Great Leap Forward – which would create conditions for a stable 'Socialism in One Country'.

Nature of genocide: Secret Politburo orders for the treatment of kulaks placed them in three categories, the first of which was reserved for 60,000 of the most 'dangerous' and 'vicious' kulaks who were marked down for immediate OGPU execution with the remainder of their families being deported to the Gulag.[132] The chaotic as well as extremely brutal nature of the initial spring 1930 campaign, however, and the tendency to treat kulaks as households, often determined that the fate of the male head of family was in effect also that of his related women and children. Additionally, ill-organised deportation by rail cattle-truck of milllions of other 'kulaks' to distant, isolated settlement camps, was responsible for a huge mortality, particularly of young children. Renewed bouts of dekulakisation, in the following two years, embraced even wider sections of rural and town populations with many simply shot out of hand. There was a later bout of mass executions of 'kulaks' in the camps, during the 'Great Purges' in 1937.

Perpetrator defence/rationalisation: The collectivisation of the countryside in the interests of Soviet state development could not proceed without the removal of class enemies and counter-revolutionaries. Food shortages, or supposed contamination of food, were evidence of kulak sabotage. The alleged aim, however – except in specifically 'dangerous' cases – was the mass removal of kulak elements, not their extermination.

Actual target group danger to state: Problematic. Collectivisation was bound to be resisted in the countryside by the majority of peasants. Eliminating an arbitrary tier of them may have served an instrumental purpose to cow the rest. There was massive peasant intransigence and resistance but as this was localised, uncoordinated and hence patchy, the degree of threat that it posed to a state apparatus committed to its programme through the use of massive violence and coercion is debatable. All of the peasant resistance was reactive to state policies and not in any sense proactive.

Other related killings: Specific assaults on national groups of whole regions, notably the Ukraine, Kazakhstan and the North Caucasus – and in part via man-made famine – either synchronised with or immediately followed the dekulakisation campaign. These continued in spasms throughout the 1930s alongside more stochastic 'purges' in the period 1937–9.

Exemptions: In principle, kulaks in Category One were only to be shot if they resisted while their families were to be deported. Category Two kulaks – earmarked for deportation *in toto* – and those in Category Three were to be spared their lives. These guidelines were rarely adhered to in practice. However, at various points in succeeding years significant numbers of 'kulaks' who had survived deportation and or the labour camps, especially children, were released.

Termination of genocide: By 1933 'dekulakisation' of the countryside was effectively completed.

Estimated deaths: Estimates vary widely from the very high figures of around 1.5 million people by the end of the first dekulakisation campaign, in July 1930, rising to 3.5 million by 1933,[133] compared with a low of 'at least 30,000 shot out of hand'.[134] Part of the issue at stake is the distinction between those who were immediately physically liquidated and the very much larger number, generally agreed as being in millions, who were deported and as a result perished in the Gulag, or other settlement camps. The statistical evidence from KGB archives is still be fully and comprehensively analysed.

Khmer with 'Vietnamese Minds'

Timespan: Six-month period from summer 1978 to January 1979.

Geographical range: Eastern Zone (regions 20–4) of Democratic Republic of Kampuchea (Cambodia), much of it contiguous with Vietnamese border and in other zones to which Eastern Zone people deported.

Organiser of genocide: Central leadership – the *Angkar Leu*, or 'Centre' – of communist Khmer Rouge regime, led by Pol Pot.

Perpetrators: Party-organised army and cadres from zones neighbouring the Eastern Zone.

Targeted population status as defined by perpetrator: 'Khmer bodies with Vietnamese minds'.[135]

Targeted population status as self-defined: Clearly no such self-definition. However, there was some sense of an historic autonomy in this region and some awareness, too, that the local Khmer Rouge commanders were operating a regime somewhat 'less harsh' than elsewhere in the DRK. Eastern Zone people would normally have been part of indigenous, interrelated, mostly peasant communities or recently displaced ones deported to this region.

Targeted population status as defined in law: Not applicable. Targeted population came both from the so-called 'New People', namely all those who, before April 1975, had been living in areas – notably the capital, Phnom Penh – still controlled by the preceding Lon Nol regime, or from the more favoured 'base people' who had been living in Khmer Rouge territory 'liberated' in the pre-1975 civil war period.

Warning signs (genocidal process): Mass death had been symptomatic of the Cambodian situation both before 1975, when the country had been sucked into the Vietnam conflict – as well as suffering a civil war between the US-backed Lon Nol regime and its Khmer Rouge adversaries – and the period, more particularly after 1975, when the Khmer Rouge had taken complete control. The new regime's agenda for the creation of a single, unified, entirely classless Khmer society of atomised individuals working solely for the good of the country on its unquestionable command, implicitly carried with it a warning that any individual or group which could not meet these specifications would be eliminated. This forecast was vastly amplified by the Centre's reading of Khmer history as a mythic saga of classical greatness in which the Cambodian race-nation had been pure and authentic, juxtaposed with more recent decay due to foreign encroachment or influence. As such, the Khmer Rouge recipe for a return to greatness was predicated on the liquidation of all elements – again, as determined by itself – which were tainted by such foreign, colonial or imperial legacies. Sealing the country off almost in totality from the outside world, and evacuating all the towns in order to put everybody to work in the countryside, thus became both the touchstone for the regime's vision of revolutionary reawakening and, at the same time, the route by which its dystopian experiment began to disintegrate under the weight of the impossible rice-harvest targets it set itself. Mass killings began to extend, throughout 1976 and 1977, to regional party cadres who were blamed for the encroaching starvation. Even so, the drive towards racial purification not only was intensifed but began to focus increasingly on the alleged danger from an historic Vietnamese enemy. Despite the fact that at the time Vietnam was supposed to be a fraternal, communist ally, the Centre's forces began to make repeated armed border-incursions into its territory. As relations between the two countries deteriorated so too did those between the Centre and its cadres in the Vietnam-bordering Eastern Zone.

Trigger/immediate catalyst: Arrest and execution of leading Eastern Zone cadres by the Centre in May 1978, sparking a largely reactive insurrection in the Eastern Zone.

Wider context: Massive destabilisation and loss of life in Cambodia, as a result of the physical destruction wrought by American bombing in the early 1970s, paved the way for the total social revolution conceived by the Khmer Rouge ideologues. Their notion of a 'super-great leap forward' which would transcend Cambodia's weakness on the international stage has to be set against the reality of the regime's dependence on violence as its only instrument for survival. A country both internally, and internationally, in a prolonged spasm of potentially terminal crisis.

Nature of genocide: Troops from the South-West Zone sent to quell the insurrection perpetrated repeated massacres of Eastern Zone cadres, plus whole villages and districts. Tens of thousands of survivors were subsequently deported to neighbouring or more distant zones on foot, by boat, or train. They were issued with specially imported blue scarves to mark them out as 'Vietnamese', from the rest of the Khmer population and as a clear signal that they were to be liquidated.

Perpetrator defence/rationalisation: The Eastern Zone commanders were plotting the overthrow of the Centre and were in cahoots with the Vietnamese enemy. The Eastern Zone population was also collectively tainted by its Vietnamese association and was, thus, effectively a fifth column.

Actual target group danger to state: There may have been a planned insurrection by Eastern Zone cadres. The blanket ascription of guilt to the population of the region as a whole only makes sense, however, in the context of the obsessive, conspiracy-laden and entirely phobic worldview which was a Khmer Rouge hallmark. But there was also an element of self-fulfilling prophecy. The cross-border war that the Centre had precipitated galvanised a Vietnamese invasion which was supported by surviving elements of the Eastern Zone apparatus.

Other related killings: Wide swathes of majority Khmer society plus definable ethnic minority groups, notably Vietnamese, Chinese and Muslim Cham.

Termination of genocide: January 1979 with the liquidation of Democratic Kampuchea by the military forces of neighbouring Vietnam.

Estimated deaths: While the acknowledged Cambodia genocide expert, Ben Kiernan has estimated that 1,671,000, or 21 per cent of Cambodia's total population perished under the Khmer Rouge regime,[136] mostly through mass starvation, disease and execution, he proposes that something between 100,000 and 250,000 of these came from the Eastern's Zone's population of 1.7 million.[137] It is generally acknowledged by other Cambodia experts that, even in terms of the Khmer Rouge bloodbath, what happened to the Eastern Zone population was exceptional, Kiernan himself describing it as a 'genocide against a part of the majority national group'.[138]

*

How then do these two additional case histories impact on our quest for genocide's ideal type? Certainly, neither of them detracts from the basic contours we have already observed. Genocide remains the result of massive state, or state-regime crisis in which an aggregate population is accused of malevolent and dangerous antagonism, not to say huge disruptive potential to the regime's agenda or purpose, justifying in the regime's mind the *necessity* of a physical-cum-biological assault, with the aim of destroying it, if not in totality, then in such numbers – at least as perceived by the regime – that it no longer represents a threat. However, the kulak and Khmer cases extend our conceptualisation in two important ways.

The first actually eliminates the necessity for genocide to take place within a broader war context. Certainly, the destruction of the kulaks was against a backdrop of almost constant Soviet fears of imminent foreign invasion. Certainly too, the Eastern Zone destruction was a prelude to inter-state Cambodian–Vietnamese conflict. Going back a few steps one might note that neither Soviet nor Khmer Rouge regimes were conceivable without mass state and societal dislocation brought about by war. And one might add that the sort of attacks launched upon kulaks and Khmer alike were not simply conducted as if they were military campaigns but were also the products of massively militarised polities. In these cases, as with those of Tutsi, Armenian and Jew, physical annihilation was accomplished as a form of special warfare. All that said, however, we could not say that the kulak and Eastern Zone genocides were undertaken either in conditions of, or under the cover of more general war. In other words, while genocide is a product of state crisis, war as such is not a absolute requirement for its crystallisation.

More tellingly, and arguably more problematically, our kulak and Khmer examples also reinforce and indeed confirm what has been implicit in our discussion throughout: victim groups in genocide cannot be viewed as fixed entities as in some Linnaean system of plant or animal classification but rather, as Lynne Viola has stated specifically with relation to the kulaks, 'to be largely in the eye of the beholder'.[139] This does not mean, of course, that a victim group may not define itself using the same nomenclature ('Jews', 'Armenians', 'Tutsi' for example) as the perpetrator, or even that the two definitions may not be in agreement. It may even be the case that the perpetrator regime's assessment of the threat which the victim group allegedly poses is, if not entirely accurate, then at least bears some passing resemblance to reality. However, our Stalinist example would rather suggest that even this need not be fixed in the perpetrator's mind. A statement one week of the 'kulak' enemy as someone who owned a horse, lent money or grain to fellow peasants, or hired family or friends for the harvest – all at least, however nebulously something to do with peasant life – could be vastly and entirely arbitrarily extended, in another, to include all manner of allegedly dubious people living in or at the margins of the countryside; ex-tsarist estate stewards, teachers, artisans, seasonal labourers, those who had fought with the Whites in the civil war, even single women.[140] Perhaps this goes some way to explaining why the contours of 'kulak' destruction were never absolute, let alone consistent or coherent; the perpetrators could never decide what it was *exactly* that defined the menace.

The kulak example, of course, is rather idiosyncratic as, arguably more so, is the quite fabulously concocted image of a Cambodian Eastern Zone population mentally transmuted into diabolic Vietnamese. But, in other respects, these are just very extreme aspects of a consistent truth. As Straus has perspicaciously put it: 'Genocide is not carried out against a group bounded by essential internal properties. Rather, genocide is carried out against a group that the perpetrator *believes* has essential properties ... however fictive such a belief may be.'[141] Moreover, it is it interesting on this score to note that in our two more obviously confabulated examples, perpetrator hatred against the created victim group was no less capable of being corporealised, even racialised than in our more obviously ethnically grounded cases. Beyond charging peasants with being 'ideological kulaks', 'sub-kulaks', 'kulak hirelings', kulak 'choirboys' and the like – all rather ridiculous in themselves – Communist Party activists who participated in the round-ups were quite capable of descending into the sort of dehumanising vitriol in which their victims – whether adults or children – became bloodsuckers, parasites and vermin.[142] And, in this mindset, wrecking their homes or devastating their churches became a logical assault on their supposed collective existence as 'kulak' enemies. The way that Eastern Zone people were slated for extermination, on the grounds of their contamination by something ugly, poisonous and alien, is equaly palpable in its viciousness. Indeed, it is exactly this sort of phobic aspect of genocide which we must address in our next chapter.

All this, however, leads this author to conclude that in addition to the eight attributes central to our idealisation as stated earlier on in this section, there is one final ninth attribute:

> The targeted group is the product of the perpetrator's assemblage of social reality.

As such, any *idealisation* of genocide cannot consider the group as anything other than an aggregate population. That said, there remains a certain niggling little problem as to where such an idealisation exactly leaves the *genos* in Lemkin's terminology. If, as is accepted here, ethnic categories are essentially porous, shifting and malleable and in many cases what we are actually dealing with are imagined or fictive groups, or numbers of individuals who share no obvious kinship, then it could be argued that repeated recourse to the term 'genocide' is a matter of habitual default rather than careful, good design. Is it therefore enough that, if people define a situation as real, it is real in its consequences, and hence the perpetrator's criteria for target group identification becomes sufficient unto itself?[143] Reification is certainly fundamental to what actually happens in genocides. A slightly more nuanced approach, however, is that taken by Straus. He proposes that where the term genocide is applied to 'groups not commonly thought to have a biological foundation the task is to demonstrate an organic logic in the perpetrator's conception of the group'.[144] At the very least, in other words, the perpetrator must perceive the group as an organic collectivity and seek to annihilate its supposed *genos*. It is this premise to which this work subscribes.

This still squarely rests the group identification on the shoulders of the perpetrator. Yet it also puts the onus on the scholars of the subject – for instance if we were trying to follow this through as anthropologists – to plot something of the consanguineous relationships of the murdered victims. In the absence of comprehensive data for all five of our idealisation-building cases we might not be able to produce a conclusive result. Accepting some considerable fuzziness round the edges, however, I suspect that we would find what we were looking for in each case. If the verdict is the mass murder of females of all ages equally and without discrimination from the males who are their blood relatives and with the purpose of denying or seeking to deny their biological as well as social reproduction there are surely grounds here for accepting that Lemkin's terminology is still the best and most appropriate available.

There remains, however, a perplexing – not to say dreadful – enigma. Our idealisation would seem to pose an acute discrepancy between the alleged danger which the group poses in the heads of the perpetrators and the group's actual defencelessness in practice. The example of the Holocaust would appear to represent this discrepancy most sharply but it is nevertheless apparent, to greater or lesser degrees, in all our cases. But if that is so, then rationally and logically speaking, genocide should not be an outcome. Rather, the sensible course of action for the regimes in question ought to be to avoid confrontation, or to circumvent it, or even to come to an arrangement with their communal adversary. The idealised model thus points to the resort to genocide being either, or both, irrational and illogical. Yet, if that is the case, why in recent history have so many states conducted these hideous assaults on populations under their control? It would appear that our quest for the well-springs of modern genocide has only just begun.

2. Perpetrators, Victims and Collective Unreason

He dreamt that the whole world was ravaged by an unknown and terrible plague that had spread across Europe from the depths of Asia. All except a few chosen were doomed to perish. New kinds of germs – microscopic creatures which lodged in the bodies of men – made their appearance. But these creatures were spirits endowed with reason and will. People who became infected with them at once became mad and violent. But never had people considered themselves as wise and as strong in the pursuit of truth as these plague-ridden people. Never had they thought their decisions, their scientific conclusions, and their moral convictions so unshakable or so incontestably right.

Fyodor Dostoevsky, Crime and Punishment (1866)[1]

What makes people behave and act as they do? Is it nature or nurture, the way they are genetically formed or the socio-economic, cultural and institutional environment in which they are weaned, socialised and then live out their lives? More keenly, do we see people's actions as motivated by behaviour which can be analysed as essentially coherent and consistently grounded in these factors? Or are there occasions when human beings would appear to say and do things that would seem to make no rational sense whatsoever? Now try and apply this not very profound statement to the stuff of history, a picture of whole human societies operating over time and place. Or even to critical moments when day-to-day societal normality appears to rupture in the face of a man-made catastrophe, for instance an event such as the 11 September 2001 attack on New York's twin towers. The need for cool, detached – even scholarly – explanation in the face of such trauma is rapidly buffeted, engulfed and overwhelmed by a welter of much more intense emotions: disbelief, disorientation, acute pain and seering anger. Personally and collectively people's very beings seem to cry out for release. But what can soothe such massive psychological shock and hurt? One answer came the very next day from a leading American paper:

Revenge. Hold on to that thought. Go to bed thinking it. Wake up chanting it. Because nothing less than revenge is called for today ... the grief for our dead will be deep and enduring ... in the days that are coming ... as the dead are finally counted our rage will only build. And every time we look at the skyline ... we will remember your actions and crave for only one thing: blood for blood.[2]

This editorial from the *Philadelphia Daily News* might serve to remind us of something about the universality of the human condition in the face of an event such as 9/11. All the carefully constructed theories about the origins and nature of mass killing seem to simply fall away in its path, as do any fanciful notions that liberal society of itself can act as some sort of prophylactic. Here, instead, we have a mirror-image of ourselves in the raw. And of a straightforward, visceral human need: for retribution.

But perhaps it takes an event like this to remind us of those psychopathological elements which bind us all together. In 1993, in a House of Commons speech, British Prime Minister John Major described the increasingly genocidal conflict in Bosnia as a product of 'impersonal and inevitable historical forces beyond anyone's control'.[3] A hundred years earlier, the French foreign minister, Gabriel Hanotaux, shrugged off the first great wave of anti-Armenian massacres in the Ottoman empire as 'one of those thousand incidents of struggle between Christians and Muslims'.[4] The implication that it is only societies 'out there' that are massacre- or genocide-prone has had its corollary in a further long-standing assumption that it must be something about the way Balkan, Near Eastern or other societies are wired up, something in their cultural or religious make-up, or some pecularity or idiosyncrasy in their developmental path, which explains their misfortune. Not only are we – Western societies – thereby absolved of any inference of similitude but allowed to continue to bask in the light of our own ethnocentric moral standard in which the non-genocidal society is coterminous with the West's supposedly tolerant, rational, civic liberalism as compared with other types of society whose structural underpinnings are so obviously, fundamentally flawed.

Building on the findings of the previous chapter, the purpose of this one is to propose that it is such assumptions themselves that are flawed. Genocide cannot be explained solely or straightforwardly as a rational or utilitarian act. It is dependent on crisis situations, usually a whole series of them, in which collective agglomerations of human beings are not simply blamed for visible aspects of the crisis but in which antagonisms, antipathies and resentments directed by the dominant society toward them take on extreme forms. It can happen to such an extent that a defining word such as hatred becomes quite insufficient for what is entailed. A much more exact term, however, would be phobia, in other words, a tendency for individuals and/or societies to become so obsessively haunted by their own worst fears that these take on very tangible sensory and bodily manifestations when projected onto the assumed culprit or scapegoat. Modern Western societies may claim that they have divested themselves almost entirely of these atavistic tendencies and, as such, the 'object' of study for researchers of genocide in such countries is essentially divorced from their own 'safe' environments. It is rather appropriate, therefore, that we should begin our discussion with reference to mid-twentieth-century Germany, a country so mindful of its own utterly rational, scientifically informed, non-fearful persona yet one which, in the face of massive societal dislocation, gave itself up almost totally to phobic projection. Indeed, it is the very fact that the resulting total genocide is also the one least amenable to *rational* interpretation which provides us with our primary goad. To interrogate the dilemma further we will seek in this chapter to consider in general terms who exactly are the organisers and perpetrators of genocide. Equally importantly, we are concerned with understanding the nature and dynamics of the relationship with those who become their victims and what it is about such relationships that can produce a psychopathology leading to extreme and unmitigated violence. As previously, the five cases we utilised for our idealisation will be critical points of reference with occasional other examples added as and where appropriate.

Moving Beyond the Structure versus Intent Dichotomy

If nature versus nurture is the dichotomy around which much modern science and social science has considered human behaviour with respect to the world at large, the specificity of extreme violence in the form of the Holocaust has produced its own ongoing dichotomy in historical analysis. 'Intentionalism' versus 'functionalism' has now been around for several decades, but, far from running out of steam or producing a consensual resolution, rather continues, albeit with all manner of variations on a theme, to provide studies 'for' or 'against' often notable for the intensity of conviction with which they are upheld.[5] Perhaps it is not surprising: a lot is at stake.

As is well known, intentionalists argue that the primary motor-force explaining the 'Final Solution' is the person of Hitler – arguably supported by Himmler and other leading Nazis. It was this single person, or coterie, who conceived, planned and put into action the destruction of European Jewry according to a scheme already in his (or their) heads prior to June 1941. By contrast, functionalists reject any notion of a preconceived extermination plan, proposing instead that the issue of causation is embedded in the bureaucratic underpinnings and socio-economic configurations of the Nazi (and pre-Nazi) state apparatus. The genocidal outcome thus lies less in specific high-level decisions – not least when state departments and party agencies were often in chaotic competition with one another – and more in the crisis-ridden circumstances emanating from the war itself.

Equally well rehearsed are the moral dilemmas which come out of these two contrasting positions. If the former intentionalist position is true then culpability for mass genocide can be levelled at a handful of known named actors motivated by a perverted ideological worldview or even the result of some flawed genetic make-up or deficiency in childhood socialisation. How the rest of the German population became inveigled into the genocide project, however, then becomes more problematic as this would suggest that they were manipulable or seducible into participation by the propagandist fervour and rhetoric of the party-led state. Worse, if something like the Holocaust could happen this way once, there are no obvious reasons why it could not repeat itself in some other time or place again. In sharp relief, the primarily German scholars of functionalism whose work began in the 1960s and 1970s were impelled by the contrasting need to show their fellow Germans that the extermination and mass murders of the Nazi era were not some aberration for which only a small core of – by possible implication – psychopathic lunatics were to blame but something which came out of German society at large. It was the course of German historical development, including that prior to Nazism itself which was seriously dysfunctional, demanding a challenge as well as moral imperative to change it. The problem here, however, was if the Holocaust itself evolved step by step out of a long and convoluted process or series of processes which nobody had actually foreseen, then conceivably nobody exactly could be held responsible for it.

Of course, these are not the only conceivable positions available, Daniel Goldhagen represents the most notably distinct, if hardly original, entry into the recent field, with what amounts to a broad intentionalist argument in which more or less all Germans of the era are implicated.[6] Goldhagen's intervention notwithstanding, there is something interesting about the way the structure–intent debate is framed; or, perhaps more accurately, about the way the debate absents from the frame aspects of the dichotomy which are the most morally challenging. For instance, although intentionalism foregrounds actors, it is much less willing to consider the efficacy, purposefulness or otherwise, of their genocidal actions which clearly, thereby, implies that there *might be* some utilitarian logic to the programme of Jewish extermination. Obversely, to propose that masses of planners, administrators and technical support staff were engaged in a great institutionally led programme for the destruction of people, which was actually, empirically-speaking, entirely *pointless*, would be to go beyond functionalism's insight with regard to a specific German state mal-function to concede that state bureaucracies can and do undertake agendas which are completely irrational.

But then can genocide be, at one and the same time, both purposeful and absurd? If the implication is that there is an important paradox here it is one which only begins to be bridgeable by a willingness to engage with the socio-psychological and cultural aspects of the Nazi–Jewish relationship; however disturbing they may be. Intentionalists, for instance, are perfectly willing to emphasise the regime's anti-Semitism but much less to empathise with what-ever it was about Nazi *perceptions* of 'the Jews' which drove them to apoplexy. Functionalists, by the same token, are more than ready to consider the intri-cate twists and turns in the process by which Jews came to be exterminated, but as often as not, in a way as if the Jews themselves were an irrelevance. Indeed, by relegating them to the role of passive, one-dimensional, pieces on a chessboard, functionalists often quite inadvertently assist in the very project of dehumanisation which was the actual genocidaires' intention. But then the very labels 'victim' and 'perpetrator', largely bequeathed to genocide studies as a whole through their persistent usage in Holocaust literature, not to say weighed down as they also are with moral and criminological overtones, may be exactly the sort of linguistic turn which blocks us off from getting to grips with the very nature of the dynamic which leads to genocide.[7]

This is not to suggest in this case that Jews had any notable leverage on the direction in which this dynamic went or even that one can really conceive of them as protagonists at all when the dynamic was essentially played out in the Nazis' heads. This is, after all, one feature of the Holocaust that makes it very singular. This is not, however to deny the value of intentionalist or functional-ist approaches to the broader field of genocide studies, nor their potential for being melded into a synthesis which equally values people, underlying social structure and contingency. Consider, for instance, some of the most provoca-tive empirical Marxist analyses of recent times – the work of E. P. Thompson, for instance, or, much closer to the subject of the Holocaust, Tim Mason – and the contours of historical change are found to be less the inevitable con-sequence of inherent social or economic forces and more an outcome shaped and transformed by human agency.[8] 'People' – including those whom we think of as victims – can become protagonists in their own fate. In the case of those we might deem perpetrators, Mason has even suggested how a Nazi party in power in a society ostensibly dominated by ruling bourgeois elites could, through its own volition, move outside their influence and rule the state contrary to those collective interests.[9]

All this provides sufficient grounds to concur with Martin Broszat's plea at the heart of the 1980s *Historikerstreit* for a proper historicisation of the Holocaust[10] and, indeed, of genocide more generally. But, unless such a project could engage with those elements in the phenomenon which would seem implicitly to resist a commonsensical historical line of reasoning, it would be unlikely to succeed. Mason discerned Nazi politics going against the grain of coherent self-interest. By the same token many other state perpetrators of genocide seem to be motivated by quite singular perceptions about the victim group which bear little or no relationship to outside empirical observation. The possibility that genocide might have as its core a driving force which at the very least defies normative political processes thus would seem to contradict not only those experts who would consider it 'a rational, calculated act, involving cruelty without passion'[11] but more particularly any study aspiring to embed its specifically human ingredients within a clearly defined structural framework.

Does this mean, therefore, that historians and political scientists who wish to pursue the phenomenon really would do better to leave the field to other professionals more aptly qualified to deal with mental sickness and trauma? Some comfort for the former might be derived from the concluding remarks of Douglas Kelley, the chief investigative psychiatrist at the IMT trials at Nuremburg. Referring to the surviving Nazi leaders, Kelley proposed that: 'such personalities are not unique or insane but ... could be duplicated in any country of the world today'.[12] This would appear to rule out clinical madness – at least in this worst-case – though it would also seem to leave the door tantalisingly open for other supposedly normal people in different cultural, social and political frameworks to behave in similar ways. A more populist approach, however, would simply not accept these findings. For a general Western public, indeed, genocide is first and foremost about dictators who are not simply ruthless and cruel but phobic, paranoid and deluded. And where they are not these things they are certainly evil. This is the word which is most commonly and repeatedly used to describe a Hitler, Stalin, Saddam Hussein, Pol Pot or Milosevic.[13] Significantly, this roster of wickedness is highly dependent on media presentation at any given time. As a result Saddam would not have been well to its fore until the 1990 invasion of Kuwait, two years after his genocidal assault on Iraqi Kurds; Milosevic certainly not at the 1995 end of the war in Bosnia, when he was being heavily cajoled and feted by Western leaders; while Indonesian President Suharto, a notable recidivist in the perpetration of genocide against fellow Indonesians and East Timorese but also a close Western ally, would not have been present at all until very close to his dumping by the West and his consequent fall. By comparison, there are other names such as Colonel Qaddafi, the highly independent if idiosyncratic ruler of Libya who has never committed genocide *per se* but has (until a dramatic change of Western policy towards him in March 2004) maintained a rather constant profile as evil madman, even if clearly and overwhelmingly gazumped in recent years by Osama bin Laden, anti-Western mass murderer and terrorist *par excellence* but, according to this book's groundrules, not a genocidaire.

If the roster, thus, is highly variable and not in itself an accurate guide to genocidal leaders in modern times, it does, however, provide us with a general insight about the human condition which might be helpful towards resolving our paradox. What it tells us is that the human capacity to demonise is a psychologically *normal* part of our everyday make-up. Indeed, in 'seeing' genocide as diabolical, mad, even quintessentially and unadulteratedly evil, human beings could be said to be simply attempting to protect their own sense of social reality and well-being against something – particularly where it involves the breakdown of religious and legal restraints on killing – which appears to be acutely at odds with it. The response is necessarily ethnocentric or at least egocentric. It assumes that we, ourselves, and/or our own societies are rational and sound and that we therefore look onto a world through a clear, focused and unobstructed lens. By contrast, the perpetrators must either be looking at it through a very distorted one and/or, must have something psychologically wrong with them. Perhaps this also explains why intentionalist arguments about the Holocaust and by inference all genocide are so much more accessible and graspable than their structuralist counterparts. The latter tend always towards institutional, if not complex abstractions; the former provide us with nasty individuals whom we can unashamedly hate.

Of course, while these tendencies to projection may be part 'of the inner life of every normal human being',[14] *on their own* they offer no explanation for genocide. If they did, we would have exterminated ourselves as a species long ago. However, suppose we were to turn the subject on its head, so to speak, and assume that genocidal perpetrators *see themselves* very specifically and actively battling against demonic evil. Armed with Kelley's proviso that we are not as a rule dealing with people who are clinically insane, nevertheless, would we not be providing ourselves with an additional variable which might in turn help bridge both the tension and dichotomy between intent and function, human agency and context? This, to be sure, is not an argument for cultural relativism; that if genocidal perpetrators sincerely and genuinely perceive that as part of their own social reality they are under threat from malevolent, conspiratorial or even diabolical forces whose bodily manifestation is in specific population groups, then their striking out at them must be somehow accept-able or exonerable. It is a tentative proposal, however, that in the ongoing debate both as to the long-term causation as well as immediate unleashing of genocide, the transformation of our normally self-protecting psychological mechanism into something both destructive and potentially self-destructive must be at the core of any – even ultimately historically pragmatic – analysis. It is also, hence, a proposition largely dependent on the specific political and cultural *conditions* in which that latent potential is realised. This is a question to which we will return in the next chapter.

That still leaves open the question of how it is that a non-quantifiable psy-chological variable, particularly in relation to whole groups of people, can be effectively examined by an empirical historian. The best that can be proposed in response is to make pointers towards a number of discrete examples, both genocidal and non-genocidal, where the historical record seems to suggest either projection or some other form of irrational behaviour impinging directly on the practice of statecraft. But even then there would still remain a residual moral dilemma. Put starkly, where does all this leave human agency? Are human beings predetermined by their psychological (as well as physiological) make-up to become killers in particular circumstances or are they ultimately autonomous masters of their own destinies whose free will enables them to deflect or deny these particular outcomes? The answer may to some extent be a matter of whether one starts from an essentially optimistic or pessimistic view of humankind.[15] Alternatively, it might simply reflect the degree to which underlying relations of power have become so skewed in favour of a core, genocidally inclined elite that only the most exceptionally single-minded or courageous individuals will be able to stand out unequivocally against them.

But if this is true, then it can only serve to highlight a whole tranche of more specific questions. Are we really assuming that in most or all genocides there is a core group of people particularly predisposed psychologically or emotionally to be the prime movers? If that is the case, what is it about their particular cultural, social or occupational backgrounds, for instance, their day-to-day relationship with members of other communal groups which particu-larly upsets, excites and incites their phobic reactions? Moreover, how then do other people become involved in the genocide? Are the greater number of par-ticipants or sympathetic bystanders simply suggestible to the inflammatory pronouncements of the core group? In which case, again, is it perhaps this 'received' projection which is the decisive factor impelling the followers to act as they do? Or are their reasons for mass participation actually a good deal more venal, sadistic or even banal? Alternatively, is this need to find a connection between core group and wider participation a false line of reasoning? Is it rather that what we assume to be true for the core protagonists is actually also so for ordinary participants; namely a general cultural patterning which enables the actions of the prime movers to be acknowledged and even enthusiastically endorsed by very wide sections of the dominant society?

At stake here, in fact, are some rather fundamentally distinct routes by which we might further approach the broader subject of perpetrators.

Perpetrators

In the hundred days of the country-wide Rwandan genocide in the spring and early summer of 1994, in which at least 800,000, and possibly 1 million people died, Gérard Prunier estimates the number of killers at between 80,000 and 100,000.[16] This out a total Rwandan population of 8 million. In leading executive roles were the architects of the genocide, the interim government (which had taken over the reins of power after the assassination of President Habyarimana) composed of long-standing career politicians and other party leaders who had coalesced around the concept of 'Hutu Power'. Prime movers also included the brothers and wider entourage of Mme Habyarimana, the wife of the assassinated president – all of whom held senior government, administrative or military posts – as well as other high-ranking generals and intelligence chiefs in FAR, the Rwandan army. At the regional level prefects with few exceptions acted as willing transmitters for the killing orders, down to the more local level of district bourgmestres and local councillors.

Professional military or para-military forces were at the forefront of the killing operations. These included the 1,500 members of the Presidential Guard, recruited almost exclusively from the home district of the president and his wife,[17] the 1,700 French army-trained government militia, the Interahamwe, which was largely recruited from young unemployed men or those living in displacement camps as a result of the civil war, as well as the smaller Impuzamugambi, the youth group militia of the Coalition for the Defence of the Republic party (CDR). As the killing accelerated in the first few days of the genocide, many other young men, again recruited from the unemployed or displaced became part-time Interahamwe, swelling its numbers to 20,000 or 30,000.[18] Equally active were the gendarmerie and some, though not all, elements of FAR. So too were a wide range of middle-ranking party activists and professional people of all types including doctors, teachers, lawyers and businessmen. Human rights activists figured amongst this tier of perpetrators as did college students.[19] These more educated people also tended to play key roles directing others in the mass slaughter.

At the local level, however, the 'main agents' of killing, whether acting on the orders of bourgmestres or activists, or on their own volition, were wide swathes of the largely illiterate majority of Hutu peasantry.[20] Gender proved no barrier to participation. Women from across the occupational spectrum were killers, from leading government ministers through to school administrators, nurses, teenaged girls, domestic servants and slightly built mothers with infants on their backs who bludgeoned with sticks their female neighbours with their own infants on their backs. Children, too, some reported to be as young as eight, were often amongst the killers.[21] There were also Hutu men who killed their Tutsi wives and children (Tutsi husbands in mixed marriages were simply rarer) and many members, some quite high-ranking, of the important Catholic and other clergy, including nuns. Other participants included Burundian Hutu refugees who had themselves fled massacres at the hands of Tutsi army and militias in that neighbouring country.[22] Occasional members of the minority Twa and a very few 'Tutsi', including Robert Kajuga, overall president of the Interahamwe (whose family had opted to become Hutu in 1959), and Angeline Mukandutiye, district president of the same militia in Rugenge, also figured among the perpetrators.[23]

Why begin here with this most extreme of genocides of recent times, one, moreover, where the degree of people mobilised was arguably much greater than in most other cases? The answer – albeit with some important caveats about those Hutu who did not participate in the killing but were often themselves slaughtered for their efforts to defend their Tutsi neighbours – is that Rwanda's perpetrator profile far from being entirely different to these other cases is actually entirely paradigmatic. Of course, the social and occupational composition of participants will vary from example to example, just as will the form of killing. And where the scope and scale of the genocide is less intense, one might equally expect the number of participants also to be reduced. That said, the organising pyramid of the Rwanda genocide is the norm; at the top a small group of core planners and directors in control of the key apparatus of state, government as well as army including military intelligence; below them a significantly larger group of administrators, army officers and police chiefs as well as, where appropriate, professional specialists – in other words middle managers who ensure that the orders and directives from the top can be carried out and are acted upon – finally at the bottom of the pyramid a mass of hands-on operatives.

This much larger group always contains some or all of the following: the military, especially military police and elite units, secret or special police, and specially organised para-military militias recruited from party activists, particularly from closely aligned party youth movements and/or from criminal elements in society. Ideological fellow-travellers and mercenaries from foreign countries as well as those with foreign citizenship but with ancestral or family ties to the perpetrator state may also sometimes be recruited. These participants tend to represent the front-line strike-forces. But they are nearly always reinforced – not least because the execution of genocide usually requires significant manpower inputs – by a range of other auxiliaries. The social composition of this element tends to be considerably more diverse. In addition to ordinary police it regularly includes units and militias recruited from displaced elements of the ethnic majority population, though also often from other ethnic or minority groups (sometimes including 'loyal' or subservient members of the targeted victim group). Sometimes, these may be only nominally under central command and hence operate quasi-autonomously. Ordinary civilians may also participate on direction of the authorities or of their own volition, sometimes forming themselves into vigilante bands for the purpose. Thus, while as a rule the front-line strike-forces tend to be temperamentally well-suited as well as inured to killing, a broader percentage of participants have no special qualifications and will react to their involvement in a variety of ways. There is no good evidence, however, to suggest that only particular types of personality are capable of committing such acts – or *enjoying* them.[24] While, thus, at the heart of genocide the killing is often conducted by hyperactive young men, the male age range can be very broad and in some instances include children. Women may also be participants or alternatively may be active bystanders egging on male relatives or colleagues to pursue their quarries.

One might also note as an additional rider, that where a state lacks specialist military hardware, logistical assistance or training for genocide (usually for its front-line strike-forces) it may seek this support from other better organised and usually stronger polities, who thereby become – whether they are aware of what the training and hardware is for, or not – accessories to the act. On some of these occasions foreign military specialists, with or without their own country's authorisation, also become active participants.

What we can say with some certainty from the above is that genocide usually involves a high degree of people-participation. We are thus back with our essential conundrum about the nature of that participation: is it the result of a state imposing itself on the majority or – for instance in colonial settler societies, dominant population – thereby forcing their unwilling participation in the act; or rather is it a reflection of the *demos* itself and hence of the people's will? Put more crudely, is causation top–down or bottom–up? Let us consider three broad models.

1 The (Impersonal) Modern State as Perpetrator

This model tends to start from the premise that genocide is a function of advanced modernity and hence is entirely rational, the product of good organisation and planning and supported by a scientifically informed, efficiently managed, coordinated and technically resourced society. Thus, the more a society is of this nature the more effective and sustained the genocide. Indeed, in its most influential recent rendering Zygmunt Bauman has gone to great lengths to stress that the Holocaust should not only be regarded as a legitimate resident in the house of modernity and could not be 'at home in any other house' but that there is an 'elective affinity' between it 'and modern civilisation'.[25] What we have here, however, is not only a view of genocide which is almost entirely Holocaust-centric but predicated on a particular and rather selective interpretation of its morphology. In this it is the Holocaust machinery, most particularly the apparatus of streamlined death, the gas chambers, which are at the centre of the picture, though significantly not as an aberration so much as a logical extension of a complex industrial landscape in which mass murder works efficiently because that is the way modern time-compartmentalised society operates. If we were to apply this reasoning, for instance, to the near-extermination of Hungarian Jewry in the summer of 1944, what thus becomes significant is not *why* so late in the war – when it was turning utterly catastrophic for the Nazis – they should attempt to marshall extremely scarce resources for a programme which could not conceivably make an iota of difference to its outcome, but rather *how* the complex movements and interactions necessary to transport 400,000 people several hundred kilometres to a fixed liquidation site at Auschwitz could be scheduled and sequenced so that the gas chambers could operate both at maximum capacity while ensuring target completion in the minimum time.

> Precision, speed, unambiquity, knowledge of the files, continuity, discretion, unity, strict subordination, reduction of friction and of material and personal costs ... bureaucratisation offers ... the principle of specialising administrative functions according to purely objective considerations ... The 'objective' discharge of business primarily means a discharge of business according to *calculable rules and without regard for persons*.[26]

But this was not simply with disregard for Hungarian Jewish or other victims. In the Bauman version, as in many of the studies upon which he draws,

the perpetrators' only role seems to be one of functional cogs. Any requirement for these human beings to think for themselves, let alone have opinions,
or feel aroused by their tasks does not seem to enter into the equation. As the
whole thing, moreover – like other aspects of modernity – is simply another
impersonal routine, these perpetrators might as well be invisible. Indeed,
where identified at all they are usually a particular type of appropriately faceless bureaucrat, a high-level planner working from behind a desk, a medium-
level functionary in charge of a death camp, a specialist providing expert
assistance to ensure the smooth, unglitched running of the liquidatory
machinery. Studies of some these figures repeatedly emphasise their rather
dull, uninspiring qualities or lack of them: Himmler, the puritanical, uncharis-
matic card-index architect of the 'Final Solution',[27] Eichmann, 'the terrifyingly
normal' chief controller,[28] Franz Stangl, 'the gentle-voiced, courteous and aff-
able' ex-policeman-commandant of Treblinka, and later Sobibor, running his
camps 'with clockwork efficiency'.[29]

Working within the framework of a super-bureaucratic killing agency, the
SS, which prided itself on its *Sachlichkeit* – its objectivity and hence, clinical
detachment from the task in hand – many studies similarly emphasise that
what drove at least some of these prime actors was not hostile feelings towards
the victims but rather a desire to prove to superiors their responsibility and
ability in executing their assignments. A degree of competitiveness seems to
have thus developed amongst the commandants of the major death camps on
Polish soil in 1942–3, as each vied to prove that his gassing agent, chambers,
crematoria and overall operation were the most efficacious, cost-effective and
worthy of emulation. The very fact that the SS had streamlined the operation
of the 'Final Solution' with these fixed units, moreover, seems to have anaes-
thetised some of the potential for these mass murderers to become emotionally
involved with, or disturbed by the killings. As Rudolf Hoess, commandant of
Auschwitz recalled from his Polish prison cell, in the winter of 1946:

> I must admit openly that the gassings had a calming effect on me ... I was
> always horrified of death by firing squads, especially when I thought of the huge
> numbers of women and children who would have to be killed. I had had enough
> of hostage executions, and the mass killings by firing squad ordered by
> Himmler and Heydrich. Now I was at ease. We were all saved from these blood-
> baths.[30]

Supposedly liberated, thus, from the problem of having to think of mass liquidation as mass murder, Hoess and his colleagues could instead concentrate
their emotional energies on matters which harassed middle managers in industrial units confront everywhere: problems of manpower or other resource
allocation; technical problems which threaten to cause log-jams in their pro-

duction systems. The fact that in this instance the latter most frequently centred on wider environmental or health hazards which were the industrial by-product of the hundreds of thousands of corpses which their units annually 'produced' would surely have meant that the commandants' mental confrontation with the visceral reality of their task could never be entirely displaced. However, the argument of this model would continue that these problem-solving aspects could be farmed out to a range of industrial scientists, architects, engineers and doctors specifically on hand for this purpose. Moreover, as the ultimate aim in so doing was the entirely *logical* one of refining the process so that the disposal, obliteration as well as recycling of the human remains would be achieved not only more hygienically but as a contribution to optimal goal-implementation, the perpetrators could continue to sleep easily at night.

What we seem to be back with here is Lifton's case for 'a genocidal mentality', less as a specific product of Nazism and more of a highly scientistic yet also occupationally segmented society in which complex compartmentalisation both obscures and indeed deprives the atomised individual participant of any sense of his (or her) own responsibility or guilt. This is equally applicable to any large-scale modernist project of mass destruction; the mentality being further enabled by various psychological traits which have allegedly come into their own in a contemporary modernist niche. Certainly, notions of dehumanisation, disassocation and doubling (this last, in effect enabling participants to switch from their killing to their 'normal' selves as they literally clock off from their working day) all seem to relate plausibly to mass murders conceived and planned in conference rooms or offices, to be then put into effect through bombs dropped from a great height or even at a press of a button.[31] Nevertheless, while a sanitised mental or geographical space between killer and killed may be preferable for this *modus operandi*, it is not a prerequisite. *Einsatzgruppen* units who slaughtered hundreds and sometimes thousands of Jews daily on the Eastern Front in late 1941 were able to report their massacre tallies 'couched in cold, official language as if recording production figures for refrigerators or numbers of vermin destroyed'.[32] In this way, while the core perpetrators in the modernist model remain the administrators, technocrats and specialists whose professional mindset is already supposedly predisposed to the depersonalisation of slaughter, the implication must be that in an advanced and highly organised society, there is no reason why whole populations cannot be similarly assimilated to this collective mindset and trained up to adopt it in hands-on situations in the field. The result, in the language of military jargon, is 'standard operating procedure'. In other words, routinised mass murder.

Powerful endorsement for the assumption has existed since the 1960s as a result of American social psychologist Stanley Milgram's famous and at the time controversial experiments dressed up as routine learning studies.[33] These revolved around subjects – mostly college students – being required to administer what they believed were increasingly painful levels of electric shocks to other subjects when the latter answered a set of questions incorrectly. Milgram's findings strongly suggested that the majority of subjects, even when protesting, continued to administer the shocks as directed, even up to the point of lethality. He concluded that human beings in general will respond to authority provided it is 'single-minded, unequivocal and monopolistic'.[34] Bauman has taken his cue from this, thus: 'The more rational is the organisation of action, the easier it is to cause suffering'.[35] Similarly, Christopher Browning's close study of the killing operations of the German reserve order police battalion, 101, operating in the Lublin district in 1942 and 1943, would also confirm with some embellishments the general contours of the Milgram 'agentic mode' hypothesis. In a period of some sixteen months these very 'ordinary men' repeatedly carried out mass executions of Jewish men, women and children *as ordered*. By the end of their Polish tour they had notched up a staggering 38,000 murders, to say nothing of the additional 45,200 they helped deport to the Treblinka death camp.[36]

The fact that only a very few desisted – to be, incidentally, relieved of their immediate duties but not otherwise punished – seems to suggest that the majority of men and women, in modern societies will do more or less unquestioningly whatever authority tells them to do, including, in circumstances of their mobilisation for war, the discharge of mass murder. If there is any doubt on the matter, Raul Hilberg, the outstanding expert on the apparatus of Holocaust, scotches it thus:

> The German perpetrator was not a special kind of German ... We know that the very nature of administrative planning, of the jurisdictional structure and of the budgetary system precluded the special selection and special training of personnel. Any member of the Order Police could be a guard at a ghetto or on a train. Every lawyer in the RSHA was presumed to be suitable for leadership in a mobile killing unit: every finance expert to the Economic-Administrative Main Office was considered a natural choice for service in a death camp. In other words, all necessary operations were accomplished with whatever personnel were at hand.[37]

However, if all this provides overwhelming grounds for pessimism with regard to contemporary man's ability to stand against modern state-willed projects of destruction, conversely, these explanations are much less cogent in offering grounds for why states or possibly their mass adherents are willed against particular targeted groups in the first place. Or why, for that matter, specifically in examples of genocide, the behaviour of the perpetrators towards the victims both before and at the point of murder, far from being detached and dispassionate, is actually often extremely intimate, gratutious if not sado-erotic. Even in the case of the Holocaust, the example which is meant to buck this trend, Dan Stone, from a new generation of Holocaust scholars, is quite right to complain that:

> the emphasis in the literature on 'industrial killing' – the perverse fascination with 'modernity' equated with 'emotionless technology' – ignores the fact that in every testimony from those days there are so many acts of extreme violence that they cannot all be dismissed as isolated incidents of sadism. Instead, the evidence is overwhelming that brutality was a fact of everyday life, and that factory-line genocide was only a part of what constitutes the Holocaust.[38]

Of course, the issue of 'why the Jews?' is not exactly circumvented in Bauman's critique, though the exact grounds for their 'incongruity' in a modern experiment whose supposed aim – metaphorically-speaking – is the creation of an 'objectively better more efficient, more moral and more beautiful garden'[39] is never entirely made clear; nor why, according to Bauman's own logic, it is not the United States rather than Germany that is the perpetrator. This, in itself, does not necessarily discount his gardening metaphor insight that genocide is about removing the weeds which stand in the way 'of a grand vision of a better, and radically different, society'.[40] Using similar reasoning with regard to the *Aghet*, Michael Arlen has postulated that:

> The Armenian genocide was based on the imperfectly utilised but definitely perceived capacities of the modern state for politically restructuring itself which were made possible by the engines of technology ... In virtually every modern instance of mass murder, beginning, it appears, with the Armenians, the key element ... which has raised the numerical and psychic levels of the deed above the classic terms of massacre has been the alliance of technology and communications.[41]

The argument is at least partly correct. Even the largely rudimentary weaponry of the Rwandan case hides the degree to which the accomplishment of genocide was dependent on an organised, rigorously efficient, modern administration operating within a state communications infrastructure which included sound roads, working telephone and fax links as well as state or quasi-state radio stations. Utilising the most efficient, cost-effective technology for dispatching the targeted group was as relevant for Hutu Power as it was for Nazi Germany. That the latter, the innovation notwithstanding, opted for gas chambers is not in itself that surprising or remarkable in a polity which in its broader war was developing advanced missile ballistics or – albeit unsuccessfully – its own atom bomb. Thus, whether the proposed delivery is gas chambers or the use of air- or water-borne chemical weapon 'mixes' (including various types of toxic gas) as the Iraqi Ba'ath attempted in their 1988 anti-Kurdish 'Anfal' campaigns,[42] focusing on the cleverness, or for that matter crudity, of the technology utilised in mass murder should not blind us to the cause. It is people not machines who make genocide possible. Studies that veer towards describing the Holocaust as about 'inexorable momentum', or like some runaway machine, are being disingenuous or lazy. Certainly, bureaucratic momentum, as well as technical capacity and efficiency has to be built up and sustained to make a genocide work just as it clearly helps to be serviced by 'colourless and mediocre' functionaries, as Ezhov, prime organiser of the Soviet great purges of 1937–8, has been described – rather in the manner of portrayals of Eichmann.[43] But to take these facets as explanations for what drives genocide and enables people to participate in it is a little like conceiving and then building a very streamlined car and then assuming it will run without a motor.

Arguably, the nearest 'the genocide as modernity' camp comes to locating that motor is in Lifton's 'healing–killing paradox'.[44] This entails the very modernistic premise that mass killing, whether it is Auschwitz or Hiroshima, is entirely justifiable because its ultimate purpose is to make the world a better place. This incidentally transforms our faceless bureaucrats and technocrats into heroes and saviours. Equally interesting, however, is that if something needs saving one must also assume that there is something 'out there' which mortally threatens and therefore must be unequivocally cast out and destroyed. If the 'healing–killing paradox' is thus at first sight a modern rationalisation its sense is actually derived from a much more ancient archetype in which the source of goodness must be in some combative juxtaposition with 'a source of pure evil'.[45] According to Lifton and Markusen, Nazism on this score has parallels with 'nuclearism' – the neologism they use to describe the post-1945 US nuclear weapons programme. Both are thus millenarian ideologies. But if that is the case and perpetrators of mass extermination see themselves as latter-day salvationists why should we be treating our phenomenon as a singularly contemporary one at all?

2 The Ideologically Driven Elite as Perpetrator

The problem is not easily resolvable and actually sets up a tension between assumptions that modernity represents a definite rupture with the pre-industrial past and an acceptance that we are still socio-psychologically the same beings that we always were throughout the human record. If modernists might thus concede that the often prophet-like statements and claims to a monopoly of truth of a Hitler or Mao have similarities with the utterances of self-styled Messiahs of the past, the critical difference would be that the formers' vision of a better world is one which will be transformed not by god but by men themselves, albeit as if they were gods. This vision is in the certitude that rational-purposive, scientifically based action, rather than blind, obscurantist belief makes this not only theoretically imaginable but practically achievable. If this thereby seems to be an extension of the Bauman line, an alternative starting point for the study of perpetrators might be Norman Cohn's exploration of the persistence of apocalyptic and millenarian tendencies from the religiously saturated High Middle Ages through to our own supposedly very secular, contemporary times.[46]

In this reading, what many core Nazis, for instance, would share with flagellants, illuminati and other chiliasts would be two critical things. First is the sense of having lived through circumstances of acute societal dislocation in which the world as they know and understand it has been turned upside down, not simply as a temporary set-back but as a sign of some deep-seated and potentially fatal malady. Secondly, there is the sense of having some visionary insight as to both cause and cure of that malady. In this lies the claims of the core group – whether medieval or modern – to their special powers; the powers to reveal the secrets of past health and present decay; the ability to interpret the signs by which society can be finally and unequivocally purged of its misery; and finally, not only restored to former glory but dramatically reborn for the initiation of a perfected future without end. But it is only possible through their special mediation. Without the *prophetae*, the secret society, the vanguard party – call them what one will – there will be no basis for things to turn out right, no hope for humanity, only the certainty of calamitous perdition. To be redeemed, to be saved, is thus wholly dependent on imbibing the authentic message; a message that can only be assured by the complete and unquestioning coming together of the people behind the prophetic voice.

We could be certainly speaking here of the radical anabaptists of the sixteenth-century Low Countries, or the drum-men whose magic turned them into the leaders of proto-states in the west Africa of the eighteenth century.[47] But could this also be a very contemporary narrative, one which stripped of its sacred or cultic overtones actually takes us into the mental world of otherwise stridently secular modern ideologues? Perhaps one does not even need to remove the religiously saturated elements. Read Hitler's *Mein Kampf* and one

is immediately struck by elements of eschatological Manichaeism; dark warn-
ings that 'If the Jew triumphs over the peoples of the world, his crown will be
the dance of death for mankind', side by side with premonitions of the day
when another power will stand up against him 'and in a mighty struggle casts
him, the heaven stormer, back to Lucifer'.[48] In the late 1970s, members of the
Argentine Junta conducted their genocidal 'dirty war' against a largely unde-
fined subversive enemy as if impelled by 'signs' of some last millenial battle in
which they were 'Christ's vicar ... heir of the heavenly militias of Genesis ...
and the Virgin General' and their adversaries 'pagan agents of the Anti-
christ'.[49] Just a few years later the war against the Highland Maya of
Guatemala reached its genocidal apotheosis on the diktat of a much self-
proclaimed 'born-again' Christian, General Efraim Rios Montt.[50] Of course,
these two last cases demonstrate that an open and strident religiosity can be
well to the forefront in the modern state. But then, by comparison, what is
one to make of the inference that the entirely atheistic Soviet regime during
the 1930s – albeit under that most famous of all ex-seminarians, Joseph Stalin
– was not only permeated 'by magic and rituals'[51] but saw itself arrayed
against 'evil forces, spirits or demons'?[52]

True, by venturing that religious aspirations and anxieties have persisted
well into contemporary times – even where they have metamorphosed into an
avowedly atheistic 'political religion'[53] – one could be accused of simply missing the point. After all, one of the distinguishing features of our second
perpetrator model is the leading role of named, foregrounded actors who not
only appear to be in full possession of their faculties but know exactly what
they are doing and why. To bring in extraneous factors when we already have
self-conscious and self-willed individuals organising and directing genocide for
very specific, calculated and terrestrially grounded ends might thereby seem
superfluous. Yet, equally, could it be that it is in the very ideological purpose-
ness of leading actors operating either at the limits of, or indeed beyond
normal social and political constraints which illuminates beneath genocide's
superficial instrumentality a much more emotionally charged even psycho-
religious underpinning? Hitler's declamation: 'I believe that I am today acting
according to the purposes of the mighty Creator. ... I am fighting the Lord's
battle'[54] with its anti-Jewish object and overtly Christian imagery might represent a particularly extreme rendition of this tendency.

Nevertheless, the sense of having a special mission answerable not so much
to fellow-men as to some higher authority would appear to be a significant
feature in the key genocidaire profiles of at least our five illustrative cases. This
hardly makes the core regime leaders in the CUP, Stalin's USSR, Nazi Germany, the Khmer Rouge, or Hutu Power politically of the same hue. Rather

their shared affinity would seem to lie in the absolute conviction that what they are striving for is not simply right but is the *only* path towards political and societal redemption. Indeed, it is the very moral rectitude implicit in the conviction which both denies any alternative path of compromise but also makes mass atrocity allowable. Himmler's infamous self-exculpatory secret speech to Higher-SS officers, in October 1943, after much of the 'Final Solution' had been completed, when he proclaimed: 'We had the moral right, we had the duty with regard to our people to kill this race that wanted to kill us',[55] exemplifies this mindset. The obligation on the core protagonists of genocide to justify their actions thereby only exists in the entirely abstract sense of submitting themselves before a court of history. Of course, this does entail the implicit recognition of a transgression. But, like the belief of devotees of some visionary sect, it is one that not only is justifiable because it involves 'hidden' knowledge of some ultimate historical – even cosmic – purpose, but is decreed from on high and thereby transcends temporal jurisdictions whether of a national or international kind.[56] Not only are those who are wiped out as a result thus deserving of their fate, but the real *sacrifice* is of those who knew they had to commit the act on behalf of future generations, even though this conceivably might mean facing the penalty of the profanely institutional, everyday law.

Clearly, an inferred or actual invocation of some higher, sacred sanction, not to say elements of visionary fervour to go with it would lend weight to the thesis that core protagonists in modern genocide are essentially latter-day variants of earlier breeds of religious fanatic. So too are all their efforts to invest their temporal power, once achieved, with symbolic meaning, mystical aura and personalised cultic authority. But this still begs some rather important questions. Even supposing, for instance, that this core perpetrator profile, while potentially appropriate to our five 'idealisation' cases, is also transferable to other less extreme or chronologically dispersed examples, there remains a basic problem of transmission. If, for instance, our key protagonists see themselves, Nietzsche- or Sorel-like, as apart from the common fray and hence apart from the normal social and judicial conventions, rules and restraints that govern profane society, the question must arise as to how they become leaders of modern polities at all? If the answer is a populist demagoguery – in which their claim to represent the wishes of the people or nation in its struggles for fulfilment or transcendence is acknowledged by wide sections of the *demos* – this, however, might suggest less a closed and unrepresentative group whose thought processes are essentially peculiar unto themselves and more one that is the product and even accurate reflection of much broader cultural mores and grievances.

A model based on social separateness would certainly dovetail with standard intentionalist assumptions while also chiming in with the classic totalitarian thesis in which genocide, or democide, not only takes place against the interests or wishes of the majority but in which that majority itself is coerced or terrorised.[57] This would further assume that the ideologically driven group – via a coup or some other revolutionary act – takes over, subverts or reduces the apparatus of state to its will, including its entire military, judicial and institutional machinery. Vahakn Dadrian's work on the CUP in the context of the Armenian genocide offers an interesting and plausible variation on this theme. Dadrian argues that the CUP, even had it wished to utilise the official structures of the Ottoman state to accomplish its agenda, would have found itself stymied by inbuilt legal processes and procedures at complete odds with the CUP's own requirement for an absolute, unfettered power. The way round this problem of accountability was to set up an alternative *informal* authority based on the inner party itself. Thus, the preplanning for the Armenian genocide was not conducted through the political or military organs of state *per se* but by way of secret conference, or conferences, conducted by a handful of CUP loyalists, the implementation of whose orders were then transmitted by cipher either through the tightly controlled ministries of interior and war or through specially appointed and trustworthy CUP representatives operating in the field. Genocide, in this way, is seen as a conspiracy planned, organised and mounted by an ideologically driven and monolithic party or clique operating in contradistinction to the state.[58] Moreover, similarities in the relationships between the core groups and their respective official organs of state in all of our 'idealisation' cases would certainly seem to lend some weight to Dadrian's thesis. Genocide is not only rarely, if ever, actually conceived by popular acclaim but – at least in the post-1914 record – is usually the outcome of decisions taken secretly in the very inner sanctums of state power, a tendency only further underscored by the organising and executive role in the process of the highest military intelligence and secret police chiefs of state. But if this again would seem to distance the core perpetrators from society at large, is there some definable and measurable quality that makes them different in the first place?

One interesting, if problematic hypothesis on this score is that offered by R. Hrair Dekmejian.[59] Like Dadrian, Dekmejian's reading is based on a comparison of core CUP Turkish and Nazi German perpetrators but with an emphasis firmly focused on their social and geographical origins. Both groups were growing up before the First World War, the older Turkish group reaching adulthood and maturity prior to, or in the first decade of the century, the later German group more obviously on the cusp of war itself. The common denominator Dekmejian claims to find between the two groups is in their status: they are outsiders. He posits this as both a social and geographical composite. Not only are his core perpetrators outside their country's historic governing elites but their social origins are often very lowly. In addition, they are usually distinctly non-metropolitan, coming from regions often very remote or removed from the polity's traditional power centre, even possibly beyond the boundaries of the 'national' state itself. One outcome of this is an issue of access. Dekmejian's subjects belong to a generation, very possibly a first generation of children of humble background, who receive some secondary, possibly seminary-style education; a condition which provides at least for the possibility of position within and even mobility through the growing administrative or military functions of the state. If this sets up a premise that these people will be very grateful for the opportunity thus provided by the system and will loyally defer to it – however traditional, hierarchic and hide-bound it might be – obversely, the fact that they have had a sort of education gives them not only a sense of the wider world but of their own worth within it.

The crunch, however, comes if social or political conditions deteriorate to such a point that in place of successful integration the result is actually an ongoing and very self-conscious frustration. Thus, Dekmejian's reading of what makes core perpetrators special is that they are individuals with a deep identity crisis. Nor can the psycho-social element here be divorced from the issue of geographical origins. Far from making them want to be different, this latter factor actually has the opposite effect, producing intense, passionate and often very violent urges to belong. The problem is that this itself may be symptomatic of a deep uncertainty and confusion about their very sense of who they are, and this against a background of rapidly changing ethnic, social and demographic realities in the regions from which they came, further exacerbated by emerging counter-national or other ideological currents openly questioning previously given, politically anchored assumptions about custom, language and cultural values. Dekmejian cites some well-known names to support his case. Amongst Nazis is the half-educated Hitler, brought up close to the ethno-linguistic German–Czech boundary in a multi-national empire whose traditional German dominance could no longer be taken for granted, as well as Alfred Rosenberg, the *Volksdeutsche* Baltic German whose partially Lett background he seems to have gone out of his way to disown.[60] As for the CUP inner circle, Ziya Gökalp, the actually half-Kurdish theoretician of pan-Turkism whose formative years were spent in the ethnically mixed but volatile eastern Anatolian province of Diyarbekir, is placed prominently alongside prime genocide perpetrator, Talaat Pasha, whose formative experience was in Macedonia, another very contested province in a turn-of the-century Ottoman

empire.[61] Dekmejian's case for a distinct and separate group of core perpetrators in the *Aghet* and Holocaust thus suggests an intimate linkage between
their agendas for radical social change and the psychology wound up with
their 'outsider' status. It is not an argument for political religion *per se*. It is,
however, a proposition that what these 'demented souls' do at a state level is a
form of working through their 'feelings of past deprivation'[62] – Dekmejian
actually uses the word 'therapy' here – and with the genocidal assault on
Armenians and Jews, though proclaimed as the route to national salvation,
actually a very crude attempt at 'the definitive resolution of their identity
crisis'.[63]

The paradox in Dekmejian's argument, however, lies in the fact that, far
from simply offering an explanation for the personal incubi which drive our
core perpetrators, it actually offers a potential bridge to much broader patterns
of social behaviour, including those that might allow for active participation in
genocide. After all, a proposition that the resolution to commit or at least carry
through the act is nearly always taken by a small tightly knit group, or even by
one leading individual, should not in itself surprise. All high-state political
decisions are taken in this way. Equally, it is not unusual to have people who
are not simply like-minded in this critical role but with all manner of social,
regional, family or other prosopographical connections binding them together.
Hence the marriage ties linking key CUP perpetrators, for instance, are closely
replicated in Pol Pot's governing Khmer Rouge circle and in Rwanda's *clan de
Madame*.[64] By the same token, leading Western liberal democracies, notably
the United States, just as many up and coming emulants including India, Sri
Lanka, Bangladesh, Pakistan and Israel have regularly opted through the ballot box to elect individuals to high office whose main claim to fame rests on
their family ties to some previous or still incumbent family member. Nor is it
necessarily social or ethnically marginal origins that are the defining difference
in cases of genocide. While it is certainly true in the backgrounds of leading
CUP players, many Khmer Rouge, or for that matter Stalin and other core
Bolsheviks, the premise does not work in the case of Rwandan President Habyarimana's entrenched Gisenyi and Ruhengeri based-entourage, while in the
Nazi instance one has the problem that the geographically peripheral (but
actually university-educated) Rosenberg, like many other virulently anti-
Semitic *Alte Kampfer*, was actually quite irrelevant to, or forcefully pushed to
one side by the thoroughly mainstream professional, technocratic and academic experts who actually organised the 'Final Solution'.[65]

Thus, Dekmejian's model is persuasive and compelling, not for its flawed
and empirically suspect conclusions but, arguably, inadvertently, for the way it
pinpoints a more general psychological angst in the context of acute social and

political change. How can one imagine the CUP or Nazis coming to power and maintaining it without at least significant parts of the population responding to their message? Again, one does not need to look to the most extreme situations to see how this might operate. Consider, for instance, the British Thatcher administration of the 1980s. This distinctly radical Conservative, overtly nationalistic, anti-trade union and anti-welfare state regime came to power on the back of a broad electoral mandate, yet one in which a significant number of its most high-profile, tub-thumping flag-wavers – Mrs Thatcher included – were themselves well-known in coming from socially 'upstart', petit-bourgeois, or white-collar backgrounds, much against the grain of traditional 'ruling-class', one-nation Conservatism.[66] Could it be, therefore, that their elevation to power through the ballot box had as much to do with broad feelings of *relative* deprivation – that is, the system was awarding some people but not others, and certainly not the ones who *ought to be* doing nicely – as much as anything to do with a specific desire to demolish the last vestiges of state socialism in Britain? The emergence of potentially new and significant social strata in what remained an actually quite stultified political environment was a notable aspect of this development. The new 'insiders' were the ones who gave a voice to grass-roots cavils both against the rules and conventions of an entirely outdated class-based *noblesse oblige* within the political and economic establishment but also much more pointedly in the form of an often thinly disguised xenophobia and racism focusing especially on supposed threats from ethnic minority 'outsiders'.[67]

Granted, the Thatcherite 'outsiders' who had become insiders were able to legitimise their proposed response to social discontent through a democratic process. But because other societies are more politically restricted or even lack democratic procedures entirely, this hardly requires us to accept a totalitarian-style thesis discounting any tendencies, opinions or grievances coming from at least sections of the *demos*. We do not have to assume all of society in Britain was pro-Thatcherite. By the same token nor do we need to perceive of pre-1933 Hitler or Rosenberg, or pre-1908 Talaat and Ziya as completely isolated cranks whose opinions were of interest to no one but themselves. On the contrary, the empirical evidence would suggest that, far from being off the mental map, their views not only had a currency in broad circles but provided them with the basis for a viable political constituency. A resonance, in other words, which can only signify that a great many people felt marginalised in similar ways or, alternatively, understood and accepted their explanation for society's ills as accurate and indeed relevant to their own lives.

One must emphasise that the background of social and political dislocation inherent in our five key cases is of an entirely different order to that pertaining to 1980s Britain. By the same token, the Thatcher administration, for all of its implied or actual aggressiveness, did not commit or contemplate anything remotely approaching genocide. But then the grievances and more specifically *ressentiments* – the unsatisfied or suppressed feelings of existential envy and hatred[68] – of this time and place were simply not equal to those in our genocidal examples. With this in view, one might argue that the degree of radical compensatory action undertaken by a socio-political organism is in inverse proportion to the degree of embitterment and anomie locked up within it. 'Powerful ideologies are at least highly plausible in the conditions of the time and they are strongly adhered to',[69] argues Michael Mann, forcefully implying that it is where groups of people are culturally and socially situated within a society, rather than the empirically observed facts of the situation, that determine their recognition of social reality. What the actual undertaking of genocide would suggest, however, given all its actual human and resource demands, is that a critical mass of people, over and beyond our core perpetrator group, would need to be similarly ideologically impelled in order to provide it with its necessary momentum.

Again, this does not have to be all of society. Model Two could still adequately operate on the assumption that specific elements within the social matrix were either prepared to act as a unilateral strike-force (for instance as army, militia or police), or alternatively through coaxing, coercing or dragooning broader elements of the population in the required direction. The latter scenario would not discount the possibility that a broader populace might be drawn into a killing process for other ideological or non-ideological reasons of its own, or because ultimately, through inculcation, it did take on board and accepted the worldview of the avant-garde. But whatever the role and purposiveness of these other belated, half-hearted, unwilling or unwitting perpetrators, it is inconceivable that genocide as imagined in the heads of its core initiators could proceed into practicable implementation without the motivated engagement of many thousands of like-minded cadres.

Certainly, one strength of Model Two might be that where the overall number of participants might be insufficient for the task in hand it could be compensated for in the ideological zeal of politically conscious acolytes. We know, for instance, that the ultra-nationalist perspective of the CUP was initially only shared by a relatively narrow strata of Ottoman-Turkish society, mostly among people in very similar social milieux, educative backgrounds and generational outlooks, who tended to receive their tertiary training in particular institutions and/or followed through their formative professional experiences along closely parallel lines. Nevertheless, it was the commitment of these same doctors, surgeons, teachers, administrators, journalists, military

officers and other professionals or would-be professionals to lend their hands-
on support to the effort which was a critical element enabling the *Aghet* to
happen.[70] In very much the same way, albeit in an entirely different context
and ideological framework, it was the millenarian-type convictions of often
very youthful student cadres which determined that the anti-kulak directives
in the Soviet collectivisation drive were carried out with an unflinching sense
of duty. Here is Lev Kopelev, an activist in a grain procurement brigade recalling his role in the Ukraine in 1932–3:

> With the rest of my generation I firmly believed that the ends justified the
> means. Our great goal was the universal triumph of Communism, and for the
> sake of that goal everything was permissible – to lie, to steal, to destroy hun-
> dreds of thousands, even millions of people, all those who were hindering our
> work or could hinder it, everyone who stood in the way. And to hesitate or
> doubt about all this was to give in to 'intellectual squeamishness' and 'stupid
> liberalism', the attributes of people who 'could not see the forest for the trees.'
> That was how I had reasoned, and everyone like me, even when … I saw what
> 'total collectivisation' meant – how they 'kulakised' and 'dekulakised', how they
> mercilessly stripped the peasants in the winter of 1932–3. I took part in this
> myself … for I was convinced that I was accompanying the great and necessary
> transformation of the countryside.
>
> In the terrible spring of 1933 I saw … women and children with distended
> bellies, turning blue, still breathing but with vacant, lifeless eyes. And corpses –
> corpses in peasant huts, in the melting snow of the old Vologda, under the
> bridges of Kharkov … I saw all this and did not go out of my mind or commit
> suicide. Nor did I curse those who sent me out to take away the peasants' grain
> in the winter, and in the spring to persuade the barely walking skeleton-thin or
> sickly-swollen people to go into the fields in order to 'fulfill the Bolshevik sow-
> ing plan in shock-worker style.' Nor did I lose my faith. As before, I believed
> because I wanted to believe.[71]

Thus, it might be argued that it is primarily the Kopelevs of the world who
turn the idea of genocide, as conceived by a smaller elite, into the actual act.
Front-rank perpetrators, usually in the uniform of a military or para-military
officer, nevertheless these men – and sometimes women – are more than likely
to have had a schooling, a good career, or the prospects for one, read serious
newspapers and books, have pronounced cultural interests and certainly
informed opinions. That commanders of the *Einsatzgruppen*, the units responsible for the massacre of at least 1 million Jews, Roma and others, in the eastern
theatre of operations in 1941–3, were made up of people most of whom considered themselves to be intellectuals, is well known. Indeed, they included a
director of a research institute, a Protestant pastor, a doctor, several lawyers
and a professional opera singer.[72] Such professional types may not only, in

everyday terms, have been living at considerable remove from street violence but they may have had moral qualms about inflicting hurt or pain, not to mention conceivably have been quite squeamish about its results. Fifty years later, the shakers and movers in the Rwandan genocide were again drawn from a not dissimilar cross-section of the country's professional classes.

But if this is so have we not grounds here for closing the gap between Models One and Two? Whether they are visionaries or technocrats – or actually very often both – the key actors in genocide thus become those who not only *believe* that what they are doing is *necessary* and *right* but also assume that they can make call upon the apparatus and human resources of the modern body-politic with which to actualise their vision of a cleaner, safer, more just and sound world-society. The question that follows, however, is what of the rest: the large bottom of the human pyramid who may actually carry out the vast bulk of the dirty work? Should we assume that genocide in action is essentially divided between those who lead and those who follow, with Milgram's hypothesis about authoritative command being the determining factor which neutralises 'the impact of primeval *moral* drives' among the latter?[73] Or are the great mass of participants even more behaviourally hide-bound, having succumbed like Pavlovian dogs to stimuli consciously bombarded at them with a view to the activation of their emotional arousal?[74]

A great deal of recent literature has certainly focused on a particular vehicle for this formula, namely modern mass media. All contemporary polities, of course, either in the form of their state radio and television networks or, at one remove, through private, commercial media, offer a very selective view of what is happening in the world, nearly always buttressed on matters considered sensitive to 'national interests' by either completely omitting to report information or alternatively, broadcasting reports which are so skewed that their purpose can only be one of disinformation. If this 'propaganda model' is obviously true for tightly controlled societies, the radical critiques of Edward Herman and Noam Chomsky in America, and the late E. P. Thompson in Britain, would strongly infer that it is also integral to Western, supposedly open and accessible ones.[75] This being the case, we would expect state elites considering the perpetration of genocide to do no less than utilise the media as a control mechanism both to lull and incite. During the hundred days of the Rwandan genocide, for instance, the Hutu Power-sponsored Radio Télévision Libre des Milles Collines (RTLM) became almost archetypal in this way, spewing out an almost equal but constant diet of anti-Tutsi hate, interspersed with lively music and chat. The basic message – go out and kill Tutsi, and any of their sympathisers, before they get you – was necessarily crude yet it is attested that everybody who had a radio listened, while in some areas the government even handed out radios for free, presumably so that the people would not miss it.[76]

Less than two years earlier, at the height of the the ethnic cleansings initiated by the Milosevic regime, primarily against the Muslims in neighbouring Bosnia, Radio Television Belgrade similarly served up for its home audience its own coarse diet of entirely concocted horror stories, including several in which uncensored footage of women being brutalised and raped purported that the victims were Serbs and their tormentors Muslim or Croat. In fact, it was exactly the other way around, a fact that was blatantly obvious from the clumsy editorial efforts to conceal it.[77] Yet there is no reason to doubt that many Serbian men must have been receptive to these free images, not least because so many of them, mobilised via the Yugoslav People's Army (JNA) or proxy militias for active service in Bosnia, were themselves prepared to participate in mass rapes conceived or sanctioned by the military high command.[78]

3 The People as Perpetrator

This question of mass rape as prelude to, or intrinsic to the course of genocide arguably, more than any other, highlights the problem of whether our broader phenomenon is a function of a utilitarian calculus defined and determined *only* by an elite, or an activity in which 'ordinary men' – and often women too – are prepared to knowingly lend themselves, even to the point where we might argue that the state's role is to reflect this more general societal will. Certainly, the issue of how rape in genocide ought to be interpreted is not as clear-cut as it might superficially seem. In contradistinction to popular assumptions that it is essentially an extension of male sexuality, combined with cultural infusions of machismo and misogyny unfettered by normal societal restraints – in other words, men behaving badly according to some assumed socio-biological condition – many commentators who have scrutinised the Bosnian and other examples charge that its practice is a quite systematic and hence deliberate policy 'chosen to humiliate, intimidate and demoralise a victim group' thus 'making resistance to genocide more difficult.'[79] Or to put it more bluntly, mass rape makes hard-headed military sense for genocidal planners, given that an onslaught on what most patriarchal communities would consider their most valued, valuable yet vulnerable commodity, namely their child-bearing women, is the quickest way to disorientate, dislocate and generally sap their will to resist. Other critical analysis, not least with regard to the sexual abuse of men in the Bosnian conflict, would certainly problematise this issue of sexual atrocity as gender-specific.[80] That said, if rape in genocide, whether of women or men, is primarily a planner's instrument, then it follows that the men who are required to carry it out are also such instruments. Raping may be part of their training induction so that, suitably brutalised, they can move on to become fully-fledged killers but the inference would be that they are as much the 'innocent'[81] dupes of the core perpetrators' design as are those equally encouraged to go on looting sprees of victims' property.

However, one problem with this assumption is that if rape and other ancillary onslaughts on genocidally targeted communities serve such specific purposes, then we might expect their operation to be carried out, if not necessarily mechanically and dispassionately, then at the very least efficiently. Yet as soon as we begin to examine the anatomy of such actions, we increasingly find that they are very often nothing of the sort. The perpetrators start lingering, time-wasting, devising stratagems so that they can go on inflicting humiliation and pain for as long as possible. Take one single example. At the epicentre of the *Aghet*, in the summer of 1915, was the town of Bitlis, rapidly made Armenian-free either through wholesale massacre or death-march deportation. However, according to the testimony of a Turkish staff officer, 300 young girls belonging to 'the best Armenian families' were reserved – or perhaps the term should be 'preserved' – from this fate so that the army might enjoy them. Detained in a church, regiment after regiment on its way to the front passed through it to avail themselves of this service, the result of which was that within a short while not only were all the girls diseased but they were passing it on to all the officers and soldiers who raped them. At this point the town's commandant charged the girls with 'exhausting the vital forces of the Ottoman army and poisoning with their infection the children of the Fatherland'. The girls were summarily put to death by execution or poisoning.[82]

The example is morbidly illuminating on a number of levels. Not only was the serial rape of the unmarried teenage daughters of the most wealthy and hence genteel Armenian burghers the most viciously unpleasant violation of the whole Armenian community that our Bitlis heroes could dream up, but they excelled themselves in terms of sado-eroticism by doing it in the very place Armenians would have considered most sacred, and indeed sacrosanct, to their individual and collective identity. Yet the Turks also physically harmed themselves in the process – despite the fact that such a danger was blatantly obvious from the outset – leading classically to further blame and annihilation finally being visited on the victims.

Much of this would seem to bear out Philip Zimbardo's psychological experiment at Stanford University – carried out almost in parallel with Milgram's Yale observations – that if ordinary people (young male students in his case) are placed in situations where they have complete power over other people they will start devising the most extraordinary, even complicated ways of mentally and physically torturing them.[83] Are these 'rituals of degradation' further evidence that this is how human beings 'naturally' respond under a given set of conditions regardless of the subject or subjects against whom they are directed, i.e. an endorsement of the Pavlovian line, or does it suggest rather particularly strong antipathetic feelings towards a specific subject, or subjects? Certainly, the more one reads about different cases of genocide, the more one senses the perpetrators' desire to turn the actual moment of killing into an event, a spectacle, an entertainment. In Rwanda, Tutsi men were made to watch their pregnant wives or daughters being disembowelled before their own agony of death, often by having their genitals cut off and stuffed into their mouths.[84] Crowds were very often on hand to watch these and other spectacles – another favourite was what was called cutting the usually tall Tutsi 'down to size' by chopping off their feet and hands with machetes.[85] Frequently, as with the Armenian episode previously described, this was done in churches. Often too, on these occasions, Hutu women cheerleaders sang and ululated their menfolk into action in what Adam Jones describes as 'a kind of gendered jubilation at the "comeuppance" of Tutsi females'.[86] Nor were the latters' children spared the equally public yet vicious humiliations and mutilations before their own horrendous deaths.

Of course, one could argue that what this propensity to inflict not simply gratuitous but specifically inscribed violence on victims tells us most about, is the cultural underbelly of *particular* societies. Christopher Taylor's recent work on Rwanda, for instance, highlights the degree to which the highly ritualised forms of mutilation, impalement, breast oblation, male emasculation and so on – as visited on the still living bodies of the victims of Hutu Power – had its own profoundly symbolic relationship to Rwandan understandings of bodily health and illness (both individual and collective) for sufferers and tormentors alike.[87] In similar vein, the quite extraordinary range of tortures – the whittling down of noses, the drawing out of teeth, hair, finger- and toe-nails, as well as repeated bastinadoing – which were visited on Armenian men often for many days or even weeks *before* their liquidation in the *Aghet*,[88] were not specially invented for this occasion but, as noted by Dadrian, regular fare when supposed criminal suspects, especially Christians, were brought before the authorities.[89] There is, he proposes, something about the interaction of Turkish martial values and a society founded on Islam which explains an Ottoman culture of cruelty particularly directed against its non-Muslim minorities.[90] Michael Vickery is another who, in considering the well-springs of the Cambodian genocide, has sought to dispel Western notions of the Khmer people as a gentle people living in a gentle land, in favour of a more realistic picture in

which everyday violence could often be endemic and extremely cruel.[91] These
ideas, even with Vickery's caveats, tend to buttress rather than negate general
Western assumptions that other societies' proclivities towards genocide are
something to do with their not-yet-quite-modern, uncivilised, even tribal
nature. It is doubly paradoxical, therefore, that when German *Einsatzgruppen*
and Wehrmacht units operating in the Balkans and east in 1941 witnessed the
liquidation of Jews, gypsies and others by their Croat and Romanian allies,
their commanders found themselves greatly shocked by what they saw, repeatedly writing reports or complaints detailing these abuses and, in the case of
one Wehrmacht commander, General Wöhler, even issuing the following
extraordinary order to his men:

> Because of the eastern European concept of human life, German soldiers may
> become witnesses of events (such as mass execution, the murder of civilians,
> Jews and others) which they cannot prevent at this time but which violate Ger-
> man feelings of honour most deeply. To every normal person it is a matter of
> course that he does not take photographs of such disgusting excesses or report
> about them when he writes home. The distribution of photographs and the
> spreading of reports about such events will be regarded as a subversion of
> decency and discipline in the army and will be punished strictly ... To gaze at
> such procedures curiously is beneath the dignity of the German soldier.[92]

What is immediately obvious here is the gaping double-standard in operation. It is certainly true that there were German military notions as to what
was correct, orderly and 'civilised' conduct in the execution of their mass murder remit. And that certain ways of behaving were therefore supposedly
disallowed. For instance, front-line German perpetrators were under very
strict orders not to rape, or personally appropriate their victims' valuables, or
generally go berserk and this, at least in theory, suggests a major divide
between their behaviour *in extremis* and that of their Romanian allies. Yet even
putting aside the absurd contradiction between the notion of orderly conduct
and mass slaughter, it is increasingly clear that Nazi killings involved 'incredi-
ble excesses of brutality, cruelty and at times carnivalesque or "sublime"
elation'.[93]

One small example of these tendencies has been described by both Christopher Browning and Daniel Goldhagen in their studies of Police Battalion 101.
It involved the manhunt or more specifically 'Jew-hunt' in which members of
the battalion would make sweeps of the Polish countryside to flush out Jews
who had escaped massacre or deportation and had literally gone to ground in
forest bunkers and hide-aways.[94] It might be noted that hunts, by their very
nature – having developed out of man's traditional pursuit of animals – have
been traditionally considered vastly exhilarating undertakings in themselves

and not least because the lack of serious danger to the hunter is in direct juxta-position with the power he has to cause absolute fear and terror in his prey. Whether it is this factor alone which explains the repeated use of manhunts on native peoples, especially in Amazonia and Australasia[95] is not the issue here. What is, is the fact that the recorded conduct of Battalion 101 in its 'Jew-hunt' missions displays exactly these features and more. Indeed, far from being detached automatons responding unthinkingly to orders, what we see instead is soldiers revelling in the opportunity to roam the forests unfettered by authority – the hunts were usually conducted in small groups with only an NCO in charge – in order to gratify their blood-lust through often very inti-mate and gratuitous murder. From among innumerable episodes of this kind Goldhagen thus alights on a participant's testimony regarding a group of cor-nered Jews who were meant to be conveyed elsewhere by their captors. Instead their NCO Sergeant Bekemeier

> had the Jews crawl through a water hole and sing as they did it. When an old man could not walk anymore, which was when the crawling episode was fin-ished, he shot him at close range in the mouth ... After Bekemeier had shot the Jew, the latter raised his hand as if appealing to God and then collapsed. The corpse of the Jew was simply left lying. We did not concern ourselves with it.[96]

This was hardly efficient genocide, even though hundreds and possibly thou-sands of Jews were caught and murdered in this way. Indeed, contrary to the German penchant for streamlined and audited massacre there were no tallies requested nor given for these operations, no burials made – despite, again, the normal German obsession with untended corpses leading to epidemic – and certainly no check on how many Jews remained unaccounted for. Yet despite the fact that operations tallies were decreasing to the point of non-existence, the hunts, with all the time, manpower and cost implications involved, contin-ued unabated for months. Like the Soviet or Cambodian Gulags where vast numbers of 'examiners' used up even vaster number of man-hours extracting confessions of guilt from people who were going to be killed anyway,[97] some-thing other than a straightforward utilitarian approach to mass murder seems to be demanded by way of explanation here.

Of course, there is a counter-argument. This might posit that genocide remains essentially top–down and instrumental but as the exercise can neither be contemplated nor completed without the participation of thousands of ordinary people some method of compensating them for their efforts has to be brought into the equation.[98] In the absence of more tangible or long-term rewards the quickest, most effective way to enjoin a populace or even army to such a purpose is to give them a sufficient degree of latitude so that their participation becomes pleasurable – even if that means a degree of deviation from the immediate purpose of the exercise. This certainly seems to be Prunier's implication regarding the disaffected and utterly impoverished Kigali 'street boys, rag-pickers, car-washers and homeless unemployed' who joined the Interahamwe:

> For these people the genocide was the best thing that could ever happen to them. They had the blessings of a form of authority to take revenge on socially powerful people as long as they were on the wrong side of the political fence. They could steal, they could kill with minimum justification, they could rape and they could get drunk for free.[99]

This reading would seem to posit a basis for broad people-involvement in genocide predicated on little more than the opportunity for some quick kicks intermixed with some equally quick pickings in a recognisably ephemeral, *charivari*-like orgy allowed at the behest of the powers that be. Of course, one might take the inference further; that once set in train this sort of mob violence might actually become so mindless, open-ended and for its own sake that any original strategic purpose might itself end up becoming quite lost. A more radical interpretation still, entered into in some recently scholarly speculation, is that it is the very defiance of such strategic purpose which *is* the purpose of its unleashing.[100] This is not, however, the conclusion which Prunier himself draws, at least not with regard to the testimony of a seventy-four-year-old peasant 'killer' whom he cites. This man claimed to being ashamed and regretful of his involvement but almost in the same breath went on to expostulate: 'but what would you have done if you had been in my place? Either you took part in the massacre or else you were massacred yourself. So I took weapons and I defended the members of my tribe [sic.] against the Tutsi.'[101]

The implication from this statement could be one of two things. Either, as Prunier himself interposes, the man participates according to the dictates of the dominant ideology, not because he believes in it but because he has no choice in the matter. Alternatively, he does so because he genuinely and sincerely accepts that what the government is saying is true; namely that the Tutsi – including those who are his neighbours – are dangerous and therefore must and ought to be killed. Prunier himself shrinks from this possibility though Mahmood Mamdani, another analyst of the Rwandan genocide, does not, making it the lynchpin of his explanation.[102] Far more controversially, Goldhagen, in his study of ordinary Germans and the Holocaust, radically develops this tack, proposing that far from being an example of elite ideology, let alone modernity, the genocidal onslaught on Jews was a reflection of how

Germans at large felt about them. The implication is that this deep-rooted and pervasive hate-system was something peculiarly *sui generis* to the German condition. However, if Goldhagen's 'cultural cognitive model' were applicable to genocide *tout ensemble* it would throw an extremely different light both on its general nature and indeed on the relationship between its elite planners and a *vox populi*. In this way, rather than a radical ideology being genocide's driving force, it could be argued that it is actually the other way round, ideology actually following popular opinion. As Irving Louis Horowitz suggests, 'totalitarian regimes can elevate or dampen certain policies but they seem incapable of addressing those cultural formations that lead to genocide in the first place'.[103]

Certainly, one of the most perplexing conundrums for the totalitarian thesis is the apparent popularity of leaders who ultimately drive their countries to war, mass misery and the committing of genocide. The charismatic fascination that Hitler held over large sections of the German and Austrian people is well known and well attested, not least from the vast crowds which greeted him on his nationwide trips.[104] The death of the much less charismatic Stalin, in spite of the crescendo of mass deportations and killings, to say nothing of the secret police terror which were the hallmarks of his last years, appears to have elicited genuine nationwide grief.[105] His mythic standing remains high in Russia even today. Saddam Hussein, whose private office was reportedly full of books on none other than Stalin, was another absolute dictator who in the view of one entirely dispassionate expert has 'demonstrated a greater understanding of ordinary people than any leader in the history of Iraq'.[106] All these three leading genocide practitioners of the twentieth century had grass-roots followings not because they were great ideologues who presented themselves as at one remove from the masses – even though once in power this is exactly how they conducted their existences – but rather because they strove to identify themselves as sons of the people, at one not only with the aspirations but also the basic homespun virtues of the common man. Saddam, the 'Son of the Alleys' whose childhood of poverty was like their own; Stalin – unlike those too-clever-by-half party intellectuals of the ilk of the 'Jewish' Zinoviev and Trotsky – a *praktik*, someone you could depend on to get things done; Hitler, a man you could genuinely trust above all those conniving Weimar politicians and generals, because he had been in the trenches and fought like a hero, even though at the end of the day he was just a salt-of-the-earth, plebeian ex-corporal.

If, thus, one were to extrapolate from the Goldhagen reasoning that the common trajectory of these regimes towards genocide was an extension of a popular will, then the questions which would legitimately arise would revolve

around the cultural origins and causation of the dominant society's antagonism towards specific 'out' groups. Even then, however, making a direct
linkage between popular antipathies and the actual act of extermination
might be tenuous. As one significant commentator, Professor Wladislaw Bartoszewski, has cautioned:

> Alienation does not always have to be synonymous with enmity, as a lot of peo-
> ple in New York consider the Puerto Ricans to be foreign, but do not kill them.
> Many people do not like blacks but do not kill them. A large number of people
> can be antagonistic towards another national group but it does not mean there
> has to be some ultimate reckoning. But it is bad. It is always bad, because dis-
> like and alienation are the beginning of a far-reaching dislike, perhaps prejudice,
> perhaps hate. That is bad, but it does not have to all be thrown into the same
> pot, as it is not the same.[107]

Bartoszewski would have known all this from harsh personal experience. As
a Pole observing Polish–Jewish relations in the 1930s and then 1940s – in the
latter years of which he was co-founder of Zegota, the underground organisation that sought to give assistance to the Jews during the Holocaust – he
observed at first hand the nature of Polish anti-Semitism, an arguably much
more widespread, resilient and deeply embedded variety than existed in neighbouring Germany. But if this is the case, why, in Goldhagen terms, is it not
Poles rather than Germans who committed genocide? Goldhagen's answer, in
so far as he responds to the comparative problem at all, is to propose that German anti-Semitism cannot be compared with any ordinary ethnic hatred;
rather its operation is on an entirely different 'demonic, hallucinatory and
metaphysical' plane.[108] How Germany came to adopt this 'eliminationist' variant given the ubiquity of anti-Semitism throughout the European continent is
not clarified. Nor, perhaps even more tellingly, is there any explanation of why
this phenomenon – which Goldhagen treats as a continuum in the cultural life
of Germany – only comes to genocidal fruition under Hitler and not fifty, a
hundred or two hundred years earlier.[109] If Goldhagen's much criticised ahis-
toricality is an additional burden for a thesis which operates on the level of
sweeping generalisations, nevertheless, the fact that he directly confronts the
extraordinary nature of the animus and implicitly suggests that this might be
shared by elites and masses alike, represents in one sense a critical break-
through for genocide studies. Low culture and high culture may, after all,
share common ground just as socio-cultural phobias might have their place in
state-building agendas. But if the interconnections, as well as stepping stones
between these elements, are in need of further exploration, the only way we
can really pursue this with reference to Goldhagen, is to go back to our original question of perpetrator–victim interaction. What exactly is it about some

real or even imagined groups which turns them into the target for this murderous assault? Or more exactly, what is it about these communities which – despite their objective vulnerability as communities – so frightens and terrifies a considerable section of dominant state and society that the latter feel they can only resolve it by their physical annihilation?

'Victims'

To propose that it is something about the nature of the targeted group that explains the genocide might sound like a wanton capitulation to the perpetrators' logic itself. Perpetrators, after all, always blame their victims for the 'punishment' *that they have to* inflict on them. For our exercise, however, if we could locate particular attributes which victim groups share, just as we have attempted to locate common attributes to perpetrators, it would make our task a whole lot easier. So could we not for instance return to our five core groups – European Jews, Ottoman Armenians, Rwandan Tutsi, Soviet 'kulaks' and Khmer 'blue scarves' – in the respective periods when they found themselves under genocidal threat and find some commonalities between them?

Unfortunately not – or at least not across the board. The first three groups in the most general sense, given the qualifications we have already raised about the fluid nature of ethnicity, do evince some traits in common. Each of them, at least in significant part at the time of their genocides, are self-defining minority groups within the confines of the perpetrator state, with the additional clarification that the vast majority of targeted Jews were actually minority communities within Nazi-occupied or allied states. Each, too, displays occupational tendencies as well as socio-cultural customs which add an element of distinction between them and the majority community. A marked educational and/or commercial orientation, for instance, underscores a profile in usually quite specific areas of business, academic or professional life; certainly disproportionate to their numbers in the overall population. That said, to attempt to embrace all three groups within a category of 'middleman minority'[110] would be quite specious. Jews alone – and then only in the most general terms – would fall within it, contrasting with the majority of Armenians and Tutsi who remained peasants or pastoralists within a rural economy. One could therefore not infer a class hierarchy nor the assumption that to be a member of one of these groups was to be necessarily economically better-off than any other member of society. Issues of economic wealth and mobility are a factor in a broad societal versus minority group dynamic here but founded less on actual social and economic indices and more on dominant social perceptions.

Already, our tangible, shared victim groups' attributes are giving way to views of them by others. The Tutsi and Armenians in our genocide contexts may have been viewed as 'outsiders' but, notwithstanding their connections to broader diasporas, they were as indigenous – in the Armenian case, where they were still living in their historic heartlands, even more so – as anybody else. Similarly, Jews may provide the quintessential model of a diaspora but especially in eastern Europe they had been living in the interstices of broader but also ethnically and religiously very diverse communities for hundreds of years. If one might still fairly argue that European Jewry, taken as a whole, was dispersed, ubiquitous and geographically mobile, our further two kulak and Khmer groups being mostly peasants were, by contrast, firmly rooted in their rural milieux. In short, there is no single common denominator which would explain these five groups' dubious status as victims.

Applying other possible criteria, for instance, trying to chart social, geographical or cultural patterns in the nature of the interaction between perpetrators and victims also does not produce uniformly congruent results. 'The closer a relationship the more intense the conflict'[111] – the formula of J. T. Sanders with regard to Jewish–Christian relations in their first hundred years – seems a neat and efficacious starting point but would be well-nigh useless on the 'kulak' score, as Bolsheviks hardly had a relationship with them before 1917. Add other victim groups – notably native peoples – at the literal margins of many perpetrator societies' geographical, let alone cognitive, maps and the formula becomes even less persuasive. Michael Ignatieff's use of Freud's insight on the 'narcissism of minor difference' – namely the need to amplify little differences between oneself and one's neighbours in order to convince oneself of a separate identity – as developed by Ignatieff in his study of contemporary nationalism,[112] again might be useful in some of our examples. For instance, Hutu and Tutsi might fit his criteria well but only if explored in isolation from other factors. Try and apply it, however, to Christian Armenian vis-à-vis Muslim Turk, or for that matter European Jew with regard to (at least nominally) German Christian, and its conceptual value might seem to wane, just as a Samuel Huntington-style thesis might seem to rise.[113] The Huntington argument that what really causes conflict in the modern world is the clash of intrinsic 'civilisational' values again has a certain resonance, but then most German Jews did not regard themselves as socially or culturally anything other than part of Western, including German civilisation, while, even more prosaically 'Eastern Zone' Khmer remained entirely indistinguishable from other Khmer. If all this is beginning to seem like a case of chasing round in ever-decreasing circles, then that is exactly what it is. Middlemen groups, peasant groups, pastoralists and nomads, political insiders and social outcasts, the religiously committed and the vociferously atheistic, people living in tropical forests, deserts or metropolitan cities, people who are neighbours or living far away on some distant frontier, people who look and behave the same as the perpetrator group, as well as people who look and behave entirely differently, have all fallen prey to genocide: and it is only the perpetrator who determines why.

So, if there is a question of victim commonality at all, it can only be by dint of the perpetrators' perception of them; even if that entails affixing to the victim a yellow star or blue scarf to make visible a difference which otherwise would have remained invisible. Let us then attempt to posit what in the most general terms one can say about the victim as *characterised* by the perpetrators of genocide. Firstly, the victim is not a victim but the perpetrator. The roles are always entirely reversed, the victim group being accused of a crime so heinous that it is perceived as a direct threat to the body and soul of both state and 'people'. *Ipso facto* anybody who is charged with the crime is 'an enemy of the people'. This will include not only named actors who by dint of their alleged actions are known 'terrorists', 'subversives', 'bandits' but any other people who – whether they are, or are not directly or indirectly related to, or associated with these specific accused persons – are also collectively bracketed with them as enemies. In this way, whether 'the group' consists of those who are genuinely 'involved' in opposition to the state, or entirely oblivious of what is going on, indeed whether they are babes in arms or even not yet born, they are all reified into 'a single organised actor'.[114] Thus, secondly, however politically or socially diverse in actual practice, the victim group in genocide is always defined as a monolith whose sole and single-minded *raison d'être* is to accomplish the destruction of the 'perpetrator' community.

Here are some relatively mild examples of perpetrators elucidating their response in terms of the alleged victims guilt:

Talaat Pasha, (posthumous) memoirs, 1921, recalling events in Ottoman Armenia, 1915:

> I admit that we deported many Armenians from our eastern provinces, but we never acted in this matter upon a previously prepared scheme. The responsibility of these acts falls upon the deported people themselves. Russia ... had armed and equipped the Armenian inhabitants of this district [Van] ... and had organised strong Armenian bandit forces .... When we entered the Great War, these bandits began their destructive activities in the rear of the Turkish army on the Caucasus front, blowing up the bridges, setting fire to the Turkish towns and villages and killing all the innocent Mohammedan inhabitants regardless of age or sex ... All these Armenian bandits were helped by native Armenians.[115]

Interview with journalists given by Francis Bianchi, press secretary to Guatemalan dictator, Rios Montt, at the time of army massacres in the Mayan highlands, 1982:

> The guerrillas won over many Indian collaborators. Therefore the Indians were subversives. And how do you fight subversion? Clearly you had to kill Indians because they were collaborating with subversion. And then it would be said that you were killing innocent people. But they weren't innocent. They had sold out to subversion.[116]

Fatwa by Sudanese imams endorsing *jihad* (holy war) against Nuba people, 1992:

> The rebels in South Kordofan and southern Sudan started their rebellion against the state and declared war against the Muslims. Their main aims are: killing the Muslims, desecrating mosques, burning and defiling the Koran, and raping Muslim women. In so doing, they are encouraged by the enemies of Islam and Muslims: these foes are the Zionists, the Christians and the arrogant people who provide them with provisions and arms. Therefore an insurgent who was previously a Muslim is now an apostate: and a non-Muslim is a non-believer standing as a bulwark against the spread of Islam, and Islam has granted freedom of killing both of them.[117]

The nature of the self-exculpation in these three examples is framed in the language of an actual, tangible two-sided armed conflict. None appears to make outrageous claims, for instance that the communal enemy is contaminating the food-supply – a common theme in Stalin's Russia – or the working of some devilish scheme to sexually ravish every young Aryan maiden – at the very heart of Hitler's feverish nightmares. Yet in each case the explanation involves either such an extraordinarily selective reading or even complete reversal of the truth that one has to wonder how they came to be constructed. Are we to assume that their creators knew that they were perpetrating falsehoods but that it was politically expedient to keep up the lie? Or alternatively, can we possibly countenance that they genuinely believed that the Armenians, the Mayan Indians, the Nubans, really were a clear and present danger? Which answer, moreover, is the more problematic? If our perpetrators or perpetrator-justifiers are not being Machiavellian but just plain honest, this would cast their responses in very strange light. Can such projection really operate at the highest levels of state?

Projection, Conspiracy and Paranoia

One thing that the above statements seem to suggest is that an outcome of genocide cannot properly develop without the perpetrators' conviction that there really does exist an intense struggle between themselves and the victims. And in it, it is they – those representing state power – who are on the defensive. Objectively speaking, this last point cannot be true. As Dadrian correctly and astutely points out: 'In any conflict involving a disparity of power relations the underlying power differential is apt to enable the more powerful group to control the direction of the conflict.'[118] The point in *these* conflicts, however, is that it is not the way it *seems* or at the very least is not the way it is portrayed by the state power. On the contrary, what is presented to the world is a situation where the state is having to exert all its energies, resources and manpower to fending off forces which threaten to overwhelm it.

How, then, do we as observers disentangle what is an actual, empirically verifiable threat from that which exists only in the heads of the perpetrator? Perpetrators do not come to their conclusions about the nature of threat in a complete vacuum. Conflicts that involve genocide do indeed include those where the struggle for the control of land, resources and people, is genuinely real and intense just as they include others, most notably in the Holocaust and related Roma *Porrajmos*, where it is pure fantasy. But if these two examples seem to offer us the absolution of certainty – that the only perpetrator–victim interaction that exists is one which is going on in the befuddled brains of the Nazis – the problem still remains: where do we draw the line with the rest of the field? The otherwise crass adage 'just because you're paranoid, it doesn't mean that they're not out to get you' seems to have a certain application here. If there is not a speck of truth in the thrust of Talat, Bianchi and the Sudanese imams' statements above, are then they not simply engaging in the same sort of diabolisation (or alternatively complete disingenuity) as the Nazis? Do we simply discount each of their individual inferences that behind their communal adversary lurks some other more powerful, sinister, outside force which is going to help it bring down the state: the Russians behind the Armenians; guerrillas (for which read the forces of 'international communism') on behalf of the Indians; 'Zionism' backing the Nuba? Or should we even go one stage further still and posit that these charges of dark, international forces at work are not so very different in kind from those that the Nazis projected onto the Jews?

Paradoxically, part of the inference here relates to an entirely legitimate unease we may feel about conceding anything to the perpetrators' perspective, thereby in turn running the risk of displacing a neat black-and-white ascription of guilt in favour of a much more murky grey. More to the point, however, the aim is to remind ourselves that any broad historical examination of the phenomenon of genocide cannot fruitfully proceed without engagement with issues of collective human psychopathology. We have already signalled that projective tendencies seem to be intrinsic to the human condition and that even in 'normal' circumstances this can lead to quite exaggerated, frightening and even diabolically 'bogeyman' images of the 'other'. What concerns us here is how such tendencies manifest themselves in times of acute societal stress, both individually and, perhaps more importantly, across significantly large human collectivities. As this study is about modern and even contemporary history, one riposte might be that the advent of a reason-based, advanced scientific society rules out the need to factor in this consideration. Unfortunately, there is no evidence to support such bland optimism. On the contrary, the very nature of modern societies, usually made up of millions of human beings melded together through the infrastructure of states, yet provided with rapid access to information through modern mass media, may actually provide a much more obvious and potent pathway for the transmission of the tendencies in question.

Consider, for example, the most powerful, wealthy and materially sophisticated modern state of all: the United States. This is not a state most people in the West immediately associate with genocide. And it is not one which we tend to think of as having suffered mass societal dislocation, at least not comparable with other societies in the last century. Yet the important point here is not what historians dispassionately adjudge to be the truth but what people *feel* to be true. And if those people happen to be, if not whole national groups, then significant segments of national society, and if they all simultaneously start feeling that it and its values, as they understand them, are going seriously adrift – and moreover have it confirmed from their neighbours' hearsay, in the newspapers and in repeated statements from opinion formers and policy makers – then we might expect some of this to register in their outward behaviour.

'The years from 1917 to 1921', says historian, David Brion Davis, 'are probably unmatched in American history for popular hysteria, xenophobia and paranoid suspicion'.[119] Objectively speaking, this makes little sense. The USA had just helped win a global war at relatively little material or manpower cost to itself, and in so doing had established itself as the leading industrial society on the planet. Yet its mental state was as Davis described it. Why? Primarily because the successful Bolshevik Revolution in Russia, with its internationalist agenda, challenged the very ideological basis of homespun, individualistic, apple-pie America. Russia was a long way away, but it did not stop the first great wave of reds, especially Jewish 'reds under the beds' scares. Workers' strikes, a financial down-turn, the activities of 'foreign' immigrant anarchists and left-winger pro-Bolshevik sympathisers, not to say black restiveness, were all interpreted by 'believers' as portents of the great plot to destroy America. Yet Davis is probably wrong to say this was the highpoint of the conspiratorial craze. In the wake of a successful global war, and with the USA firmly acknowledged as 'the greatest power of earth', Senator Joseph McCarthy's June 1951 speech, in which he claimed to have uncovered 'a conspiracy on a scale so immense as to dwarf any previous such venture in the history of man',[120] far from being greeted with howls of derision became the basis for a nationwide, publicly endorsed 'witch-hunt' against the high-level subversives and saboteurs, both in government and outside, supposedly masterminding this plot on behalf of 'World Communism'.

At this juncture, in the early 1950s, not only were average white Americans enjoying a security, life expectancy and material benefits streets ahead of their contemporaries in most other countries, but on the world stage the United States was *the* hegemonic power. True, this was being militarily, politically and ideologically challenged by the Soviet Union, China and other emerging third-world national-communist states and movements. Yet these undoubted set-backs seem to have had such a severe psychological effect on many 'ordinary' Americans' feelings of poise and equilibrium that the only way they were able to cope with their confusion was by endorsing an explanation which blamed it all on secret 'enemies within', or envisaging that what was going on – as another contemporary commentator put it – entailed 'phantasies of apocalyse and destruction, of the battle between the children of light and the children of darkness'.[121] The fact that during subsequent years almost every moment of political crisis or set-back, whether it were the Bay of Pigs fiasco, or the Kennedy assassination, had Americans reaching anew for the conspiracy motif is again, surely, telling. As too, is the persistence of a strong cultural ingredient within it: the idea that the subversion was not simply political but was being conducted by almost invisible stealth – through the schools, the arts and the above all the media – all with the ultimate aim of so sapping and debilitating the physical and moral vitality of American life that it would ultimately fall apart. Even after the collapse of the Soviet 'great Satan', the American penchant for conspiracy continued: most obviously attested in the cult-following for the 1990s television series *The X-Files* with its storyline of an inner government cover-up to deny knowledge to the broader population of its machinations to control and manipulate para-normal 'powers' 'out there'.[122]

The purpose of this digression has not been to highlight some weird and singular dysfunction peculiar to Americans. What it has aimed to demonstrate is that widely held feelings of angst, anomie and disorientation – even in otherwise relatively stable conditions – are quite capable of manifesting themselves in collective tendencies 'to obliterate the distinction between the symbolic plane and that of reality' allowing for, 'by definition, the interlocking of fantasm and reality assessments'.[123] The statement is that of Saul Friedlander, and he is referring not to the United States but to Nazism. Any inference that this might provide some basis for comparison between Nazi Germany and the United States may alarm some readers. The aim, however, is not to compare like with like: the contemporary United States is not the same sort of society as Nazi Germany. Nor has it recently committed any genocide as a *direct* or, at least, sole result of its collective paranoias; though how latent Islamophobia in the wake of 9/11 is likely to unravel is still uncharted if potentially highly disturbing terrain. Nevertheless, what this paradoxical superpower culture of vulnerability surely does offer is a window into some of the universal conditions and preconditions from which projection can become volatile. And in this sense the gap between American conspiracy myths and arguably the most potently genocidal conspiracy myth of modern times – 'the international Jewish conspiracy' – becomes less improbable.

The hypothesis that the well-springs of the Holocaust can be found in the obsessive fantasies which many Germans projected onto Jews – in other words, Jews in German heads, not in reality – has been developed most cogently and convincingly by Norman Cohn. His starting point is the infamous turn-of-the-century Russian forgery, the *Protocols of the Elders of Zion*. This purports to show how a collective Jewry, since the birth of Christianity, has been plotting its revenge with the aim of destroying all known civilisation in favour of a complete, irrrevocable and utterly totalitarian Jewish world domination.[124] However, as Cohn shows, the *Protocols* is only part of a much wider trans-European genre and, indeed, integrates into its grand narrative many additional elements current in other conspiracy stories from this period. The grounds for its particular and quite sensational success lie, in the first place, in its apparently comprehensive explanation for all the ills, dislocations and miseries that afflict the modern world. These include the erosion of religious and moral values as well as economic and political disasters. In this sense, the storyline of the *Protocols* is simply an updated version of the sort of Manichaeism preached by the medieval millenarians who had been the subject of Cohn's earlier study, and so, supposedly of succour and relevance only to a limited and dwindling audience of cranks in the increasingly secular and rational world of the twentieth century. That its audience actually proved to be both mainstream and massive is due to the fact that the forgery fortuitously emerged out of Russian obscurity at the very moment when Western civilisation was *genuinely* in danger of dissolution, in the critical months at the end of the First World War, when Germany had been defeated and the Bolshevik-Communist alternative to the traditional order seemed to be dramatically on the march.

Herein lies a second critical element in the specific potency of the *Protocols*. In conditions which could fairly be described as 'almost eschatological'[125] and in which whole sections of European society had lost their normative social and political moorings the *Protocols* provided something firm, sure and consoling upon which to grasp. Its message – for anybody willing to listen – was simple. What had happened in the war: mass death, starvation, revolution and social collapse was neither the Europeans' fault, nor the fault of their chosen or acknowledged leaders. It was all instead part of an evil plan manipulated into play by the only group who could have such an all-encompassing grudge against the whole of Europe's Christian heritage. Who else were the Bolsheviks in Russia but a load of Jews? Who else were causing chaos and havoc on the streets of Kiel, Berlin and Munich, but the Jews? Who else were manipulating Wall Street and the stock exchanges to makes vast financial killings out of all this disaster, but the Jews?

Thus, the *Protocols* provided more than simple explanation. Like the millenarianism of old this was also visionary prophecy, foretelling of an enslaved future which awaited ordinary folk if they succumbed to the false Jewish promises of egalitarian democracy, and of the true promise of redemption if they only could awake and see through the great deception being perpetrated upon them and in so doing cast asunder the bonds of their affliction. Ignore the fact that this mish-mash of half-truths, lies and misconceptions made no logical sense. In the apocalyptic climate of 1919 the last thing people wanted was to be told that the sacrifices they had made were the totally pointless result of the tunnel-visioned stupidities of their great political and military leaders and thus, arguably, symptomatic of a much more complex and deeper-seated social and political malaise. What people did want was something to take away their mental anguish and pain and at the same give them some sense that – at the end of the day – justice and retribution would prevail. That this need was felt by possibly millions in far away America, leading to significant receptiveness to the conspiracy fantasy, is at least as significant as the fact that it had a powerful promoter in Henry Ford, who serialised the *Protocols* in his own *Dearborn Independent*. Just as, in Britain, it was not only a coterie of right-wing politicians but hundreds of thousands of ordinary middle-of-the-road conservative readers who continued to buy their copies of the serious 'broadsheet' *Morning Post*, with its own ongoing *Protocols* serialisation, and all, doubtless, musing that there must be something in the story after all.[126]

In Britain and America, the *Protocols* sensation did gradually wane, not least because, after much prevarication on the matter, *The Times* published evidence proving it to be a blatant forgery.[127] This makes its persistence in Germany all the more telling. Here not only was the post-war trauma as a result of defeat that much more intense but also what went with it was complete incomprehension and bewilderment as to how that had happened. A country awash with demobilised soldiers – many of whom, like Hitler himself, were to become core members of the then protean Nazi party – was full of persistent stories that there had been no capitulation on the battlefield and that the explanation, thus, had to be elsewhere. Again, in these conditions of acute national fracture the one thing that only a minority would, or could countenance was the actual truth: that army and state had been dumped by Germany's military leaders, who, unable to accept responsibility for either military defeat or its consequences, had instead chosen to hide behind the civilian politicians who had been forced to accept the terms of Allied armistice and dictated peace. Indeed, any attempt to offer a rational explanation – going against the grain of the now increasingly shrill but persistent cry that it was the Jews who were to blame – was likely to be rounded on forcefully. Here is an extract from a book written in 1922 in the 'scholarly university tradition', by Hans Blüher, a major intellectual mentor to German youth movements:

> It is useless to 'refute' the fable of the 'stab in the back'. Everything can be refuted and everything can be demonstrated. But every German already had in his blood this existential fact. Prussianism and heroism go together. Judaism and defeatism go together ... On that score, all proof, either pro or con, is pointless, even if 100,000 Jews died for their country. Germans will soon know that the Jewish question is at the heart of all political questions.[128]

If Bluher's chop-logic was widely accepted, then Goldhagen's thesis in essence is right. The cultural underpinnings for Germany's 'eliminationist' – or to use Saul Friedlander's more penetrating term, 'redemptive' – anti-Semitism[129] were already firmly in place before Hitler came to power. And it was shared by all sorts of people; not just front-line veterans desperate to share their prophetic insights from the trenches but all those students, officers, graduates of technology institutes, professors, schoolmasters, civil servants and businessmen who were both the most avid readers and disseminators of the *Protocols*.[130] Where Cohn, in effect, provides a corrective to Goldhagen is in offering us a moment of crystallisation for this intense animus. Hatred of Jews may have been embedded for hundreds of years in German culture just as it was elsewhere. But its genocidal potentiality was not so much a constant, as Goldhagen seems to imply, but latent. It was dependent, in other words, on the sort of massive societal crisis and hence psychic rupture which would have an educated intellect like Dr Otto Ohlendorf, the Einsatz commander responsible for hundreds of thousands of Jewish deaths on the eastern front, looking back from his prison cell, in 1947, to plead 'What else could we have done when confronted with demons at work?'[131]

Role-Reversal: 'The All Powerful' Victim

One obvious way of considering the issues raised by the *Protocols*, and the whole nature of Western fantasy construction around the Jews, is simply to underscore its exceptionality. After all, even if we are to accept that during the last century large sections of American society were at critical points swept up by similar psychoses, there is no comparable 'take-off' during this period in the direction of *genocide*. There is a 'fixed' perceived 'enemy' in the form of international communism and, indeed, quite conscious and persistent responses from the apparatus of the US state to counter it, most notably through a massive nuclear-cum-conventional arms build-up. Yet interestingly, after the initial McCarthyite scare, there is no further cultural or political attempt to pin down the image of this 'enemy' to specific 'internal' ethnic, religious or social groupings, again in spite of the initial potential for Jews to fulfil this role.[132] One might at this point make a further long digression about democratic checks and balances in US society, or its traditions of pluralistic tolerance. Or one might simply note that America's political-military response to its sense of threat has been expressed in a form which is equally exterminatory but paradoxically non-genocidal: at least in its own domestic context. Alleged 'reds under the beds' have been certainly vilified and harassed but the weapons of mass annihilation remained pointed outwards at the Soviet Union, Red China, little Cuba. By the same token, to date, the US post-9/11 'war on terrorism' has been directed against Afghanistan and Iraq, not through overt state assaults on American Arabs and Muslims.

Thus, one might legitimately pose that the overtly Manichaean-style demonisation of Jews in the modern German context, not to mention its apparent resilience for the twenty years from its first flowering in the aftermath of the First World War through to its exterminatory actualisation in the Second, would superficially seem to suggest a peculiar psycho-social-historical aspect which is not replicated elsewhere. As we have already hinted, some of the most perspicacious historians of the Holocaust have emphasised how this is bound up not so much with the specificity of Nazi racism so much as Nazi proclivities towards millenarianism as if they believed themselves to be genuinely involved in a cosmic struggle between good and evil, with the earth as its arena, and the Jews their satanic adversaries. All this would point back to the very deeply embedded origins of anti-Semitism reflecting not the Jewish but the essentially European Christian problem of 'self'. As George Steiner has noted: 'When it turned on the Jew, Christianity and European civilisation turned on the incarnation – albeit an incarnation often wayward and unaware – of its own best hopes'.[133] But in trying to understand how this eventually would lead to genocide Steiner seemed to be groping for some further insight:

> In the Holocaust there was both a lunatic retribution, a lashing out against intolerable pressures of vision, and a large measure of self-mutilation. The secular, materialist, warlike community of Europe sought to extirpate from itself, from its own inheritance, archaic, now ridiculously obsolete but somehow inextinguishable carriers of the ideal. In the Nazi idiom of 'vermin' and 'sanitation' there is a brusque insight into the infectious nature of morality. Kill the remembrancer, the claim-agent and you will have cancelled the long-debt.[134]

Or, to put it another way, the Nazis *had to* wipe out the Jews because they too painfully reminded them of what they were and what they were not. It is not simply that Jews represented some archetypal 'other' by which one could recognise one's own kind, nor did they represent the basis, as Hegel proclaimed, of national self-awareness, as might come about through engagement with an adversary in war. Instead, what Steiner seems to be pointing to is a much more intense and all-pervasive crisis of identity; the sense that not only are the ideological or material foundations upon which one makes claims to power and legitimacy in danger of being revealed as nothing more than a bogus sham but with them are shattered one's public image of hubristic certitude, confidence and power. This surely is why Nazis particularly loathed the Jewish association with intellect and went out of their way to denigrate and destroy everything to do with it. Thus, in 1980, the writer, Primo Levi, musing in not dissimilar vein to Steiner, postulated:

> Auschwitz may be the punishment of the barbarians, of barbarian Germany, of the barbarian Nazis, against Jewish civilisation – that is the punishment for daring ... I was thinking of that vein of German anti-semitism that struck chiefly at the intellectual daring of the Jews, such as Freud, Marx and all the innovators, in every field. It was that daring that irked a certain German philistinism *much more* than the fact of blood or race.[135]

Jewish 'power' vis-à-vis the Nazis thus rested on the Nazis' fear that they – the Jews – had the ability to see through their claptrap to its hollow core[136] while offering their own alternative vision of society which, far from needing mystical ties of blood-soaked community to hold it together, was genuinely founded on reason, science and modernity. This may have had little or nothing to do with ordinary Jewish people ekeing out their existences just like other people. But Nazi projection did not operate on this ordinary plane. All Jews whatever their backgrounds were guilty by association with this threat, just as all Jews everywhere were 'internationalist', 'cosmopolitan', purveyors of 'cultural-Bolshevism'. Yet these symbol-laden representations also – exasperatingly for the Nazis – cut the other way. Jews might be both the organisers and carriers of anti-national dissolution but while Nazism struggled to re-create an authentic *Volksgemeinschaft*, the Jews utterly perversely had preserved theirs since ancient times. Or so the Nazis imagined. The same was supposedly true for the Roma; another ubiquitous, dispersed, and – so the Nazis assumed – nomadic people, yet with all the apparent and genuine trapping of a race-community. The fact that Reich experts found it difficult in practice to provide a common denominator definition of 'gypsy' was beside the point.[137] What mattered at heart was that Jewish and Roma 'magic' was far more potent than all the noise and thunder of the Nuremberg rallies.

If this, then, is the critical and absolutely bizarre paradox of both Holocaust and *Porrajmos*; that behind the race science-validated image of Jews and Roma as inferior, mentally and physically debilitated, vapid and weak, there lies an altogether different image in which the Nazi perpetrators fear that what they are really dealing with is, in effect, races of 'supermen', this surely of its own makes Nazi projection wholly unusual and distinct from that operating in the broader run of genocides. Or does it? Certainly, the gaping chasm between the perpetrators' projective vision of contamination, dissolution and destruction, which these victim groups were supposed to have been able to wield, compared with the actual reality of their absolute physical defencelessness, is nowhere greater than in these cases. Nowhere is the victim–perpetrator dynamic more tenuous. Nowhere, equally, is the perpetrator's need to compensate for its fear of the victims by providing medical-scientific proof that they really are utterly deficient, sub-human and worthless, more pronounced. Yet, in varying, albeit lesser degrees, these symptoms are evident in most cases of genocide. If they were not – if the perpetrators did not 'imagine' the group as a formidable danger – why would they resort to marshalling manpower and resources for the undertaking in the first place? They would simply ignore the group, or, as nineteenth-century imperialists were wont to pronounce with regard to indigenous peoples, let them simply *fade away*. All this is egregious enough and telling evidence of the emergence of race theory and social Darwinism. But it does not of itself account for genocide.

Genocide implies that the perpetrator *has to go to the effort* of extirpating a perceived threat. Not something which just happens to be in the way of its domestic or colonial agenda, but some group of active protagonists who are going to oppose and halt that programme in its tracks. As we shall see, the Germans in *fin-de-siècle* South-West Africa may have become accustomed to referring to the native black population as 'baboons', and treating them accordingly, but when one of these peoples, the Herero, rose against German rule and, for a few brief days, looked as if they might eject the colonialists forever, the German military commander responded not simply by putting down the revolt but attempting to exterminate the Herero *in toto*. What drove him to this genocidal policy was none other than the fact that the 'baboons' 'had shown a potential well beyond their allotted station'[138] and, in so doing, unmasked German racial superiority for what it was; an unmitigated lie. The Herero, in fact, did not have the 'power' or resources to confront the Germans for long, the dynamic of conflict, in other words, rapidly descending into a vastly uneven one. Yet even as the Germans continued to exterminate them as if they were 'baboons' or 'savages', and thus beneath contempt, the linguistic denigration suggests its own hidden sting in the tail. Who were the more potent: the civilised, masterful Teutons or the tribal, 'animalistic', black men? Nor was this case of the Herero peculiarly unique in the colonial record. On the contrary, over and over again, European conquerors in the Americas, antipodes, Asia, Africa and even on their own domestic frontiers, found themselves repeatedly hoist on this dichotomy of their own making.

That said, 'deceitful', 'treacherous' and 'murderous', 'barbarians,' 'cannibals' and savages' were at least visible. The language of 'scientific' racism arguably amplified and exacerbated the angst of the more modern potential genocidaire by introducing an entirely novel range of unpredictable, not to say unseeable elements. 'Armenian traitors had found a niche for themselves in the bosom of the fatherland: they were dangerous microbes', insisted the CUP physician, Muhmat Reshid, as he duly pronounced his medical duty to destroy them before they liquidated the Turks and became 'the proprietors of this land'.[139] Microbes, infection, corrosion, or, to continue with the medical analogy, of a disease in need of bodily remedy, or worse, of 'a cancer of the living organism' for which only surgical amputation would bring relief: this is hardly the sort of vocabulary likely to assure a group of anxiety-ridden protagonists that it is they, rather than their adversaries, who are in control of a situation,[140] anymore than if they were to use more traditional terms like 'vermin', 'poison', or perhaps worst of all 'invisible'. On the contrary, what all this conveys is not simply a tension between 'our' power and 'theirs' but that the 'they' are, at the very least, already one step ahead of the 'us'. *The truth is* that all non-Serb ethnic groups, especially the Croats, are at this very minute preparing the genocide of all Serbs',[141] exclaimed Batric Jovanovic, in the Serb parliament in June 1991.

This projective potency can also manifest itself in other ways. One is when the victim group's women and children are embraced within its frame. By social and biological definition these two critical elements of the communal triad not only stand in juxtaposition to the adult male third but in the context of the larger world are dependent on it to protect their vulnerability. This has never prevented dominant cultures investing the women of 'outsider' groups with both open and hidden powers. To what extent the dangerous sexual allure of female Roma and Jewess, or their alleged skills, especially in the Roma case, as clairvoyants and sorceresses, are reflections of a broader culture of European misogynism or, rather, are logical gender extensions of archetypal Jewish and Romani male 'constructions' is not quite the issue here. This is partly because any special female potency, bar of course their all-important reproductive power to bear more Jewish and Romani children, was excluded from the Nazis' genocide equation. Subsequently, Jewish (though not Roma) women deported to death camps alongside their menfolk were more likely to be killed immediately, especially if accompanied by children and babies but in all other senses, their threat as female Jews – or Roma – did not require specific exorcism.[142] If this would make them part of a generalised but essentially 'male'-labelled adversary (signficantly reversing the Christian medieval and early modern archetype where Jewesses, in spite of their alleged sexual potency, were considered sufficiently passive, malleable – and beautiful – to be worthy of redemption through predatory marriage and conversion)[143] there are other instances where the specificity of female potency is quite transparent.

Again, there were persistent charges made by Jean-Baptiste Carrier, or more particularly General Turreau, the main agents of the Jacobin onslaught on the Vendée in 1793–4, that it was the Vendéan women who were primarily responsible for the anti-government insurrection which preceded this – arguably the first genuinely nation-state case of genocide.[144] But whether these charges owe more to European misogynist traditions from the period of witchcraft scares and earlier, or are specific to the circumstances of the Vendée itself, are somewhat tangential to the argument here. What is clear is that Carrier and Turreau oscillated between viewing the women as the special instruments of the Vendéan priests (another source of cosmic 'power') or as the key fomenters and sustainers of the insurrection in their own right. Worse, it was the women who were primarily culpable for the slaughter of captured Jacobins.[145] The idea that women might be self-propelled agents at all was about as serious a challenge to social order as anyone could envisage in the mental climate of the late eighteenth century. That they might have used this unfettered liberty not simply to kill but by implication mutilate their prisoners smacked of a sexual transgression which demanded their deaths alongside that of their menfolk.[146]

Some 170 years later, the accusation was explicitly made in the great genocidal massacres of Indonesian communists. The army-directed killings had been preceded by an attempted coup in which a number of generals had been killed. But the story rapidly took hold that women communists ('Gerwani') had not only been responsible for this outrage but had engaged in a lurid sexual orgy with the dismembered corpses. Everywhere popular wall slogans read 'Hang Gerwani, Crush Gerwani, the Gerwani are Whores'. Allied with an intensely vitriolic media campaign specifically focusing on the alleged sado-erotic mutilations committed by the female communists, it is clear that the fantasy had touched a raw nerve which, in giving an additional potency to the communists, also further fuelled demands for their complete extirpation.[147]

If specific instances such as this may also suggest how rape and murder in modern genocide may follow the contours of more traditional ritualistic-style efforts at exorcism, then equally the killing of children might also be seen as a frantic attempt to ward off the return of 'evil' danger at some future date. As a participant in the Guatemalan killings attempted to exonerate himself:

> We have to go on finishing them off house by house because the parents pass on the poison [of subversion] to the children. You have to kill the parents and children of ten, eight, five years, you have to finish them off because they've already heard the things their father says, and the children will do it.[148]

To suggest, thus, that genocidal perpetrators mass murder 'innocent' men, women and children for no good reason, or for no reason other than that they belong to a particular ethnic or social group critically misses the point. More often that not genocide is committed because its protagonists *see* the victim group as *representing* something that challenges their sense of identity, well-being, purposefulness or collective vision. As recent work has suggested, much of this sense of threat may be very specifically culturally conditioned, gendered or both.[149] It may be also be very functionally grounded. The perceived need for land, for resources, for popular empowerment, for the unfettered mobilisation of national assets, or the opening up of a frontier region – all of which a real or imagined communal group may resist or deny – is certainly intrinsic to the majority of genocides. Of the Kurds in Saddam's Iraq, Kanan Makiya notes that they 'suffered more than others not because they were Kurds, but because they resisted and fought back hard'.[150] So, the motive for murder here appears to be essentially political, underscored by the fact that some Kurds fought on Saddam's Ba'athist side. If this makes this particular genocide less all-embracing, less obviously 'ideological' than that perpetrated by the Nazis on Jews and Roma, we need to be cautious, however, before carrying the distinction too far. The Kurds of Iraq, like the Armenians of Ottoman Turkey before them, may not have been labelled according to some specially designed racial template but the reason why a significant portion of their women, children and old people – as well as men – were, nevertheless, targeted for death, lay in the fact that as a communal entity they appeared to pose a direct and potent *alternative* to their state and dominant society's value-system. The threat, in other words, was much more in the idea or ideas which, in reified form, they represented rather than in their specific persons or any tangible physical assets that they could bring to a potential political or military encounter.

What was this 'idea' that the leaderships in CUP Turkey, Ba'athist Iraq or, for that matter, Nazi Germany could not handle? The idea – certainly in these cases – was that, instead of society's strength being founded on assumptions of a unitary, homogeneous and streamlined polity determined and developed according to unilinear criteria set by a single, political party elite, it might instead be multi-cultural, plural, heterodox, a society of diverse peoples, rather than 'people', even a society where power and resources might be shared. How such aspirations came to be associated with particular groups may have had much to do with their deep cultural or religious background, or it may have been much more prosaically the result of immediate social and political circumstances. Certainly, we need to be very careful here of ascribing a one-dimensional, plaster-cast sainthood to the victims just as we do of blanket-charging their killers as evil monsters. Genocidal 'victim' groups, after all, can also become – in changed circumstances – perpetrators,[151] suggesting too, that the sort of pathologies which we have charted as potential informers and galvanisers of the act, are universal to the human condition.

However, the fact that genocidal process emanates from situations where the perpetrators' sense of society *as it ought to be* is confronted by groupings – whether they are indigenous natives at the geographical margins or 'cosmopolitans' at its heart – whose resilient non-conformity not only defies but makes a transparent mockery of its hegemonic and monolithic wisdom – gives an often unusually heightened or symbolic twist to the subsequent dynamic which regularly mixes with, where it does not entirely overwhelm its political dimensions. In some cases this is very overt. When, in 1959, a Tibetan attempt to re-assert their former autonomy from China was met by massive physical assault from the communist People's Army, the outcome of the military struggle was in no doubt. But, on the moral plane, who held the upper hand in this encounter between two great world systems: communism or Buddhism, was less obvious.[152] Again, reduced to its entirely political or geo-political dimensions, China's resort to genocide could be appraised as the out-come of its need to control fully the Himalayan plateau and of the party's determination not to let the Tibetan bad example infect the state's many other non-Han ethnic and religious minorities. But if that was the case why not simply quell the uprising. Why kill great swathes of the Tibetan population as well?

This suggests to this author that that while – to revisit Dadrian's termin-ology – the perpetrators in genocide have 'preponderant access to the overall resources of power',[153] in other words, they have the operating capacity with which to commit mass murder, their own sense of control is very far from absolute. Paradoxically, this is the very reason why they ultimately resort to mass murder: because they fear the victim; if not physically, in terms of *his* military prowess, or demographic numbers, then in some other much less definable and possibly much more frightening way. Not only are 'ethnic' 'ene-mies' in this process translated into political enemies, blurring any distinction in the perpetrators' perception of them, but their potency becomes magnified by their alleged or real connections with political movements or organisations beyond the boundaries of the state. From being the tool or agents of foreign powers working their malevolent machinations against the interests and well-being of the nation – no more and no less than the McCarthyite projection and paranoia we have already noted – it is not such a giant step to see the victims as international conspiratorial forces in their own right, or even, to turn up the amplification of this terrifying broadcast, as demons working their own dark spells and black magic. The struggle, thus, is finally joined as the last great battle between good and evil.

If this is a view into the mindset of the perpetrators of the Holocaust and with it into 'the interaction of entirely heterogeneous phenomena: messianic fanaticism and bureaucratic structures, pathological impulses and administra-tive decrees, archaic attitudes and advanced industrial society,'[154] it is, in fact, only the phenomenon at its most extreme and absolute. If something between 1 and 1.5 million Jewish children could perish as a result,[155] the collapse, or more exactly extrusion of moral restraints on the murder of children did not end here. The usually brutal and often wholly sadistic physical torture and annihilation of babies, their mothers, their whole families, the sequestration of their communities' valuables and property, the laying waste of a landscape in which those people lived and worked and with it the conscious obliteration of the elements most sacred to those people in that landscape, as if those commu-nities and with them their belief-systems had never existed – not to mention the absolute denial that any such act has taken place – all these, the *common* ingredients of genocide, suggest something more than a simple, straightforward utilitarian calculus. Let alone the workings of a well-oiled – or alternatively, if one does not like that reading – misshapen modernity.

But if that is the case, if at the centre of our phenomenon is the ongoing fragility of the human psyche and its proclivity, under circumstances of acute stress, to be pushed over the edge, it begs one critical question: why is genocide something which has specifically come of age in the contemporary era?

3. Continuity and Discontinuity in the Historical Record

The century of the nation-state. The century of genocide. A key proposition running through this work is that the crystallisation of the phenomenon we call 'genocide' – as opposed to other categories of mass murder – could only be really achieved in the context of an emerging, global, interlocking system of nation-states which finally came to its *fullest* fruition in the twentieth century. The emphasis, to date, on five core examples spanning this epoch underscores this contention. Necessarily it also raises a further question as to whether, with the foreseeable completion of the nation-state building process – arguably with the collapse of the communist neo-'alternative' – in the final years of the century, the danger of genocide has passed its apotheosis and is now in decline. Discussion of this issue must wait for a later, more contemporarily focused volume.

The purpose here, however, is to investigate how we arrived at the specificity of the phenomenon in the first instance. Assuming that human beings in recent history have been wired up in essentially the same way as our forebears were a thousand, ten thousand years or even nearer a hundred thousand years ago, and that this carries with it a certain propensity or at least potentiality to kill members of our own kind, the charge that genocide is actually an outcome of a quite recent turn in human development is a rather serious one.[1] All the more so when the accusation is implicitly levelled against a political transformation which – at least in the West where it originated – is considered both normative and sound.

The way this author proposes to develop this argument is counter-intuitive, that is, by consciously raking over pre-modern, including quite ancient historical terrain where the term genocide might seem appropriate. This does not imply some attempt to arrive at our preordained hypothesis by a process of elimination. On the contrary, it is a paradox that the path to genocide is in part, deeply embedded in the human record and that facets of it are actually very evident in ancient, classical, as well as more recent, pre-modern times. Nor is it easily discernible at what point exactly genocide – or at least a modern variant of it – overtly takes shape. It might be convenient to begin with critical break-points in the rise of the West, such as 1789 or, for that matter, 1492. But that in itself would be to assume the overriding role of decisive rupture against that of long-term processes of historical change. In this sense, the dilemma for historians of genocide is no different from that of historians more generally. Moreover, this alone hardly provides an explanation for the specific recourse to genocide engaged in by some 'nation'-states rather than others. If the aim of this final chapter, thus, is to provide an overarching historical framework for the occurrence of genocide, equally the aim is to locate within it the specific conditions and preconditions which have driven some states to this entirely extreme response.

Extermination, Hyper-Exploitation and Forced Deportation in Pre-Modern Times

A prevailing feature of much of contemporary culture and society is the assumption that our ancestors, lacking the technological sophistication we possess or even the same degree of social organisation, were quite incapable of accomplishing systematic mass murder on the scale of our achievement. Avers one Holocaust study: 'Within certain limits set by political and military power considerations, the *modern* state may do anything it wishes to those under its control'[2] – as if traditional states did not have this capacity. This is all the more peculiar when those the modern mind does sometimes remember for mass murders on a significant scale appear not to be states at all but hordes of apparently disorganised, rampaging Huns, Mongols, Zulus or other 'barbarians'. In so doing, we set up another dichotomy: that between civilisation and barbarianism, almost the very starting point of Lemkin's thesis.[3] As if to turn the problem yet again on its head, if the population of states – i.e. civilised societies – are not exactly incapable of mass murder, then they are socialised in a such way that any proclivity to killing has been ironed out, at least from their 'normal', everyday behaviour.

To be fair to 'civilisation' in the pre-modern record, it does, at least superficially, seem as if the 'barbarians' have the edge in the murdering stakes. For instance, the Mongol conqueror, Genghis Khan, on the estimation of one historian, was responsible in the early thirteenth century for the eradication of some four-fifths of the population along the belt of Arabic Iranian civilisation,[4] while his latter-day successor, Timur, better known in the West as Tamerlane, in his great rampage across the great cultural and commercial centres of Central Asia and Northern India between 1379 and 1403, sufficiently excited Arnold Toynbee, another great comparativist, to comment that in the span of these twenty-four years Timur perpetrated as many horrors as the last five Assyrian kings had achieved in the space of 120.[5] Yet it is arguable whether Timur can really be described as a barbarian at all, while his descendants were to found India's great Mogul civilisation, before this too was brought to an apparent terminus in 1739, when the forces of another central Asian adventurer, Tamas Kuli Khan (Nadir Shah), concluded his campaign by putting the entire population of Delhi to the sword.[6]

The paradox here should be obvious. Genghis, Timur, Nadir Shah or the Zulu leader, Shaka – primarily responsible for the great waves of extermination known as the *Mfecane*, the Great Crushing in which upwards of a million people were killed in southern Africa in the early nineteenth century[7] – may have started their murderous careers as archetypal 'barbarians'. But the havoc and depredations which they wrought, far from being intended for their own sake, were their chosen route to the achievement of supremely strong, centralised imperial polities. Once there, the mass killing did not stop. Indeed, 'without gas chambers, machine guns or the guillotine, Shaka managed to establish one of the most effective regimes of terror on record'.[8] But did this make him a wolf of war, or, as the historian, A. T. Olmstead, describing Assyrians or Romans would have put it, a shepherd dog of civilisation?[9]

If the barbarian–civilised dichotomy, thus, is a largely false one – though with some interesting and pertinent pointers to the mindset of those mass murderers who perceive themselves to be 'civilised' – a common argument deployed to defend the distinction of twentieth-century 'totality' in genocide is the notion that in the past perpetrators rarely, if ever, set out to kill everybody in the target group. Men would be killed or enslaved but at least the younger women and (male as well as female) children would often be spared and even assimilated into the victor's population as chattel or spouses. This was certainly the case in Shaka's wars. But even in some of the best-documented cases of unmitigated mass murder in antiquity, like the Athenian onslaught on the Aegean island of Melos, in 416 BC, or the Roman destruction of its great rival, Carthage, in 146 BC, enslavement rather than extermination seems to have been the fate of many female and child survivors.[10] The issue, in such instances, thus becomes whether this would constitute a distinction between genocide now and then. It is true that slavery in the classical world, as well as being the economic underpinning of the social fabric and, therefore, a practice considered perfectly functional and normal, did not *necessarily* have to lead to either a short and brutish life or painful death. With this in mind it is hardly surprising that Steven Katz has been particularly at pains to stress these least unpleasant contours in order to reinforce his case that there can be no comparison with the sort of hyper-exploitation practised against Jews in the Holocaust.[11] Moreover, statistical evidence confirms that Jewish life expectancy in Nazi labour camps compares entirely unfavourably with inmates from other ethnic groups, underscoring the argument that forced labour was primarily a technique for working both Jewish men *and* women to a rapid death.[12]

Yet if this highlights the extremity of the Holocaust it does not invalidate the general rule that enslavement and hyper-exploitation on the one hand, combined with the separate treatment of males and females on the other, have provided an effective tool for emasculating and indeed dissolving targeted national or communal groups *throughout* history. While hyper-exploitation has been mostly conducted for entirely venal purposes, resulting, as in the wake of European conquest and spoliation of the Americas in millions of Amerindian and African deaths, most infamously in the Bolivian mines at Potosi and Huancavelica, and in the 'Middle Passage' of the Atlantic slave trade,[13] it has also been part of a consistent battery of methods utilised by polities for the extirpation of perceived ethno-political threats. From this perspective, the labour camps of the Soviet Gulag, or the Nazi *Zwangarbeitslager für Juden* (ZALs), while undoubtedly statements of modernity in terms of scope and scale, do not in themselves represent a major rupture with the past, any more than the abduction and/or sexual violation of thousands of young Armenians in the *Aghet*, can in itself be considered a new method in the disposal of troublesome populations.[14] Indeed, the context in which these latter mass violations took place – namely, the mass deportation of a people from their settled homelands to another distant and inhospitable frontier – has been practised, particularly in this Middle (or Near) Eastern region, against rebellious, recalcitrant or militarily subjugated peoples on a regular basis by Ottomans, Safavids, Byzantines, or, for that matter, by Babylonians, Assyrians and Akkadians, for thousands of years.[15] True, deportation in itself does not have to lead – as in the case of the Ottoman Armenians – to a total genocide. In the ancient, as in the modern, the nature and severity of the deportation process is at least partially dependent on the degree to which the perpetrating state seeks to punish or revenge itself on the deportees. But the fact that the very process of uprooting and forced migration cannot but lead to mass mortality underscores the fact that the perpetrators' motivation has always been in the broadest sense genocidal. That it is nearly always accompanied by efforts to erase the human topography of the ethnically cleansed region – as if those

people never existed – is further confirmation of this intent, while the historically consistent ability to carry out both deportation and culture-obliteration
should, incidentally, remind us of the military-bureaucratic power and organising outreach of *pre-modern* states.[16]

That forced deportations involved the targeting of specific communal
groups must also cause problems for any contention that the extermination or
near-extermination of aggregate populations until the early modern period
was largely a product of *where* they were rather than *who* they were. Certainly,
Roger W. Smith is correct to suggest that the most likely pre-modern cause for
the slaughter of whole communities without regard to age or gender was
because they happened to be in the way of an enemy's military campaign.[17] In
this sense, the obliteration of Baghdad with its 1 million inhabitants by Hul-
agu, one of Genghis' successors in 1258, or Timur's destruction of Isfahan in
1387, or for that matter General Tilly's sack of Magdeburg, in 1631, during
the Thirty Years War, represent only some of the most celebrated, if infamous
examples of indiscriminate massacre, regardless of the social, religious or any
other background of the victims. Besieged towns that refused the terms of the
besiegers – terms which usually involved the sparing of their inhabitants –
knew perfectly well that the laws of war entitled the latter to offer no mercy
thereafter.[18] By the same token, the nature of the majority of traditional polities with their markedly heterogeneous populations, segmental loyalties and
often high degree of localised self-rule, in principle, might appear to mitigate
against either a ruling elite or foreign invader's destruction of communal
groupings on specifically ethnic or religious grounds.

However, we should be wary of assuming that issues of ethnic difference
had no place in the political calculations of those who engaged in traditional
wars of extermination whatsoever. Even if we leave to one side the contentions
of those who argue that exterminatory or sub-exterminatory warfare against
other tribal groups was massively endemic in tribal prehistory and thus the
violent conflicts of the ancient world, had millennia of precedents,[19] the written and broader record associated with Assyria from the eleventh century BC
certainly suggests repeated attempts to eradicate entire collective identities.
True, much of the evidence of this kind points towards the deportation of
quite specific political and cultural elites as well as craftspeople in the wake of
the subjugation of vassal state rebellions rather than 'national' exterminations
tout court. Even then, a programme of massive social engineering, in which as
many as 4.4 million human beings over the following centuries were shifted
around the empire's domains,[20] certainly dissolved one famous identity, that of
the biblical state of Israel (as opposed to that of its southern neighbour, Judah)
in the eighth century BC, while also pointing to more than simply utilitarian

considerations being at the root cause of its actions. Mario Liverani in his studies of the Assyrian state in the context of international power relations in the
ancient Near East, for instance, points towards recurrent anxieties and fears
about the empire's fluid and porous frontiers and margins. Lilliputian states
like Israel and Judah were much less worrisome on this score than the warlike
nomadic peoples of the Central Asian steppes, two of whom, the Medes and
Babylonians, were ultimately responsible for Assyria's total destruction in the
seventh century BC. Liverani's exposition thereby juxtaposes an Assyrian sense
of hubristic self, founded on the sacred order at its reassuring imperial centre,
contrasting with the disorder, chaos and abnormality represented by the
strange, anarchic and incomprehensible sub-humans at its periphery. When
these barbarians sometimes refused to submit to the rule of the centre this was
thus interpreted by the Assyrians not simply as rebelliousness but as the committing of a sinful, mad and unnatural challenge to cosmic harmony.[21]

That the Assyrian response was always to strike out and extirpate this opposition, whatever its actual danger, presents us with the image of an all
powerful hegemon terrified of its own shadow. But it also brings us much
closer to the sort of psychological catalysts that we have already considered as
integral ingredients of modern genocide. Interestingly, the fear of 'otherness'
presenting an alleged threat to societal well-being, combined with the need to
justify its annihilation by extra-political, religious sanction was hardly unique
to the Assyrians in ancient times. As a further case of note, there is the story
related by the Roman historian, Curtius, of the extermination of the Branchidae, in 329 BC, in the course of the conquest of the Persian empire by
Alexander the Great. Again, given the way the Macedonian conqueror had
already cut a murderous swathe through scores of Persian imperial towns and
communities which had resisted his advance, the story of the liquidation of a
single town in an far-away province hardly seems remarkable. Yet this community was not Persian but Ionian Greek – that is, culturally, if not ethnically
akin to Alexander – and, far from resisting him had welcomed his arrival with
libations and olive branches. So why did Alexander mercilessly massacre
them? The Branchidae, it turned out, were the descendants of priests who,
some 150 years earlier, had failed to guard the sacred Greek sanctuary of
Apollo when it fell to the then westward advancing Persians and thereafter
they were forcibly resettled by them in central Asian Bactria. Actually, Alexander's campaign attempted to justify itself as a war of revenge – as ordained
by the gods – not against this particular Persian assault on the Greek world
but against a slightly later and more infamous campaign that included an even
more wholesale destruction of the holiest Greek shrines, Apollo's included.
According to Curtius, however, Alexander *believed* that the Branchidae had

betrayed the sanctuary to the Persians in this later cause célèbre.[22] As a result, the gods were invoked in order to destroy a passive, compliant community who offered no immediate or likely threat to Alexander's agenda on the grounds of their probably mistaken, albeit potent, association with a moment in the distant past when renegade Greeks *had been* the agents of an outside powerful, international constellation ranged against Hellenic 'civilisation'.

The idea of a transmission belt of this nature, in other words, of a notion of the 'sins of the fathers' being tied in with theological injunctions not to forgive but to punish, even if this means killing descendants of an alleged insult, danger or pollution several generations later, suggests a motif hardly specific to any particular period in the human record. That said, its discomforting resonance at least for modern Western man, is greatly amplified by its repeated yet integral outings in the Old Testament:

> When the Lord your God brings you into the land which you are about to enter and to occupy, when He drives out before your face Hittites, Girgashites, Amorites, Canaanites, Perizites, Hivites and Jebusites – seven nations more numerous and more powerful than you – and when the Lord delivers them into your power so that you overcome them, you must exterminate them.[23]

This specific text, from the book of Deuteronomy, refers to the early period when the twelve tribes arrived and began to settle in what they came to know as the land of Israel. What is most interesting about it, however, is not the straightforward utilitarian issue of controlling the land and its resources – the obvious point of departure for conflict – but the way this is markedly heightened if not subsumed in a much more angst-laden tale in which specific prescriptions are made incumbent on the Israelites to burn the sacred altars and sites of their enemies – clearly a rite of cleansing – combined with further orders neither to make peace nor enter into social or sexual relations with them. That similar texts from these chronicles repeatedly return to this question of sexual relations also rather suggests that, far from exterminating all these peoples as commanded in the Lord – Yahweh's – divine injunction, the Israelites were in practice acting very much like other Near Eastern peoples: that is, killing their adversaries' menfolk but enslaving and probably assimilating their women and children.

Here, indeed, is a further ingredient which is not so far from aspects of modern ideologically based genocide. Legitimacy for the Israelites' actions is predicated on a special sense of who they are: a people with an entirely unique God-given identity. Yet in spite of divine commandment to be separate and to behave accordingly, the sexual attraction of the ethnic 'other' repeatedly asserts itself to wreck this agenda. The result, in Numbers 31, is the story of

Moses leading a war of extermination against the Midianities, in Moab, on the grounds that their women have lured the Israelite men into their embrace and thereby encouraged them to participate in sacrifices and worship before the idolatrous god, Ba'al. Objectively speaking, it should seem obvious that if blame is to be meted out at all for these alleged misdemeanours it should be to the craven Israelite men. In the subsequent war, however, the Israelite warriors are required to undergo a purifying ritual not for having killed Midianites but for having defiled themselves through bodily contact with them.[24] When, moreover, in the most unequivocally extirpatory of these Old Testament texts, Samuel 15, the first Israelite king, Saul, is commanded by Yahweh to go and kill all and every last one of the Amalekites and all they possess, 'man and woman, infant and suckling, ox and sheep, camel and ass',[25] the latter's crime is not simply that they are 'an untameable race of savages',[26] but that in the past they were linked to that old enemy, the Midianites. In other words, their crime is a hereditary one.

Of course, these narratives are a mythical rendition of possible events dating back to 1200 BC and, in the absence of precise archaeological data to prove or disprove them, we cannot know how systematically genocidal was the actual nature of the Israelites' warfare with their neighbours. Moreover, the texts themselves provide plenty of grounds for ambiguity. Numbers 31, for instance, avers that while all the men, men-children and many women were killed, the Israelites saved the Midianite virgins and she-children – as well as the nation's plentiful flocks – for themselves, while Saul's failure to carry out Yahweh's injunction to the letter, in Samuel 15, may explain why his successor David is still exterminating Amalekites later on in the biblical narrative. More to the point, the purpose of this exercise has not been to single out the unusual proclivities of the Israelites towards unrestrained massacre when this was clearly an ancient Near Eastern norm. Rather it has been to suggest how the particular justifications for these actions – even possibly where they were not fully committed – have close parallels with their more modern variants. While, thus, the actual competition for land and resources in the Near East of antiquity was undoubtedly intense, these conflicts were regularly presented in terms of the preservation of ethnic identity and national cohesion. Similarly, though theological rationalisations, then as now (in their secularised form), were used as cover for political-economic agendas, more often than not they were fervently, even fanatically accepted as the heart of the matter. On one level, it could not be otherwise, as constraints on killing – the Old Testament as best testament to this – were also embedded in the moral and legal systems of the ancient world and had to be overcome to excuse and justify the act.[27] Indeed, the warriors of antiquity, like the mass murderers of the twentieth century – whether they have committed partial or in rare cases total genocide – have not simply been comforted but driven on in the relentlessness of their killing by the belief that they are engaged in life and death struggles with forces of an unquenchable infection and unmitigated evil.

The Riddle of the Modern Variant

If the point, thus far in this chapter, has been to highlight aspects of human psychology and social or political behaviour which suggest linkage and even continuity between the wars of people-extermination of the distant past and genocides in the historical present, one might well ask what makes this modern variant different? We have already by implication, if not more explicitly, ruled out various possibilities. The *form* that modern genocide takes is not a critical disjuncture, the technological innovation of gas chambers notwithstanding. A Foucauldian discourse on modernity might emphasise the institutionalisation of punishment and the way, for instance, having removed public executions from the spatial foci of everyday life, it has also detached state-legitimised violence from either the common people's gaze or participation.[28] However, while this argument may be convincing in general, not least with regard to the modern state's monopolisation of the apparatus of violence, it works less well with an extraordinary contingency such as genocide where the state very often has to redeploy and redistribute that monopoly through the rapid mobilisation of citizens as active, hands-on participants. This does not mean that genocide does not often take place in out of the way places and sometimes literally off the map, especially when the killing is on the state's unconsolidated domestic or colonial frontier – just as was the case in antiquity. But genocide can equally be committed against people who live in the next valley, the nearest village, or literally next-door. Thus, in such circumstances, far from access to violence being denied to ordinary people, or being mediated through some faceless bureaucracy of state, the onus is actually on them to join in, often with similarly crude implements as were ever available to accomplish such tasks.

Certainly, when one reads of exterminatory wars from the pre-modern record one is regularly struck by the extraordinary levels of cruelty that accompany them. The ninth century BC Assyrian emperor, Ashurnasirpal, after having taken one enemy city had it written in the chronicles '… many of the captives taken from them I burned in a fire. Many I took alive: from some of these I cut off their hands to the wrist, from others I cut off their noses, ears and fingers, I put out the eyes of many of their soldiers … I burnt their young men and women to death'.[29] Some two millennia later the obliteration of the Bulgar threat to the Byzantine empire was inscribed with the blinding of the surviving 15,000 prisoners from the defeated army 'leaving every hundredth man with one eye to guide his companions back to the royal capital at Prespa'.[30] When the cortege reached the capital, the Bulgar king is said to have died of shock. Coming across these atrocity stories many years ago this author was also horribly shocked. Only later, after many similar encounters, did he realise that these were classically utilitarian examples of victorious polities literally putting the fear of god into their opponents or would-be opponents.[31]

Perhaps here one can discern a possible distinction between classical exterminatory warfare and modern genocide. If people are willed to participate in the latter, the notion of some clinical detachment from the act is difficult to swallow. There is a paradox, of course, in the way that modern perpetrators often attempt to cover up the violent heart of what they are doing with terminologies of sanitisation. Yet even these half give the game away. The *noyades* (drownings) of the Vendée, the *nettoyage* (cleansing) of Rwanda and Burundi, even bizarrely (and possibly inadvertently) the way we have adopted 'Holocaust' for the Nazi genocide, a term whose actual Greek origins denotes a sacrificial burnt offering to the gods, all bespeak of efforts by the protagonists to give a deeper meaning to their actions, as if what they are actually engaging in is a form of ritual purification. Cruelty, as ever, remains fundamental to any act of mass hands-on killing.

This does not mean that changing logistics or technologies have not infomed the anatomy of people-extermination. To what extent a new 1870s invention like barbed wire offered a quantum leap in the isolation or concentration of targeted populations is a valid question.[32] Obversely, the degree to which the deployment by modern governments of systematic famine or mass rape as techniques in the perpetration of genocide is evidence of major departures from a deeper record of warfare is also open to debate. Even the marshalling of advanced technologies of communication, so integral to the rationally streamlined infrastructure of the twentieth-century polity, does not necessarily amount to some grand discontinuity. True, much more pedestrian communication systems alongside usually diffused power structures in the past resulted both in considerably longer time-lags with which to mobilise an army of extermination or expedite it to its destination. At the end of the day, however, if Akkadians, Assyrians, or Alexander wanted to exterminate a War Type Two or Type Three enemy they generally had the ability and capacity to do it. Indeed, if Alexander's example is anything to go by, they might even follow their quarry to the ends of the earth,[33] suggesting that, in antiquity at least, what perpetrators lacked in support systems they made up for in willpower.

Thus, if there is a dichotomy between exterminations of people in the modern as opposed to the pre-modern era it does not primarily come down to a question of means. Or, as a logical extension of this line of thought of differing institutional or administrative arrangements between traditional compared with more modern polities. Nor, however, does the scale of killing provide sufficient grounds for discontinuity. Certainly, the last century has been a staggeringly murderous one but it is hardly unique for that. Demographic catastrophes emanating from programmes of state-organised violence have regularly punctuated the human record. State extirpation of the Taiping and other rebellions in China are estimated to have reduced its population from 410 million in 1850, to 350 million in 1873.[34] In the two centuries after the first landing by Columbus in 1492 the demographic profile of the New World, estimated by some scholars to be in the range of 70–100 million – in other words, equivalent to or even greater than contemporary European numbers – collapsed by as much as 90 per cent.[35] Taking into account the general global human population rise of 250 per cent since then, this would make it *homo sapiens'* single greatest demographic disaster.[36] Admittedly, in critical respects the New World catastrophe could be said to be as much about pathogens as policy, European diseases cutting a devastating swathe through the Amerindian population at least as dramatically as plague had done in Eurasia since the first great surge of the 'Black Death', in the late 1340s. But this cannot obviate the fundamental difference that the New World tragedy emerged out of a conscious agenda of European conquest and continent-wide subjugation, resulting in fatalities on a scale so much greater than anything in the Old World record that the resulting demographic reshaping of the Americas, has been described by one perspicacious scholar as 'an ontological attempt to refashion humanity'.[37]

Granted, there may be inexactness in the statistical compilations available for these pre-modern catastrophes. But again this does not offer the basis for a distinct separation from the contemporary record. On the contrary, arguably it invites comparisons. Soviet premier, Khrushchev, asked to give some account of his predecessor Stalin's mass murder programme, once retorted: 'I can't give an exact figure because no one was keeping count: All we knew was that people were dying in enormous numbers.'[38] Even that most sacrosanct of figures associated with genocide – the 6 million of the Jewish Holocaust – is not necessarily exact. As one statistically minded expert quite fairly remarks: 'Although the Germans are noted for their rule-following and record keeping, and the relevant German archives were available after the war and participants could be systematically interviewed, there is still considerable disagreement – a range of over a million – among experts over the number of Jews actually murdered.'[39] If this statement is contentious it is only by dint of the fact that we have invested the 6 million figure in our latter-day heads with the aura of a sacred and hence incontrovertible veracity, and because the Holocaust has come to occupy the centre-stage of Western self-examination and reproach, hence acting as a benchmark by which to judge the scale of other atrocities. In terms of this study, however, its major usefulness might be instead as a warning that numbers of dead, though important, are not by themselves determinants of genocide, or for that matter distinguishing markers between some less grisly past and an all too obviously blood-soaked present.

So, if all these lines of enquiry lead nowhere in particular, why not accept genocide as an aspect of the human condition which has been with us since time immemorial? Lemkin himself would have accepted the proposition; after all, he was trying to right what he perceived to be an atavistic tendency through recourse to a legally *internationalised* modernity. Nor has this examination sought to refute either individual or collective psychological tendencies within the human make-up which, if over-excited under conditions of acute extreme political, societal or cultural stress, are prone to lead to murderously catastrophic results whatever the historical period. All this said, the fullness of the phenomenon we call 'genocide' – as opposed to other forms of mass murder – can only be fully understood and explained within the context of the very dramatic and accelerated process of global historical development we associate most specifically with the rise of the West over the last few hundred years. Or to restate the case in a slightly different way: the specificity of genocide cannot be divorced from the very modern *framework* within which it occurs.

Indeed, what we are proposing here is much more than an amorphous entity called modernity. The framework rather, is an overtly political one, founded on a bedrock of state formation and reformulation under the exigencies of chronic inter-state war initially in a single, core Western European testing ground. The resulting first nation-states were paradigmatic, becoming the model for what would eventually become an interlinked global system. So much so that as Anthony Giddens has stated: 'Nation-states only exist in systemic relations with other nation-states ... International relations is co-eval with the origins of nation-states.'[40] Certainly, the way this emerged cannot in itself explain either the attributes or exact causation of each and every genocide. Nevertheless, one can hardly overemphasise the importance of Giddens' statement for its bearing on our phenomenon at the macro-level. Far from being an act perpetrated in hermetic isolation from other states and societies, what it points to instead is one that is actually an expression of a state regime's relationship with other such polities. Genocide thus remains a state attack on one or more communal populations. But it is also one that emanates from a crisis response to a problem of integrity, or sovereignty, or place, as *perceived* by that state within the international system. This does not always mean that the act is literally directed outwards as much as it is inwards; there are many examples in this study's pages, especially in a colonial context, where this would not apply. That said, not only are all modern genocides perpetrated with an eye to the integrity of the state vis-à-vis other competitor states, the linkage regularly manifests itself in the way that regimes repeatedly accuse the targeted communal population of being collective agents of outside, extra-state forces whose alleged aim is the undermining of the state's own efforts towards covering up, or rectifying its international *weakness*.

Yet again, we are in the realm of the projective, phobic and paranoid and hence a realm where the dichotomy between modern and pre-modern is largely irrelevant. Certainly, because the stakes for state success and survival within the modern system are that much higher than in earlier times the possibilities for forms of collective hysteresis[41] are that much more intense. What is entirely novel, however, is the way the exterminatory potential operates against the grain of emerging system rules which are meant to give to all aggregate populations within each and every nation-state's confines the guarantee of personal security if not necessarily equality and liberty. Indeed, it is exactly on this universal supposition of obligation[42] that the Lemkin thesis came to be propounded. Taking the nation-state model to be normative and hence benign, Lemkin's conceptualisation of genocide as an act outside the framework of the international system of nation-states could thereby be elevated into a *United Nations* Convention aimed at genocide's international outlawing.

Our argument is that precisely the opposite is true. The system is itself a root cause of modern genocide, not least through its self-recognition enshrined in the UNC as a world community of self-determined *sovereign* states.[43] Whereas, however, most Western liberal assumptions are predicated, like Lemkin's, on the system's essential benignity, this in itself provides for a distinctive feature with regard to people-extermination by contemporary states which could not have arisen in pre-modern centuries. This entails a notably schizophrenic attitude towards the act whether viewed from the perspective of perpetrator or bystander states.

Of course, it is absolutely correct that in parallel to the Western creation of the nation-state system there has evolved a post-Enlightenment human rights discourse which has informed the system and led, over a period of time, to its acceptance of a rule-book of ideas and values, inscribed in a series of international conventions, the most important of which is the 1948 UN Declaration of Human Rights, and to which the UNC arguably stands as a critical adjunct. One might wish to dispute whether these developments are actually the result of the system *per se* when it has actually been jurists and campaigners like Lemkin himself actively working in favour of the idea of an international *society*. The distinction is actually a very important one, not least given that the behaviour of the 'system' is primarily determined by hegemonic interests, compared to that of a legally regulated and convention-bound 'society' where the primacy is that of (an otherwise system-dependent) United Nations. Even so, the very nominal subscription of the system to a regime of human rights instruments as propounded by the institutions of international society – and the general erroneous confusion between the two[44] – have tended to assist the notion that the system *qua* system both repudiates and criminalises acts of genocide.

The result is that, whereas in the past state-perpetrators were able to publicly proclaim the political and even theologically ordained legitimacy of their actions and celebrate the consequences – Roger Smith, for instance, notes the Assyrian predilection for stelae, bas-reliefs and obelisks as well as public festivals and sacrifices to commemorate the extirpation of their enemies[45] – such openly, self-congratulatory behaviour is expressly disallowed in the modern context. Equally marginalised, however, is self-exoneration. On paper the committing of genocide is as morally unacceptable as it is internationally illegal – whatever the circumstances – and so the modern protagonists of exterminatory power have indeed been forced into entirely new modes of behaviour. Henceforth, genocide is always presented to the world as something other than what it is: as 'civil war, the destruction of terrorists, or the repulsion of external invasion'.[46] Alternatively, it has to be dressed up as something being done for the targeted group's own good and protection, 'resettlement' being the favoured Ottoman and Nazi euphemism. This entirely surreal tendency at its most extreme can even lead, usually as a matter of posthumous justification, to claims that the victim group never existed – or at least certainly not in significant numbers – on the territory of their 'alleged' extirpation.[47] Whatever the story, forceful denial often linked to vigorous efforts at dissembling or obliterating the evidence, most obviously in the form of masses of unburied bodies, is a distinctly modern if standard perpetrator practice.

However, this hardly exhausts the paradoxical and with it schizophrenic tendencies peculiar to the modern variant. Subterfuge and disinformation may be the perpetrators' preferred strategy for avoiding international public attention or at least obviating its censure. Yet once we have arrived in the twentieth century, acts of genocide are also very often intended as a conscious shot across the bows not only of international society but of the system itself. This would not have fully applied when the system only comprised a handful of prototypical Western states. With its emerging crystallisation in the post-1914 era, however, genocide almost by definition became an adjunct of aggrieved regimes claiming to seek redress from the perceived ills or failings of the system, either by circumventing its rules, avoiding them, or simply tearing them up with a view to denying the validity or the system's right to impinge on their state sovereignty or independent action. Yet one obvious paradox in this situation is that no twentieth-century state has openly challenged the criminality of the act by broadcasting its perpetration. On the contrary, genocide has become specifically associated with the avoidance of 'normal' administrative or politico-military procedures in favour of extraordinary, emergency or extra-judicial measures. And, for that matter, it is usually carried out in the greatest secrecy. Even when the evidence of what a government is doing filters out, the public visage remains one of absolute denial, buttressed by official statements or communiqués of outraged *amour-propre* when accusations are levelled against it. Only in private do chief perpetrators acknowledge and articulate their true feelings, thereby linking them with the unrepentant mass murderers of the past. Both leading CUP players and members of the SS Ahnenerbe organisation founded by Himmler, for instance, identified closely with Genghis Khan.[48] Hitler's embrace of Genghis is equally revealing. In an infamous secret speech to his senior Wehrmacht commanders in August 1939, just prior to the onslaught on Poland, he is said to have proclaimed:

> Our strength is in our quickness and our brutality. Genghis Khan had millions of women and children killed by his own will and with a gay heart. History sees only in him a great state builder … . Thus, for the time being I have sent to the East only my 'Death Heads Units' with the order to kill without pity or mercy all men, women and children of Polish race or language. Only in such a way will we win the vital space that we need. Who still talks nowadays of the extermination of the Armenians?[49]

If this statement seems to starkly and chillingly confirm Lemkin's great fear that genocide represents a return to some ancient barbarism, there is here, however, a second, arguably equally chilling, certainly entirely schizophrenic paradox concerning its more pointed relationship to modern times. The system, in principle, has been committed to a repudiation of genocide. Yet at the same time the very reason the system exists in the shape that it does is because it is beneficial to its members, most particularly those Western states who were both its founding fathers and the ones who continue to control, direct,

regulate and where necessary enforce its will in the pursuit of their own hegemonic self-interest. Rather than this amounting to a best defence against mass
murder, however, Leo Kuper's sober assessment referred to in our first chapter,
has, at least until very recently, been largely an accurate one.[50] The system has
colluded with genocide because to do otherwise would have been massively to
destabilise the sophistry upon which the system rides: namely, that it is a global family of bounded but equally independent sovereign states. While, thus,
acts of genocide are mostly committed by states challenging or defying the
system ground rules, the system leaders themselves – that is those who have
the power to respond – have either condoned, or turned a blind eye, or in
some cases, even covertly abetted such acts in complete contradiction of their
own UNC rubric.

The long-term consequence has been that while attacks on the territorial
integrity of a nation-state by one or more others have been treated as a griev-
ous violation of the system-rules, with a very few notable exceptions – usually
where criminal charges have been brought within the context of a War Type
One situation – the system leaders have gone to inordinate lengths to obfus-
cate or obviate accusations of domestic genocide made against fellow but
usually lesser states. The added irony is that this conscious international acqui-
escence in the face of genocide is as much what gives the phenomenon its
peculiarly modern aspect as the actions of the perpetrator regimes themselves.
Indeed, in a critical sense what we witness here are two sides of the same damaged coin. On the one, the perpetrators have been those seeking means with
which to either beat or wreck the system but without going public on their
genocidal actions. On the other, the system's guardians have been those seeking to deflect the challenge by doing nothing about it, or pretending that
nothing amiss has occurred. Additionally, of course, they may have been further hesitant to make a cause out of the issue for the simple reason that this
might highlight a tranche of historic cases where they themselves might be
found guilty.

Of course, it may be that this situation is now fundamentally changing. The
rise of the United States as hegemonic superpower and with it of a New World
Order (sic.) may be the basis for a different sort of international system in
which the genocidal potentiality exhibited by some states – if not necessarily
others – will be rigorously policed or punished. Alternatively, though much
less probably, the creation of the UN *ad hoc* tribunals on former Yugoslavia and
Rwanda as well as the founding of the International Criminal Court suggest
an international society route through which the inviolability of the genocidally inclined could be more vigorously monitored and challenged. Our concern
here, however, is not to speculate about these future prospects but rather to

determine the exact relationship between genocide and nation-states within an international system of such states in the recent past.

Plotting a Pattern

Two problems immediately arise. First, is it really nation-states who are the fundamental transmitters of genocide? The question is pointed because it assumes that fixed, stable political entities operating according to that approximate description are our primary if sole culprits. Yet in the course of these four volumes the diversity of political entities encountered will be rather marked. There will be self-governing colonial administrations, in some cases run by chartered companies who are technically subordinate and accountable to metropolitan governments thousands of miles away. There will be communist regimes that, because they ostensibly repudiate nationalism as a 'false consciousness', would not seem obviously to fit the appellation 'nation-state' at all. Then, too, there are newly formed, protean or putative states whose de facto existence may be so precarious that *de jure* recognition by the prime arbiters of the international system may be withheld or withdrawn. Cases such as the Ukraine, in 1918–19, or Denikin's Southern Russian administration from this same Russian civil war period, themselves become interesting as well as perplexing because the systematic anti-Jewish massacres perpetrated by their retreating armies also raise questions about the capacity of imploding or 'failed' states to commit genocide.

But then what of instances where authority does not appear to lie with the state but some other locus of power? In 1965 Indonesia it was the military high command, operating on its own volition – albeit under crisis – rather than that of the state *per se* which organised genocidal massacres. The notion that rogue elements, for instance, within the secret intelligence services, might act either behind the back or in wilful opposition to government, has also been propounded by Rummel, arguably as a way of distancing Western and more specifically US democracy from complicity in genocide.[51] Dadrian has gone further by arguing that the 'normative' state's genocidal potential can only be realised if it is first hijacked by a party consciously and conspiratorially intent on utilising for its own nefarious ends the state's machinery.[52] All five of our primary perpetrators would certainly seem to fall within this pattern. That said, the very desire to capture the political, administrative and judicial apparatus would also seem to confirm that regimes, whatever their political colouring, need states however strong, or weak they might be, to perpetrate the act.

That surely must lead one to ask what are the specific contexts in which intolerable pressures build up within specific states to lead to their radical reformulation, metamorphosis or even extinction. In other words, crisis conditions out of which genocide might emanate. This takes us to our second problem. If the aim here remains to demonstrate that acts of genocide are committed by polities within the framework of an emerging international formulation of such states *as* nation-states it would seem to require some empirical data or other evidence to show how the relationship over time or space has worked. But again lining up our key cases: Nazi Germany, Ottoman Turkey, Rwanda, the Soviet Union under Stalin, and Khmer Rouge Cambodia, and it will be obvious that dissimilarities between these polities, societies and cultures massively outweigh any obviously discernible similarities. How, for instance, can one begin to compare the stunningly poor, largely rural, underdeveloped not to say Lilliputian post-colonial backwater of Rwanda with a giant of an advanced, industrial, heavily urbanised and extremely powerful, centre-stage, international actor such as Germany? Adding a second tier of major twentieth-century perpetrators to our equation would hardly advance clarification. What, after all, do China, Indonesia, Pakistan, Bangladesh, Burma, Iraq, Burundi, Ethiopia, the Sudan, Romania, Croatia, Serbia or Guatemala[53] exactly have in common other than being signed up members of the United Nations club?

There are possible ways in which we might seek to interpret this information. In terms of political geography, for instance, we might note that there has been less *recent* genocide in the Americas (remembering that it has played host to plenty of other types of mass killing and structural violence) than in Africa or Asia, while a lot of the overall incidence has been in regional clusters: the Great Lakes region of east-central Africa, the north Caucasus, eastern Anatolia, the western Russian borderlands, the Balkans, or on the hill margins of south-east Asia. This might suggest a reading of genocide that again is less state-bound and more nuanced towards ethnographic and other regional variations. Morever, the fact that these 'zones of genocide'[54] are notably heterogeneous in ethno-religious and linguistic terms, yet also cross modern national state boundaries, is surely significant when one considers, for instance, that in eastern Anatolia, both Turkey and Iraq have committed genocide against the dominant Kurdish population on both sides of the international border. On the other hand, the fact that these two states are also notable recidivists, who have made genocidal assaults on a number of other distinct communities, both in eastern Anatolia and beyond, would tend to detract from an approach based on ethnic interactions *alone* in favour of a broader survey of these states' overall national development. The lack of synchronicity between Turkey's great genocidal surge, between 1915 and the late 1930s, and the peak of Iraq's comparable activities, in the late 1980s, would also seem to demand a more precise chronological input to our hypothesis before we are able reach any convincing conclusions.

Such a broad chronological plot – alongside that of geographical locations – would necessarily be geared towards drawing parallels between the emergence and changing contours of the international system and the actual incidence of genocide. That immediately raises questions about the origins of the system and indeed whether its formation should be traced back to the European inter-state competition of the early modern period, from c. 1500, or even three or four centuries earlier still, to the very shaping of the medieval European state system, not least through colonisation and conquest.[55] By the same token, it would raise some difficult questions about where and when we would locate the first genocides or at least proto-genocides associated with this trajectory. However, whether we choose to argue for Ireland in the seventeenth century, the Canaries in the fifteenth, or for that matter Prussia in the thirteenth, as our quintessential starting point, the longer time period certainly offers us a rather different perspective on the carriers of genocide than if we were to restrict ourselves to the twentieth century.

In the time of intense nation-state formation, specifically in the late eighteenth and early nineteenth centuries, for instance – itself closely related to the rise of the West as a world system[56] – arguably the two most notable repeat-perpetrators of genocide were Britain and the United States. The geographical relationship is again important, as incidences of genocide would appear to relate closely to regions on their domestic or colonial frontiers where state consolidation remained incomplete, or where expansion continued to be contested by native peoples. That said, as the old system of world empires began to implode or disintegrate in the face of the Western advance, we also find some of these traditional polities also committing the act. The fact that, as radically reformulated entities in the twentieth century: Russia (USSR) China (People's Republic of China) and the Ottoman empire (Turkey) again were notable perpetrators, sometimes specifically involving renewed exterminatory assaults on the peoples of frontier regions as in the previous century or two, might suggest, moreover, an essential continuity of state geo-strategic policies – or, more accurately, sensitivities – regardless of the radical change of regimes.

Political transformation may clearly be an important variable, particularly when it is closely associated with crisis. The revolutionary emergence of modern France, which many would consider the first authentic nation-state, has, as its corollary, the extirpation of the Vendée revolt, considered, in Volume II, as a major staging post in an emergence of modern genocide. Again, the genocide plot we might associate with the emergence of authentic Western nation-states in the period from the 1800s through to the outbreak of the First World War is to be found post-Vendée, not in conflicts in their metropolitan heartlands but rather on their extreme colonial peripheries. Indeed, the contrast between the absence of genocide in Europe, before 1914, and the crescendo of genocidal assaults in response to native resistance in Africa, Asia and the Pacific at the *fin-de-siècle* highpoint of the Western imperialist surge, is very noteworthy. Again it would suggest that the real crises of the avant-garde states (by this time a much extended, mostly European, ménage) and hence of their relationships to the emerging international system were at points not of strength but of implicit weakness; that is where their expansionist projects were most prone to challenge: either from native forces holding onto what was left of their traditional autonomies, or, for that matter, from their other imperial competitors.

If this is transparent evidence of the acute destabilisation wrought on discrete, often relatively self-contained pre-modern societies through the advent of Western dominance on the global stage, all this nevertheless precedes the creation of a 'normative' interconnected world system of nation-states. The co-relationship between the first intense phase of this particular development in the era of the two global wars (1914–45), and a great wave of mega-genocides is thus of crucial significance. Important too is the fact that the loci of these genocides lack a truly colonial dimension, being much more associated with processes of immediate state building and social engineering. Necessarily we associate these trajectories most obviously with the massive upheavals and attempts at radical societal reformulation in Nazi Germany, the USSR and late Ottoman, or post-Ottoman Turkey, all of which provide classic examples of revisionist polities resisting or challenging the nation-state system as reconfigured and extended by the victorious Western allies after the First World War. Closer examination in Volume III of this study, however, will suggest a wider set of such revisionist states which committed genocides: in some instances acting quasi-autonomously under Nazi aegis, as in the case of Romania and Croatia in the period 1941–2, and in others, such as that of early 1930s Iraq, making a specific point of their new-found status as independent national entities in defiance of Western supervision.

What is significant overall about the range of these genocides, however, is the way they are essentially circumscribed by the political-cum-geographical dimensions of the nation-state system as it existed at this point. Only states that saw themselves contesting an implicit Western domination of it in some shape or form, primarily in Central or Eastern Europe, or in the newly formulated 'Middle East' become archetypal genocide perpetrators. Nevertheless, these were all states which potentially had the right to be recognised within the system if they so chose to accept its terms. Colonial peoples in the pre-1945 Western empires were clearly outside this universe. Only after the Second World War and, more specifically, in the era of European post-colonial retreat did genocide become a truly global phenomenon, most obviously facilitated through the extension of the Western-created concept of the nation-state to all hemispheres, and with it of the embrace of the entire world's population as citizens of such states within its international nation-state framework.

There is, of course, something doubly paradoxical about the near-culmination of this process. As we have already suggested, it enabled the creation of a UN and through it of a UNC umbrella under which the act of genocide became internationally outlawed. Yet, at the same time, the very creation of a mass of newly independent sovereign nation-states recognised as authentic system members provided the most obvious and persuasive goad for the commencement and then acceleration of their own agendas towards people-homogenisation. That this could lead to the most extreme measures was demonstrated even as the UNC was being formulated, through the violent expulsion and/or murder of excess millions of Germans from Poland and Czechoslovakia as these nation-states refound their original 1919 Western-granted independence after the Second World War.[57] The precedent was ominous. The post-colonial world of nation-states would be particularly characterised by dominant ethnic groups and the marginalisation of others as ethnic 'minorities', vastly exacerbating the potential either for ethnic struggles to reshape the unitary nation-state or, alternatively, to attempts at ethnic territorial secession by subordinate groups, usually leading in turn to violent, if not genocidal, resistance by the dominant majority.

One could counter that these tendencies had less to do with the international system *per se* than with the particulars or peculiarities of specific newly created polities. In the same way, one might also argue that the underlying toxicity associated with so much of the violence of the post-1945 third world was heavily determined by the way the US versus Soviet bi-polar struggle intruded into all spheres of human interaction. It is absolutely correct to posit that much of the genocide of this period was a result of social or ethnic communities being literally caught up as proxies in these Cold War machinations. But neither was this entirely monocausal. Tribal peoples at the remote frontiers or inaccessible regions of, for instance, central America or south-east Asia often found themselves willing enlistees in pro-communist or, alternatively, pro-'free world' militias because they were already seriously marginalised, threatened and/ or immiserated by the diktats of sovereign states intent on the control and consolidation of their land and resources. In other words, they were sidelined by modernising agendas which had become the norm everywhere because these had become the recognised and accepted post-colonial price of participation in a global political economy. Even the very attempt to create alternative, avowedly non-national, political systems, in the form of the Communist blocs (both Soviet and Chinese) – thus carrying with them their own immense potential for mass violence against internal dissenting populations – were primarily shaped and determined as conscious counters to the dominant Western model.

However, the end of the official Cold War, with the collapse of the USSR in 1990–1 signalling both the apparent triumph of the West and of the dominant mode of state-organisation around the idea of the 'nation', perplexingly and again paradoxically did not lead to a cessation of genocide. On the contrary, its incidence or potential incidence appeared to be re-ignited not only in locations where it had been dormant since the Second World War or earlier, including in the trans-Caucasian margins of the USSR, and in the imploding Yugoslav entity, but also, most devastatingly of all, in Rwanda. So what, might one ask, has any of this to do with relationships between, on the one hand, nation building or state formation and, on the other, pressures emanating from an already well-established international system?

Disputing the Pattern

Why not, for instance, simply concede that in the place of some overarching framework each case of genocide is explicable within a matrix of primarily domestic socio-economic, political, cultural and environmental interactions specific unto itself? Thereby, one is different from the next, and that next different from a third, the only commonality being an outcome of extermination or attempted extermination of some defined population group. Michael Vickery, for instance, reviewing the causes of the Khmer Rouge regime has pronounced that 'foreign relations and influences are very nearly irrelevant to an understanding of the internal situation';[58] a launching pad from which to posit that what happened in Cambodia was specific to the conditions and culture of that country and should not be directly related or compared with anything else. Perhaps, one could go further in support of Vickery – who pointedly refuses to countenance that what happened in Cambodia was genocide – and argue that the very usage of the term carries expectations which simply are not supportable. After all, just because we have gone to the trouble of attempting a definition it does not have to signify that its basic common features necessarily prove each example to be figures in the same large canvas.

Actually, on one level, Vickery's position is an isolated one. The general wisdom of leading comparativists in the field is to provide a template for what genocide is, and then to posit a range of categories into which individual examples – Cambodia included – might be placed. Fein, for instance, proposes a four-fold developmental, despotic, retributive and ideological typology. The 'developmental' refers to genocides committed against indigenous people who have not yet been integrated into the majority culture and stand in the way of the economic exploitation of resources. The 'despotic' relates to those where a strong man attempts to monopolise power, usually in a new, untried but ethnically diverse, post-colonial state by, in effect, 'getting his retaliation in first' against real or potential bidders for power, and with the 1970s Ugandan dictator, Idi Amin, as the obvious archetype. The 'retributive' would seem similar to the 'despotic' but with an emphasis on examples – Fein cites the military-organised genocides in East Pakistan in 1971, and Burundi in 1972 – where the state unleashes its vengeance against genuine rebellion or political dissent. Finally, 'ideological' genocides are those motivated by regimes with strong, if not all-encompassing prejudices or grievances against minority groups who then set about their destruction as a quasi-religious injunction with Fein particularly having in mind the Holocaust and the *Aghet*.[59]

This sort of categorisation, however, in a different sense follows the Vickery premise in the way that it avoids either the connecting threads between genocides or countenance of the possibility that there might be very general structural or systemic underpinnings to the phenomenon overall. Instead, genocides are decipherable as the outcome of varied, essentially localised causes – even if they can then be put into discrete categories – rather than the 'developmental', 'retributive' or 'ideological', being treated as facets of what is identifiable in all genocides, not to say dependent on preconditions which are general rather than specific. Suffice to say this author does not adopt this model. This does not mean, in fairness to Fein, that her typology does not have a heuristic value, not least when she herself has pointed out that it is not intended to amount to hard and fast categories.[60] By the same token, she and most other comparativists certainly offer partial or more accurately serial explanations for the causes and processes of genocide. Nevertheless, in many cases the principle desire to get to the heart of the matter is often tempered by a perhaps understandable reluctance not to be seen to be putting all one's eggs into a single basket.

Leo Kuper, for instance, while refuting an all-embracing theory of genocide clearly had his hunch as to what was at its 'structural base'.[61] This pointed back in his view to what – following the work of J. S. Furnivall – he called the plural society, that is one where the relationships between two or more usually ethnic groups is marked by distinctions not only of culture but also of respective position with regard to access to and control over political power. The processes of African decolonisation in the 1960s and 1970s, where the recurrent legacy of the departing colonisers was exactly such ethnically diverse polities, usually resulted in the domination by one tribal or ethnic grouping over one or more others. A close observer of this process, Kuper foresaw outcomes where ensuing struggles for the redistribution of that power might lead, in the most extreme of these situations, to the wholesale extirpation of the subordinate by the dominant group. Certainly, recent surveys of post-1945 genocides, have produced findings which would appear to corroborate aspects of Kuper's thesis and worst fears, one important nuance in that of Fein being that the danger of genocide is at its greatest when the dominant group might be on the cusp of conceding some of its power monopoly to its contenders.[62]

The problem is that Kuper's predilection for this model led him to consider a range of cases of ethno-class domination including apartheid in South Africa, Protestants vis-à-vis Catholics in Northern Ireland, plus diverse inter-ethnic conflicts in 1947 India, 1960s Nigeria, and the Lebanon of the 1970s and early 1980s, which, while involving either considerable violence or mass death, rather distract attention away from consciously organised state programmes of communal extermination. This certainly does not negate in entirety the value of this approach. Kuper's emphasis on the centrality of a two-way dynamic of conflict, developed by Fein as an issue of competition rather than simple static domination,[63] plus its empirical observation of the many cases where such conflicts develop an acute toxicity – often in post-colonial circumstances of marked transition – offer important insights into some necessary elements and contours of genocide. Yet given that most modern societies are to greater or lesser degrees 'plural' – notwithstanding their usually desired intention to be homogeneous – and that many of these are not overtly genocidal though not necessarily lacking in symptoms of mass structural violence and even serious ethnic conflict, there has to be a question mark over how far we can travel on this single track. The fact that some of the most serious cases of genocide such as the Holocaust, the extirpation of the kulaks and Khmer Rouge atrocities are hardly amenable to this interpretation at all, moreover, leaves little option but to create a typology of categories which Kuper, like Fein and others, ultimately employ.

Offering Different Explanations:
Totalitarianism and the Revolutionary State

The tendency towards categorisation does not mean that there are not experts who have thrown caution to the winds in favour of a single common denominator. For instance, the sheer scale and totality of major genocides has certainly led some to argue that the phenomenon is primarily an outcome of 'totalitarianism'. This concept, which enjoyed considerable vogue in Western academic circles in the Cold War era, owes much to the work of the German-Jewish political philosopher, Hannah Arendt. According to Arendt, totalitarian regimes differ from others not only in their desire to have complete control over the political, social and economic lives of their inhabitants but in their willingness to use the apparatus of state as an instrument with which to perpetually terrorise these inhabitants into complete submission to their will. Arendt acknowledges that the politics of the *demos* is part of the route by which such regimes capture power, but, having achieved it, their aim is not a 'normal' state function of achieving limited goals but one governed by ideological imperatives aimed at 'transcending' such limitations. This is, in effect, what makes the two most obvious models for the 'totalitarian' thesis – Nazism or communism – more similar than different. In this way the incongruent content of their two ideologies – the one governed by a 'law of nature' worldview in which race is all, compared with the latter where class struggle is the driving force of history – is not allowed to stand in the way of the basic congruence of their 'totalising' agendas. As a result, the drive to mass murder is a logical consequence in both systems, the victims 'chosen without reference to individual actions or thoughts, exclusively in accordance with the objective necessity of the natural or historical process'.[64]

It is this tendency to pick and choose 'enemies of the people' almost at random, however, that makes the totalitarian–genocide equation a less than perfect fit. In so doing, it greatly strengths the case for Rummel's much broader and less specific democide framework. Thus, while Arendt's historical analysis of anti-Semitism leading to Jewish destruction under the Nazis – and its potentiality under Stalinism – is linked to assumptions of the need to find a scapegoat for national and political failings, this constituting either the actuality or possibility of genocide, a wide range of other Nazi victims would include the mentally and physically disabled, as well as homosexuals, whom one would be hard-pressed to place within our rubric. Stalinist Russia is actually even more problematic as, alongside specifically targeted national groups, are a whole range of people incarcerated in the Gulag, or directly murdered because they were POWs or slave labourers under the Germans during the war, party members who had followed a particular line or been supporters of a particular party boss who belatedly – perhaps twenty years on – had been denounced as deviant, or simply those who had at some stage lived abroad or had had foreign acquaintances.[65] Intriguingly, while these features might underscore the proclivity for 'totalitarian' regimes to conjure up collective or communal enemies, thus providing grounds for their inclusion as genocides, one cannot circumvent Rummel's implicit insight that a great deal of these mass killings cannot possibly be categorised as such. Nor, nevertheless, can one deny that the chief regimes that he ascribes as totalitarian; namely Soviet Russia, Communist China and Nazi Germany, have been far and away the prime mass murderers of the twentieth century.

The problem, however, with the totalitarian argument – at least so far as this thesis is concerned – is three-fold. First, as already implied, it cannot provide a streamlined, explanatory template for genocide. It would leave out many key perpetrator regimes, such as the Turkish CUP or their Kemalist successors, whom Rummel would consider authoritarian rather than totalitarian, while ignoring acknowledged totalitarian ones such as East Germany which clearly – in spite of massive police surveillance of ordinary peoples' daily lives – was neither a democide nor genocide perpetrator. Secondly, the very conceptualisation of 'totalitarian' as if we are dealing with an utterly distinct mode of governance at complete odds with some normative presumably Western liberal model, is both unconvincing, not to say ahistorical. As students of, for instance, Nazism have been pointing out for years, while Nazism smashed parliamentarianism and with it any system of checks and balances on untrammelled government, drove democratic opposition underground and bent a juridical order founded on the notion of Germany as a *Rechtsstaat* (constitutional state), to its own perverted will, for the majority of Germans Nazism was neither vastly intrusive nor even overtly coercive in matters of their normal daily lives: certainly not when one compares it with a genuinely extreme example such as the Khmer Rouge or, for that matter, Shaka's Zulu kingdom. There was, albeit limited, scope for individual autonomy. More to the point, however, the majority did not feel pressurised on this score as the very strong base of popular support for the regime precluded the need for secret or uniformed police on every street corner,[66] an aspect, incidentally, in marked contrast to a regime such as Francoist Spain,[67] which Rummel would consider as an example of the less onerous authoritarian type. Moreover, Rummel's idealised notion of 'totalitarian governments as the contemporary embodiment of absolute Power'[68] would have to contend with the fact that during the Second World War, for example, Nazi Germany – with its well-attested polycratic nature, replete with administrative departments and organisations vying with, overlapping and often duplicating functions – was positively shambolic by comparison with the centralised, tightly controlled planning of manpower, resources, information and so on of supposedly liberal, democratic Britain.[69] Even in the case of Stalin's Russia, increasing access to the Soviet archives has led to a recent, notably iconoclastic historical revisionism highlighting the degree to which not only was this supposedly tightly controlled police-regime and 'command' economy utterly disorganised and persistently inchoate but even the great waves of purges seem to have developed less as thought-out, centrally preconceived programmes and rather more as reactive, on-the-hoof responses to perceived, if usually wildly imagined threats to the state's integrity.[70]

None of this is to fault Rummel's contention as to the 'mega'-murderousness of the Soviet regime – even with the proviso of the revisionists that the actual numbers killed may have to be significantly downgraded.[71] Nor is it to somehow shift the blame, as *The Great Soviet Encyclopedia* once attempted in its brazenly monocausal depiction of genocide as 'an offshoot of decaying capitalism',[72] as if the 'alternative' communist system as led by the USSR was not somehow in the vanguard of its operation. However, the encyclopedia's statement does, quite inadvertently from its intention, have a certain merit. For it raises the third and arguably most myopic weakness in the totalitarian thesis, namely the place of such states within the dominant, normative and 'liberal' international system. Neil Gregor cogently posits mass support for fascism emerging 'out of a series of crises of capitalism and a concomitant crisis of bourgeois liberalism, albeit one conditioned strongly by the specific cultural impact of the First World War'.[73] The statement is equally applicable to communism. In other words, it is insufficient to consider simply what is perceived as a totalitarian deviation by way of juxtapostion with a liberal-universalist norm but rather requires study and explanation as something emanating out of the latter's very own dysfunction.

Thus, a further key question that must arise out of this liberal state–totalitarian state dichotomy is one of the comparable coherence and strength of the latter compared with the former. Are states of the totalitarian variety so absolutely unfettered in their power and so in control as Rummel assumes them to be, or is their persistent recourse to overt, mass violence actually the most telling statement of the fact that they are not only very unsure of themselves but wrestling with some innate or systemic febrility? After all, if these states were genuinely strong they would be hardly likely to throw up regimes driven by the need to transcend the limitations upon them at all. They would rather be, and as Arendt constantly reiterated, founded on the rule of law, dealing with their internal problems through duly authorised and constituted bodies emanating from and with a popular democratic mandate from civil society, acting where need be against those who persistently transgressed their social rules, according to open, publicly recognised and agreed procedures. If this may be an idealisation in itself, it is clearly something which totalitarian states could never hope to be, except by abolishing themselves. The best they might conceivably achieve in its place would be some form of internal pacification. The one thing, however, that they could not be would be societies at basic peace with themselves.

Yet if we were to apply this rule to genocide perpetrators in the broad sense, regardless of the type of nomenclature we might ascribe to them, the same general contours would hold. States that commit genocides are almost by definition not only ones lacking a sound and stable underpinning but subject to acute convulsions. We have already noted the close relationship between genocide and one such destabilising factor, namely external war. A further sure sign of weakness – very often itself emanating from war – is revolution. This is Robert Melson's starting point for his important comparative study of the *Aghet* and Holocaust.

Melson has not been alone in drawing upon the comparison in these specific cases[74] but his specific strength has been in establishing a particularly strong historically contextualised framework for his study. Thus, the revolutionary elites who capture power, both in 1908 Ottoman Turkey, and in 1933 Weimar Germany, and then drive their respective polities towards a further nemesis of war and genocide, are only able to do so because of the quite extraordinary concatenation of circumstances which enable their success in the first place. Similarly, the high degrees of popular receptiveness – albeit more in some sections of society than in others – to their radical proposals, including their virulently xenophobic nationalism is also a critical reflection of the extremity of the situation. Once in power, however, our untried and inexperienced protagonists are able to promote their extreme ideology as the essential glue for their programmes aimed at reasserting state power and resolving its societal crisis through a revolutionary style social and political transformation. The corollary is that this can only arise by reference to communal – in Melson's view, pariah – 'outgroups' who are accused of malevolence to the new, all-encompassing national project, both by dint of their alleged record of past transgressions against the nation's existence as well as their predictable efforts to sabotage its future hopes of redemption. The rest of the Melson thesis thus more or less falls into place behind this basic argument. With the resurrected nation defined and legitimised in large part by reference to its anti-national 'enemy', all it really requires is a renewed bout of external war instigated by the regime for the achievement of its ideologically driven, revolutionary goals, for genocide to be activated.

The thesis is certainly both bold in its attempt to offer an overriding explanation yet also astute in narrowing down its field to a handful of 'total' cases where the relationship with revolution and war is most acute. Thus, while the argument also owes something to Arendt's work on totalitarianism, and in particular its emphasis on ideology as a tool for transcendent empowerment, it also recognises that this alone cannot account for a total genocide such as that committed by a CUP-led Ottoman Turkey, not least when, according to the totalitarianism advocates, the 1915 empire lacked 'totalitarian' criteria. If this represents further grounds for disputing the value of the concept in the first place, Melson's own response is to seek an alternative conceptual framework which he finds in the work of Theda Skocpol.[75] Here Melson potentially engages a guide who might be very useful. Skocpol's work on revolutions and in particular the causes of the French, Russian and Chinese versions is at its most suggestive for our argument, not so much in its emphasis on the role of grass-roots social classes in fomenting revolutions from below, as in pinpointing aspects of the broader international environment which might help catalyse such tendencies. Indeed, at a critical point in his own thesis Melson articulates Skolpol's findings thus: 'The causes of modern social revolutions are linked to the spread of capitalism and the modern state on a world stage. Old regimes that are "situated in disadvantaged positions within international arenas" in the sense of being militarily backward or politically dependent are especially vulnerable.'[76]

It is at this juncture that Melson comes closest to deciphering the bigger picture. But, by binding his thesis on the cause of total genocide to revolution and revolutionaries, he somewhat overlooks the possibility that interactions between ostensibly 'disadvantaged' states and an increasingly hegemonic international system might in itself be at the root of our phenomenon *with or without revolution*. All such regimes, after all, whether we choose to use the term revolutionary or not – and there are certainly grounds for disputing whether CUP or Nazis really meet these criteria[77] – were bent on ambitious projects of massive state and societal transformation, whose take-off can be located in their cadres' direct experience of conditions of acute societal dislocation and collective trauma. Practically all genocide experts are in agreement that such 'difficult life conditions'[78] are a major element in the formulation of the genocidal perpetrator's mind, even if – as in the Rwandan case thirty years on from the moment of revolution – the actual crystallisation of this state of mind into the actuality of genocide may require a further spur in which the original transformative ideal is finally and irrevocably confronted with a defining moment of crisis. This also, of course, raises further questions as to the degree to which a 'revolutionary' regime can remain so many years down the line, though this in itself would again not preclude a genocidal reaction from a government which refuses to come to terms with the redundancy of its own, or its predecessor's, visionary message.

However, the really important question here is whether these various transformative projects emerge out of entirely domestic conditions or as a response to a single extrinsic source; for which the simplest term is 'the rise of the West'. It is certainly curious that until very recently almost no major genocide scholar, monocausalist or otherwise, with the fleeting exception of Melson was prepared to engage properly with this possibility.[79] At first sight this is all the more curious given that the vast majority of scholars working in this field are Westerners. But perhaps, on reflection, this myopia is not so odd. Looked at from the standpoint of 'the West' genocide is something which happens 'out there', the product of societies that lack the civic institutions, the separation of executive and legislative branches, and above all the democratic, liberal traditions which act as a bulwark against the overwhelming and untrammelled power of the state and, hence, of its genocidal tendency. It is not, then, that Western states are incapable of committing genocide or have not in the past done so. Horowitz, for example, acknowledges systematic US extermination of the Native Indians. But he also offers an eight category measurement of political societies, with genocidal at one end and tolerant and permissive at the other, the strong inference of which is that 'systems' which offer the fullest basis for pluralistic, democratic participation also offer the surest grounds for genocide avoidance.[80] Rummel is more forthright still. Democracies do not go to war with one another, and they only commit mass killing or support it by others when this is 'carried out in secret behind a conscious cover of lies and deceits'.[81] By implication, if Western states commit genocide it must be a regrettable oversight, whereas if carried out by 'totalitarian' ones it is par for the course. Indeed, if we were to develop this tenor of argument with reference to *The End of History*, the influential thesis offered by American guru Francis Fukuyama[82] in the immediate wake of Soviet demise, then capitalism supported by the liberal ideology of the West is the goal towards which all mankind is striving, other ideologies or system are basically redundant or offtrack, and recurring incidents of genocide nothing but a series of aberrations committed by non-Westerners.

Certainly, not everybody who writes on genocide starts from this Western equals 'normal', genocide equals aberrant premise. Some, such as David Stannard and Sven Lindqvist, who have charted Western colonialism and conquest in the Americas and Africa, have, indeed, almost turned the premise on its head by arguing that the wellsprings of modern genocide are to be found in the hubris, racism and even Christian underpinnings of European-cum-Western thought systems.[83] For them it is not so much that genocide is a reaction to the West but quintessentially *is* the West. At first sight this also seems to be what Bauman, from a somewhat different perspective, is arguing when he propounds that Nazi Germany and Soviet Russia are really modern societies very much like our own. But his argument is about the features which make these societies 'the most consistent uninhibited expressions of the spirit of modernity'[84] rather than an examination of the processes of history by which they arrived there. Bauman, in other words, seems to read modernity as an ahistorical given, rather than considering that it is the drive towards it, in a world where some states are in modernity's van and others struggling to catch up, which is actually the most significant element in this equation.

Certainly, Stannard, Lindqvist, and others, cannot be faulted on the matter of history. However, by arguing in effect, that genocide's crystallisation lies in various post-1492 phases of European colonialism and imperialism, they do not entirely satisfy as to what the exact relationship is between these events and the significantly greater incidence of twentieth-century mass murders whose hallmarks more closely resemble that of our specific phenomenon, and whose context is often only marginally colonial, non-colonial or definitively post-colonial. To be sure, the historical process by which we arrive at the marked contemporaneity of genocide is not always an easy one to unravel and one to which we will return in greater depth in our second volume. The Western forerunner nation-states were clearly both integral and essential to the process. But working from the proposition that the full crystallisation of genocide in the twentieth century lies not in the *direct* outcome of these forerunners' actions *per se* but in the drive to modernity of some of their immediate, or latter-day competitors, or at least would-be competitors, our immediate aim must be to offer some broader brush-strokes as to its realisation.

The Rise of the Modern World

The first point to emphasise – once again – is that the nature of genocide in the modern world cannot be explained except by way of its relationship to recent history, any more than that history can be understood without reference to genocide. This statement may be a truism but we should not ignore it. At its core is one central paradox, namely 'the dynamics of uneven historical development'.[85] This may sound too readily Marxist in its terminology but one hardly has to be *marxisant* to accept its basic veracity. Indeed, what it refers to here is not development in terms of a dialectic of class struggle but rather a very particular model of political and social development, as represented by a very select handful of *states* who arrived there first, became the required standard for the rest of the globe while largely leaving this handful not only pre-eminent with regard to the rest but signficantly positioned to determine the trajectory of global modernisation to their own continuing advantage.

The modern world has been shaped, argues Giddens, by 'the intersection of capitalism, industrialism and the nation-state system'.[86] More specifically he has noted its following general but critical features as they apply to the development of the nation-state:

a) the creation of economic interdependence of those living within its frame so that the possibility of living apart or outside it through, for instance, an economic subsistence separate from others, becomes outmoded and unattainable. Indeed, the very idea of 'the economy' as we have come to use it, would suggest not society and state as separate spheres but largely inseparable from one another. If private economic space is thus precluded in the modern nation-state – a form of totalitarianism which certainly precedes the creation of states specifically so named – modernisation, notes Giddens, is significant in the degree to which, 'technologically based transmutations of the natural environment far beyond anything seen in prior types of society' divorce modern man 'from the given world of nature'.[87]

b) An assumption that this state consolidation will include major infrastructural change associated with communications and transport systems linking all of its perhaps once remote or self-governing parts with the centre and thereby asserting its defined territorial oneness and unity.

c) A conscious drive to cohere socially – at least in principle – all the state's inhabitants as 'aware' members of the same collectivity, a process of nation building, in other words, which can only be comprehensively accomplished by the state itself creating or taking charge of an all-encompassing school curriculum aimed at inculcating not simply universal literacy but common aims and values. Whereas, thus, the traditional state consists of numerous, heterogeneous 'societies' speaking possibly many languages or dialects, the modern nation-state almost by definition implies the aspiration for a homogeneity of its people founded on linguistic uniformity.

d) By the same token, the modern nation-state demands a high degree of hegemonic control, surveillance and supervision over the daily and thus intimate lives of its inhabitants. Such emphasis on its absolute sovereignty and monopoly of power – which crucially involves a monopoly of violence – thus negates or makes redundant traditional patterns wherein the state's rule is negotiated and/or diffused through tribal, segmental or other intermediate arrangements.[88] The relationship between state and subject, or – to use the more modern post-French revolutionary conceptualisation – 'citizen' is thus administratively direct and in juridical terms uniform. Class divisions may, as Giddens notes, be normal and intrinsic to the modern nation-state but they stand alongside notions that citizens normally have equality before the law, regardless of background or, to use Durkheim's slightly different formulation, are embraced within its universe of obligation. This in turn, perhaps paradoxically, assumes that relationships between state and society are not simply a question of rulers and ruled but that the state derives its sovereign legitimacy, at least in principle, from the will of the people.

e) The domestic nation-state development only makes sense within a global pattern of nation-states, not least because each such state is dependent for its existence and survival on economic, political and military relationships with other nation-states in the system.

If our implication from all this is that it is the process of modernisation rather than the state or modernity *per se* which should be our fundamental reference point, its specifically genocidal toxicity only makes sense in the context of a broader international reality where the perceived price of failure to modernise is perpetual thrall to the system's leaders. Modernisation, thus, is not proposed here in the same terms as 'modernisation theory' – which, much in vogue with US social and political scientists of the 1950s, was seen a passport to the unadulterated, material benefits of Western-led 'progress' – but, rather, as a poisoned chalice. Nation-states once constituted as such, and hence members of the international system of nation-states have little or no choice but to modernise. The only issue, at stake is how they do it: whether they do so according to the rule-book provided by the system's Western capitalist leaders – in effect the wisdom of Fukuyama – or they instead choose only the elements they consider most efficacious to their goal, discarding the rest. Or, again, they choose to tear up the rule-book in entirety in favour of their own entirely independent route to change. The charge made by Michael Burleigh and Wolfgang Wipperman in their study of Nazism that to consider its development in terms of modernisation is egregiously at fault given its clearly barbaric complexion thus misses the essential point.[89] There is no *a priori* requirement to treat modernisation as some undiluted good.[90] On the contrary, the fact that the primary goad to its achievement is either a fear of loss of authentic state integrity or that of falling behind in the international race for position, means that the methods states adopt to get there may often contravene or even challenge the human rights standards latterly enshrined in UN conventions. Nazism may certainly represent one of the most pathological routes to modernisation of the contemporary era, but its behaviour as such represents an extremity on a general spectrum; not a condition which is entirely *sui generis*.

This should be apparent by reference to the core protagonists of the system at its point of departure in early modern Europe. Already highly distinctive in the degree to which these relatively small polities were at considerable remove from that of the historic world empires, their almost constant martial competition with one another for territorial aggrandisement, wealth and primacy became the major impetus not only to develop technologically in terms of weaponry – the so-called 'military revolution' – but also to overhaul themselves structurally in such a way that they could more seriously meet the challenge. In place of the relatively loose organisation of other pre-modern polities these states were thus forced to adapt to a political environment of almost perpetual crisis. Advantage logically went to those who could not only innovate militarily but also be most efficient in developing and maximising their available human and material resource base, not least in fiscal and administrative terms. It also drove all of them, by degrees, aggressively to seek out resources, markets and a basis for fiscal accumulation via maritime expansion in the world beyond Europe.[91]

Even so, some of these early contenders, notably Spain and Portugal, were unable to stay in the race and eventually fell by the wayside. So too did another potentially serious competitor, the Dutch Netherlands. By contrast, Britain and France, the two players to emerge as clearly dominant at the end of the eighteenth-century phase of the struggle – by this stage being increasingly fought in a global arena – were also the two who had come nearest to transforming themselves into something prototypically modern. The two states were now a fiscally and administratively coherent British state operating in the interests of an increasingly capitalist-orientated ruling class; and France, forced into massive 'revolutionary' streamlining exactly as a result of combined fiscal, social and political blows largely brought on by repeated war with Britain.[92] They were almost immediately joined by a third contender, the United States, out of its own revolutionary rupture with Britain. However, not only were these three distinct prototypes for the modern nation-state significantly driven by a *Wille zu macht* urgency to remain sovereign and strong with regard to each other and any other regional or global competitors that they encountered, but they also demonstrated a marked willingness to bend or break their own emerging programme of Enlightenment-assisted rules governing domestic and foreign relations, whenever they perceived it to be in their national interest to do so.

All three, thus, in these critical early periods of their nation building resorted repeatedly to aggressive external war. All three, too, practised hyperexploitation based particularly on slavery on a significantly modern scale. And all three proceeded without any evident self-reproach to ethnically cleanse, deport or entirely eliminate peoples who stood in the way of national and territorial consolidation, settlement and/or control of economic or actual resources, either within their expanding home boundaries (as in the case of the United States), or in the case of the British and French, increasing imperial sway overseas. These would be the very sort of acts which, as leaders of the international system, these core nation-states would later seek in principle to disallow, repudiate or outlaw in others. Yet through these very same acts, including notable episodes of genocide, or proto-genocide, usually initiated at crisis moments under the cover or in the aftermath of war, these same system leaders provided themselves with some critical short-cuts with which to assist their state formation and sometimes crucially supplement their mainstream market-place, accumulation of capital.[93]

If, thus, the motives of these avant-garde nation-states was entirely one of self-interest, nevertheless we can discern their impact on the eventual emergence of a systemic genocide framework in three important respects. Firstly, because they were significantly ahead of other states, and able to use this power to dictate their own strategic and commercial advantage vis-à-vis other countries, their position as global leaders quickly became hegemonic. Granted, US immersion in its own domestic but trans-continental national consolidation plus its lack of a major foreign venture for much of this period, masked its actual global clout until at least 1917. Nevertheless, it is surely accurate to state that not only was 'a new world order', founded particularly on British and to a lesser extent French primacy already strongly in the ascendant by the early to mid-nineteenth century but perhaps more accurately a 'new world pecking order'.[94] There were, to borrow Immanuel Wallerstein's formulation, advanced industrial states at its core, a semi-periphery of mostly European or new Latin American states with varying degrees of economic and political independence, but still considerably lagging behind in the modernisation stakes, and finally a large – what we today would consider 'third world' – periphery whose position in the system was entirely one of economic and political dependency and/or, subservience to the core group.[95]

Moreover, if this emerging three-tier system profile was already evident two centuries ago, what is more remarkable is how little it has changed since then.

Granted, a number of states have moved position to become significant members of the select core, including a Japan which thereby somewhat paradoxically becomes embraced within 'the West', while the US has indisputably replaced Britain as the hegemonic leader of the pack. In the third tier, of course, regions of the globe which were literally on the rim of the system have subsequently moved through a colonial to a post-colonial existence to become fully recognised members of the nation-state club. If this would suggest a significant shift founded on the notion of the sovereign equality of all nation-states, bolstered by broad industrial and technological exchanges which appear to confirm and concretise a much more complex global interdependency, Wallerstein's location of power still holds. A world still surviving into the early eighteenth century, where centres of powers were founded on a plurality of civilisations from east to west and north to south, has since been replaced by a universal political and economic system clearly led, supervised, regulated and ultimately dependent on a select group of Western states (albeit in the contemporary era with key non-state institutions as the most obvious foci of real power) and with periphery and semi-periphery remaining as such. In short, the modern world is one where the liberal capitalist West – whether loved or hated – is the centre of the human universe, incorporates the rest and rules it.[96]

This brings us on to our second point of significance with regard to the emerging system leaders. Though their existence as nation-states was, of course, in every sense prototypal for the simple reason that no coherent blueprint or agenda previously existed for what they should be, their very success, once up and running – not only domestically but in their apparently unfettered political and economic penetration into all corners of the globe – ensured that their example would be paradigmatic. No traditional state or society which wanted to maintain its integrity vis-à-vis these frontrunners could afford to ignore the model. Indeed, the more aware became forward-looking elites in neighbouring countries of the disparity, the more they sought to learn, imitate or emulate the forerunners' best practice. This embraced not only aspects of technological innovation, industrial development and capital formation. It also assumed taking on board Western ideas, institutional and juridical arrangements, even social, linguistic and cultural borrowings. If this was particularly true of still pre-industrial European countries in the nineteenth century struggling to catch up, it had become by the twentieth, a practically universal norm. The assumption was plain. The price of staying afloat in the dominant political economy was to be like the West. The alternative was political and, or economic subjugation: in other words, eternal weakness.[97]

The paradoxical problem was that for many societies attempting to make this quantum leap, various aspects of the model proved less than perfect for its accomplishment. Partly this might be a matter of Western institutional arrangements failing to match the social environment or practice where the attempt at transplantation was being made. The result could be acute social alienation, leading often to the creation of radical, though often traditionally voiced protest movements. More systemically, however, state elites in a position to plan structural overhaul on the basis of Western economic prescriptions of laissez-faire found that the resulting terms of trade seemed to ensure to themselves a permanent disadvantage. The emerging international system had not started as a level economic or political playing field nor, as emerging modern states quickly discovered, was it likely to change. The result was that instead of adopting a British or French template for development, an emerging characteristic of the system was states attempting their own separate, usually more obviously hands-on, *dirigiste* programmes, often in some degree of tension with, or even collision with the assumed Western liberal 'norm'.

There was, however, a further problem for contenders. Karl Marx might state with some optimism in 1867 that 'the country that is more developed industrially only shows to the less developed, the image of its own future'[98] but the rate of industrial-cum-technological change was becoming so rapid by this stage that latecomers to it were in danger of being left far behind. Some might evince relief and even opportunity in this historical backwardness. Trotsky, for instance, en route to his theory of permanent revolution some two generations after Marx, envisaged savages 'skipping a whole series of intermediate stages' and throwing away 'their bows and arrows for rifles all at once, without travelling the road which lay between those two weapons in the past'.[99] This was all well and good. 'Savages' might be able to acquire rifles for a time by trading them for quite finite and ultimately unrenewable primary resources to which they had access but the critical issue was who was manufacturing the rifles in the first place and how quickly they would move on to a new generation of rapid-firing guns with which to then make the rifles obsolete, and with them the 'savages'. A more sober and accurate assessment of the problem from the latecomers' perspective is that offered by Moshe Lewin:

The very difficulty of the task of industrialising any country is actually a result of powerful pressures that more developed predecessors exercise on the newcomers. It is the predecessors, objectively who define the task, the intensity of the effort, and the span of the leap to be accomplished by the developing pretender, who has to acquire and develop the complex and costly technologies that the former created and mastered. The option of going, at least at the beginning, for some older, cheaper, and simpler gear does not exist in the real world. It is, in a nutshell, the dilemma of a transition straight to the jet and computer or continued underdevelopment and decay.[100]

Lewin may have specifically Russia in mind here, a country dogged by its actual ongoing backwardness. However, the ramifications of the latecomer–forerunner gap is equally applicable to countries that seem to have made the transition more successfully. Germany and Japan are the two most obvious examples. Having rapidly industrialised with a view to taking on, if necessary, the system leaders on their own military terms, their elites still remained persistently fixated on the notion that all the critical cards were held by the forerunners. The third key impact of the transformation of the few avant-garde states on the many who followed thus relates to the time factor; not only in terms of lost time which the latecomers never had to launch their process of modernisation *at their own pace*, but also as a corollary, the much shorter time curve they required to ensure both their own economic take-offs and the ability to keep going at the pace set by the avant-garde. The elites of new or would-be states might thus willingly embrace the merits of modernisation but coming from behind they were bedevilled by the constant anxiety that they were engaged in a contest that they could never hope to win. Here is the CUP theoretician, Ziya Gökalp, in his poem 'Esnaf Destani', written in the wake of catastrophic Ottoman military reverses in Tripolitania and the Balkan wars:

> We were defeated because we were so backward,
> To take revenge, we shall adopt the enemy's science.
> We shall learn his skill, steal his methods.
>
> On progress we will set our heart.
> We shall skip five hundred years
> And not stand still. Little time is left.[101]

It is the last sentence that gives the game way. This is a race, a race against the more advanced states who have all the advantages but also a race against time. The opportunity 'to maintain a precarious equilibrium that will prevent the occurrence of desperate situations, of intolerable choices', the late Isaiah Berlin's suggested prescript 'to avoid extremes of suffering' which he considered 'the first requirement of a decent society'[102] is, by cross-reference to Gökalp, almost completely ruled out by the acute social Darwinian competition inherent in the system's function. Dynamic, hothouse, dependent on rapid yet ongoing acceleration for latecomer states to make good, its nature could not but breed instability, obsession and paranoia, in other words the very psychological conditions likely to give rise to genocide. Yet none of this inevitably *has* to lead to it. If that were the case, practically every state would have committed the act at some stage and gone on doing so. What we we have outlined, thus far, are only genocide's general *preconditions*; albeit ones which emanate out of the historical framework of the nation-state system. For the actual conditions we need to probe a little further.

Specific Conditions for Genocide

Why then, to go back to the $64,000 question, have some countries committed genocide, sometimes repeatedly so, and other have not? And why, for that matter, are we dealing with such a disparate agglomerate of offenders? We have already proposed in the previous chapter that human agency is an important ingredient in the equation and that without the motivation to commit the act genocide *qua* genocide could not happen. But we have equally proposed that the sort of people who might be more willing to contemplate such a policy usually only come to prominence under conditions of the most acute stress also usually accompanied by a more general socio-psychological dislocation, or breakdown, in the population at large. It is surely no accident, for instance, that the first great wave of contemporary genocides comes out of the actuality and aftermath of that great twentieth-century catastrophe and watershed, the First World War, in which *particular* states and their societies, the ones which collapsed, or were defeated, or were most obviously embittered by the war and post-war outcome – and not least by the post-1929 economic aftershock – were the ones who were most likely to go down this path. But in a sense this tells us both everything and nothing. Is genocide entirely contingent on a shock to the collective organism such as war or does such an event simply catalyse latent tendencies which were already embedded in that society? After all, the list of most obviously disgruntled states includes a number that one might have expected to respond rather differently. The first post-1918 fascist state, for instance, was not Germany but Italy, technically a major war victor. Japan was another victor whose behaviour in the inter-war period, though arguably non-genocidal, was certainly extremely aggressive. A third, Romania, in spite of doubling its territorial holdings simply by joining the right – Allied – side in 1916, went on, a global war later to be, in its own terms, a major genocide perpetrator.[103]

One can certainly discern a general pattern in this broad grouping, whatever their respective positions at the end of official hostilities, in late 1918. All at varying stages in its aftermath become 'revisionist' states in the sense that they challenged the post-war world order as laid down at Versailles by its self-appointed arbiters – Britain, France and the United States – and therefore with it the received wisdoms of the Western-led system. That this repudiation was generally accompanied by the discrediting and removal of regimes who had either traditionally aligned themselves with, or at that juncture were adherents to the liberal-capitalist path, in favour of alternative 'second' or 'third' ways to progress and ultimate triumph, simply reinforces the message that these were explicit and conscious efforts to renege on, or override, the accepted rules of the modernisation game by which developing states were supposed to abide. With regard specifically to Germany, the historians Horst Matzerath and Heinrich Volkmann posit this tendency thus:

> National Socialism is the attempt at a special path *out of the problems of modernisation* [my emphases] into the utopia of the third way, beyond the internal social crises and conflicts of the parliamentary, democratic capitalist society and beyond the concept – releasing anxiety and aggression – of a communist total alteration (of society), but essentially without giving up the capitalist and industrial economic bases of this development.[104]

While one might wish to dispute some of the terminology of this statement, not to say its glaring omission of a racial policy which arguably made Nazi Germany *sui generis*,[105] its general thrust has an applicability far beyond this genocide perpetrator *par excellence*. Indeed, its inference that what is at stake here is some method to defy, defeat, buck, circumvent, or simply find some technical fix with which to avoid the rules of, and thereby ultimately transcend the requirements of the Western liberal template is *a* if not *the* common ingredient of all genocide perpetrators. It is as applicable to Stalinist Russia – with the proviso that the state accumulation of wealth with which to drive modernisation was supposed to be derived from 'socialist' rather than 'capitalist' control of the means of production – as it is to democratic Kampuchea – albeit recognising that though Khmer Rouge utopian ends are similar, the means by which they aimed to arrive there were both stridently anti-capitalist and anti-industrial – as it is also, in its own bizarre way, to MRND Rwanda, whose method for bucking the terms of the international system – carried off with consummate skill for thirty odd years – was by milking it for all it was worth. Most paradoxically of all it is also applicable to the Western states who set the ground rules, though at an earlier stage of their rise to power. There is obviously sufficient divergence here to remind us that ensuing genocidal outcomes are always, on one level, uniquely peculiar unto themselves. The general rule nevertheless applies. States who end up committing genocide whether they are Western states in the van of the development process, or sub-Suharan or Asian states notably in the rear, are all, in varying degrees, in search of some radical, or accelerated short-cut to empowerment.

This still, however, leaves a gap in our transmission belt. Some states have sought and achieved accelerated development without recourse to genocide.

The problem of how to accomplish modernisation is, after all, a general and prevalent one. Moreover, with the notable exception of the forerunners themselves, crossing the Rubicon to commit the act and thereby at the very least risking incurring the wrath of the international community in the process would appear to be both illogical and self-defeating. The problem becomes even more perplexing when we consider states who have sought to buck the received rules of the game yet at the same time would appear to have been remarkably successful at modernising according to those rules. Let us for a moment return to the classic example: Germany, or more accurately the state which grew out of Wilhelmine Prussia into a unified German nation-state.

Granted, Germany does, in a critical sense, break some of the rules. For instance, it keeps on going to war in the period 1864–71, to further its unification and consolidation, just as it studiously ignores the tenets of Manchester liberalism in favour of its own Listian-style state-directed and centralising drive to industrial mastery.[106] But it is so successful through these expedients that no avant-garde leader is in a position to halt it. France's efforts to do so come crashing down in her humiliating military defeat of 1870–1 while Britain is forced to look on largely from the sidelines as Germany's industrial output indices over the next several decades rapidly begin to close the gap with Britain's own and, in so doing, confirm the Germans' future position as the major long-haul competitor for the also up-and-coming United States.[107] Thus, despite some potentially wayward tendencies Germany's pre-1914 record does not add up to either a complete rupture with the rules of the liberal system nor to a notable prefiguring of Nazism. Certainly, this has not prevented a whole range of commentators – going back to Thorstein Veblen, the economist and social critic writing during the First World War[108] – to propose that there has been something rather odd, malformed, and even retarded about Germany's historical trajectory, meriting its consideration as a *Sonderweg* – a quite special and singular path to development. The problem with this approach, however, is that the term could be equally if not more appropriately applied to any of Britain, France or the United States on the grounds that their prototypicality made them a great deal more unusual than a Germany whose *dirigiste* response was very much the example adopted by other modernising latecomers. Nor is it always obvious, as some historians seem to detect, what exactly it is in the social structure or political arrangements of the new Germany which make it so very distinct from other emerging industrial powers. It could be argued in rather reductionist Marxist terms that the required 'bourgeois revolution' as necessary precondition for an untrammelled capitalist development is arrested in the Bismarckian state, modernisation thus being carried forward to a significant degree under the political control of a markedly conservative, authoritarian and even anti-modernistic traditional ruling elite. But this contradiction is hardly specific to Germany. Indeed, one might even characterise the nineteenth-century British political economy in rather similar terms.[109] Yet neither in the German nor the British case do these supposed social and political idiosyncrasies seem to have noticeably sabotaged the general modernising thrust.

If, then, the origins of Germany's Nazi challenge to the rules of the international system cannot be found in straightforward economic, political or even social indices from the pre-1914 period, can some other cultural factor or predisposition account for it? A number of historians and political scientists, usually coming at the issue from the standpoint of class analysis, have certainly paid some considerable attention to the particular *mentalité* of the German *Mittelstand* or lower middle class, and not least because it is they who have been most regularly identified as the backbone of the Nazi Party. The innovative Marxist thinker Ernst Bloch, whose original observations were contemporaneous with the party's rise, has accounted for the *Mittelstand*'s well-known resistance to modernising trends, for instance, by arguing that this was a regressive social formation, living out of step with actual reality, 'a non-synchronous remainder' who were not living 'in the same now'.[110] Working along the lines of this same argument, Ron Aronson, more recently, has proposed how this explains the Nazi attempt 'to reshape society *against* its actual historical possibilities'.[111] However, this dialectic between the Nazi's apparent power – geared towards a past which no longer existed – and impotence in the face of the actual present, could, argues Aronson, ultimately only lead through a 'fantasy-driven process of transformation' in one direction – towards 'a rupture with reality' and with it 'a kind of suicidal vengeance on the twentieth-century world'.[112]

Aronson's extrapolation of Bloch, to produce his own double dialectic of power and impotence, reason and madness – a dialectic of disaster – is to this author's mind, an extremely important contribution to the study of genocide and most particularly because of its willingness to seriously engage with the acting out of psychological volatility and collective unreason in the political arena as a direct outcome of dysfunctional social and cultural factors. The problem with the thesis in so far as Germany is concerned is two-fold. Firstly, though a reactionary desire to return to some mythical past may be an important part – though only part of the Nazi programme – the more prevalent and ultimately significant fear is one of somehow being left behind in the present. Nor is this anxiety specific to the Hitler 'class', nor indeed only to the immediate pre-1933 period. If we were to return to the political culture of pre-1914 Germany we would find the anxiety at many levels of German society, but particularly in elite circles, where its hold was little short of obsessive. The almost constant Wilhelmine refrain, 'Weltmacht oder Niedgergang' – 'world power or collapse', more fully spelt out in the dire forecast of Admiral Tirpitz that it was 'a life and death question … to make up the lost ground'[113] – speaks volumes as to the nature of the mindset. The great paradox, as we have already noted, is that Germany had no sound empirical basis for this fear. So the problem has to be somewhere else; not so much in political or socio-economic realities *per se* as in their perception.

However, this is where Aronson's power–impotence dialectic does seem to have a certain resonance. After all, what is Germany pre-1914 but a new state which, on the one hand believes itself to be incredibly strong and is indeed overbrimming with hubristic self-confidence about its potential as a world power yet, on the other, seems to be quite terrified that sooner later someone is going to demonstrate that the image is a case pure and simple of the emperor's new clothes? In this tension lies a national self-destruct mechanism which precedes the Nazis. Indeed, their own radicalised efforts to overcome the tension only makes proper sense in the context of the previous conservative-led attempt at resolution, whose apotheosis is the 1914 declaration of war and whose denouement is the 1919 internationally imposed peace of national humiliation. Stage one of Germany's efforts to assert its position in the international system against what it perceives to be consistent thwarting at the hands of the other dominant Great Powers is thus enacted in 1914 without the genocide but it is still, to use Aronson's terminology, an attempt to 'realise' the unrealisable[114] or, in Fritz Fischer's words, amounts to 'a war of illusions'.[115] Following this argument, stage two – Nazism – might thus be viewed as an extraordinary ratcheting up of the stage one effort, the new regime, however, clearing out of its path any vestiges of deference to the Western-led 'mainstream' in order to resume its own entirely uncompromising, alternative, yet still fatally flawed, drive towards transcendence.

In this way, the German example may help identify a particular type of state with the potentiality for genocide not so much on the basis of whether it is labelled as authoritarian, revolutionary, ethnically stratified or whatever, or for that matter whether it is one which is industrially advanced, middling or backward, so much as one which suffers from what one might call a chronic 'strong' state–'weak' state syndrome. By this is meant a state that believes that it is strong, or at least should be strong but at the same time perceives all sorts of limitations preventing this from being recognised. Indeed, such states seem to have what one might only describe as a collective inferiority complex: that is, of a conviction shared by policy makers, opinion formers and possibly significant sections of their general population that the position which they believe *ought* to be theirs in terms of international status is forever being denied or blocked off to them.[116] From this standpoint one could assert that Germany not only has something in common with Russia, China or Turkey but also with Cambodia, Ethiopia, or, for that matter even Rwanda or Burundi. But if this is the case, if all these societies have evinced in their recent political culture persistent, even acutely pathological symptoms of envy, resentment and anomie, whence does the tendency emanate?

Presumably any state which has a strong sense of its own worth does so – correctly or incorrectly – by reference to some understanding of its recent or more distant past when its claims to status were recognised by others. This would seem, at first sight, to be quite at variance with Chalk and Jonassohn's proposition that 'It is new states or new regimes attempting to impose conformity to a new ideology that are particularly likely to practice genocide.'[117] As the above-mentioned states would all claim a considerable provenance, newness in itself would, therefore, not seem to be a necessary premise. On the other hand, particularly bearing in mind that genocide is notably associated with often prolonged moments of massive state or societal rupture and crisis, perhaps Chalk and Jonassohn's focus on new *regimes* is perfectly valid, suggesting that what is at stake is not the state *per se* but some radical restatement or possibly even reinterpretation of its relationship to its past. This might further suggest that it is not necessarily states 'of lesser international status',[118] as Harff and Gurr infer, that are the most likely contenders – when we have already seen that our prime perpetrator Germany, objectively speaking, was and remains a leading world power – so much as any state whose vivid sense of a powerful and resplendent past is mirrored, if not in the reality, then at least in the perception of a diminished and enfeebled present.

If thus, genocide states are likely to be ones obsessed by their 'strong–weak' contradictions, they are also ones whose anxiety on this account are often enfolded in an 'old state–new state' dichotomy or discrepancy. Here again, the issue is not whether states really were so historically strong or even whether a contemporary state which bears the same or a similar name as a past one is its authentic heir. All modern states reinvent or repackage their past in order 'to mobilise change in the future'[119] and where no such state called Turkey or Indonesia ever existed until created by newly self-aware 'national' elites out of receding imperial or colonial constructions, the necessity to demonstrate a relevant ancestry is all the more pressing. Yet it is in this very effort to assume an often entirely 'mythic' genealogy with which to prove not only continuity but to press claims for contemporary recognition or restitution that we can locate further aspects of Aronson's dangerous dialectic. Conjuring up a fantasy past might sound fairly harmless. Even national palingensis – the idea of a 'national community rising phoenix-like after a period of encroaching decadence which all but destroyed it'[120] – which, for Griffin, is at the mythic core of fascism (though equally it could be applied to a significant proportion of latecomer regimes here under discussion)[121] might not in itself be cause for undue alarm.

The problem is that the past revisited in such a way implies some critical ingredient missing in the present. What 'we' lack now is what 'we' had then, a then when 'we' were a mighty and unified people, when others treated 'us' with respect, when 'we' were not afraid, or cowed by borrowed, enfeebling sensibilities to prevent 'us' striking down 'our' mortal enemies. We have already noted the Nazi glorification of Genghis, though he was hardly an authentic ancestor for any self-proclaimed Aryan. This, however, did not prevent Nazi genealogists looking back beyond conquering Teutonic knights to Goths credited with ravaging the Roman empire, to some deep past when their original Aryan warrior forbears were – highly imaginatively – supposed to have clambered down westwards from the Tibetan plateau or even from an Arctic 'lost civilisation' of Atlantis.[122] Nor did historical fact stop the CUP leader Enver Pasha and his friends from seeing the true modern-day Turk in terms of some 'ur' ancestor called 'grey wolf' whose Turanian warrior-descendants freely roamed the great steppes of central Asia.[123] Yet again, reality did not deter the Khmer Rouge from compensating for Cambodia's weakened present by immersing themselves in the 'lost world' of the powerful Khmer medieval kingdom founded around the great temple complex of Angkor Wat.[124] The fact that Angkor's glory had been entirely uncovered by nineteenth-century French scholars, the very conveyors of a Western Enlightenment-based epistemology which the Khmer Rouge in power so vituperatively rejected, adds a certain piquant irony to the story. But then, all manner of historians, archaeologists, ethnographers, anthropologists, geographers and others found their work unwittingly appropriated and often mutilated in the interests of modern nation and/or state building, though there were also, at times, plenty of others more than willing to lend their scholarly imprimatur to the cause.[125]

This leads us to conclude that genocide-proneness – at least in its most contemporary twentieth-century crystallisation – is usually associated with states with a very strong sense of contemporary grievance against the world at large, for which they not only compensate by wrapping themselves up in images of past grandeur, innocence or purity but which they intentionally utilise as tools with which to articulate their resentment and anger at other states or societies who, in their minds, have been the undeserved gainers from their loss. Moreover, the very fact that new, often ideologically motivated regimes are able to come to power in such states in the first place, usually superseding in the process more traditional-minded 'mainstream' governments also suggests that their feelings of frustration, relative deprivation or hatred are actually widely shared by large sections of society. The consequent efforts of these regimes to radicalise their domestic arrangements as well as foreign policies in ways that consciously contravene or challenge the rules of the liberal, Western-led system is thus often legitimised – even, paradoxically, in cases of communist rupture[126] – by an appeal to *national* history.

We should be wary, however, of assuming that Western states are exempted by their very self-definition from these tendencies. The primary disjuncture between the genocidal acts of the eighteenth and nineteenth century and those of the twentieth lies in the facts of historical development. Because the avant-garde nation-states achieved their global ascendancy first and went on to maintain it, their recourse to a rampant xenophobia, closely linked to a strong exclusivist definition of the 'people' founded on a mythic if not utterly false reading of history, was largely eased or obviated. Being at the top of the global hierarchy, 'weak–strong' or 'old–new' anxieties did not generally apply. However, this did not negate the potential for sustained moments of collective psychological over-excitement during periods of usually war-related national crisis, or for recourse to retributive over-kill when their imperial trajectories were challenged by colonised or native peoples at the frontiers of state-development.

By the same token, other states with obviously more recent and identifiable 'weak–strong'/'old–new' tensions have not always ended up committing genocide. Iran, for instance, is a notable exception, even though its recent history – culminating in a definitive, overtly anti-Western but popularly based revolutionary rupture in 1979, immediately followed by a catastrophic decade-long war with neighbouring Iraq – provides it with exactly the sort of conditions from which we might expect genocide to emanate. Certainly, this is not to disavow Iran's considerable post-1979 domestic blood-letting, significant human rights abuses and one very specific case of persecution, amounting to the early stages of a 'genocidal process'. The fact, moreover, that the focus of this assault was the Baha'i, a youthful, small, entirely pacific yet internationally connected and indubitably visionary religious community, is surely significant, not least in the context of a post-revolutionary society where the route 'out of the problem of modernisation' was perceived to be a religious uniformity founded on theocratic Islam.[127] Yet, if one can see in this the potential for the sort of demonising projection one might expect from a would-be monocultural, religious-led state against a notably liberal and tolerant religious alternative the fact remains that the mullahs did not pursue it to its genocidal end. Perhaps it is equally significant that this was in a country where local clan, tribal linguistic, and sectarian solidarities – whether emanating from the dominant Persian group or the various Turkic, Arab, Kurdish and other constituent parts – have for centuries always managed to impede any attempt to impose a national (as opposed to religious) uniformity.[128] If this would suggest Iran's particular structural underpinnings militating against the high probability of a state-led genocide one should not discount the human and contingent factors either. We must insist once more that genocide, even under crisis conditions, is the coming together of several factors in a particular matrix and certainly never a foregone or inevitable conclusion to a preordained blueprint.

There again, other states, while evincing a strong list of potential genocide characteristics, may have in their makeup, or mindset, other factors or elements mitigating against its likely outcome. Early twentieth-century Japan, for instance, displayed significant comparability with Germany, both in its break-neck speed modernising and industrialising drive to Great Power status – in its case very much against the odds – and in its huge frustration, once there, at being blocked off by the other powers from what it perceived to be its rightful place in the first rank. Like Germany, its political culture had its own hubristic notion of being a master race, founded on a quite quirky racist-cum-mystical rendition of a Japan-centred universe. Like Germany, too, its leadership did not baulk at defying Western hegemony by attempting its own dramatic military short-cut to national salvation.[129] Pre-1945 Japan was thus as good an example as any of a state in thrall to its 'strong–weak', 'old–new' contradictions. And, of course, it committed mass murder on a truly gigantic scale, its War Type Two campaigns in northern China in the 1930s and 1940s alone, according to Rummel, reducing the population in the region from some 44 million to only 25 million.[130] If this confirms a Rummel verdict of democide, there is less evidence, however, that Japanese occupation forces started out from a premise that the Chinese were anything other than subordinate, certainly pitiable but nevertheless related members of the same family as themselves.[131] Moreover, the persecution and near-extirpation of its 'problem' Christian population back in the early seventeenth century, and most of its Ainu people bar a tiny and isolated northern remnant at a much earlier date still,[132] ensured that by the contemporary age of genocide Japan had an unusually high degree of ethnic and cultural homogeneity for a nation-state and hence less scope with which to accuse any particular social or ethnic grouping of being the 'enemy within'.

None of this would have precluded or prevented the Japanese state, or for that matter any other, from a fantasy invention of a communal fly in the ointment or – in conditions of an active resistance to their occupation – from overturning the image of a nominal friendly foreign population into collective enemies. That exemplar of genocide, Saddam Hussein, famously said in 1978: 'The revolution chooses its enemies and we say chooses its enemies because some enemies are chosen by it from among the people who run up against its programme and who intend to harm it. The revolution chooses as enemies those who intend to deviate from its main principles and starting points.'[133] While this may remind us that a regime already inclined in this direction will make up its own rules with which to assault, terrorise and murder those it chooses to target, the Iraqi example actually reinforces a more general rule that the specificity of genocide – in Saddam's case against the Kurds, and arguably more debateably against the Marsh Arabs – is usually directed against ethnic populations who are perceived as problematic by successive regimes, sometimes over many generations. Genocide, thus, rarely comes out of the blue anymore than it picks on a group of people for no reason whatsoever. True, among the archetypal genocides we have noted, the two examples of kulak and Eastern Zone Khmer seem, at one level, to contradict this argument. It is certainly not evident that kulaks were socially – let alone ethnically – overtly distinguishable from the rest of peasant Russia, while Eastern Zone Khmer were only definable as 'enemies' on the basis of their chance territorial location at the time. Yet even here state objections to these groups do not appear to have been entirely arbitrary. In the first instance, regime perceptions of kulaks were of a distinct and compact 'problem' group who both stood in the way of and were perceived as challengers to the Soviet Union's drive to modernisation. In the second, the alleged danger from the 'eastern' Khmer lay in their proximate and allegedly too cosily co-existent relationship with Cambodia's historic arch-enemy, Vietnam, the country perceived as most likely to sabotage democratic Kampuchea's own entirely self-determined drive 'out of *its* problems of modernisation'.

The modern but highly authoritarian pre-1945 Japanese state escaped these sorts of dilemmas, at least in its domestic frame, because it perceived its integral population as homogeneous and hence implicitly loyal. Authoritarian, mullah-led Iran, by contrast, has avoided them, to date, for the entirely distinct reason that its broad but closely balanced multi-ethnicity in effect precludes any regime from forcing this issue: societal homogenisation instead following an essentially religious route. Yet if Japan and Iran represent examples of a debatable genocide-avoidance, their good luck on this score paradoxically underscores the further feature which distinguishes those states most prone in this direction: their desire for people uniformity.

Expressing what exactly is meant here in a single all-encompassing term is difficult. As so often, Nazi terminology would seem to offer the most cogent pointer; the term *Gleichschaltung* representing more than simply a streamlining of party regime and state but also the aspiration towards an organic society where distinctions between Germans in terms of their regional, religious or socio-economic backgrounds are deemed redundant. One might add, of course, that the tendency towards a state-centred and controlled social and cultural process of homogenisation is hardly peculiar to Nazi Germany but is part of the general preconditions for genocide in the modern world, further evidence, indeed, of the legacy of the forerunner states who first defined themselves as nations as well as goad to any latecomer with aspirations to compete in their emerging global framework.

What makes Nazi Germany and the bulk of most genocide-prone states different from the general run of state homogenisers, however, is the degree to which they are prepared to go down this route. Again this is first and foremost a function of their desperation. More driven than other states by anxieties about being left behind in a modernising race in which they believe they ought to be ahead, yet finding themselves often unable to adapt those elements of the Western template – whether it be technological innovation, capital formation, democratic participation or whatever – to their own advantage, these states have been usually the ones most eager to latch on to the national issue as the one remaining element of the Western recipe with which to attempt to state-build their way to enhanced power or, in the case of some communist states, to counter it with an entirely alternative, ostensibly anti-national programme. It is noteworthy that in this process they have often either dispensed with elements of the original Western formulation of nation – the rights of the individual being one common casualty deemed surplus to requirements – or significantly redefined it in such a way as to eliminate those elements, and peoples, considered to be an inertial drag on it. Whereas, thus, Western principles (if not necessarily practices) posit an essentially liberal-universalist and inclusivist conception of the citizen as having equality before the law whatever his (though not always her) racial, religious, social or indeed ancestral origins – enshrined in the legal concept of *jus soli* – the emerging late-Wilhelmine wisdom adopted not only by Germany but by other latecomer European states was one where the national community was composed only of those who could prove their blood-ties to it.[134]

Granted, this principle of parentage – *jus sanguinis* – rather than place of birth as the defining quality which entitles someone to be 'in' rather 'outside' the society of the nation-state does not necessarily or decisively have to point in the direction of genocide. But its emphasis on *ethnos* rather than *civitas* in states that were yet to go fully down the path of overtly radical system-defiance, was ominous in the historical trend it set. Combined with supernationalist prescriptions to create pan-Germanic, pan-Slavic or later pan-

Turanic or pan-Arab entities, its implication was wholly exclusive for those who could not meet its requirements. When Gökalp in 'Esnaf Destani' thus spoke of 'we' it could not mean an Armenian, Greek, Kurd, or Arab, despite the fact that all these peoples had lived since time immemorial in the lands of the Ottoman empire. It could only mean a Turk. Whether the majority of people Gökalp would have defined as such in 1913 would have understood or appreciated either his embrace or clarion-call is another matter. But then the sort of ultra-nationalism which Gökalp espoused did not require people to discuss the matter, only willingly agree. If beyond ultra-nationalism there were even more radical departures from the vapid Western model; the Nazi concept of a *Volksgemeinschaft* – a racial Aryan community over and beyond that of simple nation – or communism's stridently *anti-national* ideal of a 'Homo Sovieticus' being among the most extreme, all these were conceptions which highlighted not only the nature of these driven regimes but their rationale to utilise the basic building-blocks of the Western Enlightenment project to socially engineer their way toward population aggregates more coherently powerful than anything the nation-state forerunners had or could have envisaged.

Such agendas also suggest that the ordinary desires or aspirations of the people who are meant to be their beneficiaries count for little compared with the abstract idea of the 'new men' to which each of these formulas, in its own way, is geared. But equally the very notion of some new one-dimensional archetype almost by its own logic must have as its corollary something which it is not: an anti-type. The 'new man' thus can only become complete and go on from this to succeed in his special mission in life by vanquishing if not extirpating his mortal adversary.

Binary opposition: the 'us' and the 'them', as has already been suggested in the previous chapter, is hardly something invented by the modern world just as Manichaean divisions between black and white, good and evil, could and did lead in the past to veritable explosions of mass murder. If pre-modern Christian Europe thus particularly witnessed the most horrendous assaults on Jews, heterodox sectarians and women charged with 'witchcraft', it is also noteworthy that here, as elsewhere, such raw hatreds, loathings and phobias were for the most part restrained by and contained within the very structure of traditional societies. By their very definition populations were segmented, corporate and hierarchical; crossing social, cultural or sexual boundaries between different tiers or groups within them was explicitly to transgress. But the political-legal restraints that enforced these rules also offered some degree of protection and security, especially for 'outsiders' such as Jews. Pre-modern societies may have been generally intolerant, prejudiced and prone to violence.

And they certainly did deny to nearly all Jews, Armenians or, for that matter, Tutsi, any alternative, simply by the fact that they delineated their exact roles and position within the society by a series of social, cultural and economic markers. Yet whether offering privilege and prerogative or downright discrimination, their structures had at least the potential to provide for a wide degree of cultural diversity and practice.

Which is why, of course, they stand in such stark if not dangerous juxtaposition with the societal framework of the nation-state. In the latter there could be no boundaries or half-way houses between state and ordinary citizen, no basis for autonomous self-rule, no principle to which one could turn to negotiate a separate existence in some way apart from the general rules and regulations of the dominant mainstream. The best one could hope for as a minority – the very terminology underscores its implicit anomalousness – was that the state would assimilate you to its aggregate requirements in a benevolent manner, allowing you to go on practising your linguistic, religious or cultural idiosyncrasies not only in the privacy of your own home but through institutional arrangements – schools, religious centres and so on – which confirmed these particular freedoms. This, of course, was the liberal Western model of the nation-state, whose most full and mature rendition was the United States.

The fact, however, that this particular state's universe of obligation did not apply to one huge category of society – black African Americans – even in practice long after emancipation, suggests either a major flaw, or alternatively a double-standard implicit in the model. That the elites of latecomer states or would-be states read the concept of nation to mean people who not only behaved and spoke but also racially looked like themselves entitled them – but not the others – to equal rights, thus owed more than a little to Western practice. That this could also combine with supposedly scholarly, Western-informed historical discourses to produce some murderous concoctions is also amply demonstrated in the notion of the 'Hamitic thesis'. This late nineteenth-century European imperial wisdom which explained the alleged aesthetic, cultural and political superiority of the Tutsi of the Central African lakes region on the grounds of their supposed provenance much further to the north in Ethiopia implied that this was because they were racially much closer to Europeans than Negroid Africans.[135] If this provided the minority Tutsi with a suitable justification for lording it over the Hutu masses, in both colonial Burundi and Rwanda, it also provided the counter-argument, when the Hutu majority seized power in post-colonial Rwanda, that not only did Tutsi not belong there but, as in one infamous public speech by a Hutu Power ideologue in 1992, that they ought to be dispatched back to Ethiopia by the way

of the Nyabarongo River.[136] The use – or rather abuse – of an already significantly problematic, Western-created, historical tool to create narratives of
struggle between the supposedly authentic holders of land and state and their
allegedly illegitimate, parasitic contenders thus becomes a critical weapon in
the hands of any regime trying to forge its own *Gleichschaltung*. And if this
involved turning history on its head – as Turkish school texts did after the
Aghet by painting the Armenians as a nomadic 'tribe' intruding onto the sovereign territory of the 'civilised' Turk where they ungratefully abused his
hospitality[137] – then there was always the plea of historical necessity with
which to justify the lie.

System-defying regimes are the ones most likely to use such defamatory
and pathologically perverse accusations about 'problematic' constituent elements of their own subject or citizen population because they also have the
most to lose by coming to a *modus vivendi* with them. The whole justification of
such regimes, after all, is founded on the premise that to resolve their state's
perceived weakness requires, as its prerequisite, a much more state-organised,
controlled – and if necessary regimented – social cohesion. If forerunner states
could offer some latitude on this score because they had already found their
way to success – usually *after* having eliminated, or at least subjugated groups
who had stood in their way in the first place – system-defiers are the ones who
are most obsessed that such an approach is really offering a hostage to fortune,
impeding their path to progress and foretelling of ultimate disaster. The best,
therefore, that such regimes can ever offer to those who do not or will not fit
their prescript for social harmony is coercive assimilation. One possible route
to this goal is to 'de-imagine' problematic groups and pretend that they do
not exist, thereby providing a smoke-screen for attempts to force them into
the required national straitjacket. This was Turkish policy as attempted for
decades vis-à-vis their Kurds,[138] as it was equally that of Bangladesh in its
sophistry that its whole population was ethnically Bangladeshi, conveniently
ignoring, amongst others, the Chittagong hill tribes who vehemently contested the assumption.[139] This certainly suggests that such regimes do not
necessarily start out by contemplating genocide, though the fact that they may
have no line of retreat should the policy fail certainly begs the question. But
the parameters for even this sort of a draconian solution rapidly fall away
where a regime commences from some basic reductionist class analysis or
racial worldview. In these circumstances the only non-genocidal possibility
available is the isolation and exclusion of the allegedly troublesome group or
groups from the state's universe of obligation; in other words, from its moral,
legal, social, economic and cultural framework, from its aspirations and *raison
d'être*. This could be argued to be tantamount to the true beginnings of a

genocidal process. Even then, whether it is a 'sufficient condition of genocide' is another matter.[140]

The Perpetrator's Version of 'Never Again':
The Final Piece of the Jigsaw?

Putting together a series of key critical ingredients – as if it it were some laboratory experiment – does not make genocide inevitable. On the other hand, if we could chart the behavioural responses of system-defying states to the problem of existence as they see it, and in particular to their sense of what went wrong before they attempted to put it right, we might be able to come finally to some sense of how genocides ultimately occur. If we were to return, for instance, to our five core examples, one notable feature in four of of them – Kampuchea being the exception – is that genocide does not synchronise with the emergence of the regime but happens some years down the line. Thus, Hitler comes to power in 1933 but initiates the 'Final Solution' in 1941, the CUP seizes power – first time round – in 1908 but do not commit genocide until 1915. Similarly the time gap between Bolshevik takeover and its onslaught on the kulaks is a twelve-year one, from 1917 to 1929, while the hiatus between the initiation of the original Hutu regime in Rwanda and its authentic successor's genocide is a period of thirty-five years, between 1959 and 1994.

Again, one might argue that there is nothing very noteworthy here. There is no particular pattern to these time-lags which, in any case in the Khmer Rouge example are hardly applicable. The initiation of each regime, moreover, is itself accompanied by varying degrees of extreme violence. In Rwanda's case, for instance, the killings in the wake of the original 1959 Hutu takeover of power were regarded by some contemporary observers as genocide.[141] The significance thus is not in the length of time-lag between the first initiating event and the second full or fuller outbreak of genocide but the fact that the regime's later response is conditioned by something it remembers as happening previously and which it wishes now to correct. Indeed, the memory may not be specifically of the circumstances in which it itself came to power at all but of some other national trauma or sequence of traumas which are its critical – even mythic – point of historical reference. The obvious example, as always, is the Nazi genocide of Jews. When was it initiated? In the high summer of 1941; at the critical make-or-break moment of the regime's existence, when, having consciously set itself on an agenda – the destruction of Soviet Russia and so the ultimate short-cut to German world power – it recognises what will be the consequences if it should fail: utter and total German destruction? Yet what is the reference point uppermost in Hitler and the core Nazi leadership's mind? Not January 1933 but November 1918, the moment of German defeat and humiliation at the end of the First World War.[142]

Hitler goes to war with Soviet (but also in his mind Jewish-Bolshevik) Russia, in 1941, not just for *Lebensraum* but to wipe out the fractured memory of impotence and humiliation which denied Germany her alleged rightful destiny and birthright in 1918. Everything, thus, is geared up in this second attempt to ensure that this time there will be no repeat failure: this time Germany *will* succeed. It is, to repeat Aronson's phraseology, the classic case of 'realising the unrealisable', the ultimate expression of an entirely self-willed audacity directed towards overturning the intrinsic framework of contemporary reality. It can only, of course, be achieved through massive violence, a statement in itself of why genocide generally is so intimately linked with war, or at the very least war-like emergencies. But it also carries with it by dint of its mythic linkage to 1918 a Nazi leadership promise to itself that *the specific causes* – as they see them – for that earlier catastrophe will not be allowed to repeat themselves in this second run. In the specifics of the Nazi case, when Operation Barbarossa starts to snarl up (as, almost inevitably it must), the response hence is not simply one of having a violent tantrum against the nearest and most obvious scapegoat or even simply taking revenge on that scapegoat for the Nazis' own failings. Rather, the complete and systematic extermination of the Jews takes off at this point because the potentiality of another looming disaster is immediately connected to that previous historic blot on the landscape for which the Jews as a collective are held singly and entirely responsible. 'They should not have staged 9 November 1918 with impunity', Hitler raged some twenty years later. 'That day shall be avenged ... The Jews shall be annihilated in our land.'[143] This is the classic example of what is referred to here as the perpetrator's 'never again' syndrome.

Of course, on one level, one could attempt to avoid any potential connectedness between this and other genocides by treating the events of 1941 as a full and final explosion of two millennia of damaged Christian–Jewish relations; in other words of something entirely specific to the Holocaust. Yet, on another level, one could equally propose that the contours and trajectory of the Nazis' 'never again' fixation are quite relateable and comparable with that of many other perpetrators. For instance, in all of our archetypal cases, Cambodia's included, the genocidaire perception of a particular moment or moments of previous societal trauma when the 'enemy' group almost succeeds in sabotaging the state's initial drive to achievement are broadly linked to some more general wrong-turn in the country's history when its leaders, perhaps inadvertently, or even perhaps traitorously, handed to this 'enemy' the wherewithal with which it would later attempt later to strike the state down. For the Nazis – as for many other Germans – the wrong turning is to be located in the wholly misconceived attempts of their Wilhelmine predecessors to include the Jews within the framework of national existence, by giving them equal rights. The same is true for the CUP looking back to the period of the high Tanzimat when the Ottoman state bequeathed citizenship on its Armenian and other non-Turkish populations. For Hutu Power the key wrong turning is in the Belgians' favouring of the minority Tutsi over the majority Hutu, while for Stalinists vis-à-vis the kulaks, it is Stolypin's first-decade-of-century reforms that build them up as a class. If a single moment is less identifiable in the Khmer Rouge case, the general rule still holds: the error is to be located in the French colonial and post-colonial Sihanoukist tendency to favour the urban, professional and/or non-racially Khmer people over the majority rural population.

In each of these instances, the charge is, in effect, the same: these historic enemies of the true, authentic, grass-roots and 'pure' forces of national or societal progress, the ones, in other words, who ought to be kept out, down, or preferably both, are actually given an unfair advantage with which not only to challenge but even undermine true society's heroic even Herculean path towards independence and salvation.[144] What may, thus, for Armenians or Jews, be seen as a brief window of opportunity, an occasion for celebration that here they were at last to be properly included in society on equal terms, is instead remembered by Nazi or CUP regimes as the real beginnings of the malaise, the moment when societal corrosion sets in, when its vital forces are sapped and traditional anti-Semitic or anti-Armenian antipathies proved to be entirely accurate.

But there is a further aspect as to why traditional boundary-contained prejudices begin to crystallise around this point into active and highly charged vehicles of hate. In each of our core examples alleged advantage being given to the enemy group is seen as closely aligned with a renewed surge of Western political or economic penetration, domination, influence or ideas. Of course, becoming more like the 'West' was welcomed in all our core cases by elite groups sympathetic to their country's essential alignment with the liberal-capitalist system. Nor was this goal necessarily the exact opposite of all of our system-defiers, MRND Rwanda, as we have seen, being one case almost entirely dependent on Western largesse to survive. Yet it is also a fact that the reason all our five archetypal genocide regimes are able to seize power in the first place or sustain it once there, is because they have sufficient popular backing for programmes or agendas which are grounded in notions of freeing themselves from foreign, meaning essentially Western, shackles or inter- ference. Which is exactly why the position of the targeted groups in each of these cases becomes so perilous. If these groups were always seen in essentially negative terms as alien 'others', 'foreign bodies', and/or as social and economic parasites, it is only in the context of their being seen *as somebody else's 'foreign bodies'*: as the stooges, agents or auxiliaries of interfering outside powers trying to undermine, even sabotage the state's self-styled drive to independence that the potentiality for genocide against them starts to become fully apparent.

Even then, the relationship between the crystallisation of that potential and its ultimate actualisation is determined by a regime's willingness to revisit the arena of its own or its predecessor's previous trauma: the moment, in other words, when the state's previous efforts at breaking free from its constraints are supposedly spiked through the alleged malevolence of the enemy group. For the Turks, that moment is really a continuous period of crisis stretching from at least 1878, through the 1890s and culminating in the Balkan wars of 1912–13, during which repeated Armenian political efforts to engage the Great Powers on behalf of their own agendas are seen as evidence of a collec- tive Armenian willingness to stab the empire in the back. Students of modern Germany history will be familiar that this very term, 'stab in the back' – *Dol- chstoss* – is the very refrain repeatedly intoned by wide sections of German society when, in November 1918, and the tumultuous months which follow it, responsibility for defeat at the hands of the Allies is laid at the door of Jews accused of inciting, orchestrating and leading the revolutions on the streets of German cities.

The kulaks, by contrast, are not a social group one would immediately identify with Western capitalism, or for that matter Soviet Bolshevism (Jews, of course, being regularly accused of being in cahoots with both). Yet, in 1921, when under the weight of international – Western – intervention in support of the forces of reaction, as well as the impossible task of social and economic transformation which it had set itself, the Bolshevik party was forced to call a halt to its agenda and instead initiate a New Economic Policy (NEP), in effect bowing to market forces, the prime beneficiaries of this humiliating retreat and Soviet Thermidor are Russia's peasants. For which the Bolsheviks specifi- cally read kulaks. For many among the Hutu elite in Rwanda looking back at their recent history, their moment of truth is the period 1959–64. Here, on the one hand, they achieve a signal two-fold victory, sweeping away Belgian control and monarchy, yet on the other hand they face repeated and almost fatal counter-revolutionary attacks from both inside and outside the country. Again, the accused party, the Tutsi, are branded not only as perpetual enemies of majority-rule Rwanda but a grouping willing to act as agents of foreign powers in order to bring the state down and so enslave its 'authentic' people once again. Cambodia's Eastern Zone genocide may be somewhat at variance from this rule in the lack of any specific historic reference point. But arguably, not unlike Ottoman Turkey, this may simply be because there are so many catastrophes and traumas acting as grist to the Khmer Rouge mill – and not just in the immediate prequel to their takeover, but also in a pre-colonial record where the Vietnamese, above all, are seen as the liquidating force of the historic Khmer polity. Here again, 'never again' antipathies against any communal group seen as assisting the historic enemy could not fail to be massively reactivated.

Genocide, then, does not have to follow a two-stage process, nor even be impelled by a perpetrator's promise to itself that 'never again' will it allow some communal adversary, or adversaries to disrupt or sabotage its transformative-salvationist agenda. It is, however, difficult to imagine without at least something similar to these sort of contours or ingredients how genocide can be translated from something in the thought processes and discussions of regime leaders into an active policy requiring the allocation of major state resources and personnel for its implementation. The very fact that somebody, some group, some committee at the highest level of state must make that decision certainly suggests something considered and thought through, implying similarly that the end result is expected to be of net benefit to both state, and society, if not in the immediate, then at least in the longer term. This would seem to favour an explanation for genocide in purely 'rational choice' terms. Yet, as we have seen, the circumstances in which such decisions are reached are almost never ones of calm, clinical detachment but of acute, crisis-laden desperation. Certainly, perpetrators may rationally weigh in their minds at this given point that to go forward is potentially to burn their bridges to the international community and thus put their regime and state in even greater jeopardy. This may, indeed, be a factor as to why they usually go to such inordinate lengths to dissemble their actions. Yet at the same time what equally seems to drive them – informed, as it usually is by that sense of some calamitous loss of nerve in the country's historic experience – is an almost pathological conviction that this is the only way out of their country's all-pervasive crisis and sense of impending doom.

That certainly – and, one might argue, very conveniently – throws responsibility for genocide onto the victims rather than the perpetrators. But it would also seem to suggest a perpetrator's mindset in which the victims *really are seen* as the agents of an international malevolence whose sole aim is to deny their state its rightful future. Tutsi in Rwanda, Jumma in Bangladesh, Karen in Burma, Dinka and Nuer in southern Sudan, Assyrians and Kurds in Iraq, Harkis in Algeria; the more one looks, the more one finds examples in the recent history of genocide of minority groups whose fate hinges on their historic connections with Western, usually former imperial powers. Where the connections hardly exist then they can also be invented. When the Herero began their fatal insurrection against Germans in 1904, the latter's immediate response was to assume that the British were behind it.[145] If this was entirely untrue, genuine British machinations a half-century earlier to utilise Circassian tribes against the Russians in the Caucasus proved critical to a near-exterminatory outcome for these native peoples.[146] Nor, as we have come closer to the present-day, does the big, bad power have to be a Western one. In the era of the Cold War if Tibetans could be collectively tarnished as proxies of the CIA by the Chinese, equally so could anybody in some states if they were, or were deemed to be, communist. Such, for example, was the fate of great swathes of Indonesia's population when, in 1965, the military, impelled by their 'never again' memory of communist uprising in 1948, launched their own major genocide.[147]

Yet in all these instances, perhaps, the most startling aspect is the way that the power of the group targeted for destruction is nearly always exaggerated out of all proportion. If the 'international Jewish conspiracy' stands as by far and away the most fantastical of these imaginings – the Jews being seen not so much as the proxies of a foreign power as the power itself – in nearly all cases where this projection occurs the discrepancy between the actuality of the threat posed compared with the way it is portrayed by the perpetrating regime is so great as to implicitly confirm Aronson's notion of 'a rupture with reality'. If such confabulations were isolated and not a part of a general pattern we might more readily dismiss them as examples of a regime's conscious but mischievous disinformation whose primary purpose is to deceive and manipulate their supposedly gullible wider population. The importance of such intentional propaganda is not to be denied; it is an essential part of the backdrop to genocide. But neither does it seem to negate often genuinely held convictions on the part of the core – and not so core – perpetrators that they really are confronting forces of such potency as to bring about the disruption if not dissolution of their state's imperial, colonial or national agendas.

We have previously suggested that these socio-psychological tendencies to projection are not in themselves peculiar to the phenomenon of genocide but are an aspect of the human condition. Applied by Bloch and other members of the Frankfurt school to societies in crisis, or more particularly those parts of society which feel left behind, frustrated or resentful of change, the results may indeed be a rampant and barbaric rebellion against civilisation, albeit with Aronson's proviso about their 'using the technical and organisational sophistication available only in that civilisation' to accomplish it.[148] Yet the problem is not ultimately one peculiar to social formations or classes left stranded in the rock-pools of an advancing tide; nor is it exactly a question of wanting to return to a fantasy past. In the world of increasing global modernisation conceived of and driven by Western capitalism, it is almost impossible for societies to cut themselves off in this way. There is no choice but to play the system's game. But to do so requires at the very minimum nation-statehood, an assumption which in turn demands not simply attempting to keep abreast of fellow nation-states but actually accelerating one's developmental drive in order to compete more effectively in the wider international political economy.

The states, or more specifically regimes to which we have paid most attention to date in our archetypal cases, are not ones who do not want to be there, they want to succeed – albeit on their own terms – and to be acknowledged as such. Indeed, on one level they seem to evince signs of enormous confidence, if not overconfidence as to their abilities, accompanied often by a jarring hubris. The problem is that historical development seems to be working against them. Or so they perceive it. They see no option thus but to make up lost ground or at least assert their goal of independent development by taking some short-cut, a direction which may involve a strident and dangerous defiance of the system, or possibly the covert assistance of the system leaders. Either way, as their goals are not realisable by normal everyday methods, indeed, as there clearly is a discrepancy between the projected goals and the plausibility of arriving there, something has to give. If the result is very much a self-inflicted crisis or series of crises of state and society, the only way it can be obviously deflected is through projecting it onto those who stand in its way, or oppose it, or, through their very existence, show the state agenda to be the unattainable mirage that it is. Genocide may not result immediately through the full crystallisation of this projection. But in circumstances where a regime renews or more forcefully attempts the realisation of the unrealisable, and the potentially life-threatening crisis to state and society ensues, the drive to nemesis may become unstoppable.

*

Summary

Let us then very briefly attempt to state the main conclusions of *The Meaning of Genocide*. The first chapter hinged on the problem of what we actually mean by genocide. The question may sound trite but without being able to provide some coherent formulation it might be better to concede that genocide is simply another word we use for 'mass murder' or one we should jettison in favour of a more all-encompassing term such as 'democide'. This study, however, is predicated on the assumption that genocide – the state organised partial or total extermination of perceived or actual communal groups – is distinguishable from other forms of mass murder and that it is important to understand the mechanisms of its particular operation. But it also concedes that it cannot be absolutely categorised. There are grey areas. In fact, there are a lot of grey areas. There is also an essentially cultural problem, or more specifically Western cultural problem which we acknowledged at the outset, that the very term has become so charged and carries such a weighty emotional load, that almost any attempt at definition is likely to run up against any number of interest groups demanding their pet issue for inclusion or exclusion. But even were we in a position to act as some all-powerful arbiter offering guidance on each case we might be hard-pressed to always provide a crystal-clear verdict.

Consider, for instance, eastern Anatolia, a key zone of genocide to which we have referred. A whole range of ethnic groups, Armenians, Assyrians, Kurds, Pontic Greeks have all been systematically and repeatedly assaulted by Ottoman and successor Turkish and Iraqi states in this area over the last 120 or more years. There have been massive human rights abuses, draconian coercion, massacres, communal pogroms and mass deportations. But not each and every one of these events in itself constitutes a policy of extirpation. Even when it has occurred we can see important differences. The genocide perpetrated against the Turkish Kurds of the Dersim area in 1936 was essentially partial and local, while that against Iraq's Assyrians in 1933 was aborted almost as it began.[149] Compared to what happened to the Armenians in 1915, or, for that matter, what happened to them nearly a generation earlier in 1894–6, these other events were smaller scale, ultimately somewhat less systematic, and less total not only for the victim groups involved but also for their implications for the dominant state and society. The point of stating these different contours, however, is not to promote a hierarchy of suffering but simply to remind ourselves that genocides are not all the same in scope or scale just as genocide itself is only one, albeit the most extreme outcome on a spectrum of possibilities which a state might consider for dealing with what it perceives to be a troublesome communal population. This should also confirm that the study of genocide is nine-parts that of genocidal process and only one-part that of a particular outcome. But this does not obviate the problem that some genocides blur into other scenarios where the term might not apply, or the fact that the phenomenon never emanates out of a vacuum but more often than not out of conditions of civil conflict or inter-state war which sometimes become confused with the act itself. Indeed, it is these very complications which make it essential to chart as closely as possible the interactions between state and communal group through which genocide specifically emerges.

In Chapter 2, thus, we proposed that genocide always involves this dynamic. But the very fact that this in turn involves relationships of power may also require us to consider the targeted group – or more particularly its political elites or leaderships – less in the conventional sense of a one-dimensional group of passive innocents and more as protagonists in their own right. We have not found any easy or obvious way round the terms 'perpetrator' and 'victim' to describe those who are responsible for the killing and those who are killed. Yet we also consider that these criminological referents do not do proper justice to the political ramifications implicit in genocide. Certainly, many targeted groups either do not have political agendas or if they do, have very diverse ones. However, these are nearly always treated as monolithic by the perpetrator regime which in itself blurs the distinction between genocide and politicide as posited by Harff and Gurr.

Yet there is a further two-fold paradox here. Firstly, genocide can only become genocide by dint of the state–community relationship being totally asymmetrical – at least at the moment of genocide – enabling the state to strike at the (real or perceived) communal group with complete impunity to itself. Objectively, thus, genocide might be understood as simply an extreme variant of radical state developmental agendas geared towards seizing the land, resources and/or property of recalcitrant, resistant or intransigent population groups through their physical elimination. The second part of the paradox, however, lies in the fact that the perpetrator rarely sees the conflict *only* in these utilitarian terms. Targeted groups may certainly be marked off from the 'loyal' population by any number of (real or perceived) ethnic, social or religious differences, which in itself lends some weight to the argument that it is regimes which put a particular premium on some racial, ethnic, social or other basis for organic unity which are more likely to be predisposed towards genocide. Whether this is the case or not, however, and remembering that pre-twentieth-century Western colonial polities were also notable recidivists, a much more regular and common characteristic in nearly all such regimes which commit the act is the belief – however spurious or misconceived it may be – that the victim group wields a political, cultural or even spiritual, and hence demonic, power which poses a clear and present danger to the state, demanding that the state defend itself accordingly. The evidence, moreover, overwhelmingly suggests that this is not simply a convenient rationalisation but is genuinely held. Understanding genocide as a result, is very dependent on probing the mindset of the perpetrator's regime and of its supporting demotic culture in order to tease out the anxieties, phobias and obsessions which not only drive it but drive it to act in often highly conspiratorial and even deeply *irrational* ways. This is all the more so given that in *some* cases of genocide no actual, objectively determined communal enemy exists: it is instead largely conjured into existence through the perpetrator's own distorted, or even fantasy version of reality.

If one might be inclined thereby to interpret this as another problematic facet of the human condition, in Chapter 3 we have gone to some lengths to propose that this has developed into what we think of as the specific phenomenon of genocide primarily through the historical transformation of human societies worldwide as a politically and economically interacting and universal system of modern – mostly nation – states. Wars of people-extermination are clearly as old as history. Even in quite recent times, contemporaneous with the advent of our emerging framework, mass murder of this sort, such as that initiated by Shaka in southern Africa, was being perpetrated. But whether we consider what Shaka was doing as genocide or not, his relationship to the processes and patterns described herein remains essentially tangential. Certainly he was intent on creating a strong, even 'totalitarian' state but his agenda, except in a peripheral way, was neither to engage with nor indeed circumvent the emerging international system itself.

This study thus sees in the processes whereby that system was created both the primary well-springs and continuing motor to genocide. At the outset it was the avant-garde modernising states, usually in their colonial or imperial guise, who were its prime exponents. Later it was primarily their foremost global challengers, later on still, all manner of post-colonial polities as the system itself became truly globalised. Genocide as such is a systemic dysfunction and cannot be simply or solely dismissed as the aberrant or deviant behaviour of rogue, revolutionary or 'totalitarian' regimes or for that matter ones with particular, one might say peculiar, types of political culture or social and ethnic configuration. On the contrary, the very fact that genocide is the by-product of such states' drives towards development and/or empowerment only makes proper sense within the context of the system's fundamental disequilibrium as determined by a hegemonic leadership which either abets, ignores or anathematises breaches of its rule-book.

This does not mean that the causes of much contemporary extreme violence cannot be found in more nationally bounded communal, often ethno-religious interactions, though even here explaining a pogrom in northern Nigeria, or inter-ethnic massacres in the Indonesian archipelago without due reference to a range of global political, economic, demographic and environmental factors and pressures would be rather nonsensical. This certainly would suggest that the relationships between broader patterns of conflict and what we specifically refer to here as genocide are themselves in serious need of further analysis. Nor, particularly as the scope and scale of these broader conflicts continue to expand, are such mass killings somehow less important or serious than cases of genocide. The fact that the massive inter-ethnic bloodletting of the Indian sub-continent in 1947, or, the inter-tribal massacres of Nigeria which preceded the Biafra war in 1965, or for that matter the wave of killings perpetrated by Idi Amin in Uganda in the 1970s, will remain essentially marginal to a later volume of this study is not because they are less noteworthy or significant than some of what has happened in Rwanda, Burundi or the Chittagong Hill Tracts. It is simply that they do not fall squarely into the immediate parameters of our definition of genocide.

We have sought to develop that definition primarily by reference to five key twentieth-century cases. But if this thereby emphasises the degree to which genocide has become a function of unusually driven latecomer states attempting to assert their integrity and independence in a system created by and operated on behalf of its forerunners, seeking the true origins of the phenomenon demands engagement with precisely that group of Western avant-gardists, *their* explosion onto the global stage, and the consequences for the rest of humankind. It is pursuit of this pre-1914 quarry that will be the goal of *The Rise of the West and the Coming of Genocide*, the second volume of this study.

Notes

Preface

1 See Ernst Nolte, 'Vergangenheit, die nicht vergehen will', *Frankfurter Allgemeine Zeitung*, 6 June 1986, for Nolte's opening tirade. Idem., *Der europäische Bürgerkreig. Nationalsozialismus und Bolschewismus* (Frankfurt on Maine and Berlin: Propylaen, 1987), however, for the more interesting, if still flawed thesis concerning the idea of a European civil war between 1917 and 1945. Charles S. Maier, *The Unmasterable Past, History, Holocaust and German National Identity* (Cambridge, MA, and London: Harvard University Press, 1988); Peter Baldwin, ed., *Reworking the Past, Hitler, the Holocaust and the Historians Debate* (Boston, MA: Beacon Press, 1990) for analyses of the *Historikerstreit* and its repercussions.

2 See Richard G. Hovannisian, *The Armenian Holocaust. A Bibliography Relating to the Deportations, Massacres and Dispersion of the Armenian People 1915–1923* (Cambridge, MA: Armenian Heritage Press, 1980); Hamo Vassilian, ed., *The Armenian Genocide: A Comprehensive Bibliography and Library Resource Guide* (Glendale, CA: Armenian Reference Book Co., 1992); G. A. Abraamian, *Russkie Istochniki o genotside Armian v Osmanskoi imperii, 1915–1916 gody* ['Russian Sources on the Genocide of the Armenians in the Ottoman Empire in the Years 1915–1916'], (Yerevan: Areresum, 1995), for details.

3 A. Dirk Moses, 'Conceptual Blockages and Definitional Dilemmas in the "Racial Century": Genocides of Indigenous Peoples and the Holocaust', *Patterns of Prejudice*, 36:4 (2002), 28.

4 Raphael Lemkin, *Axis Rule in Occupied Europe* (Washington, DC: Carnegie Endowment for International Peace, 1944).

5 Ian Buruma, *Wages of Guilt, Memories of War in Japan and Germany* (London: Jonathan Cape, 1994), 295.

6 Dominick LaCapra, *Writing History, Writing Trauma* (Baltimore and London: Johns Hopkins University Press, 2001), 22–3; Moses, 'Conceptual Blockages', 11; Alain Finkelkraut, *The Future of a Negation, Reflections on the Question of Genocide,* trans. Mary Byrd Kelly (Lincoln, NB, and London: University of Nebraska Press, 1998), 112–17; Omer Bartov, 'Defining Enemies, Making Victims: Germans, Jews and the Holocaust', *American Historical Review*, 103 (1998), 811–12, for further commentary.

7 Gavriel D. Rosenfeld, 'The Politics of Uniqueness: Reflections on the Recent Polemical Turn in Holocaust and Genocide Scholarship', *Holocaust and Genocide Studies*, 13:1 (1999), 28–61.

8 Moses, 'Conceptual Blockages', 18. See also Dan Stone, 'The Historiography of Genocide: Beyond "Uniqueness" and Ethnic Competition', *Rethinking History*, 8:1 (2004), 127–42.

9 Karl Marx, 'Thesis on Feuerbach' (1845), quoted in Sidney Pollard, *The Idea of Progress, History and Society* (London: Pelican, 1971), 128.

Introduction

1 Leo Kuper, *Genocide: Its Political Use in the Twentieth Century* (New Haven, CT, and London: Yale University Press, 1981), 40.

2 Ibid., 101.

3 Helen Fein, 'Genocide: A Sociological Perspective', *Current Sociology*, 38:1 (1990), 56.

4 Maier, *Unmasterable Past,* 69.

5 Moses, 'Conceptual Blockages', 21.

6 Frank Chalk and Kurt Jonassohn, *The History and Sociology of Genocide* (New Haven, CT, and London: Yale University Press, 1990), 32.

7 Ibid.

8 Max Horkeimer and Theodor W. Adorno, *Dialectic of Enlightenment*, trans. John Cumming (New York: Continuum, 1972 [first published 1944]). See also Enzo Traverso, *Understanding the Nazi Holocaust, Marxism after Auschwitz*, trans. Peter Drucker (London: Pluto Press, 1999), chapter 3, 'On the Edge of Understanding: From the Frankfurt School to Ernest Mandel', and the wide range of essays, some of which deal critically with Horkheimer and Adorno, in James Kaye and Bo Strath, eds, *Enlightenment and Genocide, Contradictions of Modernity* (Brussels: P.I.E-Peter Lang, 2000).

9 Richard L. Rubenstein, 'Afterword: Genocide and Civilisation', in Isidor Wallimann and Michael Dobkowski, eds, *Genocide and the Modern Age* (Westport, CT: Greenwood Press, 1987), 284.

10 Zygmunt Bauman, *Modernity and the Holocaust* (Oxford: Blackwell, 1989), 12.

11 C. A. Bayly, 'The British and Indigenous Peoples 1760–1860: Power, Perception and Identity', in Martin Daunton and Rick Halpern, eds, *Empire and Others: British Encounters with Indigenous Peoples, 1600–1850* (London: UCL Press, 1999), 27.

12 See Immanuel Wallerstein, *The Capitalist World-Economy* (Cambridge and New York: Cambridge University Press, 1979) for the emerging relationships between metropolitan core, peripheries and semi-peripheries.

13 See E. P. Thompson, *Customs in Common* (London: Penguin, 1993), chapter 3, 'Custom, Law and Common Right'; Pierre Bourdieu, *Outline of a Theory of*

Practice, trans. Richard Nice (Cambridge and New York: Cambridge University Press, 1977), 16–17, 78–87, for the concept of 'habitus' and chapter 4, 'Structure, Habitus, Power: Basis for a Theory of Symbolic Power', for its application to the peoples of the Algerian Kabyle.

14 As stated in John Gray, 'Blair is in Thrall to the Myth of a Monolithic Modernity', *Guardian,* 19 April 2003. See idem., *False Dawn, The Delusions of Global Capitalism* (London: Granta Books, 1998), for a fuller exposition of this theme.

15 Tzvetan Todorov, *The Conquest of America, The Question of the Other,* trans. Richard Howard (New York: HarperPerennial, 1984), for the classic discussion of this theme. Also Norbert Finzsch, 'Settler Imperialism and Discourses of Genocide in Eighteenth and Nineteenth-Century America and Australia', in A. Dirk Moses, *Genocide and Colonialism* (New York and Oxford: Berghahn Books, forthcoming, 2005)

16 James Kaye and Bo Strath, 'Introduction', in idem., *Enlightenment,* 15.

17 Quoted in Chandak Sengoopta, *Imprint of the Raj, How Fingerprinting Was Born in Colonial India* (Basingstoke: Macmillan, 2003), 43.

18 John C. Mohawk, *Utopian Legacies, A History of Conquest and Oppression in the Western World* (Santa Fe, NM: Clear Light Publishers, 2000), chapter 1, 'Utopia and the Pursuit of the Ideal'.

19 Alexander Laban Hinton, 'The Dark Side of Modernity: Toward an Anthropology of Genocide', in idem., *Annihilating Difference, the Anthropology of Genocide* (Berkeley and Los Angeles: University of California Press, 2002), 13.

20 Sengoopta, *Imprint,* chapter 3, 'A Signature of Exceeding Singularity', for William James Herschel's original explorations of the uses of fingerprinting.

21 See Gretchen E. Schafft, 'Scientific Racism in the Service of the Reich: German Anthropologists in the Nazi Era', in Hinton, *Annihilating Difference,* 117–34.

22 Hinton, 'Dark Side', 12–14.

23 Ibid., 12.

24 Gerard J. Libaridian, 'The Ultimate Repression: The Genocide of the Armenians', in Wallimann and Dobkowski, *Genocide,* 216–17.

25 Sengoopta, *Imprint,* 42; Kaye and Strath, 'Introduction', 15. More generally on the rise of race as a concept and its linkage to modernity see Eric D. Weitz, *A Century of Genocide, Utopias of Race and Nation* (Princeton and Oxford: Princeton University Press, 2003), chapter 1, 'Race and Nation: An Intellectual History'.

26 James C. Scott, *Seeing Like a State, How Certain Schemes to Improve the Human Condition Have Failed* (New Haven, CT and London: Yale University Press, 1998), 47, 11. See more generally chapter 1, 'Nature and Space'.

27 Ibid., 11.

28 Norbert Elias, *The Civilizing Process,* vol. 2: *State Formation and Civilization* (Oxford: Oxford University Press, 1982).

29 Barrington Moore, Jr., *Social Origins of Dictatorship and Democracy* (London: Penguin, 1967); Charles Tilly, *Coercion, Capital and European States AD 990–1990* (Oxford: Blackwell, 1990), esp. 205–7. See also Mark Mazower, ' Violence and

the State in the Twentieth Century', *American Historical Review*, 107:4 (2002), 1158, for commentary.

30 Scott, *Seeing*, 11. See also Peter Holquist, '"To Count, to Extract and to Exterminate", Population Statistics and Population Politics in Late Imperial and Soviet Russia', in Ronald Grigor Suny and Terry Martin, eds, *A State of Nations, Empire and Nation-Making in the Age of Lenin and Stalin* (Oxford: Oxford University Press, 2001), 112–13, for a searching insight into the general nineteenth-century European policy-driven application of these aspirations in the shape of 'population politics'.

31 Henry J. Steiner and Philip Alston, eds, *International Human Rights in Context, Law, Politics, Morals* (Oxford: Oxford University Press, 2000), 1376–80, for the complete text but also the verdict of Scott, *Seeing*, 32, where he likens citizenship to an 'abstract grid'.

32 See Gerard Chaliand, 'Minority Peoples in the Age of Nation-States', in idem., ed., *Minority Peoples in the Age of Nation-States*, trans. Tony Berrett (London: Pluto Press, 1989), 1–11.

33 See most obviously Michel Foucault, *Madness and Civilisation: A History of Insanity in the Age of Reason*, trans. Richard Howard (London: Routledge, 2001 [first published 1967]); idem., *Discipline and Punish, The Birth of the Prison*, trans. Alan Sheridan (London: Penguin, 1979); Colin Gordon, ed., *M. Foucault: Power/ Knowledge, Selected Interviews and Other Writings 1972–1977*, trans. Colin Gordon (Brighton, Harvester Press, 1980).

34 Human Rights Watch, *Slaughter Among Neighbours, The Political Origins of Communal Violence* (New Haven, CT, and London: Yale University Press, 1995), for some notable examples.

35 See Alexis Heraclides, *The Self-Determination of Minorities in International Politics* (London: Frank Cass, 1991), on the latter score.

36 Carole Nagengast, 'Inoculations of Evil in the U.S.–Mexican Border Region, Reflections on the Genocidal Potential of Symbolic Violence', in Hinton, *Annihilating Difference*, 328.

37 Ibid. See also James Schmidt, 'Genocide and the Limits of Enlightenment: Horkheimer and Adorno Revisited', in Kaye and Strath, *Enlightenment*, 99, for support of this line: 'The renunciation demanded by modern forms of social life may well serve as the breeding ground for explosions of rage against anyone in a society who appears (if only in the delusions of the attacker) to have somehow escaped these demands. To be different is to be at risk.'

38 However, we might be equally wary here of assumptions as to the emergence of intolerant thought systems in the Middle Ages, which might then provide another route towards an obvious point of culmination in the Holocaust. See David Nirenberg, *Communities of Violence, Persecution of Minorities in the Middle Ages* (Princeton: Princeton University Press, 1996), 4–5, for a robust refutation on this score.

39 Ward Churchill, 'Genocide: Towards a Functional Definition', *Alternatives,* 11 (1986), 403.

40 See Saul Friedlander, ed., *Probing the Limits of Representation: Nazism and the Final Solution* (Cambridge, MA: Harvard University Press, 1992); LaCapra, *Writing History,* for critical reflections on the conundrum.

41 See Rose Lindsey, 'From Atrocity to Data: The Historiographies of Rape in Former Yugoslavia and the Gendering of Genocide', *Patterns of Prejudice*, 36:4 (2002), 74; Tony Kushner, 'The Holocaust and the Museum World in Britain: A Study of Ethnography', *Immigrants and Minorities*, 21:1/2 (2002), 28–33, for important commentaries on this score.

42 Kuper, *Genocide,* 9, for similar anxieties.

43 See Jeffrey C. Alexander, 'On the Social Construction of Moral Universals: The "Holocaust" from War Crime to Trauma Drama', *European Journal of Social Theory*, 5:1 (2002), 5–85.

44 Norman Finkelstein, *The Holocaust Industry* (New York: Verso, 2000).

45 Raul Hillberg, *The Politics of Memory: The Journey of a Holocaust Historian* (Chicago: Ivan R. Dee, 1996), 105–119. Also more generally, Peter Novick, *The Holocaust in American Life* (Boston: Houghton Mifflin, 1999), chapter 6, 'Not in the Best Interests of Jewry'.

46 Sergio della Pergola, 'Changing Cores and Peripheries: Fifty Years in Socio-Demographic Perspective', in Robert Wistrich, ed., *Terms of Survival, The Jewish World since 1945* (London and New York: Routledge, 1995), 13–43.

47 See for example, Deborah Lipstadt, *Denying the Holocaust: The Growing Assault on Truth and Memory* (New York: Free Press, 1993).

48 There appears to be no comparable study to that of della Pergola with regard to the demographic profile and social mobility of American Armenians. However, considerable data relating to this can be gleaned from Anny P. Bakalian, *Armenian-Americans. From Being to Feeling Armenian* (New Brunswick, NJ, and London: Transaction Publishers, 1993), esp. chapter 1, 'Introduction: Assimilation and Identity'. See also Peter Balakian, *Black Dog of Fate: A Memoir* (New York: Basic Books, 1997), 'An Armenian Jew in Surburbia', 35–44, for a gentle insight into Armenian-Jewish affinities in the USA.

49 Alexander Solzhenitsyn, *The Gulag Archipelago, 1918–1956*, trans. Thomas P. Whitney (New York and London: Collins/Fontana, 1974), vol. 1, 24–5.

50 Mark Munzel, 'The Manhunts: Aché Indians in Paraguay', in Willem A. Veenhoven, ed., *Case Studies on Human Rights and Fundamental Freedoms, A World Survey* (The Hague: Martinus Nijhoff, 1976), vol. 4, 392–4, and idem., 'Manhunt', in Richard Arens, *Genocide in Paraguay* (Philadelphia: Temple University Press, 1976), 37–8, for sketchy attempts to assess the disaster, Munzel concluding that 900 northern Aché had been killed or kidnapped and that possibly 800–1,200 were, at that stage, still alive.

51 Mark Mazower, 'After Lemkin: Genocide, The Holocaust and History', *Jewish Quarterly*, 156 (Winter 1994/5), 8.

52 Ibid. See also Steven E. Aschheim, review of 'Journal of Genocide Research', *Times Literary Supplement,* 9 November 2001, 33.

53 See Samuel Totten, William S. Parsons and Robert K. Hitchcock, 'Confronting Genocide and Ethnocide of Indigenous Peoples', in Hinton, *Annihilating Difference,* 62–4, for discussion of the controversy.

54 Andrew Gray, *The Amerindians of South America* (London: Minority Rights Group, 1987); Survival International, *Disinherited: Indians in Brazil* (London: Survival International, 2000) and http//www.survival.org.uk.

55 Michel-Rolph Trouillot, *Silencing the Past, Power and the Production of History* (Boston: Beacon Press, 1995).

56 Robin Okey, 'The Legacy of Massacre: The "Jasenovac Myth" and the Breakdown of Communist Yugoslavia', in Mark Levene and Penny Roberts, eds, *The Massacre in History* (New York and Oxford: Berghahn Books, 1999), 270.

57 Ibid., 272.

58 Ibid., 267–68. See also Branimir Anzulovic, *Heavenly Serbia, From Myth to Genocide* (New York: New York University Press, 1999), 101–4, for corroboration of the intrinsic soundness of the Žerjavic and Kočović studies.

59 Martin van Bruinessen, 'Genocide of the Kurds', in Israel W. Charny, ed., *The Widening Circle of Genocide, Genocide: A Critical Bibliographical Review* (New Brunswick and London: Transaction Publishers, 1988), vol. 3, 177.

60 Middle East Watch, *Genocide in Iraq: The Anfal Campaign against the Kurds* (New York: Human Rights Watch, 1993).

61 David Irving, *Hitler's War* (London: Hodder and Stoughton, 1977), esp. 392. By the time of the 1991 edition of the book, Irving had radicalised his position even more thoroughly to one of blanket 'hard-core' Holocaust denial. See Richard J. Evans, *Telling Lies about Hitler: History, Holocaust and the David Irving Trial* (New York: Basic Books, 2001), 112–13.

62 Evans, *Telling Lies,* for a meticulous and detailed examination of Irving's method and motivation.

63 Tony Kushner, 'Holocaust and Museum World', 20–1, for instance, specifically notes the problems of forensic archaeology with regard to the 'hundreds if not thousands of sites of destruction'.

64 See, notably, Robert Conquest, *The Harvest of Sorrow, Soviet Collectivisation and the Terror-Famine* (New York: Oxford University Press, 1986); idem., *The Great Terror, A Reassessment* (New York and Oxford: Oxford University Press, 1990).

65 See, for instance, J. Arch Getty and Roberta T. Manning, eds, *Stalinist Terror, New Perspectives* (Cambridge: Cambridge University Press, 1993).

66 Steve Laurence Kaplan, *Disputed Legacies, The Historians' Feud 1789/1989* (Ithaca, NY, and London: Cornell University Press, 1995), chapter 4, 'The Vendée Trope and Idée France', and, more generally, Jean-Clément Martin, *La Vendée de la Mémoire 1800–1980* (Paris: Éditions du Seuil, 1989).

67 See, in a more generalised vein on this score, Stanley Cohen, *States of Denial, Knowing about Atrocities and Suffering* (Cambridge: Polity Press, 2001), esp. chapter 5, 'Blocking Out the Past: Personal Memories, Public Histories'.

1 Definitional Conundrums

1 As originally in Mark Levene, 'Is the Holocaust Simply Another Example of Genocide?', *Patterns of Prejudice*, 28:2 (1994), 11, but with a critical emendation in the borrowed term 'organic collectivity', from Scott Straus, 'Contested Meanings and Conflicting Imperatives: a Conceptual Analysis of Genocide', *Journal of Genocide Research*, 3:3 (2001), 366.

2 Chalk and Jonassohn, *History*, 44–9, for the full text.

3 See ibid., 11; Jacques Sémelin, 'From Massacre to the Genocidal Process', *International Social Science Journal*, 174 (2002), 434–5.

4 For my own doubts on this matter see Mark Levene, 'A Dissenting Voice: or How Current Assumptions of Deterring and Preventing Genocide May Be Looking at the Problem through the Wrong End of the Telescope', *Journal of Genocide Research*, 6:2 and 6:3 (2004), 153–66 and 431–45.

5 Steve Paulsson, 'The Term "Genocide"', h-holocaust@h-net.msu.edu, 11 December 2002.

6 For further examples including, in some instances, egregious examples of trivialisation see Straus, 'Contested Meanings', 349, 359; David Stannard, 'Preface', in Ward Churchill, *A Little Matter of Genocide, Holocaust and Denial in the Americas: 1492 to the Present* (San Francisco: City Light Books, 1997); Novick, *Holocaust in American Life*, 192–5, 247–53. For a more obviously post-modernist defence of the term's broad usage, see Charles Briggs, 'Genocide', in David Theo Goldberg and John Solomos, eds, *A Companion to Racial and Ethnic Studies* (Malden, MA, and Oxford: Blackwell Publishers, 2002), 31–45.

7 David Moshman, 'Conceptual Constraints on Thinking about Genocide', *Journal of Genocide Research*, 3:3 (2001), 431.

8 See Seymour Drescher, 'Slavery as Genocide', in Israel W. Charny, ed., *Encyclopedia of Genocide* (Santa Barbara and Denver: ABC-CLIO, 1999), vol. 2, 517–18.

9 However, see Kuper, *Genocide*, 197–204, for a somewhat ambiguous argument for the relationship between apartheid and genocide.

10 See Rosenfeld, 'Politics', 35–7, for the emergence of this trope; Moshman, 'Conceptual Constraints', 433–6 for its deleterious impact on comparative genocide studies.

11 Israel W. Charny, 'Introduction', in idem., ed., *Genocide, A Critical Bibliographical Review* (London: Mansell, 1988), vol. 1, xii. See also idem., 'Editor's Introduction: The Dawning of a New Age of Opposition to Genocide', in Charny, *Encyclopedia*, vol. 1.

12 For those unfamiliar with the causes of third-world mass murder – albeit at one remove – should read Susan George, *How the Other Half Dies, The Real Reasons for World Hunger* (London: Penguin, 1976). However, for a more cogent argument to the effect that genocide has to be seen as part of a continuum which begins with multitudinous, everyday forms of structural violence, see, amongst others of her works, Nancy Scheper-Hughes, *Death without Weeping: The Violence of Everyday Life in Brazil* (Berkeley and Los Angeles: University of California Press, 1993) and idem., 'Coming to our Senses, Anthropology and Genocide', in Hinton, *Annihilating Difference*, esp. 369–74.

13 Quoted in Eric Hobsbawm, *Age of Extremes, The Short Twentieth Century 1914–1991* (London: Abacus, 1995), 12.

14 Yehuda Bauer, 'The Place of the Holocaust in Contemporary History', *Studies in Contemporary Jewry*, 1 (1984), 213.

15 Ibid., 201.

16 See Alan Rosenberg, 'Was the Holocaust Unique?', in Wallimann and Dobkowski, *Genocide*, 153–6, for a discussion of Bauer's shifting, often ambiguous position on Holocaust versus genocide.

17 Saul Friedlander, 'On the Possibility of the Holocaust: An Approach to Historical Synthesis', in Yehuda Bauer and Nathan Rotenstreich, eds, *The Holocaust as Historical Experience* (New York: Holmes and Meier, 1981), 2.

18 Steven T. Katz, *The Holocaust in Historical Context*, vol. 1: *The Holocaust and Mass Death before the Modern Age* (New York and Oxford: Oxford University Press, 1994), 131.

19 See Chalk and Jonassohn, *History*, 23.

20 Katz, *Holocaust*, 131.

21 Ibid., 28.

22 See, however, Michael Freeman, 'Puritans and Pequots, The Question of Genocide', *New England Quarterly*, 68 (1995), 278–93, for one example where an earlier Katz disavowal of genocide on the grounds of absence of actualised intent (Steven T. Katz, 'The Pequot War Reconsidered', *New England Quarterly*, 64 (1991), 206–24) is searchingly repudiated.

23 The Rwanda case arguably brings the whole Katz thesis crashing down. See, however, René Lemarchand, 'Disconnecting the Threads: Rwanda and the Holocaust Reconsidered', *Journal of Genocide Research*, 4:4 (2002), 499–518, for a potential life-raft in the form of a functionalist interpretation of Rwanda events, by an area expert.

24 Moshman, 'Conceptual Constraints', 432–6, and more recently Henry R. Huttenbach, 'Towards a Conceptual Defintion of Genocide', *Journal of Genocide Research*, 4:2 (2002),168, for more on this theme.

25 Barbara Harff, 'Recognising Genocides and Politicides', in Helen Fein, ed., *Genocide Watch* (New Haven, CT, and London: Yale University Press, 1992), 27–41; Barbara Harff and Ted Robert Gurr, 'Toward Empirical Theory of Genocides and Politicides: Identification and Measurement of Cases since 1945', *International*

Studies Quarterly, 32 (1988), 359–371; idem., 'Victims of the State: Genocides, Politicides and Group Repression from 1945 to 1995', in Albert J. Jongman, ed., *Contemporary Genocides: Causes, Cases, Consequences* (The Hague: CIP-Gegevens Koninklijke Bibliotheek, 1996), 33–58. Also Mark Levene, 'Remembering for the Future: Engaging with the Present', in Elisabeth Maxwell and John K. Roth, eds, *Remembering for the Future: The Holocaust in the Age of Genocide* (London: Palgrave, 2001), vol. 1, 59–61.

26 Harff and Gurr, 'Toward Empirical Theory', 360.

27 Helen Fein, 'Accounting for Genocide after 1945: Theories and Some Findings', *International Journal on Group Rights*, 1 (1993), 79–106.

28 Kuper, *Genocide*, 181–2.

29 Ibid., 161. See also Hinton, *Annihilating Difference*, 27, for corroboration.

30 Chalk and Jonassohn, *History*, 11.

31 Mazower, 'After Lemkin', 5; Samantha Power, *'A Problem from Hell', America and the Age of Genocide* (New York: Basic Books, 2002), 23–6. See also Steven L. Jacobs, 'The Papers of Raphael Lemkin: A First Look', *Journal of Genocide Research*, 1:1 (1999), 105–14, and idem., ed., 'Totally Unofficial Man: Raphael Lemkin', in Samuel Totten and Steven Leonard Jacobs, *Pioneers of Genocide Studies* (New Brunswick, NJ: Transaction Publishers, 2002), 365–99, for an autobiographical sketch. A full biography of Lemkin, '"To Live an Idea": Raphael Lemkin and his Campaign to Outlaw Genocide', is currently being written by James T. Fussell.

32 Lemkin, *Axis Rule*, 77.

33 See Power, *Problem*, 77; Mazower, 'After Lemkin', 5.

34 Power, *Problem*, 21–2; Kuper, *Genocide*, 22.

35 Quoted by Mazower, 'After Lemkin', 5, from the Lemkin papers in New York Public Library. Mazower makes the critical point that the use of the plural – 'peoples' – demonstrates that 'Lemkin was not, and had never been concerned exclusively with the fate of the Jews'. For corroboration of the point see also Steven L. Jacobs, 'Lemkin and the Armenian Genocide', in Richard G. Hovannisian, ed., *Looking Backward, Moving Forward: Confronting the Armenian Genocide* (New Brunswick, NJ: Transaction Publishers, 2003), 125–35.

36 Lemkin, *Axis Rule*, 79.

37 Ibid., 81.

38 Ibid., 86–7.

39 Ibid., 86.

40 Ibid., xii, 196–7.

41 Ibid., 85, xi.

42 See Power, *Problem*, chapter 4, 'Lemkin's Law'.

43 Raphael Lemkin, 'Genocide as a Crime under International Law', *American Journal of International Law*, 41 (1947), 145–71.

44 See Churchill, *Little Matter*, 409–12, for details.

45 Ibid., 410.

46 William A. Schabas, *Genocide in International Law, The Crime of Crimes* (Cambridge: Cambridge University Press, 2000), 184.

47 Ibid., 195–6, where Schabas rather wryly notes that when the issue resurfaced in the 1952 session 'of the prestigious Institut de Droit International', its rapporteur, Giorgio Balladore Pallieri 'concluded, with the logic of an ethnic cleanser, that there was nothing in international law to oppose the legitimacy of population transfers and that they were even, in certain circumstances, desirable'. Further discussion of European and Middle Eastern cases of this period will follow in Volume III of this work.

48 Churchill, *Little Matter*, 410.

49 Schabas, *Genocide*, 140, where Schabas disputes 'that opposition to inclusion of political genocide was some Soviet machination'. See, more broadly, 134–45. Compare however with Kuper, *Genocide*, 24–30, where a greater onus for exclusion is put on the USSR.

50 United Nations, *Convention on the Prevention and Punishment of the Crime of Genocide* (London: Her Majesty's Stationery Office, 1966).

51 Quoted in Churchill, *Little Matter*, 410.

52 Noel Malcolm, *Kosovo, A Short History* (London and Basingstoke: Macmillan, 1998), xxvii.

53 Lemkin, *Axis Rule*, xi.

54 Ibid., 79–80.

55 See Moses, 'Genocide', 26, for a recent doubter.

56 Michael Hechter, *Internal Colonialism, The Celtic Fringe in British National Development* (London: Routledge and Kegan Paul, 1975), notably chapter 6, 'The Anglicisation of the Celtic periphery, 1851–1961'; Eugen Weber, *Peasants into Frenchmen: The Modernisation of Rural France 1870–1914* (Stanford, CA: Stanford University Press, 1976), esp. 485–91. Interestingly also note Schabas, *Genocide*, 180, where French opposition to the inclusion of cultural genocide in the UNC was on the grounds that it risked the 'political interference in the domestic affairs of states'.

57 See Robert Paine, 'The Claim of the Fourth World', in Jens Brosted et al., eds, *Native Power, The Quest for Autonomy and Nationhood of Indigenous Peoples* (Oslo: Universitetsflorlaget AS, 1985), 49–66, for the value of this term.

58 See most obviously Karl Schleunes, *The Twisted Road to Auschwitz, Nazi Policy towards the Jews 1933–1939* (Urbana: University of Illinois Press, 1970).

59 Julian Burger, *Report from the Frontier: The State of the World's Indigenous Peoples* (London: Zed Press, 1987), 264.

60 Fein, 'Genocide, Sociological Perspective', 24.

61 Harff and Gurr, 'Toward Empirical Theory', 363, 366.

62 Ismet Sheriff Vanly, 'Kurdistan in Iraq', in Gerard Chaliand, ed., *People without a Country, The Kurds and Kurdistan* (London: Zed Press, 1980), 192–203; David McDowall, *A Modern History of the Kurds* (London: I.B. Tauris, 1997), 327–37, 348–50. Further details to follow in Volume III.

63 See Vahakn N. Dadrian, 'The Role of the Turkish Military in the Destruction of Ottoman Armenians: A Study in Historical Continuities', *Journal of Political and Military Sociology*, 20:2 (1992), 282. Further details to follow in Volume II.

64 See Dan Stone, 'Genocide as Transgression', *European Journal of Social Theory*, 7:1 (2004), 45–65, for an important exploratory essay on this theme.

65 Claude Lanzmann, 'Shoah as Counter-Myth', *Jewish Quarterly*, 35 (Spring 1986), 12.

66 Michael Freeman, 'Genocide, Civilisation and Modernity', *British Journal of Sociology*, 46 (1995), 209.

67 Yves Ternon, *L'État criminel: les génocides au XXe siècle* (Paris: Éditions du Seuil, 1995), 18.

68 Quoted in ibid., 33 (author's translation).

69 Schabas, *Genocide*, 37–8.

70 Ibid., 46.

71 Harff and Gurr, 'Toward Empirical Theory'; Fein, 'Accounting for Genocide'. See also most recently Martin Shaw, *War and Genocide, Organised Killing in Modern Society* (Cambridge: Polity Press, 2003), for a sustained, conceptual analysis of the connectedness between the two.

72 Robert Jay Lifton and Eric Markusen, *The Genocidal Mentality: Nazi Holocaust and Nuclear Threat* (New York: Basic Books, 1990); Eric Markusen and David Kopf, *The Holocaust and Strategic Bombing, Genocide and Total War in the 20th Century* (Boulder, CO, San Francisco, Oxford: Westview Press, 1995).

73 Hannah Arendt, *Eichmann in Jerusalem, A Report on the Banality of Evil* (London: Penguin, 1965), 276.

74 Markusen and Kopf, *Holocaust*, 70. See David Cesarani's review of Markusen and Kopf, in *Studies in Contemporary Jewry*, 18 (2002), 271–3; Mark Levene, 'Ways of Seeing Killing', *Patterns of Prejudice*, 30:4 (1996), 65–71, for critiques of this proposition.

75 Markusen and Kopf, *Holocaust*, jacket information. More generally, chapter 4, 'The Relationship between Genocide and Total War'.

76 Quoted in Ruth Seifert, 'War and Rape: A Preliminary Analysis', in Alexandra Stiglmayer, ed., *Mass Rape, The War against Women in Bosnia-Herzegovina*, trans. Marion Faber (Lincoln, NB, and London: University of Nebraska Press, 1994), 63.

77 Gil Eliot, *Twentieth Century Book of the Dead* (London: Penguin, 1972), 215.

78 R. J. Rummel, 'Democide in Totalitarian States: Mortacracies and Megamurders', in Israel W. Charny, ed., *Genocide, A Critical Bibliographical Review*, vol. 3: *The Widening Circle of Genocide* (New Brunswick, NJ, and London: Transaction Publishers, 1994), 3.

79 See Schabas, *Genocide*, 54–5, on the French consistent preference in international law for 'crimes against humanity' as against the 'useless and even dangerous neologism' of genocide, a 'practical' position also somewhat implicit in Ternon, *L'État*.

80 Ronald Aronson, *The Dialectics of Disaster, A Preface to Hope* (London: Verso, 1983), 161–2.

81 Quoted in ibid., 164.

82 Quoted in Markusen and Kopf, *Holocaust*, 70–1.

83 Aronson, *Dialectics,* 163 (with Aronson's emphasis).

84 Peter Paret, 'Clausewitz', in idem., ed., *Makers of Modern Strategy, from Machiavelli to the Nuclear Age* (Oxford: Clarendon Press, 1986), 209–10. Also Shaw, *War*, 19–21.

85 See Colonel C. E. Caldwell, *Small Wars, Their Principle and Practice* (East Ardsley, West Yorks: EP Publishing, 1976 [first published 1906]), 21–42, for a veteran rendition of this theme effectively combining Type Two and Type Three wars but from a military strategist's perspective within the 'legitimate' (sic.) state. Also Shaw, *War*, esp. 5–6, for a not entirely dissimilar explication to that herein but with the notion of 'degenerate war' as his chosen bridge. As Shaw's work was published close to the completion of this work, I will be returning to some of his ideas and arguments, in later volumes.

86 Douhet, quoted in Markusen and Kopf, *Holocaust*, 201.

87 Geoffrey Best, *Humanity in Warfare* (New York: Columbia University Press, 1980), for more on this vast subject.

88 Lawrence Freedman, 'The First Two Generations of Nuclear Strategists', in Paret, *Makers*, 736.

89 See Mark J. White, *Missiles in Cuba, Kennedy, Khrushchev, Castro and the 1962 Crisis* (Chicago: Ivan R. Dee, 1997).

90 Fein, 'Genocide, Sociological Perspective', 21; more fully developed in idem., 'Discriminating Genocide from War Crimes: Vietnam and Afghanistan Reexamined', *Denver Journal of International Law and Policy,* 22:1 (1993), 29–62.

91 See Kuper, *Genocide*, 76, though significantly Kuper himself is prepared to countenance that what happened before and during the war to the (Biafran) Ibos is a *prima facie* case of genocide.

92 Vakahn N. Dadrian, 'The Structural-Functional Components of Genocide', in Israel Drapkin and Emilio Viano, eds, *Victimology: A New Focus* (Lexington, MA: Lexington Books, 1975), vol. 4, 123.

93 However, see David Fitzpatrick, 'Militarism in Ireland, 1900–1922', in Thomas Bartlett and Keith Jeffrey, eds., *A Military History of Ireland* (Cambridge: Cambridge University Press, 1996), 402–6, for the ratcheting up of the British-sponsored military and para-military violence. Also Charles Townshend, *The British Campaign in Ireland, 1919–1921: The Development of Political and Military Policies* (Oxford: Oxford University Press, 1975).

94 See Kenneth O. Morgan, *Consensus and Disunity, The Lloyd George Coalition Government, 1918–1922* (Oxford: Clarendon Press, 1979), 126–32; Frank Pakenham, *Peace by Ordeal: an Account from First-Hand Sources, of the Negotiation and Signature of the Anglo-Irish Treaty, 1921* (London: New English Library, 1967).

95 See Michael Farrell, *Northern Ireland: The Orange State* (London: Pluto Press, 1980), chapter 2, 'Siege or Pogrom: 1921–24'.

96 The multi-layered and often contradictory complexity of the war has been recently highlighted in Martin S. Alexander, Martin Evans and J. F. V. Keiger, '"The War without a Name": The French Army and the Algerians: Recovering Experiences, Images and Testimonies', in idem., *The Algerian War and the French Army 1954–62* (Basingstoke and New York: Palgrave Macmillan, 2002), 5–6. Along with other recent studies, it also challenges the iconic Algerian figure of 1 million Muslim deaths in the fighting, favouring a total death toll, including French and French auxiliary forces of around half a million. For a more traditional but still highly valued interpretation see Alistair Horne, *A Savage War of Peace, Algeria 1954–1962* (London: Macmillan, 1977).

97 Significantly, the western Darfur region of the Sudan appears to be one very current example where the strength of a communal insurgency against the state has been insufficient in preventing a clearly genocidal retributon against the rebels' base population. Though, hence, clearly out of date, Harff and Gurr's 'Watchlist of Potential Victims: 1994–1995', in 'Victims of the State', 54–8, still provides a useful list of some of the other potential danger zones worldwide.

98 Straus, 'Contested Meanings', 365: 'Strategies of war that destroy an entire group are genocide'.

99 Fein, 'Genocide, Sociological Perspective', 24.

100 Chalk and Jonassohn, *History*, 23.

101 Roger Griffin, *The Nature of Fascism* (London and New York: Routledge, 1991), 10.

102 Ibid., 11.

103 See Moshman, 'Conceptual Constraints', 433–6; David E. Stannard, 'Uniqueness as Denial: The Politics of Genocide Scholarship', in Alan S. Rosenbaum, ed., *Is the Holocaust Unique? Perspectives on Comparative Genocide* (Boulder, CO: Westview Press, 1996), 163–208; Rosenfeld, 'Politics', 43–6 for further discussion.

104 See Robert F. Melson, *Revolution and Genocide: On the Origins of the Armenian Genocide and the Holocaust* (Chicago: University of Chicago Press, 1992), 26–9, for the proposed distinction between 'partial' and 'total' genocide. Melson, writing before the Rwanda genocide, refers to Armenia and the Holocaust as the two clear examples of 'total genocide' but has since embraced Rwanda in this scheme. See also Alain Destexhe, *Rwanda and Genocide in the Twentieth Century*, trans. Alison Marschner (London and East Haven, CT: Pluto Press, 1995), chapter 2, 'Three Genocides in the Twentieth Century'.

105 See Moshman, 'Conceptual Constraints', 436.

106 See Richard Breitman, 'Plans for the Final Solution in Early 1941', in Michael Berenbaum and Abraham J. Peck, eds, *The Holocaust and History, The Known, The Unknown, The Disputed and the Reexamined* (Bloomington and Indianapolis, Indiana University Press, 1998), 187–96; Christopher R. Browning, *Fateful Months: Essays on the Emergence of the Final Solution* (New York and London: Holmes and Meier, 1985); Phillipe Burrin, *Hitler and the Jews, The Genesis of the Holocaust*, trans. Patsy Southgate (London: Edward Arnold, 1994), for some of the major contrasting positions in a much contested field.

107 See Christian Gerlach, 'The Wannsee Conference, the Fate of German Jews, and Hitler's Decision in Principle to Exterminate all European Jews', in Omer Bartov, ed., *The Holocaust, Origins, Implementations, Aftermath* (London and New York, Routledge: 2000), 106–61, for a notably controversial argument for December 1941; Christopher R. Browning (with Jürgen Mattaus), *The Origins of the Final Solution, the Evolution of Nazi Jewish Policy, September 1939–March 1942* (London: William Heinemann, 2004), 427, for autumn 1941.

108 See for instance, Raul Hilberg, *The Destruction of the European Jews* (New York: Holmes and Meier student edition, 1985), 37, for the case of Ministerialrat Killy, a *Mischling* 'of the second degree' (i.e. someone with a single Jewish grandparent) but also a Reich Chancellery official with significant bureaucratic functions in the implementation of the 'Final Solution'.

109 Paul R. Mendes-Flohr and Jehuda Reinharz, *The Jew in the Modern World, A Documentary History* (New York: Oxford University Press, 1980), cite the figure of 5,978,000. A more cautious Hilberg, *Destruction*, 338, estimates the figure at c. 5,100,000.

110 See Kemal H. Karpat, 'Millets and Nationality: The Roots of the Incongruity of Nation and State in the Post-Ottoman State', in Benjamin Braude and Bernard Lewis, eds, *Christians and Jews in the Ottoman Empire, The Functioning of a Plural Society* (New York and London: Holmes and Meier, 1982), vol. 1, 107–34, for more on these aspects of Ottoman-communal relations.

111 See Donald Bloxham, 'The Beginning of the Armenian Catastrophe, Comparative and Contextual Considerations', in Hans-Lukas Kieser and Dominick Schaller, eds, *Der Voelkermord an den Armeniern und die Shoah* (Zurich: Chronos Publishing, 2002), 101–28, for the most astute discussion of this controversy.

112 Melson, *Revolution*, 145–7, for a careful analysis based on contemporary sources.

113 According to the official census Tutsi constituted 8.4 per cent of the population. See Alison des Forges, *Leave None To Tell The Story, Genocide in Rwanda* (New York and London: Human Rights Watch and International Federation of Human Rights, 1999), 15. The higher figure cited in Christopher C. Taylor, 'The Cultural Face of Terror in the Rwandan Genocide', in Hinton, *Annihilating Difference*, 173, indicates both state and communal dissemblance of the reality.

114 Mahmood Mamdani, *When Victims Become Killers, Colonialism, Nativism and the Genocide in Rwanda* (Oxford: James Currey, 2001), notes figures as high as 1.1 million or 15 per cent of the population. Many of these, according to US State Department sources, had been displaced for the third or fourth time as a result of the RPF invasion.

115 See des Forges, *Leave None*, 15.

116 Straus, 'Contested Meanings', 365.

117 Patrick Brogan, *World Conflicts* (London: Bloomsbury Publishing, 1989), 604.

118 Helen Fein, 'Scenarios of Genocide: Models of Genocide and Critical Responses', in Israel W. Charny, ed., *Toward the Understanding and Prevention of Genocide: Proceedings of the International Conference on the Holocaust and Genocide* (Boulder, CO,

and London: Westview Press, 1984), 4–5. Fein has subsequently offered a more tightly constructed but also arguably more opaque definition. See idem., 'Genocide, Sociological Perspective', 24.

119 Straus, 'Contested Meanings', 366.

120 Hinton, *Annihilating Difference*, 5.

121 Ibid., 4–5; Schabas, *Genocide*, 130–2.

122 See Ternon, *L'État*, 47; Churchill, *Little Matter*, 414–15, for more on the Drost critique.

123 See Donald L. Niewyk, *The Jews in Weimar Germany* (Manchester: Manchester University Press, 1980), 98–9.

124 See Tessa Hoffman and Gerayer Koutcharian, 'The History of Armenian–Kurdish Relations in the Ottoman Empire', *Armenian Review*, 39:4 (1986), 30, n. 71, 33–4.

125 See Jacques J. Macquet, *The Premise of Inequality in Ruanda* (Oxford: Oxford University Press, 1961) for the classic study.

126 Hinton, *Annihilating Difference*, 5–6, for an anthropologist's corroboration.

127 *Documents on Ottoman Armenians* (Ankara: Prime Ministry Directorate of Information, 1982), vol. 1, doc. 76, 4 August, and doc. 83, 15 August 1915, officially exempting Catholics and Protestants from the deportation orders. See, however, Leslie Davis, US Consul (Harput) to Dept. of State, 6 September 1915, in Ara Sarafian, ed., *United States Official Documents on the Armenian Genocide* (Watertown, MA: Armenian Review Books, 1995), vol. 3, 73–4, for the essential duplicity of the exemption.

128 Annegret Ehmann, 'From Colonial Racism to Nazi Racial Policy: The Role of the So-Called Mischlinge', in Berenbaum and Peck, *Holocaust*, 128–9.

129 André Sibomana, *Hope for Rwanda, Conversations with Laure Guibert and Hervé Deguine*, trans. Carina Tertsakian (London and Dar es Salaam: Pluto Press and Mkuki na Nyota Publishers), 56.

130 Alec Nove, *An Economic History of the USSR* (London: Penguin, revised edn 1976), 107–8.

131 See Moshe Lewin, *The Making of the Soviet System, Essays on the Social History of Interwar Russia* (London: Methuen, 1985), 129.

132 Nicholas Werth, 'A State Against its People: Violence, Repression and Terror in the Soviet Union', in Stéphane Courtois et al., eds, *The Black Book of Communism, Crimes, Terror, Repression*, trans. Jonathan Murphy and Mark Kramer (Cambridge, MA, and London: Harvard University Press, 1999), 147. In fact, three pages later, Werth notes that a secret OGPU report a few days into the campaign had already reported 64,589 'liquidations'.

133 Robert Conquest, *The Harvest of Sorrow: Soviet Collectivisation and the Terror Famine* (New York: Oxford University Press), 126.

134 R. W. Davies, 'Forced Labour under Stalin, The Archive Revelations', *New Left Review*, 214 (Nov./Dec. 1995), 62–80.

135 Ben Kiernan, *The Pol Pot Regime, Race, Power and Genocide in Cambodia under the Khmer Rouge, 1975–79* (New Haven, CT, and London: Yale University Press, 1996), 406. See also Gregory H. Stanton, 'Blue Scarves and Yellow Stars: Classification and Symbolisation in the Cambodian Genocide', (Montreal: Montreal Institute for Genocide Studies, Occasional Papers, 1989).

136 Kiernan, *Pol Pot Regime*, 458.

137 Ibid., 404.

138 Ben Kiernan, 'The Cambodian Genocide: Issues and Responses', in George D. Andreopoulos, ed., *Genocide, Conceptual and Historical Dimensions* (Philadelphia: University of Pennsylvania Press, 1994), 201–2.

139 Lynne Viola, 'The Second Coming: Class Enemies in the Soviet Countryside, 1927–1935', in Getty and Manning, *Stalinist Terror*, 66.

140 Ibid., 79–80.

141 Straus, 'Contested Meanings', 366.

142 Vasily Grossman, as quoted in Robert Conquest, *Reflections on a Ravaged Century* (London: John Murray, 1999), 94.

143 Churchill, *Little Matter*, 421, for support of this position. From a somewhat different angle, the 1998 decision of the International Criminal Tribunal for Rwanda to embrace the vailidity of an emic – that is subjective – criteria as to what constitutes an ethnic group, in this case, the Tutsi, as opposed to an objective (etic) definition, also offers, from the standpoint of international law, a more empirically grounded basis for interpreting the nature of targeted groups in genocide. See Paul J. Magnarella, 'Recent Developments in the International Law of Genocide: An Anthroploogical Perspective on the International Criminal Tribunal for Rwanda', in Hinton, *Annihilating Difference*, 318.

144 Straus, 'Contested Meanings', 366.

2 Perpetrators, Victims and Collective Unreason

1 Fyodor Dostoevsky, *Crime and Punishment*, trans. David Magarshack (London: Penguin, 1966 [first published 1866]), 555. See also Tony Marchant, 'Dostoevsky Can Teach You about Terror', *Sunday Times*, 10 February 2002.

2 *Philadelphia Daily News*, editorial, as quoted in *Guardian (The Editor)*, 15 September 2001.

3 Quoted in Noel Malcolm, *Bosnia, A Short History* (London and Basingstoke: Macmillan 1994), xix.

4 Vahakn N. Dadrian, *The History of the Armenian Genocide, Ethnic Conflict from the Balkans to Anatolia to the Caucasus* (Oxford: Berghahn Books, 1996), 78.

5 See Dan Stone, 'Recent Trends in Holocaust Historiography', *Journal of Holocaust Education*, 10:3 (2001), 3–24; Mark Levene, 'Illumination and Opacity in Recent Holocaust Research', *Journal of Contemporary History*, 37:2 (2002), 275–92, for recent surveys.

6 Daniel Jonah Goldhagen, *Hitler's Willing Executioners, Ordinary Germans and the Holocaust* (London: Little, Brown and Co., 1996).

7 That said, this study will use them as sparingly as possible as a form of shorthand and on the proviso that a better, alternative terminology is not currently available. See also Tristam Hunt, 'In the Scales of History', *Guardian*, 6 April 2002, for anxieties regarding the 'judicialisation of history'.

8 E. P. Thompson, *The Making of the English Working Class* (London: Penguin, 1963).

9 Tim Mason, '"The Primacy of Politics" – Politics and Economics in National Socialist Germany', in Henry A. Turner, ed., *Nazism and the Third Reich* (New York: Quadrangle Books, 1972), 175–7.

10 Martin Broszat, 'Plädoyer für eine Historisierung des Nationalsozialismus', *Merkur,* 39 (1985), 373–85, reprinted in English as 'A Plea for he Historicization of National Socialism', in Baldwin, *Reworking the Past*, 77–87.

11 Roger W. Smith, 'Fantasy, Purity, Destruction: Norman Cohn's Complex Witness to the Holocaust', in Alan L. Berger, ed., *Bearing Witness to the Holocaust 1939–1989* (Lewiston, Queenston and Lampeter: Edward Mellen Press, 1991), 116.

12 Quoted in Fein, 'Genocide, Sociological Perspective', 45. More critically, see James Waller, *Becoming Evil, How Ordinary People Commit Genocide and Mass Killing* (Oxford and New York: Oxford University Press, 2002), 59–66, for a full exposition of Kelley's dismissal of popular 'mad Nazi' assumptions.

13 See for example, *The Roots of Evil*, dir. Rex Bloomstein (Nucleus Productions), broadcast Channel-4 (UK), autumn 1997. Also Daniel Chirot, *Modern Tyrants, The Power and Prevalence of Evil in Our Age* (New York and Toronto: Free Press, 1994).

14 Paul Parin, 'Open Wounds, Ethnopsychoanalytical Reflections on the Wars in Former Yugoslavia', in Alexandra Stiglmayer, ed., *Mass Rape, The War against Women in Bosnia-Herzegovina* (Lincoln, NB and London: University of Nebraska Press, 1994), 49.

15 In one respect, Waller, *Becoming Evil,* by reminding us of who we are in the broadest evolutionary terms does an admirable job in directing us towards ordinary, individual human potentialities for violence, or its alternatives. Read by this author in the closing stages of his own writing, it cannot be fully utilised here. That said, the very fact that this study is not about resisters or rescuers in the face of genocide may point to an implicit pessimism about possibilities for going against the collective grain. For more positive narratives amongst the burgeoning, specifically Holocaust literature, see Phillip Hallie, *Lest Innocent Blood Be Shed: The Story of the Village of Le Chambon and How Goodness Happened There* (New York: Harper and Row, 1979); Nechama Tec, *When Light Pierced the Darkness, Christian Rescue of Jews in Nazi Occupied Poland* (New York: Oxford University Press, 1986).

16 Gérard Prunier, *The Rwanda Crisis, History of a Genocide 1959–1994* (London: Hurst and Co., 1995), 342.

17 African Rights, *Rwanda: Death, Despair and Defiance* (London: African Rights, 1995), 49.

18 Des Forges, *Leave None*, 227.

19 Mamdani, *When Victims*, 225–30, for the very wide range of professional participants.

20 Prunier, *Rwanda Crisis*, 247; Mamdani, *When Victims*, 198–202, for further assessment.

21 African Rights, *Rwanda: Not so Innocent, When Women become Killers* (London: African Rights, 1995), for the full horror.

22 Prunier, *Rwanda Crisis* , 246–7.

23 African Rights, *Rwanda*, 56, 123.

24 Stone, 'Genocide as Transgression', particularly with reference to the earlier writings of Roger Callois and Georges Bataille for more on this critical aspect of genocide.

25 Bauman, *Modernity,* 17, 89, 88.

26 Ibid., 14 (my emphasis).

27 Richard Breitman, *The Architect of Genocide, Himmler and the Final Solution* (London: Bodley Head, 1991), 10, 33.

28 Arendt, *Eichmann,* 276

29 Ronnie S. Landau, *The Nazi Holocaust* (London and New York: I.B. Tauris, 1992), 186.

30 Quoted in Markusen and Kopf, *Holocaust,* 234.

31 See Lifton and Markusen, *Genocidal Mentality,* for Nazi parallels with the US nuclear weapons programme. However, see also Waller, *Becoming Evil,* 116–20, for a strong and compelling critique of Lifton's 'doubling' thesis.

32 Heinz Höhne, *The Order of the Death's Head: The Story of Hitler's SS,* trans. Richard Barry (London: Pan, 1972), 332.

33 Stanley Milgram, *Obedience to Authority* (New York: Harper and Row, 1974).

34 Bauman, *Modernity,* 165.

35 Ibid., 154–5.

36 Christopher Browning, *Ordinary Men, Reserve Police Battalion 101 and the Final Solution in Poland* (New York: HarperPerennial, 1993), 191–2.

37 Hilberg, *Destruction,* 277.

38 Dan Stone, 'Holocaust Testimony and the Challenge to the Philosophy of History', in Robert Fine and Charles Turner, eds., *Social Theory after the Holocaust* (Liverpool: Liverpool University Press, 2000), 226.

39 Bauman, *Modernity,* 92, 38.

40 Ibid., 91

41 Michael J. Arlen, *Passage to Ararat* (New York: Farrar, Straus and Giroux, 1975), 243–4.

42 Peter W. Galbreath and Christopher van Hollen, Jr., 'Chemical Weapons Use in Kurdistan: Iraq's Final Offensive', staff report to the US Senate Committee on Foreign Relations, 21 September 1988; further details in Middle East Watch, *Genocide*, Appendix C.

43 Boris A. Starkov, 'Narkom Ezhov', in Getty and Manning, *Stalinist Terror*, 22.

44 Lifton and Markusen, *Genocidal Mentality*, 95–7, 226.

45 Ibid., 87.

46 See Norman Cohn, *Warrant for Genocide, The Myth of the Jewish World-Conspiracy and the Protocols of the Elders of Zion* (London: Penguin, 1967); idem., *The Pursuit of the Millennium: Revolutionary Milleniarians and Mystical Anarchists of the Middle Ages* (London: Paladin, 1970); idem., *Europe's Inner Demons: An Enquiry inspired by the Great Witchhunt* (New York: Basic Books, 1975). See also Smith, 'Fantasy', 115–26 for valuable commentary.

47 See Eugene Victor Walter, *Terror and Resistance: A Study of Political Violence, With Case Studies of Some Primitive African Communities* (London, Oxford and New York: Oxford University Press, 1969), chapter 5, 'Invisible Government'.

48 Quoted in Cohn, *Warrant*, 209.

49 See Frank Graziano, *Divine Violence, Spectacle, Psychosexuality and Radical Christianity in the Argentine 'Dirty War'* (Boulder, CO, San Francisco and Oxford: Westview Press, 1992), 125.

50 Virginia Garrard-Burnett, *Protestantism in Guatemala, Living in the New Jerusalem* (Austin: University of Texas, 1998), chapter 8, 'The Protestant President', for connections between Rios Montt's faith and the 1983 exterminatory assault.

51 Moshe Lewin, 'Stalin in the Mirror of the Other', in Ian Kershaw and Moshe Lewin, eds, *Stalinism and Nazism: Dictatorships in Comparison* (Cambridge: Cambridge University Press, 1997), 108.

52 Lewin, *Making*, 310.

53 See Eric Voegelin, *Die politischen Religionen* (Vienna: Bermann-Fischer, 1938), for the origins of the concept. For its more recent development and academic cachet see also the journal *Totalitarian Movements and Political Religion*.

54 Quoted in Cohn, *Warrant*, 206.

55 See Breitman, *Architect*, 242–3.

56 Famously Hitler as defendant, in his 1924 'Rathaus putsch' trial, proclaimed: 'Pronouce us guilty a thousand times over: the goddess of the eternal court of history will smile … She will acquit us.' Quoted in Sean Thomas, 'A History of Forgiving', *Guardian*, 21 July 2003. However, see Berel Lang, *Act and Idea in the Nazi Genocide* (Chicago and London: Chicago University Press, 1990), especially chapter 2, 'The Knowledge of Evil and Good', for further exploration of Nazi recognition of wrongdoing.

57 See most obviously, Hannah Arendt, *The Origins of Totalitarianism* (New York: Meridian, 1958).

58 Vahakn N. Dadrian, 'The Comparative Aspects of the Armenian and Jewish Cases of Genocide: A Sociohistorical Perspective', in Rosenbaum, *Is the Holocaust Unique?*, esp. 122–6.

59 R. Hrair Dekmejian, 'Determinants of Genocide: Armenians and Jews as Case Studies', in Richard G. Hovannisian, ed., *The Armenian Genocide in Perspective* (New Brunswick, NJ, and London: Transaction Books, 1986), 85–96.

60 See also Cohn, *Warrant*, 214–18.

61 Uriel Heyd, *Foundations of Turkish Nationalism, The Life and Teachings of Ziya Gökalp* (London: Luzac, 1950); Feroz Ahmad, *The Young Turks: The CUP in Turkish Politics: 1908–1914* (Oxford: Oxford University Press, 1969), 'Biographical Index', 166–81, for broader CUP Macedonian connections.

62 Dekmejian, 'Determinants', 94, 91.

63 Ibid, 94.

64 Elizabeth Becker, *When the War was Over: The Voices of Cambodia's Revolution and Its People* (New York: Simon & Schuster, 1986), 72–4, on core Khmer Rouge marriage connections; Prunier, *Rwanda Crisis*, 85–7; African Rights, *Rwanda*, 100–2, on the *clan de Madame*.

65 See the essays in Ulrich Herbert, ed., *National Socialist Extermination Policies, Contemporary German Perspectives and Controversies* (New York and Oxford: Berghahn Books, 2000), for conclusive evidence on this score.

66 See John Ranelagh, *Thatcher's People, An Insider's Account of the Politics, the Power and the Personalities* (London: HarperCollins, 1991), especially chapter 2, 'The People: Class and Party'.

67 There was a paradox in this, in the sense that Thatcher's cabinets and advisors to an unusually high degree included Jewish staff who, in the context of the traditional British establishment, could be construed as both social and ethnic 'outsiders'. See Ranelagh, *Thatcher's People*, 55–7. However, see also Paul Gilroy, *'There Ain't no Black in the Union Jack': The Cultural Politics of Race and Nation* (London: Hutchinson, 1987) for an important corrective arguing that anti-black racism has both crossed and transcended left–right political divides in Britain.

68 Liah Greenfield, *Nationalism, Five Roads to Modernity* (Cambridge, MA: Harvard University Press, 1992), 15–17, for an important exposition of this theme.

69 Michael Mann, *Sources of Social Power*, vol. 1: *From the Beginning to 1760 AD* (Cambridge: Cambridge University Press, 1986), 22–3.

70 See David Kushner, *The Rise of Turkish Nationalism 1876–1908* (London: Frank Cass, 1977), 29–38 for the emerging nationalist nucleus; Vahakn N. Dadrian, 'The Role of Turkish Physicians in the World War One Genocide of Ottoman Armenians', *Holocaust and Genocide Studies*, 1:2 (1986), 169–92, for the consequences.

71 Extracts as telescoped in Conquest, *Harvest*, 233 from Kopelev's memoirs. For a full unexpurgated rendition see Lev Kopelev, *The Education of a True Believer*, trans. Gary Kern (London: Wildwood House, 1981), chapter 9, 'The Last Grain Collections (1933)'.

72 Hilberg, *Destruction*, 104–5.

73 Bauman, *Modernity*, 188. See, however, Omer Bartov, 'Reception and Perception: Goldhagen's Holocaust and the World', in Geoff Eley, ed., *'The Goldhagen Effect': History, Memory, Nazism – Facing the German Past* (Ann Arbor: University of Michigan Press, 2000), 78–87, for an argument with serious doubts about the Milgram behaviourist hypothesis, Bartov claiming that far from being neutral, Milgram's class and gender prejudices predisposed him to achieve the most 'moral' results from an individual who in the context of the Nazi Germany would have most likely *chosen* to support its genocidal actions. Also Waller, *Becoming Evil*, 102–11.

74 Ivan P. Pavlov, *Lectures on Conditioned Reflexes, Twenty Five Years of Objective Study of the Higher Nervous Activity Behaviour of Animals* (Oxford: Pinter Publishers, 1980 [first published 1927]).

75 Edward S. Herman and Noam Chomsky, *Manufacturing Consent: The Political Economy of the Mass Media* (New York: Pantheon, 1988); E. P. Thompson, *Writing by Candelight* (London: Merlin Press, 1980), esp. 'A State of Blackmail'. See also David Cromwell, *Private Planet, Corporate Plunder and the Fight Back* (Charlbury, Oxon: Jon Carpenter, 2001) chapter 3, 'Spotlight on the Media: How the truth is hidden from view'.

76 African Rights, *Rwanda,* 78–84; des Forges, *Leave None,* 66–71.

77 Catherine A. MacKinnon, 'Turning Rape into Pornography: Postmodern Genocide', in Stiglmayer, *Mass Rape,* 76.

78 See Alexandra Stiglmayer, 'The Rapes in Bosnia-Herzegovina', in Stiglmayer, *Mass Rape,* 82–169; Helsinki Watch, *War Crimes in Bosnia-Herzegovina* (New York: Human Rights Watch, 1993), vol. 2 for further details.

79 Roger W. Smith, 'Genocide and the Politics of Rape, Historical and Psychological Perspectives' (unpublished paper, 1994), 79–80.

80 See Adam Jones, 'Gender and Ethnic Conflict in ex-Yugoslavia', *Ethnic and Racial Studies,* 17:1 (1994), 115–34. For the development of the gendercide debate see Adam Jones, 'Gendercide and Genocide', *Journal of Genocide Research,* 2:2 (2000), 185–211 and idem, ed., *Journal of Genocide Research,* 'Special Issue: Gendercide and Genocide', 4:1 (2002).

81 With regard to Rwanda, the historian Jean-Pierre Chrétien has described the vast majority as 'innocent murderers'. See Prunier, *Rwanda Crisis,* 247.

82 Quoted in Dadrian, 'Role of Turkish Physicians', 183.

83 Craig Haney, Curtis Banks and Philip Zimbardo, 'Interpersonal Dynamics in a Simulated Prison', *International Journal of Criminology and Penology,* 1 (1983), 69–97. See also Françoise Sironi and Raphaëlle Branche, 'Torture and the Borders of Humanity', in Jacques Sémelin, ed., 'Extreme Violence', *International Social Science Journal,* 174 (2002), 539–48.

84 Richard Dowden, 'The Graves of the Tutsi are only Half Full – We Must Complete the Task', *Independent,* 24 May 1994.

85 Philip Gourevitch, *We Wish to Inform You that Tomorrow We Will Be Killed with our Families, Stories from Rwanda* (London: Picador, 1999), 202.

86 Adam Jones, 'Gender and Genocide in Rwanda', *Journal of Genocide Research*, 4:1 (2002), 84.

87 Christopher Taylor, *Sacrifice as Terror: The Rwandan Genocide of 1994* (Oxford: Berg Publishing, 1999), 105. More generally, see chapter 3, 'The Cosmology of Terror', for his 'generative scheme' of flow versus blockage. However, Taylor's more general point that this also links back to a Rwandan understanding of bodily illness and disease as also indicative of the moral well-being – or otherwise – of the state has many historic parallels. See, for instance, Nirenberg, *Communities*, 56–8, for an exposition on the medieval fears of the spread of leprosy in France, the belief that French kings might act as direct healers, and further anxieties that failure on this score might be tangible evidence of the spread of societal and political depravity, sinfulness and heresy.

88 See Lord James Bryce and Arnold J. Toynbee, eds., *The Treatment of Armenians in the Ottoman Empire: Documents Presented to Viscount Grey of Falloden,* Misc. No. 31. Command 8325, (London: His Majesty's Stationery Office, 1916), 85; Leslie A. Davis, *The Slaughterhouse Province, An American Diplomat's Report on the Armenian Genocide, 1915–1917* (New Rochelle, NY: Aristide D. Cataratzas, 1989), 51–2; Donald E. Miller and Lorna Touryan Miller, *Survivors, An Oral History of the Armenian Genocide* (Berkeley and Los Angeles: University of California Press, 1993), 66–7, for examples.

89 See Vahakn N. Dadrian, *Warrant for Genocide, Key Elements of Turko-Armenian Conflict* (New Brunswick, NJ, and London: Transaction Publishers, 1999), 17–18.

90 Ibid. See also idem., *The History*, 121–7.

91 Michael Vickery, *Cambodia, 1975–1982* (Boston: South End, 1984), esp. 5–8.

92 Quoted in Hilberg, *Destruction*, 131.

93 Dominik LaCapra, 'Lanzmann's Shoah, Here is no Why', *Critical Inquiry*, 23:2 (1997), 268–9, n. 4. For more on the discrepancy between the supposed 'inner' order of the Nazi self-perception and the 'outer' reality, see Dan Stone, 'Modernity and Violence, Theoretical Reflections on the Einsatzgruppen', *Journal of Genocide Research*, 1:3 (1999), 367–78. Interestingly, by comparision, Waller, *Becoming Evil*, 211, refuses to be drawn on 'the perpetrators' perverse enjoyment of, and sadistic pleasure in the excesses of extraordinary evil', preferring instead to highlight the 'extreme desensitisation' and 'callous attitude ... fostered by professional socialisation'.

94 Browning, *Ordinary Men*, 127–32; Goldhagen, *Hitler's Willing Executioners*, 233–8.

95 Mark Levene, 'Introduction', in idem. and Penny Roberts, eds, *The Massacre in History* (New York and Oxford: Berghahn Books, 1999), 9.

96 Quoted in Goldhagen, *Hitler's Willing Executioners*, 236.

97 See Robert Conquest, *The Great Terror, A Reassessment* (New York and Oxford: Oxford University Press, 1990), 130–1; Anthony Barnett and John Pilger, *After-*

math, The Struggle of Cambodia and Vietnam (London: New Statesman, 1982), part 4, 'The Bureaucracy of Death'.

98 See on this score Cornelia Sorabji, 'A Very Modern War: Terror and Territory in Bosnia-Hercegovina', in Robert A. Hinde and Helen E. Watson, eds, *War: A Cruel Necessity? The Bases of Institutionalised Violence* (London and New York: Tauris Academic Studies, 1995), 86, where, examining the nature of extreme violence in the recent Bosnian war, she has proposed that while its participants may have been allowed or enabled to inflict whatever disorganised tortures they could dream up, *the context* in which they did so remained a tightly organised one.

99 Prunier, *Rwanda Crisis,* 231.

100 See for instance, Wolfgang Sofsky, *Die Ordnung des Terrors: das Konzentrationslager* (Frankfurt on Main: S. Fischer, 1993); Bernd Weisbrod, 'Fundamentalist Violence: Political Violence and Political Religion in Modern Conflict', in Jacques Sémelin, ed., 'Extreme Violence', *International Social Science Journal,* 174 (2002), 499–509. Also idem., 'Qu'est-ce qu'un crime de masse? Le cas de l'ex-Yougoslavie', *Critique internationale,* 6 (2000), 157, for commentary.

101 Prunier, *Rwanda Crisis,* 247.

102 Mamdani, *When Victims*, chapter 7, 'The Civil War and the Genocide'.

103 Irving Louis Horowitz, *Taking Lives, Genocide and State Power* (Brunswick, NJ, and London: Transaction Publishers, 4th revised and expanded edn, 1997), 286.

104 See Victor Klemperer, *I Shall Bear Witness, The Diaries of Victor Klemperer, 1933–41,* trans. Martin Chalmers (London: Phoenix, 1998), for the full, unadulterated panoply of Hitler adulation.

105 See notably Roy Medvedev, *Let History Judge: The Origins and Consequences of Stalinism* (New York: Columbia University Press, 1989), 617–23.

106 Said K. Aburish, 'Father of All Despots', *Guardian Weekend,* 22 January 2000.

107 Quoted in Antony Polonsky, ed., *My Brother's Keeper, Recent Polish Debates on the Holocaust* (London: Routledge, 1990), 227.

108 From Daniel J. Goldhagen, 'A Reply to my Critics', *New Republic* (Dec. 1996) as quoted in A. D. Moses, 'Structure and Agency in the Holocaust: Daniel J. Goldhagen and his Critics', *History and Theory,* 37:2 (1998), 213.

109 See Moses, 'Structure', 214–17, for further searching questions.

110 Walter P. Zenner, 'Middlemen Minorities and Genocide', in Wallimann and Dobkowski, eds, *Genocide,* 253–81.

111 Jack T. Sanders, *Schismatics, Sectarians, Dissidents, Deviants: The First One Hundred Years of Jewish–Christian Relations* (London: SCM Press, 1993), 150.

112 Michael Ignatieff, *Blood and Belonging, Journeys into the New Nationalism* (London: Vintage, 1994), 14–16.

113 Samuel P. Huntington, *The Clash of Civilisations and the Remaking of World Order* (London: Touchstone Books, 1997).

114 Fein, 'Accounting for Genocide', 102.

115 Quoted in Vigen Guroian, 'Collective Responsibility and Official Excuse Making: The Case for the Turkish Genocide of the Armenians', in Hovannisian, *Armenian Genocide*, 143.

116 Quoted in Amnesty International, *Guatemala, The Human Rights Record* (London: Amnesty International Publications, 1987), 96.

117 El Obeid conference of imams, 17 April 1992, quoted in African Rights, *Facing Genocide: The Nuba of Sudan* (London: African Rights, 1995), 29.

118 Vahakn N. Dadrian, 'The Role of the Turkish Military in the Destruction of Ottoman Armenians: A Study in Historical Continuities', *Journal of Political and Military Sociology*, 20:2 (1992), 259.

119 David Brion Davis, ed., *The Fear of Conspiracy, Images of Un-American Subversion from the Revolution to the Present* (Ithaca, NY, and London: Cornell University Press, 1971), 205.

120 Ibid., 307.

121 Edward A. Shils, *The Torment of Secrecy: The Background and Consequences of American Security Policies* (London: William Heinemann, 1956), 71.

122 Richard Hofstadter, *The Paranoid Style in American Politics and Other Essays* (London: Jonathan Cape, 1966), for the classic study on this theme. However, see also Peter Knight, *Conspiracy Culture: From the Kennedy Assassination to the X-Files* (New York and London: Routledge, 2000) for a more overtly cultural reading of how the notion of conspiracy has developed 'as an everyday explanation of how the world works' (243). Significantly, Knight is more concerned here (in this pre-9/11 text) with what contemporary Americans feared the state was doing to them rather than anxieties directed against external threats in the era of the Cold War.

123 Friedlander, 'On the Possibility', 8.

124 Cohn, *Warrant*.

125 Lifton and Markusen, *Genocidal Mentality*, 52, quoting Robert C. Cecil, *The Myth of the Master Race*.

126 Cohn, *Warrant*, 168–70; Sharman Kadish, *Bolsheviks and British Jews, The Anglo-Jewish Community, Britain and the Russian Revolution* (London: Frank Cass, 1992), 32–7.

127 Cohn, *Warrant*, 78–80.

128 Quoted in Leon Poliakov, *History of Anti-Semitism,* vol. 4: *Suicidal Europe 1870–1933,* trans. George Klin (Oxford: Littman Library and Oxford University Press, 1985), 324–5.

129 Saul Friedlander, *Nazi Germany and the Jews,* vol. 1: *The Years of Persecution, 1933–1939* (London: Weidenfeld and Nicolson, 1997), 3.

130 Cohn, *Warrant*, 152–4.

131 Quoted in Goldhagen, *Hitler's Willing Executioners*, 393–4.

132 Roneil Radosh and Joyce Milton, *The Rosenberg File: A Search for the Truth* (New York: Holt, Rinehart and Winston, 1983); also E. L. Doctorow, *The Book of Daniel* (New York: Random House, 1971), for the hardly submerged Jewish sub-text

to the McCarthyite witch-hunt, via Julius and Ethel Rosenberg; its two most obvious sacrificial victims.

133 George Steiner, *In Bluebeard's Castle, Some Notes Towards the Redefinition of Culture* (London: Faber & Faber, 1971), 41.

134 Ibid., 41–2.

135 Quoted in Myriam Anissimov, *Primo Levi, Tragedy of an Optimist*, trans. Steve Cox (London: Aurum Press, 1998), 176.

136 Victor Klemperer, *The Language of the Third Reich: LTI – Lingua Tertii Imperii, A Philologist's Notebook*, trans. Martin Brady (London: Athlone Press, 2000), for the full exposé.

137 Wim Willems, *In Search of the True Gypsy, From Enlightenment to Final Solution*, trans. Don Bloch (London: Frank Cass, 1997), chapter 5, 'Robert Ritter (1901–51): Eugenist and Criminological Biologist'.

138 Mark Cocker, *Rivers of Blood, Rivers of Gold, Europe's Conflict with Tribal Peoples* (London: Jonathan Cape, 1998), 348.

139 Quoted in Dadrian, 'Role of Turkish Physicians', 175.

140 Paul Weindling, *Epidemics and Genocide in Eastern Europe, 1890–1945* (Oxford: Oxford University Press, 2000), part 1, 'Microbes and Migrants'; Alex Bein, 'Jewish Parasite, Notes on the Semantics of the Jewish Problem with Special Reference to Germany', *Leo Baeck Year Book* 9 (1964), 3–40; David Bodanis, *Web of Words, The Ideas behind Politics* (Macmillan; Basingstoke, 1988), chapter 2, 'Pasteur II: Hitler's Bacteria', for the emerging use of medical-scientific language to denigrate human groups.

141 Quoted in Parin, 'Open Wounds', 50.

142 See Dalia Ofer and Lenore J. Weitzman, eds, *Women in the Holocaust* (New Haven, CT, and London: Yale University Press, 1998) for further debates around this subject.

143 William Shakespeare, *The Merchant of Venice*, for the classic rendition of this 'archetype' in the person of Jessica, the 'Jew' Shylock's daughter.

144 See Volume II: *The Rise of the West*, Chapter 3, 'The Vendée – A Paradigm Shift?'.

145 Quoted in Claude Petitfrère, *La Vendée et les Vendéens* (Paris: Éditions Gallimard/Juillard, 1981), 74, where he particularly notes the insistence of the nineteenth-century historian Michelet, in his *Histoire de la Révolution*, on this score.

146 Ibid., 109, quoting Carrier to the Committee of Public Safety, 11 December 1793 justifying his proposal to kill men *and* women.

147 Julie Southwood and Patrick Flanagan, *Indonesia, Law, Propaganda and Terror* (London: Zed Press, 1983), 101; Leslie Dwyer and Degung Santikarma, 'When the World Turned to Chaos: 1965 and its Aftermath in Bali, Indonesia', in Ben Kiernan and Robert Gellately, eds, *The Spectre of Genocide: Mass Murder in Historical Perspective* (New York and Cambridge: Cambridge University Press, 2003), 298–301, for further cogent analysis. See also William G. Rosenberg and Marilyn B. Young, *Transforming Russia and China, Revolutionary Struggle in the Twentieth Century* (Oxford and New York: Oxford University Press, 1982), 115–16, for the

Kuomingtang 1927 'White Terror' in which Chinese leftist urban women with bobbed hair – a sign of liberation – were specifically assaulted, violated and often then burnt alive in tens of thousands; Taylor, *Sacrifice*, chapter 4, 'The Dialectics of Hate and Desire: Tutsi Women and Hutu Extremism', for a further example of the playing out of similarly gendered anxieties in the context of the Rwandan genocide.

148 Quoted in Amnesty International, *Guatemala*, 99.

149 Taylor, *Sacrifice*; Øystein Gullvåg Holter, 'A Theory of Gendercide', *Journal of Genocide Research*, 4:1 (2002), 11–38; Jones, 'Gendercide'.

150 Kanan Makiya, *Cruelty and Silence: War, Tyranny, Uprising and the Arab World* (London: Jonathan Cape, 1993), 219.

151 Mark Levene, 'Yesterday's Victims, Today's Perpetrators?: Considerations on Peoples and Territories within the former Ottoman Empire', *Terrorism and Political Violence*, 6 (Winter 1994), 444–61.

152 The nature of the dichotomy is perhaps best summed up by reference to Tenzin Gyatso, His Holiness the Dalai Lama, *Ancient Wisdom, Modern World, Ethics for a New Millenium* (London: Little, Brown and Co., 1999). I am indebted to David Newman for providing me with a copy of this book.

153 Dadrian, 'Structural-Functional Components', 123.

154 Saul Friedlander, 'Introduction', in Gerald Fleming, *Hitler and the Final Solution* (Oxford: Oxford University Press, 1986), xxxiii.

155 The figure quoted in Markusen and Kopf, *Holocaust*, 13.

3 Continuity and Discontinuity in the Historical Record

1 See Konrad Lorenz, *On Aggression* (London: Methuen, 1966); Ashley Montagu, *The Nature of Human Aggression* (Oxford: Oxford University Press, 1976), for radically different perspectives on 'innate violence' within human biology. Waller, *Becoming Evil*, is again a good adjudicator on this score in bringing to the fore our 'ancestral Shadow' yet also reminding us: 'There is no gene for genocide' (163). The debate about the actual anthropological-cum-archaeological record has similarly, recently crystallised around Lawrence Keeley, *War before Civilisation* (New York and Oxford: Oxford University Press, 1996), in his outright assertion of man's endemic recourse to inter-group violence. By comparison see John Carman, ed., *Material Harm, Archaeological Studies of War and Violence* (Glasgow: Cruithne Press, 1997); idem. and Anthony Harding, eds, *Ancient Warfare, Archaeological Perspectives* (Stroud, Glos: Sutton Publishing, 1999), for much more nuanced approaches. Note especially the distinction drawn by Jonathan Haas, 'The Origins of War and Ethnic Violence', in ibid., 13, between a clear *capacity* but a much less clear *predisposition* towards warfare.

2 George A. Kren and Leon Rappoport, *The Holocaust and the Crisis of Human Behaviour* (New York: Holmes and Meier, 1980), 130.

3 Freeman, 'Genocide', 207–23, for further discussion. Also George W. Stocking, Jr., *Victorian Anthropology* (New York: Free Press, 1987), chapter 1, 'The Idea of Civilisation Before the Crystal Palace (1750–1850)', and Martin Thom, *Republics, Nations and Tribes* (London: Verso, 1995), for emerging modern conceptions of progress from 'barbarism' to civilisation.

4 Harold Lamb quoted in Katz, *Holocaust,* vol. 1, 96. See more generally J. J. Sanders, *The History of the Mongol Conquests* (London: Routledge, Kegan and Paul, 1971); David Morgan, *The Mongols* (Oxford: Basil Blackwell, 1986).

5 Quoted in Kuper, *Genocide*, 12. The extraordinary Eurasian ravages of Timur are often treated as a footnote to the Mongol conquests. Harold Lamb, *Tamerlane the Earth Shaker* (London: Thornton, Butterworth Ltd, 1929), represents a colourful if now seriously outdated study. See however, Beatrice Forbes Manz, *The Rise and Rule of Tamerlane* (Cambridge: Canto, 1999), for a thoroughly serious modern analysis.

6 John Keay, *India, A History* (London and Delhi: HarperCollins, 2001), 385–86.

7 Walter, *Terror*, 111–12.

8 Ibid., 110. See, however, James Gump, *The Formation of the Zulu Kingdom in South Africa, 1750–1840* (San Fransisco: Mellen Research University Press, 1990) and John Laband, *The Rise and Fall of the Zulu Nation* (London: Arms and Armour Press, 1997), esp. 13–15, both of whom mirror a more general recent aspect of *Mfecane* historiography which contests the degree to which the drive to politico-military centralisation in the Drakensberg region was peculiar to a protean Zulu 'nation' alone.

9 Albert Ten Eyck Olmstead, *History of Assyria* (New York: C. Scribner and Sons, 1923), 654.

10 See Chalk and Jonassohn, *History*, chapters on 'Melos', 'Carthage' and 'The Zulu under Shaka'. See also the recent study of Shaka and his successors by Michael R. Mahoney, 'The Zulu Kingdom as a Genocidal and Post-Genocidal Society c. 1810 to the Present', *Journal of Genocide Research*, 5:2 (2003), 258, which confirms that while Shaka had no compunction in killing men, women and children among chiefdoms which resisted him, the emerging Zulu state often embraced all those who willingly conceded to his rule, thus demonstrating a complete absence of specifically ethnic motivation in his agenda.

11 Katz, *Holocaust*, vol. 1, chapter 5, 'Roman and Classical Slavery'.

12 Ibid., 199–200, 213–14; Goldhagen, *Hitler's Willing Executioners*, part 4, 'Jewish "Work" is Annihilation'.

13 See David E. Stannard, *American Holocaust, The Conquest of the New World* (New York and Oxford: Oxford University Press, 1992), 89–91; Seymour Drescher, 'The Atlantic Slave Trade and the Holocaust; A Comparative Perspective', in Rosenbaum, *Is the Holocaust Unique?*, 65–86.

14 See Mark Levene, 'The Changing Face of Mass Murder: Massacre, Genocide and Post-Genocide', *International Social Science Journal,* 174 (2002), 449.

15 Bustenai Oded, *Mass Deportations and Deportees in the Neo-Assyrian Empire* (Wiesbaden: Reichert, 1979); Mehrdad R. Irzady, *The Kurds, A Concise Handbook* (Washington, DC: Taylor and Francis, 1992), 101–8; for ancient and more recent examples.

16 See for example, John Perry, 'Forced Migration in Iran During the Seventeenth and Eighteenth Centuries', *Iranian Studies*, 8:4 (1975), 199–215.

17 Roger W. Smith, 'Human Destructiveness and Politics: The Twentieth Century as an Age of Genocide', in Wallimann and Dobkowski, *Genocide*, 31.

18 R. C. L. Jones, 'Fortifications and Sieges in Western Europe c. 800–1450', in Maurice Keen, ed., *Medieval Warfare, A History* (Oxford: Oxford University Press, 1990), 182–3.

19 Keeley, *War*, esp. 25–6, 93, 174.

20 Oded, *Mass Deportations*, 21, n.5.

21 See Freeman, 'Genocide', 219–21.

22 Michael Wood, *In the Footsteps of Alexander the Great* (London: BBC, 1997), 152–5.

23 Deuteronomy 7:1–2, in J. H. Hertz, ed., *The Pentateuch and Haftorahs* (London: Soncino Press, 1965), 774.

24 See Numbers 25:1–6, 31:1–53, Hertz *Pentateuch*, 681, 703–7. See also Roger W. Smith, 'Women and Genocide: Notes on an Unwritten History', *Holocaust and Genocide Studies*, 8:3 (1994), 317–19.

25 Samuel 15:3; Hertz *Pentateuch*, 996.

26 Ibid., commentary on Samuel 15, 995. See also Ternon, *L'État*, 269–70.

27 See for instance, Chilperic Edwards, *The Hammurabi Code and the Siniaitic Legislation, with a Complete Translation of the Great Babylonian Inscription Discovered at Susa* (London: Watts and Co., 1904), esp. 108–10, for those crimes which merited the death penalty under Babylonian law, thereby implying legal-political constraints on wholesale state-sanctioned murder. By contrast, for textual commentary and exegesis of the ancient Israelites' apparent cultic invocation to engage in genocidal warfare against their neighbours see Gerhard von Rad, *Holy War in Ancient Israel*, trans. and ed. Marva J. Dawn (Grand Rapids, MI: William B. Eerdmans Publishing Co., 1991 [first published 1958]); Michael Walzer, 'The Idea of Holy War in Ancient Israel', *Journal of Religious Ethics*, 20:2 (1992), 215–27 and John Howard Yoder, 'Texts that Serve or Texts that Summon? A Response to Michael Walzer', ibid., 229–34.

28 Foucault, *Discipline*. Also Bauman, *Holocaust*, 9; Horowitz, *Taking Lives*, 69–71.

29 H. W. F. Saggs, *The Might that Was Assyria* (London: Sidgwick & Jackson, 1984), 262.

30 Robert Browning, *The Byzantine Empire* (London: Weidenfeld and Nicolson, 1980), 90.

31 See Saggs, *Might*, 47–8. As Saggs, in another section on 'psychological warfare' (248–50) also notes, it was in political interest of the Assyrian state to broadcast to would-be insurgents the most terrifying possible consequences.

32 Alan Krell, *The Devil's Rope: A Cultural History of Barbed Wire* (London: Reaktion Books, 2002), 49–51; Oliver Razac, *Barbed Wire, a Political History,* trans. Jonathan Kneight (London: Profile Books, 2002) notably his section: 'The Camp'.

33 Wood, *In the Footsteps,* 154–67, for Alexander's campaigns against Bessus and Spitamenes in distant Central Asia, 328–327 BC.

34 John King Fairbank, *The Great Chinese Revolution 1800–1985* (New York: Harper and Row, 1986), 81.

35 Churchill, *Little Matter,* 97.

36 Sven Lindqvist, *Exterminate all the Brutes,* trans. Joan Tate (London: Grant Books, 1998), 111.

37 Dan Stone, 'The Historiography of Genocide: Beyond "Uniqueness" and Ethnic Competition', *Rethinking History,* 8:1 (2004), 132.

38 Strobe Talbott, ed., *Khrushchev Remembers: The Last Testament* (London: Andre Deutsch, 1974), 109. That said, Khrushchev may have been being thoroughly disingenuous, not least as he surely would have known of the predetermined OGPU directives requiring statistical quotas of 'victims'. See Stephane Courtois, 'Introduction, The Crimes of Communism', in idem., *Black Book,* 15.

39 R. J. Rummel, *Lethal Politics: Soviet Genocide and Mass Murder since 1917* (New Brunswick, NJ and London: Transaction Books, 1990), 236.

40 Anthony Giddens, *The Nation-State and Violence* (Cambridge: Polity Press, 1985), 4.

41 Holter, 'Theory', 25–6, for an interesting gendered usage of this term.

42 See Fein, 'Genocide, Sociological Perspective', 36; Michael Freeman, 'Nationalism and Genocide, A Philosophical Analysis', (unpublished paper for International Association of Genocide Scholars conference, Concordia University, Montreal, 1997), 6–9, for more on this theme.

43 See Antonio Cassese, *International Law in a Divided World* (Oxford: Clarendon Press, 1986), 398–400.

44 Levene, 'Dissenting Voice', 153–60, for efforts at disentangling 'system' and 'society'. The contemporary breakdown of the nominal *modus vivendi* between the two will be a matter for discussion in the final volume of this work.

45 Smith, 'Human Destructiveness', 28.

46 Ibid.

47 See Clive Foss, 'The Turkish View of Armenian History: A Vanishing Nation', in Hovannisian, *Armenian Genocide,* 250–79.

48 Dadrian, *History,* 405–6; Breitman, *Architect,* 39–44.

49 Quoted in Breitman, *Architect,* 43.

50 See Volume II: *The Rise of the West,* Chapter 1, 'European Conquest and Sundry "Savages"'.

51 Rummel, 'Democide', 11–13.

52 See Volume II: *The Rise of the West,* Chapter 2, 'Anglo Consolidation in the Americas and Antipodes'.

53 Harff and Gurr, 'Victims of the State', for a relatively up-to-date list of key perpetrators.

54 Mark Levene, 'Creating a Modern "Zone of Genocide": The Impact of Nation and State Formation on Eastern Anatolia 1878–1923', *Holocaust and Genocide Studies*, 12:3 (1998), 393–433, for more on this theme.

55 Charles Tilly, 'Reflections on the History of European State Making', in idem., ed. *The Formation of National States in Europe* (Princeton: Princeton University Press, 1975), 3–83; Robert Bartlett, *The Making of Europe, Conquest, Civilisation and Cultural Change 950–1350* (London: Penguin, 1994), for important examples of each position.

56 See Immanuel Wallerstein, *The Modern World System* (San Diego and New York: Academic Press Inc., 1974–89), 3 vols, for the classic analysis.

57 See Norman M. Naimark, *Fires of Hatred, Ethnic Cleansing in Twentieth Century Europe* (Cambridge, MA, and London: Harvard University Press, 2001), chapter 4, 'The Expulsion of Germans from Poland and Czechoslovakia'.

58 Vickery, *Cambodia*, xii.

59 Fein, Scenarios of Genocide', 3–31. See also idem., 'Genocide, Sociological Perspective', 28, Table 1, for a comparison of the genocide typologies of major scholars.

60 Helen Fein, correspondence with author, 1997.

61 Kuper, *Genocide*, 57, and more generally chapter 4, 'Social Structure and Genocide'.

62 Fein, 'Accounting for Genocide', 88–9. Also see Barbara Harff and Ted Robert Gurr, 'Victims of the State: Genocides, Politicides and Group Repression since 1945', *International Review of Victimology*, 1:1 (1989), 23–41.

63 Fein, 'Accounting for Genocide', 89, 98–100.

64 Arendt, *Origins*, 467. See also Zbigniew Brzezinski, *The Permanent Purge* (Cambridge, MA: Harvard University Press, 1958), for a statement of the thesis primarily with the USSR in its sights.

65 Rummel, 'Democide'; Werth, 'A State', esp. chapter 13, 'Apogee and Crisis in the Gulag System', for the post-1945 breadth of those caught in the dragnet.

66 See Robert Gellately, *The Gestapo and German Society: Enforcing Racial Policy 1933–1945* (Oxford: Oxford University Press, 1990); Eric Johnson, *The Nazi Terror, Gestapo, Jews and Ordinary Germans* (London: John Murray, 1999), for thorough and cogent studies of Nazi policing.

67 Raymond Carr, *The Spanish Tragedy, The Civil War in Perspective* (London: Phoenix Press, 2000), 257–8.

68 Rummel, 'Democide', 7.

69 See for instance, Mark Harrison, 'Resource Mobilisation for World War II: the USA, UK, USSR and Germany, 1938–45', *Economic History Review*, 41:2 (1988), 171–92; Margaret Gowing, 'The Organisation of Manpower in Britain during the Second World War', *Journal of Contemporary History*, 7:2 (1972), 147–67. For a more sober view of Britain's organisational strengths, however, see Correlli

Barnett, *The Audit of War, The Illusion and Reality of Britain as a Great Power* (London and Basingstoke: Papermac, 1987).

70 See notably J. Arch Getty, *The Origins of the Great Purges: The Soviet Communist Party Reconsidered, 1933–1938* (Cambridge: Cambridge University Press, 1985); Getty and Manning, *Stalinist Terror*; Robert W. Thurston, *Life and Terror in Stalin's Russia 1934–1941* (New Haven, CT, and London: Yale University Press, 1996); J. Arch Getty and Oleg V. Naumov, eds, *The Road to Terror, Stalin and the Self-Destruction of the Bolsheviks, 1932–1939* (New Haven, CT: Yale University Press, 1999).

71 See for instance, Getty, *Origins,* 8, for his pointed reference to the 'thousands' who were executed. By contrast see Courtois, 'Introduction', 4, which offers an overall twentieth-century roll-call of communist fatalities *worldwide* at approximately 100 million.

72 Quoted in Frank Chalk and Kurt Jonassohn, 'The History and Sociology of Genocidal Killings', in Charny, *Genocide, Critical Bibliographical Review,* vol. 1, 57.

73 Neil Gregor, ed., *Nazism* (Oxford: Oxford University Press, 2000), 125.

74 Helen Fein, 'A Formula for Genocide: Comparisons of the Turkish Genocide' (1915) and the German Holocaust (1939–1945)', *Comparative Studies in Sociology,* 1 (1978), 271–93; Vahakn N. Dadrian, 'The Convergent Aspects of the Armenian and Jewish Cases of Genocide: A Reinterpretation of the Concept of Holocaust', *Holocaust and Genocide Studies,* 3:2 (1988), 151–70; Florence Mazian, *Why Genocide? The Armenian and Jewish Experiences in Perspective* (Ames: Iowa State University Press, 1990), for further comparative studies.

75 Theda Skocpol, *States and Social Revolutions* (Cambridge: Cambridge University Press, 1979).

76 Melson, *Revolution,* 32.

77 Feroz Ahmad, *The Young Turks: The CUP in Turkish Politics 1908–1914* (Oxford: Oxford University Press, 1969), 21, for instance, describes the core CUP leadership as essentially socially conservative 'empire men'.

78 The term repeatedly employed in Ervin Staub, *The Roots of Evil, The Origins of Genocide and Other Group Violence* (Cambridge: Cambridge University Press, 1989).

79 There are now a group of young scholars seriously confronting the relationship. See notably Donald Bloxham, 'Three Imperialisms and a Turkish Nationalism, International Stresses, Imperial Disintegration and the Armenian Genocide', *Patterns of Prejudice,* 36:4 (2002), 37–58: Moses, 'Conceptual Blockages'; Stone, 'Historiography'.

80 Horowitz, *Taking Lives,* chapter 9, 'Nationalism and Genocidal Systems'.

81 Rummel, 'Democide', 12.

82 Francis Fukuyama, *The End of History and the Last Man* (London: Penguin, 1992).

83 Stannard, *American Holocaust*; Lindqvist, *Exterminate.* See also more recently Mohawk, *Utopian Legacies.*

84 Bauman, *Modernity,* 93.

85 Ron Aronson, 'Societal Madness: Impotence, Power and Genocide', in Charny, *Toward the Understanding,* 136.

86 Giddens, *Nation-State,* 5.

87 Ibid., 312–13.

88 See also David Maybury-Lewis, 'Living in Leviathan: Ethnic Groups and the State', in idem., ed., *The Prospects for Plural Societies* (Washington, DC: American Ethnological Society, 1984), 224–5 and chapters by Leo Kuper and Peter Worsley for more on this critical shift.

89 Michael Burleigh and Wolfgang Wipperman, *The Racial State, Germany 1933–1945* (Cambridge: Cambridge University Press, 1991), 2.

90 Indeed, see Detlev Peukert, 'The Genesis of "the Final Solution" from the Spirit of Science', in David Crew, ed., *Nazism and German Society* (London: Routledge, 1994), 274–99, for a famously controversial riposte to the Burleigh and Wipperman line in which Nazism is presented as a pathologically developmental form of modernity. For further doubts see Christopher R. Browning, 'The Holocaust and History', in Peter Hayes, ed., *Lessons and Legacies,* vol. 3: *Memory, Memorialisation and Denial* (Evanston, IL: Northwestern University Press, 1999), 26: 'Modernisation does not inherently mean progress or betterment … it is the experience of National Socialism and the Holocaust that has totally and irreparably severed the comfortable identity of progress and modernisation'. See also Florint Lobont and Dan Stone, 'Modernisation and Antisemitism in Romania', *Revista Psihologie Aplicata* (Timosoara), 4:2 (2002), 106: 'There is no *a priori* reason why "modern civilisation" should not encompass violence as part of itself.'

91 Paul Kennedy, *The Rise and Fall of The Great Powers* (London: Fontana Press, 1989), chapter 1, 'The Rise of the Western World'; Giddens, *Nation-State*; Tilly, *Coercion,* esp. chapter 3, 'How War Made States, and Vice Versa', for the essential contours of this argument.

92 See Wallerstein, *Modern World System,* vol. 3: *The Second Era of Great Expansion of the Capitalist World Economy, 1730–1840s,* chapter 2, 'Struggle in the Core – Phase III: 1763–1815'.

93 See Volume II: *The Rise of the West,* Part Two, 'To the Frontiers', for development.

94 The terminology of Misha Glenny's BBC broadcast, 'All Fall Down', Radio 4, 31 March 1995.

95 Wallerstein, *The Modern World System,* vol. 1: *Capitalist Agriculture and the Origins of the European World Economy in the Sixteenth Century,* for core, periphery and semi-periphery exposition.

96 The counter-arguments of Samuel P. Huntington, *The Clash of Civilisations and the Remaking of World Order* (London and New York: Touchstone Books, 1998), notwithstanding.

97 See Samir Amin, *Unequal Development, An Essay on Social Formations of Peripheral Capitalism* (Hassocks: Harvester Press, 1976); Alexander Geschenkron, *Economic Backwardness in Historical Perspective* (Cambridge, MA: Harvard University Press, 1962).

98 Quoted in Aronson, *Dialectics*, 196.

99 Ibid., 195.

100 Lewin, *Making*, 20.

101 Quoted in Heyd, *Foundations of Turkish Nationalism*, 79.

102 Isaiah Berlin, 'On the Pursuit of the Ideal', *New York Review of Books*, 17 March 1988, 18.

103 See Joseph Rothschild, *East Central Europe between Two World Wars* (Seattle: University of Washington Press, 1977), 281.

104 Quoted in Ian Kershaw, *The Nazi Dictatorship, Problems and Perspectives of Interpretation* (London: Arnold, 3rd edn, 1993), 139.

105 See Burleigh and Wipperman, *Racial State*, for an argument stressing the centrality of racism for the Nazi polity. See also Weitz, *Nation*, chapter 3, 'The Primacy of Race: Nazi Germany'.

106 See Roman Szporluk, *Communism and Nationalism, Karl Marx versus Friedrich List* (New York and London: Oxford University Press, 1988), part 2, for an admirable development of Listian nationalism, of some relevance to the tenor of this study.

107 Kennedy, *Rise*, section: 'The Shifting Balance of World Forces', 254–77.

108 See Daniel Pick, *War Machine, The Rationalisation of Slaughter in the Modern Age* (New Haven, CT, and London: Yale University Press, 1993), 98–9, for more on Veblen.

109 See David Blackbourn and Geoff Eley, *The Peculiarities of German History, Bourgeois Society and Politics in Nineteenth-Century Germany 1780–1918, The Long Nineteenth Century* (Oxford and New York: Oxford University Press, 1984); Arno J. Mayer, *The Persistence of the Old Regime, Europe to the Great War* (London: Croom Helm, 1981), esp. 88–102.

110 Aronson, *Dialectics*, 58–9.

111 Ibid., 59.

112 Ibid., 201, 58.

113 Quoted in Kennedy, *Rise*, 276.

114 Aronson, *Dialectics*, 169.

115 Fritz Fischer, *War of Illusions, German Policies from 1911 to 1914*, trans. Marian Jackson (London: Chatto and Windus, 1975).

116 See Greenfield, *Nationalism*, 15, for her *ressentiment* thesis, though minus a fuller sense of the international frame within which it operates.

117 Chalk and Jonassohn, *History*, 18.

118 Quoted in Fein, ' Sociological Perspective', 39.

119 Giddens, *Nation-State*, 12.

120 Griffin, *Nature*, 38.

121 See Stanley G. Payne, *A History of Fascism, 1914–45* (London: UCL Press, 1995), 5, for commentary on Griffin's work.

122 Bettina Arnold, 'Justifying Genocide, Archaeology and the Construction of Difference', in Hinton, *Annihilating Difference*, 105–6. Also Nicholas Goodricke-

Clarke, *The Occult Roots of Nazism, Secret Ayran Cults and Their Influence on Nazi Ideology: The Ariosophists of Austria and Germany, 1890–1935* (London and New York: I.B. Tauris, 1985), for some of the more extreme shores of protean Nazi mythologisation.

123 Heyd, *Foundations,* 113.

124 Arnold, 'Justifying Genocide', 109; Elizabeth Becker, *When the War was Over: The Voices of Cambodia's Revolution and Its People* (New York: Simon and Schuster, 1986), 53–4.

125 Arnold, 'Justifying Genocide', 95–116; Michael Burleigh, *Germany Turns Eastwards, A Study of Ostforschung in the Third Reich* (Cambridge: Cambridge University Press, 1988).

126 See Szporluk, *Communism,* 216–20, for a case of one such apparent contradiction, namely national-bolshevism.

127 See Roger Cooper, *The Baha'is of Iran* (London: Minority Rights Group, 1982); Baha'i International Community, *The Baha'i Question, Iran's Secret Blueprint for the Destruction of a Religious Community, An Examination of the Persecution of the Baha'is of Iran 1979–1993* (New York: Baha'i International Community, 1993).

128 See M. Reza Ghods, *Iran in the Twentieth Century, A Political History* (Boulder, CO, and London: Lynne Rienner Publishers and Adamantine Press, 1989), 1–3.

129 John Dower, *Japan in War and Peace: Selected Essays* (London: HarperCollins, 1993), 257–85. Also Chushichi Tsuzuki, *The Pursuit of Power in Modern Japan, 1825–1995* (Oxford: Oxford University Press, 2000), chapter 12, 'Fascism, Militarism and Thought-Control'.

130 R. J. Rummel, *China's Bloody Century, Genocide and Mass Murder since 1900* (New Brunswick, NJ: Transaction Publishers, 1991), 139.

131 Callum MacDonald, '"Kill All, Burn All, Loot All": The Nanking Massacre of December 1937 and Japanese Policy in China', in Levene and Roberts, *Massacre,* 237–8.

132 See William Wetherall and George A. DeVos, 'Ethnic Minorities in Japan', in Veenhoven, *Case Studies,* vol. 1, 335–75, esp. 344–6 on Ainu.

133 Quoted in Samir Al-Khalil, *Republic of Fear, Saddam's Iraq* (London: Hutchinson Radius, 1989), 20.

134 Rogers Brubaker, *Citizenship and Nationhood in France and Germany* (Cambridge, MA, and London: Harvard University Press, 1992), 'Introduction: Traditions of Nationhood in France and Germany'.

135 Edith Sanders, '"The Hamitic Hypothesis": Its Origin and Functions in Time Perspective', *Journal of African History,* 10 (1969), 521–32; Taylor, *Sacrifice,* chapter 2, 'The Hamitic Hypothesis in Rwanda and Burundi'; William F. S. Miles, 'Hamites and Hebrews: Problems in "Judaizing" the Rwandan Genocide', *Journal of Genocide Research,* 2:1 (2000), 108–9; René Lemarchand, 'Where Hamites and Aryans Cross Paths: The Role of Myth-Making in Mass Murders', *Journal of Genocide Research,* 5:1 (2003), 145–8.

136 Prunier, *Rwanda Crisis,* 171–2.

137　See Clive Foss, 'The Turkish View of Armenian History: A Vanishing Nation', in Richard G. Hovannisian, ed., *The Armenian Genocide, History, Politics, Ethics* (New York: St Martin's Press, 1992), 257.

138　McDowall, *Modern History,* 187–91, 402–7.

139　Mark Levene, 'The Chittagong Hill Tracts: a Case Study in the Political Economy of "Creeping" Genocide', *Third World Quarterly,* 20:2 (1999), 343, 350.

140　Freeman, 'Nationalism and Genocide', 8.

141　Bertrand Russell, for instance, described the killings as 'the most horrible and systematic human massacre we have had occasion to witness since the extermination of the Jews by the Nazis'. Quoted in Stanley Meisler, 'Holocaust in Burundi, 1972', in Veenhoven, *Case Studies,* vol. 5, 229.

142　See Robert Jan van Pelt and Deborah Dwork, *Auschwitz, 1270 to the Present* (New Haven, CT, and London: Yale University Press, 1996), 281–3.

143　Hitler to Czech foreign minister, František Chvalkovsky, January 1939. Quoted in Fleming, *Hitler,* 14–15.

144　This line of argument especially with its emphasis on the organic purity of authentic society as integral to the ideological wellsprings of genocide is more keenly pursued in Scott Straus, 'Organic Purity and the role of anthropology in Cambodia and Rwanda', *Patterns of Prejudice,* 35:2 (2001), 47–62. Also see Ben Kiernan, *Blood and Soil: Modern Genocide 1500–2000* (New Haven, CT: Yale University Press, forthcoming).

145　Cocker, *Rivers,* 315.

146　Paul B. Henze, 'Circassian Resistance to Russia', in Marie Benningsen Broxup, ed., *The North Caucasus Barrier: The Russian Advance towards the Muslim World* (London: Hurst and Co., 1992), 80–7.

147　Rather significantly, when six army generals were killed, allegedly by communists in 1965, the army commander, Nasution recalled the 1948 communist uprising at Madiun as a previous 'case of being stabbed in the back'. The accusation in turn became a pretext for the extermination of the Indonesian communist party (the PKI) 'down to its very roots so there will be no third Madiun'. Quoted in Southwood and Flanagan, *Indonesia,* 68.

148　Aronson, *Dialectics,* 62.

149　See Martin van Bruinessen, 'Genocide in Kurdistan? The Suppression of the Dersim Rebellion in Turkey (1937–38) and the Chemical War Against the Iraqi Kurds (1988)', in Andreopoulos, *Genocide,* 141–70; Mark Levene, 'A Moving Target, The Usual Suspects and (Maybe) a Smoking Gun: the Problem of Pinning Blame in Modern Genocide', *Patterns of Prejudice,* 33:4 (1999), 3–24.

Select Bibliography

This bibliography lists the principal works that supported this study.
Fuller references are to be gleaned from the endnotes.

African Rights, *Facing Genocide: The Nuba of Sudan* (London: African Rights, 1995).
———, *Rwanda: Not so Innocent, When Women become Killers* (London: African Rights, 1995).
———, *Rwanda: Death, Despair and Defiance* (London: African Rights, 1995).
Ahmad, Feroz, *The Young Turks: The CUP in Turkish Politics: 1908–1914* (Oxford: Oxford University Press, 1969).
Alexander, Jeffrey C., 'On the Social Constuction of Moral Universals: The "Holocaust" from War Crime to Trauma Drama', *European Journal of Social Theory*, 5:1 (2002), 5–85.
Alexander, Martin S., Evans, Martin, and Keiger, J. F. V., *The Algerian War and the French Army 1954–62* (Basingstoke and New York: Palgrave Macmillan, 2002).
Al-Khalil, Samir, *Republic of Fear, Saddam's Iraq* (London: Hutchinson Radius, 1989).
Amin, Samir, *Unequal Development, an Essay on Social Formations of Peripheral Capitalism* (Hassocks: Harvester Press, 1976).
Amnesty International, *Guatemala, The Human Rights Record* (London: Amnesty International Publications, 1987).
Andreopoulos, George, D., ed., *Genocide, Conceptual and Historical Dimensions* (Philadelphia: University of Pennsylvania Press, 1994).
Arendt, Hannah, *The Origins of Totalitarianism* (New York: Meridian, 1958).
———, *Eichmann in Jerusalem, a Report on the Banality of Evil* (London: Penguin, 1965).
Arens, Richard, *Genocide in Paraguay* (Philadelphia: Temple University Press, 1976).
Arlen, Michael J., *Passage to Ararat* (New York: Farrar, Strauss and Giroux, 1975).
Aronson, Ronald, *Dialectics of Disaster, A Preface to Hope* (London: Verso, 1983).
Baha'i International Community, *The Baha'i Question, Iran's Secret Blueprint for the Destruction of a Religious Community, An Examination of the Persecution of the Baha'is of Iran 1979–1993* (New York: Baha'i International Community, 1993).
Bakalian, Anny P., *Armenian-Americans from being to feeling Armenian* (New Brunswick, NJ, and London: Transaction Publishers, 1993).
Baldwin, Peter, ed., *Reworking The Past, Hitler, The Holocaust and The Historians' Debate* (Boston, MA: Beacon Press, 1990), 77–87.

Barnett, Anthony, and Pilger, John, *Aftermath, the Struggle of Cambodia and Vietnam* (London: New Statesman, 1982).

Barnett, Correlli, *The Audit of War, the Illusion and Reality of Britain as a Great Power* (London and Basingstoke: Papermac, 1987).

Bartlett, Thomas, and Jeffrey, Keith, eds, *A Military History of Ireland* (Cambridge: Cambridge University Press, 1996).

Bartov, Omer, 'Defining Enemies, Making Victims: Germans, Jews and the Holocaust', *American Historical Review*, 103 (1998), 771–816.

——, 'Reception and Perception: Goldhagen's Holocaust and the World', in Geoff Eley, ed., *'The Goldhagen Effect': History, Memory, Nazism – Facing the German Past* (Ann Arbor: University of Michigan Press, 2000), 33–87.

Bauer, Yehuda, 'The Place of the Holocaust in Contemporary History', *Studies in Contemporary Jewry*, 1 (1984), 201–24.

——, and Rotenstreich, Nathan, eds, *The Holocaust as Historical Experience* (New York: Holmes and Meier, 1981).

Bauman, Zygmunt, *Modernity and the Holocaust* (Oxford: Blackwell, 1989).

Becker, Elizabeth, *When the War was Over: The Voices of Cambodia's Revolution and Its People* (New York: Simon & Schuster, 1986).

Bein, Alex, 'Jewish Parasite, Notes on the Semantics of the Jewish Problem with Special Reference to Germany', *Leo Baeck Year Book*, 9 (1964), 3–40.

Berenbaum, Michael, and Peck, Abraham J., eds, *The Holocaust and History, The Known, The Unknown, The Disputed and The Reexamined* (Bloomington and Indianapolis: Indiana University Press, 1998).

Best, Geoffrey, *Humanity in Warfare* (New York: Columbia University Press, 1980).

Blackbourn, David, and Eley, Geoff, *The Peculiarities of German History, Bourgeois Society and Politics in Nineteenth-Century Germany 1780–1918, the Long Nineteenth Century* (Oxford and New York: Oxford University Press, 1984).

Bloxham, Donald, 'The Beginning of the Armenian Catastrophe, Comparative and Contextual Considerations', in Hans-Lukas Kieser and Dominick Schaller, eds, *Der Völkermord an den Armeniern und die Shoah* (Zurich: Chronos Publishing, 2002), 101–28.

Bodanis, David, *Web of Words, the Ideas behind Politics* (Basingstoke: Macmillan, 1988).

Bourdieu, Pierre, *Outline of a Theory of Practice*, trans. Richard Nice (Cambridge and New York: Cambridge University Press, 1977).

Braude, Benjamin, and Lewis, Bernard, eds, *Christians and Jews in the Ottoman Empire* (New York and London: Holmes and Meier, 1982), 2 vols.

Breitman, Richard, *The Architect of Genocide, Himmler and the Final Solution* (London: Bodley Head, 1991).

Briggs, Charles, 'Genocide', in David Theo Goldberg and John Solomos, eds, *A Companion to Racial and Ethnic Studies* (Malden, MA, and Oxford: Blackwell Publishers, 2002), 31–45.

Brogan, Patrick, *World Conflicts* (London: Bloomsbury, 1989).

Browning, Christopher R., *Fateful Months: Essays on the Emergence of the Final Solution* (New York and London: Holmes and Meier, 1985).

——, *Ordinary Men, Reserve Police Battalion 101 and the Final Solution in Poland* (New York: HarperPerennial, 1993).

——, with Matthaus, Jürgen, *The Origins of the Final Solution. The Evolution of Nazi Jewish Policy, September 1939–March 1942* (London: William Heinemann, 2004).

Browning, Robert, *The Byzantine Empire* (London: Weidenfeld and Nicolson, 1980).

Brubaker, Rogers, *Citizenship and Nationhood in France and Germany* (Cambridge, MA, and London: Harvard University Press, 1992).

Bryce, Lord James, and Toynbee, Arnold, eds, *The Treatment of Armenians in the Ottoman Empire: Documents Presented to Viscount Grey of Falloden*, Misc. No. 31, Command 8325 (London: His Majesty's Stationery Office, 1916).

Burger, Julian, *Report from the Frontier: The State of the World's Indigenous Peoples* (London: Zed Books, 1987).

Burleigh, Michael, *Germany Turns Eastwards, A Study of Ostforschung in the Third Reich* (Cambridge: Cambridge University Press, 1988).

——, *Death and Deliverance, 'Euthanasia' in Germany, 1900–1945* (Cambridge: Cambridge University Press, 1994).

——, and Wipperman, Wolfgang, *The Racial State, Germany 1933–1945* (Cambridge: Cambridge University Press, 1991).

Burrin, Phillipe, *Hitler and the Jews, The Genesis of the Holocaust*, trans. Patsy Southgate (London: Edward Arnold, 1994).

Buruma, Ian, *Wages of Guilt, Memories of War in Japan and Germany* (London: Jonathan Cape, 1994).

Caldwell, Colonel C. E., *Small Wars, Their Principle and Practice* (East Ardsley, West Yorks.: EP Publishing, 1976 [first published 1906]).

Carman, John, ed., *Material Harm, Archeological Studies of War and Violence* (Glasgow: Cruithne Press, 1997).

——, and Harding, Anthony, eds, *Ancient Warfare, Archeological Perspectives* (Stroud, Glos.: Sutton Publishing, 1999).

Carr, Raymond, *The Spanish Tragedy, The Civil War in Perspective* (London: Phoenix Press, 2000).

Cassesse, Antonio, *International Law in a Divided World* (Oxford: Clarendon Press, 1986).

Chaliand, Gérard, ed., *Minority Peoples in the Age of Nation-States*, trans. Tony Berrett (London: Zed Press, 1980).

——, ed., *People Without a Country, the Kurds and Kurdistan*, trans. Michael Pillis (London: Zed Press, 1980).

Chalk, Frank, and Jonassohn, Kurt, *The History and Sociology of Genocide* (New Haven, CT, and London: Yale University Press, 1990).

Charny, Israel W., ed., *A Critical Bibliographical Review* (London: Mansell, 1991), vols 2, and 3: *The Widening Circle of Genocide* (New Brunswick, NJ, and London: Transaction Publishers, 1994).

——, *Toward the Understanding and Prevention of Genocide: Proceedings of the International Conference on the Holocaust and Genocide* (Boulder, CO, and London: Westview Press, 1984).

Chirot, Daniel, *Modern Tyrants, The Power and Prevalence of Evil in Our Age* (New York and Toronto: Free Press, 1994).

Churchill, Ward, 'Genocide: Towards a Functional Definition', *Alternatives,* 11 (1986), 403–30.

——, *A Little Matter of Genocide, Holocaust and Denial in the Americas: 1492 to the Present* (San Francisco: City Light Books, 1997).

Cocker, Mark, *Rivers of Blood, Rivers of Gold, Europe's Conflict with Tribal Peoples* (London: Jonathan Cape, 1998).

Cohn, Norman, *Warrant for Genocide, The Myth of the Jewish World-Conspiracy and the Protocols of the Elders of Zion* (London: Penguin, 1967).

——, *The Pursuit of the Millennium: Revolutionary Millenarians and Mystical Anarchists of the Middle Ages* (London: Paladin, 1967).

——, *Europe's Inner Demons: An Enquiry Inspired by the Great Witchhunt* (New York: Basic Books, 1975).

Cohen, Stanley, *States of Denial, Knowing about Atrocities and Suffering* (Cambridge: Polity Press, 2001).

Conquest, Robert, *The Harvest of Sorrow, Soviet Collectivisation and the Terror-Famine* (New York: Oxford University Press, 1986).

——, *The Great Terror, A Reassessment* (New York and Oxford: Oxford University Press, 1990).

——, *Reflections on a Ravaged Century* (London: John Murray, 1999).

Cooper, Roger, *The Baha'is of Iran* (London: Minority Rights Group, 1982).

Courtois, Stéphane, et al., eds., *The Black Book of Communism, Crimes, Terror, Repression*, trans. Jonathan Murphy and Mark Kramer (Cambridge, MA, and London: Harvard University Press, 1999).

Crew, David, ed., *Nazism and German Society* (London: Routledge, 1994).

Cromwell, David, *Private Planet, Corporate Plunder and the Fight Back* (Charlbury, Oxon.: Jon Carpenter, 2001).

Dadrian, Vahakn N., 'The Role of Turkish Physicians in the World War One Genocide of Ottoman Armenians', *Holocaust and Genocide Studies*, 1:2 (1986), 169–92.

——, 'The Convergent Aspects of the Armenian and Jewish Cases of Genocide: a Reinterpretation of the Concept of Holocaust', *Holocaust and Genocide Studies*, 3: 2 (1988), 151–70.

——, 'The Role of the Turkish Military in the Destruction Of Ottoman Armenians: A Study in Historical Continuities', *Journal of Political and Military Sociology*, 20: 2 (1992), 257–88.

——, *The History of the Armenian Genocide, Ethnic Conflict from the Balkans to Anatolia to the Caucasus* (Oxford: Berghahn Books, 1996).

——, *Warrant for Genocide, Key Elements of Turko-Armenian Conflict* (New Brunswick, NJ, and London: Transaction Publishers, 1999).

Daunton, Mark, and Halpern, Rick, eds, *Empire and Others: British Encounters with Indigenous Peoples, 1600–1850* (London: UCL Press, 1999).

Davis, David Brion, ed., *The Fear of Conspiracy, Images of Un-American Subversion from the Revolution to the Present* (Ithaca, NY, and London: Cornell University Press, 1971).

Davis, Leslie A., *The Slaughterhouse Province, An American Diplomat's Report on the Armenian Genocide, 1915–1917* (New Rochelle, NY : Aristide D. Cataratzas, 1989).

Destexhe, Alain, *Rwanda and Genocide in the Twentieth Century,* trans. Alison Marschner (East Haven, CT, and London: Pluto Press, 1995).

Dower, John, *Japan in War and Peace: Selected Essays* (London: HarperCollins, 1993).

Elias, Norbert, *The Civilizing Process,* vol. 2: *State Formation and Civilization* (Oxford: Oxford University Press, 1982).

Eliot, Gil, *Twentieth Century Book of the Dead* (London: Penguin, 1972).

Evans, Richard J., *Telling Lies about Hitler: History, Holocaust and the David Irving Trial* (New York: Basic Books, 2001).

Farrell, Michael, *Northern Ireland: The Orange State* (London: Pluto Press, 1980).

Fein, Helen, 'Genocide: A Sociological Perspective', *Current Sociology,* 38:1 (1990), 1–126.

——, 'A Formula for Genocide: Comparisons of the Turkish Genocide (1915), and the German Holocaust (1939–45)', *Comparative Studies in Sociology,* 1 (1978), 271–93.

——, 'Accounting for Genocide after 1945: Theories and Some Findings', *International Journal on Group Rights,* 1 (1993), 79–106.

——, 'Afghanistan Reexamined', *Denver Journal of International Law and Policy,* 22:1 (1993), 29–62.

Finkelkraut, Alain, *The Future of a Negation, Reflections on the Question of Genocide* (Lincoln, NB, and London: University of Nebraska Press, 1998).

Finzsch, Norbert, 'Settler Imperialism and Discourses of Genocide in Eighteenth and Nineteenth-Century America and Australia', in A. Dirk Moses, *Genocide and Colonialism* (New York and Oxford: Berghahn Books, 2005).

Fleming, Gerald, *Hitler and the Final Solution* (Oxford: Oxford University Press, 1986).

Forges, Alison des, *Leave None to Tell The Story, Genocide in Rwanda* (New York and London: Human Rights Watch and International Federation of Human Rights, 1999).

Foucault, Michel, *Madness and Civilisation: A History of Insanity in the Age of Reason,* trans. Richard Howard (London: Routledge, 2001 [first published 1967]).

——, *Discipline and Punish, The Birth of the Prison,* trans. Alan Sheridan (London: Penguin, 1979).

Freeman, Michael, 'Puritans and Pequots, The Question of Genocide', *New England Quarterly,* 68 (1995), 278–93.

——, 'Genocide, Civilisation and Modernity', *British Journal of Sociology,* 46 (1995), 207–23.

——, 'Nationalism and Genocide, a Philosophical Analysis', (unpublished paper for International association of Genocide Scholars conference, Concordia University, Montreal, 1997).

Friedlander, Saul, ed., *Probing the Limits of Representation: Nazism and the Final Solution* (Cambridge, MA: Harvard University Press, 1992).

Fukuyama, Francis, *The End of History and the Last Man* (London: Penguin, 1992).

Garrard-Burnett, Virginia, *Protestantism in Guatemala, Living in the New Jerusalem* (Austin: University of Texas, 1998).

Gellately, Robert, *The Gestapo and German Society: Enforcing Racial Policy 1933–1945* (Oxford: Oxford University Press, 1990).

George, Susan, *How the Other Half Dies, The Real Reasons for World Hunger* (London: Penguin, 1976).

Gerlach, Christian, 'The Wannsee Conference, the Fate of German Jews, and Hitler's Decision in Principle to Exterminate all European Jews', in Omer Bartov, ed., *The Holocaust, Origins, Implementations, Aftermath* (New York and London: Routledge, 2000), 106–61.

Geschenkron, Alexander, *Economic Backwardness in Historical Perspective* (Cambridge, MA: Harvard University Press, 1962).

Getty, J. Arch, *The Origins of the Great Purges: The Soviet Communist Party Reconsidered, 1933–1938* (Cambridge: Cambridge University Press, 1985).

——, and Manning, Roberta T., eds, *Stalinist Terror, New Perspectives* (Cambridge: Cambridge University Press, 1993).

——, and Naumov, Oleg V., eds, *The Road to Terror, Stalin and the Self-Destruction of the Bolsheviks, 1932–1939* (New Haven, CT: Yale University Press, 1999).

Ghods, M. Reza, *Iran in the Twentieth Century, A Political History* (Boulder, CO, and London: Lynne Rienner Publishers and Adamantine Press, 1989).

Giddens, Anthony, *The Nation-State and Violence* (Cambridge: Polity Press, 1985).

Gilroy, Paul, 'There Ain't no Black in the Union Jack': The Cultural Politics of Race and Nation* (London: Hutchinson, 1987).

Goldhagen, Daniel Jonah, *Hitler's Willing Executioners, Ordinary Germans and the Holocaust* (London: Little, Brown and Co., 1996).

Gordon, Colin, ed., *M. Foucault: Power/Knowledge, Selected Interviews and Other Writings 1972–1977*, trans. Colin Gordon (Brighton: Harvester Press, 1980).

Gourevitch, Philip, *We Wish to Inform You that Tomorrow We Will Be Killed with our Families, Stories from Rwanda* (London: Picador, 1999).

Gowing, Margaret, 'The Organisation of Manpower in Britain during the Second World War', *Journal of Contemporary History*, 7:2 (1972), 147–67.

Gray, Andrew, *The Amerindians of South America* (London: Minority Rights Group, 1987).

Gray, John, *False Dawn, the Delusions of Global Capitalism* (London: Granta Books, 1998).

Graziano, Frank, *Divine Violence, Spectacle, Psychosexuality and Radical Christianity in the Argentine 'Dirty War'* (Boulder, CO, San Francisco and Oxford: Westview Press, 1992).

Greenfield, Liah, *Nationalism, Five Roads to Modernity* (Cambridge, MA: Harvard University Press, 1992).

Gregor, Neil, ed., *Nazism* (Oxford: Oxford University Press, 2000).

Griffin, Roger, *The Nature of Fascism* (London and New York: Routledge, 1991).

Haney, Craig, Banks, Curtis, and Zimbardo, Philip, 'Interpersonal Dynamics in a Simulated Prison', *International Journal of Criminology and Penology*, 1 (1983), 69–97.

Harff, Barbara, 'Recognising Genocides and Politicides', in Helen Fein, ed., *Genocide Watch* (New Haven, CT, and London: Yale University Press, 1992), 27–41.

——, and Gurr, Ted Robert, 'Toward Empirical Theory of Genocides and Politicides: Identification and Measurement of Cases since 1945', *International Studies Quarterly*, 32 (1988), 359–71.

——, 'Victims of the State: Genocides, Politicides and Group Repression since 1945', *International Review of Victimology*, 1:1 (1989), 23–41.

Harrison, Mark, 'Resource Mobilisation for World War II: the USA, UK, USSR and Germany, 1938–45', *Economic History Review*, 41:2 (1988), 171–92.

Hechter, Michael, *Internal Colonialism, the Celtic Fringe in British National Development* (London: Routledge and Kegan Paul, 1975).

Heraclides, Alexis, *The Self-Determination of Minorities in International Politics* (London: Frank Cass, 1991).

Herbert, Ulrich, ed., *National Socialist Extermination Policies, Contemporary German Perspectives and Controversies* (New York and Oxford: Berghahn Books, 2000).

Herman, Edward S., and Chomsky, Noam, *Manufacturing Consent: The Political Economy of the Mass Media* (New York: Pantheon, 1988).

Heyd, Uriel, *Foundations of Turkish Nationalism, The Life and Teachings of Ziya Gökalp* (London: Luzac, 1950).

Hillberg, Raul, *The Destruction of the European Jews* (New York: Holmes and Meier student edn, 1985).

——, *The Politics of Memory: The Journey of a Holocaust Historian* (Chicago: Ivan R. Dee, 1996).

Hinton, Alexander Laban, *Annihilating Difference, The Anthropology of Genocide* (Berkeley and Los Angeles: University of California Press, 2002).

Hobsbawn, Eric, *Age of Extremes, The Short Twentieth Century 1914–1991* (London: Abacus, 1995).

Hoffman, Tessa, and Koutcharian, Gerayer, 'The History of Armenian-Kurdish Relations in the Ottoman Empire', *Armenian Review*, 39:4 (1986), 1–45.

Hofstadter, Richard, *The Paranoid Style in American Politics and Other Essays* (London: Jonathan Cape, 1966).

Höhne, Heinz, *The Order of the Death's Head: The Story of Hitler's SS,* trans. Richard Barry (London: Pan, 1972).

Holquist, Peter, '"To Count, to Extract and to Exterminate," Population Politics in Late Imperial and Soviet Russia', in Ronald Grigor Suny and Terry Martin, eds, *A State of Nations, Empire and Nation-Making in the Age of Lenin and Stalin* (Oxford: Oxford University Press, 2001), 111–44.

Holter, Øystein Gullvåg, 'A Theory of Genocide', *Journal of Genocide Research*, 4:1 (2002), 11–38.

Horkeimer, Max, and Adorno, Theodor W., *Dialectic of Enlightenment*, trans. John Cumming (New York: Continuum, 1972 [first published 1944]).

Horne, Alistair, *A Savage War of Peace, Algeria 1954–1962* (London: Macmillan, 1977).

Horowitz, Irving Louis, *Taking Lives, Genocide and State Power* (Brunswick, NJ, and London: Transaction Publishers, 4th revised and expanded edn, 1997).

Hovannisian, Richard G., ed., *The Armenian Genocide in Perspective* (New Brunswick, NJ, and London: Transaction Books, 1986).

——, ed., *Looking Backward, Moving Forward: Confronting the Armenian Genocide* (New Brunswick, NJ: Transaction Publishers, 2003).

Human Rights Watch, *Slaughter Among Neighbours, The Political Origins of Communal Violence* (New Haven, CT, and London: Yale University Press, 1995).

Huntington, Samuel P., *The Clash of Civilisations and the Remaking of World Order* (London: Touchstone Books, 1998).

Huttenbach, Henry R., 'Towards a Conceptual Definition of Genocide', *Journal of Genocide Research*, 4:2 (2002), 167–75.

Ignatieff, Michael, *Blood and Belonging, Journeys into the New Nationalism* (London: Vintage, 1994).

Irzady, Mehrdad R., *The Kurds, A Concise Handbook* (Washington, DC: Taylor and Francis, 1992).

Jacobs, Steven L., 'The Papers of Raphael Lemkin: A First Look', *Journal of Genocide Research*, 1:1 (1999), 105–14.

——, and Totten, Samuel, eds, 'Totally Unofficial Man: Raphael Lemkin', *Pioneers of Genocide Studies* (New Brunswick, NJ: Transaction Publishers, 2002), 365–99.

Johnson, Eric, *The Nazi Terror, Gestapo, Jews and Ordinary Germans* (London: John Murray, 1999).

Jones, Adam, 'Gendercide and Genocide', *Journal of Genocide Research*, 2:2 (2000), 185–211.

——, 'Gender and Ethnic Confliction in ex-Yugoslavia', *Ethnic and Racial Studies*, 17:1 (1994), 115–34.

Jongman, Albert J., *Contemporary Genocides: Causes, Cases, Consequences* (The Hague: CIP-Gegevens Koninklijke Biblioteck, 1996).

Kadish, Sharman, *Bolsheviks and British Jews, The Anglo-Jewish Community, Britain and the Russian Revolution* (London: Frank Cass, 1992).

Kaplan, Steve Laurence, *Disputed Legacies, The Historians' Feud 1789/1989* (Ithaca, NY, and London: Cornell University Press, 1995).

Katz, Steven T., *The Holocaust in Historical Context*, vol. 1: *The Holocaust and Mass Death before the Modern Age* (New York and Oxford: Oxford University Press, 1994).

Kaye, James and Bo Strath, eds, *Enlightenment and Genocide, Contradictions of Modernity* (Brussels: P.I.E-Peter Lang, 2000).

Keeley, Lawrence, *War before Civilisation* (New York and Oxford: Oxford University Press, 1996).

Kennedy, Paul, *The Rise and Fall of The Great Powers* (London: Fontana, 1989).

Kershaw, Ian, *The Nazi Dictatorship, Problems and Perspectives of Interpretation* (London: Arnold, 3rd edn, 1993).

——, and Lewin, Moshe, eds, *Stalinism and Nazism: Dictatorships in Comparison* (Cambridge: Cambridge University Press, 1997).

Kiernan, Ben, *The Pol Pot Regime, Race Power and Genocide in Cambodia under the Khmer Rouge, 1975–79* (New Haven, CT, and London: Yale University Press, 1996).

——, and Gellately, Robert, eds, *The Spectre of Genocide: Mass Murder in Historical Perspective* (Cambridge and New York: Cambridge University Press, 2003).

Klemperer, Victor, *I Shall Bear Witness, The Diaries of Victor Klemperer, 1933–41*, trans. Martin Chalmers (London: Phoenix, 1998).

——, *The Language of the Third Reich: LTI-Lingua Tertii, A Philologist's Notebook*, trans. Martin Brady (London: Athlone Press, 2000).

Knight, Peter, *Conspiracy Culture: From the Kennedy Assassination to The X-Files* (London and New York: Routledge, 2000).

Kopelev, Lev, *The Education of a True Believer*, trans. Gary Kern (London: Wildwood House, 1981).

Krell, Alan, *The Devil's Rope: A Cultural History of Barbed Wire* (London: Reaktion Books, 2002).

Kuper, Leo, *Genocide: Its Political Use in the Twentieth Century* (New Haven, CT, and London: Yale University Press, 1981).

Kushner, David, *The Rise of Turkish Nationalism 1876–1908* (London: Frank Cass, 1977).

Kushner, Tony, 'The Holocaust and The Museum World in Britain: A Study of Ethnography', *Immigrants and Minorities*, 21:1/2 (2002), 20–33.

LaCapra, Dominick, *Writing History, Writing Trauma* (Baltimore and London: Johns Hopkins University Press, 2001).

Lang, Berel, *Act and Idea in the Nazi Genocide* (Chicago and London: Chicago University Press, 1990).

Lemarchand, René, 'Disconnecting the Threads: Rwanda and the Holocaust Reconsidered', *Journal of Genocide Research*, 4:4 (2002), 499–518.

——, 'Where Hamites and Aryans Cross Paths: The Role of Myth-Making in Mass Murders', *Journal of Genocide Research*, 5:1 (2003), 145–8.

Lemkin, Raphael, *Axis Rule in Occupied Europe* (Washington, DC: Carnegie Endowment for International Peace, 1944).

——, 'Genocide as a Crime under International Law', *American Journal of International Law*, 41 (1947), 145–71.

Levene, Mark, 'Is the Holocaust Simply Another Example of Genocide?', *Patterns of Prejudice*, 28:2 (1994), 3–26.

——, 'Yesterday's Victims, Today's Perpetrators? Considerations on Peoples and Territories within the former Ottoman Empire', *Terrorism and Political Violence*, 6 (Winter 1994), 444–61.

——, 'Creating a Modern "Zone of Genocide": The Impact of Nation and State Formation on Eastern Anatolia 1878–1923', *Holocaust and Genocide Studies*, 12:3 (1998), 393–433.

——, 'The Chittagong Hill Tracts: a Case Study in the Political Economy of "Creeping Genocide"', *Third World Quarterly*, 20:2 (1999), 339–69.

——, 'A Moving Target, the Usual Suspects and (Maybe) a Smoking Gun: The Problem of Pinning Blame in Modern Genocide', *Patterns of Prejudice*, 33:4 (1999), 3–24.

——, 'The Changing Face of Mass Murder: Massacre, Genocide and Post-Genocide', *International Social Science Journal*, 174 (2002), 443–52.

——, 'A Dissenting Voice: Or How Current Assumptions of Deterring and Preventing Genocide May Be Looking at the Problem through the Wrong End of the Telescope', *Journal of Genocide Research*, 6:2 and 6:3 (2004), 153–66, 431–45.

——, with Roberts, Penny, eds, *The Massacre in History* (New York and Oxford: Berghahn Books, 1999).

Lewin, Moshe, *The Making of the Soviet System, Essays on the Social History of Interwar Russia* (London: Methuen, 1985).

Lifton, Robert Jay and Eric Markusen, *The Genocidal Mentality: Nazi Holocaust and Nuclear Threat* (New York: Basic Books, 1990).

Lindqvist, Sven, *'Exterminate all the Brutes'*, trans. Joan Tate (London: Grant Books, 1998).

Lindsey, Rose, 'From Atrocity to Data: The Historiographies of Rape in Former Yugoslavia and the Gendering of Genocide', *Patterns of Prejudice*, 36:4 (2002), 59–78.

Lipstadt, Deborah, *Denying the Holocaust: The Growing Assault on Truth and Memory* (New York: Free Press, 1993).

Lorenz, Konrad, *On Aggression* (London: Methuen, 1966).

McDowall, David, *A Modern History of the Kurds* (London: I.B. Tauris, 1997).

Macquet, Jacques J., *The Premise of Inequality in Ruanda* (Oxford: Oxford University Press, 1961).

Maier, Charles S., *The Unmasterable Past, History, Holocaust and German National Identity* (Cambridge, MA, and London: Harvard University Press, 1988).

Makiya, Kanan, *Cruelty and Silence: War, Tyranny, Uprising and the Arab World* (London: Jonathan Cape, 1993).

Malcolm, Noel, *Kosovo, A Short History* (London and Basingstoke: Macmillan, 1998).

Mamdani, Mahmood, *When Victims Become Killers, Colonialism, Nativism and the Genocide in Rwanda* (Oxford: James Currey, 2001).

Mann, Michael, *Sources of Social Power*, vol. 1: *From the Beginning to 1760 AD* (Cambridge: Cambridge University Press, 1986).

Manz, Beatrice Forbes, *The Rise and Rule of Tamerlane* (Cambridge: Canto, 1999).

Markusen, Eric, and Kopf, David, *The Holocaust and Strategic Bombing, Genocide and Total War in the 20th Century* (Boulder, CO, San Francisco and Oxford: Westview Press, 1995).

Mason, Tim, '"The Primacy of Politics" – Politics and Economics in National Socialist Germany', in Henry A. Turner, ed., *Nazism and the Third Reich* (New York: Quadrangle Books, 1972), 175–200.

Maybury-Lewis, David, ed., *The Prospects for Plural Societies* (Washington, DC: American Ethnological Society, 1984).

Mazian, Florence, *Why Genocide? The Armenian and Jewish Experiences in Perspective* (Ames: Iowa State University Press, 1990).

Mazower, Mark, 'After Lemkin: Genocide, The Holocaust and History', *Jewish Quarterly*, 156 (Winter 1994/5), 5–8.

——, 'Violence and the State in the Twentieth Century', *American Historical Review*, 107:4 (2002), 1158–78.

Medvedev, Roy, *Let History Judge: The Origins and Consequences of Stalinism* (New York: Columbia University Press, 1989).

Melson, Robert F., *Revolution and Genocide: On the Origins of the Armenian Genocide and the Holocaust* (Chicago: Chicago University Press, 1992).

Mendes-Flohr, Paul R., and Reinharz, Jehuda, *The Jew in the Modern World, Documentary History* (New York: Oxford University Press, 1980).

Middle East Watch, *Genocide in Iraq: The Anfal Campaign against the Kurds* (New York: Human Rights Watch, 1993).

Miles, William F. S., 'Hamites and Hebrews: Problems in "Judaizing" the Rwandan Genocide', *Journal of Genocide Research*, 2:1 (2000), 108–9.

Milgram, Stanley, *Obedience to Authority* (New York: Harper and Row, 1974).

Miller, Donald E., and Miller, Lorna Touryan, *Survivors, An Oral History of the Armenian Genocide* (Berkeley and Los Angeles: University of California Press, 1993).

Mohawk, John C., *Utopian Legacies, A History of Conquest and Oppression in the Western World* (Santa Fe, NM: Clear Light Publishers, 2000).

Montagu, Ashley, *The Nature of Human Aggression* (Oxford: Oxford University Press, 1976).

Moore, Barrington, Jr., *Social Origins of Dictatorship and Democracy* (London: Penguin, 1967).

Morgan, David, *The Mongols* (Oxford: Basil Blackwell, 1986).

Morgan, Kenneth O., *Consensus and Disunity, The Lloyd George Coalition Government, 1918–1922* (Oxford: Clarendon Press, 1979).

Moses, A. Dirk, 'Structure and Agency in the Holocaust: Daniel J. Goldhagen and his Critics', *History and Theory*, 37:2 (1998), 194–219.

——, 'Conceptual Blockages and Definitional Dilemmas in the "Racial Century": Genocides of Indigenous Peoples and the Holocaust', *Patterns of Prejudice*, 36:4 (2002), 7–36.

Moshman, David, 'Conceptual Constraints on Thinking about Genocide', *Journal of Genocide Research*, 3:3 (2001), 431–50.

Niewyk, Donald L., *The Jews in Weimar Germany* (Manchester: Manchester University Press, 1980).

Nolte, Ernst, *Der europäische Burgerkreig. Nationalsozialismus und Bolschewismus* (Frankfurt on Maine and Berlin: Propylaen, 1987).

Nove, Alec, *An Economic History of the USSR* (London: Penguin, revised edn, 1976).

Novick, Peter, *The Holocaust in American Life* (Boston: Houghton Mifflin, 1996).

Oded, Bustenai, *Mass Deportations and Deportees in the Neo-Assyrian Empire* (Wiesbaden: Reidhert, 1979).

Ofer, Dalia and Weitzman, Lenore J., eds, *Women in the Holocaust* (New Haven, CT, and London: Yale University Press, 1998).

Olmstead, Albert Ten Eyck, *History of Assyria* (New York: C. Scribner and Sons, 1923).

Paine, Robert, 'The Claim of the Fourth World', in Jens Brosted et al., eds, *Native Power, The Quest for Autonomy and Nationhood of Indigenous Peoples* (Oslo: Univesitetsflorlaget AS, 1985), 49–66.

Paine, S. C. M., *Imperial Rivals, China, Russia and Their Disputed Frontier* (Armonk, NY, and London: M.E. Sharpe, 1996).

Pakenham, Frank, *Peace by Ordeal: an Account from First-Hand Sources, of the Negotiation and Signature of the Anglo-Irish Treaty, 1921* (London: New English Library, 1967).

Paret, Peter, ed., *Makers of Modern Strategy, from Machiavelli to the Nuclear Age* (Oxford: Clarendon Press, 1986).

Pavlov, Ivan P., *Lectures on Conditioned Reflexes, Twenty Five Years of Objective Study of the Higher Nervous Activity Behaviour of Animals* (Oxford: Pinter Publishers, 1980 [first published 1927]).

Payne, Stanley G., *A History of Fascism, 1914–45* (London: UCL Press, 1995).

Pelt, Robert Jan van, and Dwork, Deborah, *Auschwitz, 1270 to the Present* (New Haven, CT, and London: Yale University Press, 1996).

Perry, John, 'Forced Migration in Iran During the Seventeenth and Eighteenth Centuries', *Iranian Studies*, 8:4 (1975).

Petitfrère, Claude, *La Vendée et les Vendéens* (Paris: Éditions Gallimard/Juillard, 1981).

Pick, Daniel, *War Machine, The Rationalisation of Slaughter in the Modern Age* (New Haven, CT, and London: Yale University Press, 1993).

Poliakov, Leon, *History of Anti-Semitism*, vol. 4: *Suicidal Europe 1870–1933,* trans. George Klin (Oxford: Littman Library and Oxford University Press, 1985).

Pollard, Sidney, *The Idea of Progress, History and Society* (London: Pelican, 1971).

Polonsky, Anthony, ed., *My Brother's Keeper, Recent Polish Debates on the Holocaust* (London: Routledge, 1990).

Power, Samantha, '*A Problem from Hell*', *America and the Age of Genocide* (New York: Basic Books, 2002).

Prunier, Gérard, *The Rwanda Crisis, History of a Genocide 1959–1994* (London: Hurst and Co., 1995).

Rad, Gerhard von, *Holy War in Ancient Israel,* trans. and ed., Marva J. Dawn (Grand Rapids, MI: William B. Eerdmans Publishing Co., 1991 [first published 1958]).

Ranelagh, John, *Thatcher's People, an Insider's Account of the Politics, the Power and the Personalities* (London: HarperCollins, 1991).

Razac, Oliver, *Barbed Wire, a Political History,* trans. Jonathan Kneight (London: Profile Books, 2002).

Rosenbaum, Alan S., ed., *Is the Holocaust Unique? Perspectives on Comparative Genocide* (Boulder, CO: Westview Press, 1996).

Rosenberg, William G., and Young, Marilyn B., *Transforming Russia and China, Revolutionary Struggle in the Twentieth Century* (Oxford and New York: Oxford University Press, 1982).

Rosenfeld, Gavriel D., 'The Politics of Uniqueness: Reflections on the Recent Polemical Turn in Holocaust and Genocide Scholarship', *Holocaust and Genocide Studies*, 13:1 (1999), 28–61.

Rummel, R. J., *Lethal Politics: Soviet Genocide and Mass Murder since 1917* (New Brunswick, NJ, and London: Transaction Press, 1990).

——, *China's Bloody Century, Genocide and Mass Murder since 1900* (New Brunswick, NJ: Transaction Press, 1991).

Saggs, H. W. F., *The Might that was Assyria* (London: Sidgwick & Jackson: 1984).

Sanders, Edith, '"The Hamitic Hypothesis": Its Origin and Functions in Time Perspective', *Journal of African History*, 10 (1969), 521–32.

Sanders, J. J., *The History of the Mongol Conquests* (London: Routledge and Kegan Paul, 1971).

Sarafian, Ara, ed., *United States Official Documents on the Armenian Genocide* (Watertown, MA: Armenian Review Books, 1995), 3 vols.

Schabas, William A., *Genocide in International Law, The Crime of Crimes* (Cambridge: Cambridge University Press, 2000).

Schepper-Hughes, Nancy, *Death without Weeping: The Violence of Everyday Life in Brazil* (Berkeley and Los Angeles: University of California, 1993).

Schleunes, Karl, *The Twisted Road to Auschwitz, Nazi Policy towards the Jews 1933–1939* (Urbana: University of Illinois Press, 1970).

Scott, James C., *Seeing Like a State, How Certain Schemes to Improve the Human Condition Have Failed* (New Haven, CT, and London: Yale University Press, 1998).

Sémelin, Jacques, 'Qu'est-ce qu'un crime de masse? Le cas de l'ex-Yougoslavie', *Critique internationale*, 6 (2000), 143–58.

——, ed., 'Extreme Violence', *International Social Science Journal*, 174 (2002).

Sengoopta, Chandak, *Imprint of the Raj, How Fingerprinting was Born in Colonial India* (Basingstoke: Macmillan, 2003).

Shaw, Martin, *War and Genocide, Organised Killing in Modern Society* (Cambridge: Polity Press, 2003).

Shils, Edward A., *The Torment of Secrecy: The Background and Consequences of American Security Policies* (London: William Heinemann, 1956).

Sibomana, André, *Hope for Rwanda, Conversations with Laure Guibert and Hervé Deguine*, trans. Carina Tertsakian (London and Dar es Salaam: Pluto Press and Mkuki na Nyota Publishers, 1999).

Skocpol, Theda, *States and Social Revolutions* (Cambridge: Cambridge University Press, 1979).

Smith, Roger W., 'Fantasy, Purity, Destruction: Norman Cohn's Complex Witness to the Holocaust', in Alan Berger, ed., *Bearing Witness to the Holocaust 1939–1989* (Lewiston, Queenston and Lampeter: Edward Mellen Press, 1991), 115–26.

——, 'Genocide and the Politics of Rape, Historical and Psychological Perspectives', (unpublished paper, 'Remembering for the Future' International Conference on the Holocaust and Genocide, Humboldt University, Berlin, 1994).

——, 'Women and Genocide: Notes on an Unwritten History', *Holocaust and Genocide Studies*, 8:3 (1994), 315–34.

Sofsky, Wolfgang, *Die Ordnung des Terrors: das Konzentrationslager* (Frankfurt on Main: S. Fischer, 1993).

Solzhenitsyn, Alexander, *The Gulag Archipelago, 1918–1956,* vol. 1: trans. Thomas P. Whitney (New York and London: Collins/Fontana, 1974).

Sorabji, Cornelia, 'A Very Modern War: Terror and Territory in Bosnia-Herzcgovina', in Robert A. Hinde and Helen E. Watson, eds, *War: A Cruel Necessity? The Bases of Institutionalised Violence* (London and New York: Tauris Academic Studies, 1995), 80–99.

Southwood, Julie, and Flanagan, Patrick, *Indonesia, Law, Propaganda and Terror* (London: Zed Press, 1983).

Stannard, David, *American Holocaust, The Conquest of the New World* (New York and Oxford: Oxford University Press, 1992).

Stanton, Gregory H., 'Blue Scarves and Yellow Stars: Classification and Symbolisation in the Cambodian Genocide' (Montreal Institute for Genocide Studies, Occasional Papers, 1989).

Staub, Ervin, *The Roots of Evil, The Origins of Genocide and Other Group Violence* (Cambridge: Cambridge University Press, 1989).

Steiner, George, *In Bluebeard's Castle, Some Notes Towards the Redefinition of Culture* (London: Faber & Faber, 1971).

Steiner, Henry J. and Alston, Philip, eds, *International Human Rights in Context, Law, Politics, Morals* (Oxford: Oxford University Press, 2000).

Stiglmayer, Alexandra, ed., *Mass Rape, the War against Women in Bosnia-Herzegovina*, trans. Marion Faber (Lincoln, NB, and London: University of Nebraska Press, 1994).

Stocking, George W. Jr., *Victorian Anthropology* (New York: Free Press, 1987).

Stone, Dan, 'Modernity and Violence, Theoretical Reflections on the Einsatzgruppen', *Journal of Genocide Research*, 1:3 (1999), 367–78.

——, 'Holocaust Testimony and the Challenge to the Philosophy of History', in Robert Fine and Charles Turner, eds, *Social Theory after the Holocaust* (Liverpool: Liverpool University Press, 2000), 219–34.

——, 'Genocide as Transgression', *European Journal of Social Theory*, 7:1 (2003), 45–66.

——, 'The Historiography of Genocide: Beyond "Uniqueness and Ethnic Competition"', *Rethinking History*, 8:1 (2004), 127–42.

Straus, Scott, 'Contested Meanings and Conflicting Imperatives: a Conceptual Analysis of Genocide', *Journal of Genocide Research*, 3:3 (2001), 349–66.

——, 'Organic Purity and the Role of Anthropology in Cambodia and Rwanda', *Patterns of Prejudice*, 35:2 (2001), 47–62.

Szporluk, Roman, *Communism and Nationalism, Karl Marx versus Friedrich List* (New York and London: Oxford University Press, 1988).

Talbott, Strobe, ed., *Khrushchev Remembers: The Last Testament* (London: Andre Deutsch, 1974).

Ternon, Yves, *L'État criminel: Les génocides au XXe siècle* (Paris: Éditions du Seuil, 1995).

Thom, Martin, *Republics, Nations and Tribes* (London: Verso, 1995).

Thompson, E. P., *The Making of the English Working Class* (London: Penguin, 1963).

——, *Writing by Candlelight* (London: Merlin Press, 1980).

——, *Customs in Common* (London: Penguin, 1993).

Thurston, Robert W., *Life and Terror in Stalin's Russia 1934–1941* (New Haven, CT, and London: Yale University Press, 1999).

Tilly, Charles, ed., *The Formation of National States in Europe* (Princeton: Princeton University Press, 1975).

——, *Coercion, Capital and European States AD. 990–1990* (Oxford: Blackwell, 1990).

Todorov, Tzvetan, *The Conquest of America, The Question of the Other*, trans. Richard Howard (New York: HarperPerennial, 1984).

Townshend, Charles, *The British Campaign in Ireland, 1919–1921: The Development of Political and Military Policies* (Oxford: Oxford University Press, 1975).

Traverso, Enzo, *Understanding the Nazi Holocaust, Marxism after Auschwitz*, trans. Peter Drucker (London: Pluto Press, 1999).

Trouillot, Michel-Rolph, *Silencing the Past, Power and the Production of History* (Boston: Beacon Press, 1995).

Veenhoven, Willem A., ed., *Case Studies on Human Rights and Fundamental Freedoms, A World Survey*, 5 vols (The Hague: Martinus Nijhoft, 1976).

Vickery, Michael, *Cambodia 1975–1982* (Boston: South End, 1984).

Voegelin, Eric, *Die politischen Religionen* (Vienna: Bermann-Fischer, 1938).

Waller, James, *Becoming Evil, How Ordinary People Commit Genocide and Mass Killing* (Oxford and New York: Oxford University Press, 2002).

Wallerstein, Immanuel, *The Capitalist World-Economy* (Cambridge and New York: Cambridge University Press, 1979).

——, *The Modern World System* (San Diego and New York: Academic Press Inc., 1974–89), 3 vols.

Wallimann, Isidor, and Dobkowski, Michael, eds, *Genocide and the Modern Age* (Westport, CT: Greenwood Press, 1987).

Walter, Eugene Victor, *Terror and Resistance: A Study of Political Violence, With Case Studies of Some Primitive African Communities* (London, Oxford and New York: Oxford University Press, 1969).

Walzer, Michael, 'The Idea of Holy War in Ancient Israel', *Journal of Religious Ethics*, 20:2 (1992), 215–27.

Weber, Eugen, *Peasants into Frenchmen: The Modernisation of Rural France 1870–1914* (Stanford, CA: Stanford University Press, 1976).

Weber, Max, *The Protestant Ethic and the Spirit of Capitalism*, trans. Talcott Parsons (London: Routledge, 1992 [first published 1930]).

Weindling, Paul, *Epidemics and Genocide in Eastern Europe, 1890–1945* (Oxford: Oxford University Press, 2000).

Weisbrod, Bernd, 'Fundamentalist Violence: Political Violence and Political Religion in Modern Conflict', *International Social Science Journal*, 174 (2002), 499–509.

Weitz, Eric D., *A Century of Genocide, Utopias of Race and Nation* (Princeton and Oxford: Princeton University Press, 2003).

White, Mark J., *Missiles in Cuba, Kennedy, Khrushchev, Castro and the 1962 Crisis* (Chicago: Ivan R. Dee, 1997).

Willems, Wim, *In Search of the True Gypsy, From Enlightenment to Final Solution* (London: Frank Cass, 1997).

Wood, Michael, *In the Footsteps of Alexander the Great* (London: BBC, 1997).

Yoder, John Howard, 'Texts that Serve or Texts that Summon? A Response to Michael Walzer', *Journal of Religious Ethics*, 20:2 (1992), 229–34.

Index